Next-Gen Perspectives on Leadership

Next-Gen Perspectives on Leadership

Coalitional Strategies for Launching Careers, Renewing Curricula, and Defending Democracy

EDITED BY
Charles McMartin, Eric A. House,
Sonia C. Arellano, and Thomas Miller

UTAH STATE UNIVERSITY PRESS
Logan

© 2026 by University Press of Colorado

Published by Utah State University Press
An imprint of University Press of Colorado
1580 North Logan Street, Suite 660
PMB 39883
Denver, Colorado 80203-1942

All rights reserved

 The University Press of Colorado is a proud member of Association of University Presses.

The University Press of Colorado is a cooperative publishing enterprise supported, in part, by Adams State University, Colorado School of Mines, Colorado State University, Fort Lewis College, Metropolitan State University of Denver, University of Alaska Fairbanks, University of Colorado, University of Denver, University of Northern Colorado, University of Wyoming, Utah State University, and Western Colorado University.

ISBN: 978-1-64642-798-7 (hardcover)
ISBN: 978-1-64642-799-4 (paperback)
ISBN: 978-1-64642-800-7 (ebook)
https://doi.org/10.7330/9781646428007

Cataloging-in-Publication data for this title is available online at the Library of Congress

We want to express our gratitude for the financial support provided by the College of Arts and Humanities Book Publication Fund at Florida State University. Their generous contribution made the publication of this book possible.

Cover illustrations. Clockwise from top: Craig Lovell / Eagle Visions Photography / Alamy; Jacob Wackerhausen / istock; Valery Rizzo / Alamy; skynesher / istock.

Contents

Introduction: Supporting the Leaders Our Futures Depend On
Charles McMartin, Sonia C. Arellano, Eric A. House, and Thomas Miller   3

Section 1: Leading from the Job You Have to Create More Equitable Workplaces

Introduction to Section 1
Charles McMartin   27

1. Putting the Rhetorical Expertise of NTT Faculty to Work
   Sean Moxley-Kelly and Abigail Oakley   33

2. Crossing Over: Transitioning to Early-Career Leadership with Labor Equity in Mind
   Anicca Cox   56

3. Navigating Industry Careers through Cultural Integration
   Charisse S. Iglesias   79

   Section 1 Response: Mapping Core Leadership Competencies through Next-Gen Stories: Learning from Cultural Integration and Labor Advocacy Across Institutional Roles
   Jennifer Sano-Franchini   99

Section 2: Building Networks of Resistance to Claim Support for Your Work as a Leader

Introduction to Section 2
Sonia C. Arellano   115

4. Student-Faculty Coalition Building: Autoethnographic
   Perspectives on Leadership and Empowerment
   Felicita Arzu-Carmichael and Mena Hannakachl   121

5. Challenges and Opportunities for Teacher Leaders in K–12 Schools:
   Lessons Learned from Teachers of Color in K–12 Schools
   *Alice Hays, Shaylyn Marks, Alexandra Chapa-Kunz,
   and Amardeep (Rupsy) Bajwa*   146

6. From Perfunctory to Practice: Creating an Administrative Identity
   as Early-Career Faculty through Community Partnerships
   Adele Leon   163

   Section 2 Response: That's How They Get You
   Christina V. Cedillo   185

Section 3: On Not Getting Hustled

   Introduction to Section 3
   Eric A. House   201

7. Mothering in the Academy: Equity, Child Care, and the Tenure Clock
   Ana Milena Ribero   207

8. (Trying to) Take It "Slow": Navigating Productivity,
   Parenting, and Academic Life through COVID-19
   Brad Jacobson   222

9. Racialized Bodies Navigating White Institutional Spaces
   Tom Hong Do   241

   Section 3 Response: A Call for Progressive Leadership: Resisting
   Neoliberalism and Pluralistic Views of Tenure and Promotion
   Staci Perryman-Clark   259

   Afterword: "Can't Be Stopped/Gonna Hit the Top": When
   Next-Gen Stands at the Threshold of Reinstated White
   Supremacist Departments and Institutions
   Carmen Kynard   271

   Acknowledgments   281
   Index   285
   About the Authors   297

Next-Gen Perspectives on Leadership

INTRODUCTION

Supporting the Leaders Our Futures Depend On

CHARLES MCMARTIN, SONIA C. ARELLANO,
ERIC A. HOUSE, AND THOMAS MILLER

This collection examines the leadership strategies that early-career PhDs in writing studies and related areas are using to address the challenges facing their generation. Most of the chapters are by authors who earned PhDs in the decade between the great recession and the global pandemic. Those few who found tenure-track jobs in some of the worst faculty markets in history have not had the luxury to be able to follow the traditional advice to focus on their research and wait for the "safety" of tenure to do the work that sustains them and their communities (Lusin and Hunt; Goldstone). They have found themselves in the crosshairs of reactionary legislatures who have abolished diversity programs, rolled back support for women and LGBTQ people, and stripped billions of dollars from public education to build the infrastructure for mass deportations. To help you consider how you can resist such efforts, our collection includes case studies of the coalitional leadership strategies involved in unionizing, developing culturally responsive curricula, strengthening community engagements, and creating more equitable workplaces inside and outside the academy even if you do not have a designated leadership position.

The collaborations that led to this collection began in 2021 in the midst of the pandemic and after Trump's first term, when Charlie McMartin and Tom Miller interviewed early-career faculty across the country who were pressed to step into leadership roles as their institutions were closing down and going online (McMartin and Miller). Eric A. House and Sonia C. Arellano were part of that study and then joined in developing this collection to examine how recent PhDs were stepping up to support overwhelmed students, create more responsive departments, and lead coalitions working for racial justice—all while caring for their families and attending to their own mental health in a time of unprecedented stress and precarity. Almost all the chapter authors earned their PhDs after 2017, as did three of the four coeditors. The three respondents to the chapters received their PhDs after 2010, and our collection concludes with a summative reflection by Carmen Kynard, whose research is used to frame the three sets of readings. Kynard's scholarship examines how the vision and agency of Black students has shaped the development of writing and literacy studies, most notably in the 1970s when the student activists who were pressing for open admissions helped establish the curricular spaces that shaped the origins of composition studies—along with ethnic and women studies (*Vernacular Insurrections*; see also Epstein and Stringer).

The advances that have been made in the last half century are being rolled back by the targeting of such programs along with billions of dollars of cuts in college readiness and educational support programs (Cutler and Taylor). These efforts are implementing what Andrew Serwer has characterized as "The Great Resegregation" (see also "DEI Legislation Tracker"; "Truths about DEI on College Campuses"). Serwer examines how the "make America white again" movement is seeking to implement a "pre-civil-rights-movement vision of America" by uprooting the liberal consensus on the values of diversity and equity. This historic reaction will have a long-term impact on early-career graduates and faculty, especially those from marginalized backgrounds and others committed to working for social justice (see Knox). Their leadership has been shaped by Black Lives Matter coalitions, campus resistance to the genocide in Gaza, and grassroots efforts to protect the millions of Americans facing the threat of deportation. Researching and teaching such leadership can help writing studies proactively respond to the racism, sexism, and ethnonationalism of our times (Jones et al.; Carter et al.).

The leadership challenges that will shape the careers of recent PhDs are outlined in Brock Read's "6 Trump Trends to Watch Closely":

1. Those in formal leadership roles will often fail to serve their constituencies by adopting "low profile" positions and deferring to those in power to protect their institution's mission and their own standing within it.

2. Accreditation is a "pressure point" where education can be bent systematically to support racial, economic, gender, and political hierarchies, in part because faculty are not prepared to work collectively to articulate their curricular expertise.
3. The potentially "catastrophic" defunding of research-based graduate education will require a reorientation of traditional research hierarchies to focus on modes of collaborative problem solving that address public needs.
4. To defend their research missions, universities need grassroots leaders who are prepared and positioned to develop community partnerships with towns, regions, and states "to serve the *local* good" and articulate the mission of institutions of public education to serve as "economic drivers, cultural hubs, and knowledge centers."
5. Faculty must be prepared to do the research on student learning and articulate it to public constituencies to fill the "data gap" created by the dismantling of the Department of Education.
6. Faculty, administrative, and student leaders also need to be prepared to defend the public benefits of culturally responsive and communally engaged education against states who launch programs to defund public institutions to follow up on the efforts of the Trump administration's Department of Government Efficiency.

These state interventions in higher education are a reaction, in part, to two historic transitions. For the first time, most Americans under eighteen are people of color according to the 2020 US census. Just as more Black and Latino students are applying to college, a lower percentage are being admitted (Alonso). These transformative potentials and the efforts to limit them are converging with a second transition: Baby boomers have been succeeded by millennials as the largest generation in America. Millennial and Gen Z faculty and students are more diverse, more educated, and more liberal than their predecessors (Bialik and Fry; Fry; Barroso). Most younger voters and most college graduates supported Harris in the 2024 election, though Trump gained support among young men, especially young white men ("The Youth Vote"; Hill). The generational and educational divides in the electorate have been a major motivation behind the right-wing assault on higher education.

The work of defending diversity and equity work against this frontal assault is just one of the pressing examples of the distributed forms of adaptive leadership that are examined in this collection. Many administrators in designated leadership positions have responded to anti-DEI mandates by "bending the knee" to protect themselves and their institutions, while frontline leaders have worked among themselves to rename, reposition, and reorganize diversity initiatives and staff (Burmicky and Patrón). Diversity leaders have long recognized that entrenched institutional and personal biases cannot be fixed by mandating workshops. Advances with diversity require grassroots organizing, face-to-face collaborations, and working quietly to pressure or circumvent those in designated positions of leadership in the ways Sonia C. Arellano, José Manuel Cortez, and Romeo García discuss as "shadow work." The power of such behind-the-scenes coalitional work is apparent in the fact that almost three-quarters of the state and federal proposals for anti-DEI legislation have failed to pass, been tabled, or vetoed ("DEI Legislation Tracker"). The lessons in leadership provided by those working to sustain diversity and equity programs take on even more compelling significance when we consider how legislatures in red states such as Texas are using compliance with DEI prohibitions to assert control over shared governance, accreditation, curricula, and faculty work (Quinn).

Such lessons in leadership can enhance our undergraduate and graduate programs in the ways we will discuss in the next sections of this introduction. The subsequent sections set up our three sets of chapters on how distributed forms of leadership can be used to develop more equitable workplaces, expand our coalitional networks, and use those networks to support ourselves and those we care for. In the final section, we will outline the leadership development plan that is elaborated upon in our introductions to the three sets of chapters:

- **LEARNING WITH STUDENT LEADERS** looks to the leadership of student activists as models for renewing curricula to engage new-majority students and prepare graduate students to lead within and beyond the academy.
- **LEADING FROM THE JOB YOU HAVE TO CREATE MORE EQUITABLE WORKPLACES** examines how the early-career authors included in our first set of readings are working in academic and other professional settings to create more equitable working conditions in an era when the gig economy has been imposed on educators and other civil servants.
- **BUILDING NETWORKS TO CLAIM SUPPORT FOR YOUR SERVICE AS A LEADER** reviews the arguments in the second set of readings for moving beyond the siloed conceptions of research that have failed to recognize the service and mentoring that our institutions rely on to recruit students and build sustained and sustaining community partnerships.
- **ON NOT GETTING HUSTLED** sets up the arguments in our third set of readings that such work needs to include caring for ourselves and

others in ways that are fundamental to the forms of leadership that matter in our lives, our work, and our struggles to defend liberal education and liberal democracy.
- **LEADERSHIP STRATEGIES FOR YOUR WORK, YOUR JOB, AND "THE HUSTLE"** draws on Kynard's distinctions between the work we feel called to do, the jobs we are hired to do, and the careerist hustling that often confuses the two. This section outlines the leadership development plan that the editors of the three sets of reading follow up on in their introductions to the three parts of this collection.

Learning with Student Leaders

Carmen Kynard has examined the historic impact of student activism at critical moments in the history of higher education, most visibly in the 1960s and 1970s. Kynard's research on "vernacular insurrections" views high school and college students as leaders who have been instrumental in grassroots resistance to racist norms and assimilationist regimes. According to Kynard, Black student protests "function as a kind of counterinstitution that circulates its own specific modes of literacy learning" (30). These race-radical literacies provide a "living body of common practices and goals" that enables the collective leadership of those who foment "vernacular insurrections" (see also Brown). For example, next-gen scholars have looked to Hip Hop as a cultural and political resource for transforming the modes of engagement and guiding conceptions of writing studies, as Eric A. House has discussed in "Reflections on a Hip-Hop DJ Methodology" (see also Parker; Condon and Ashanti Young; Baker-Bell; Ore et al.; and Walton et al.).

The students, faculty, staff, and nonacademic leaders in this collection provide case studies and strategies that we hope you will find useful in considering how to develop more engaged and responsive undergrad and graduate programs (Martin et al.; Cole and Heinecke; Quinteros and Covarrubias; McMartin; Kannan). Many English and related departments are going to have to do more than treat career preparation as an extracurricular accommodation to soothe students' vocational anxieties (*ADE Ad Hoc Committee on English Majors' Career Preparation and Outcomes*). English and other humanities majors have seen long term declines in enrollments that are going to drop precipitously with the "demographic cliff" in the college-aged population. Leadership studies provides frameworks to bridge writing, literature, and media courses with community partnerships, experiential learning, network studies, and the funds of knowledge students bring to the classroom. Such frameworks are cited by the students, faculty, and staff in "The Revenge of the Humanities" episode of the *College Uncovered* podcast series.

To renew our curricula, we need to expand our focus from *preparing* students for future courses and jobs to include students' current *participation* in their communities in the ways that can be articulated as modes of coalitional leadership in experiential learning programs (Reichert Powell 118). Leadership studies can help advance the "political turn" in writing studies (Carter et al.; Kannan) by expanding upon rhetoric's concern for collective action, composition's collaborative pedagogies, and critical theories of intersectional networks in ways that have broad appeal to students, parents, and community and business partners. While leadership studies may be unfamiliar to rhetoric and writing scholars, leadership is an integrated part of communications programs, and it can play a comparable role in professional writing and new media majors seeking to expand the frame of reference beyond textual studies.

Like writing, leadership is an integrative discipline that combines practical skills, technical expertise, situational awareness, and recursive collaborative learning. Like writing across curriculum programs, student leadership programs are a strategic part of the integrative infrastructure that connects curricula with extracurricular experiential learning programs, including service-learning, internships, and student-growth and wellness initiatives. This integrative learning infrastructure provides vital resources for addressing the wicked problems facing our democracy, including resisting efforts to unbundle and commodify learning in the ways Chris Gallagher has discussed in *College Made Whole*. An attention to leadership can help departments expand the integrative capacities of their undergraduate and graduate programs by providing frameworks for bridging curricula with the experiential learning programs that can help students engage in coalitional forms of collective action.

For those considering the strategic potentials of integrating leadership studies into undergraduate and graduate programs, we recommend the cautionary advice that Staci Perryman-Clark offers in "Now What? Final Strategies of Forming Partnerships." In this concluding chapter of *The New Work of Writing Across the Curriculum: Diversity and Inclusion, Collaborative Partnerships, and Faculty Development*, Perryman-Clark advises "caution" to those looking to social-justice and anti-racist work to renew our discipline: don't take up this work "simply for financial incentives, professional recognition, or unit survival. Do it because it is the right thing to do." Perryman-Clark calls for the sorts of "strategic . . . collaborations" that our contributors are advancing "to make institutional progress and effect change" (109; see also Kynard, "Towards a Black Composition Studies"). Such coalition building is central to our arguments for studying and teaching distributed forms of leadership. Studies of collaborative networks can transform hierarchical conceptions of research, teaching, mentoring, outreach, and grassroots organizing. These areas are where next-gen faculty, students, and staff are working together to create more equitable working conditions, resist institutional racism, and establish the sustained and equitable community partnerships that are discussed by the contributors to this collection.

Such leadership begins and ends with the sort of "coalitional learning" that Natasha N. Jones has discussed. From the vantage point of the "outsider within," Jones looks to those who live and work in the contact zones where institutional hierarchies are called into question against broader social, demographic, technological, and political changes, including the historic transition to younger, more educated, more diverse, and more activist generations. Jones sees adaptive leadership as "relational, dynamic configurations" that prioritize awareness of power, privilege, and positionality (519). Jones sets out four "coalitional lessons" for how to engage in the provisional, contested, and recursive work of building collective leadership with students, collaborators, and communities: "center the marginalized," "celebrate difference," "disrupt borders and boundaries," and above all "listen." These are the skills that recent PhD authors in the next section are using to create more equitable workplaces inside and beyond the academy.

Leading from the Job You Have to Create More Equitable Workplaces

If we view leadership as a distributed process of facilitating collective action, we can begin to take stock of the contributions of the lecturers and instructors who comprise 75 percent of all instructional faculty. Drawing on his wide-ranging consultations with unions as a leader of the American Association of University Professors, Gary Rhoades has observed that just as the numbers of women and graduate students of color have increased, the proportion of tenure-track positions has declined. In "From the Margins to the Center," Rhoades discusses how the coming of "the new faculty majority" has pressed tenured faculty to get involved in union organizing, which has increasingly included coalitions with staff, teaching assistants, and student workers (see also Holcombe et al., *Leading for Equity from Where You Are*). According to Rhoades, these "wall-to-wall" unions are becoming the "new progressive normal" with the shared precarities of "academic capitalism" ("Working in Coalition"). Such coalition building is discussed by the authors in the first section (see also Holcombe et al., *Capacity Building for Shared Equity Leadership*). All are recent PhDs who are "repurposing" their doctoral studies to do environmental scans, map activity systems, and mobilize coworkers in the ways Shari Stenberg has discussed in *Repurposing Composition: Feminist Interventions for a Neoliberal Age*.

Our first chapter, by Sean Moxley-Kelly and Abigail Oakley, sets out a methodology for non-tenure-track (NTT) faculty advocacy that extrapolates from critical pedagogy's emphasis on reflection in action, rhetoric's grounding in situational analyses, and models of composing as a recursive process of collaborative problem solving. Their chapter provides a case study in how to map institutional structures and mission statements to identify conjunctions and contradictions that can be used to articulate the values of NTT faculty's contributions. They discuss how they have intervened in the activity systems that have devalued the work of NTT faculty. Their analysis shows how distributed models of leadership can be used to raise the visibility of the "leadership in place" in departmental reviews of faculty and staff work (Wergin). Resources for such interventions are provided by the Pullias Center for Higher Education at the University of Southern California, as we discuss in more detail at the end of our introduction. Moxley-Kelly and Oakley's case study shifts "our frames of leadership from individualistic to collective" in the ways Jocelyn Chadwick and her coauthors discuss. They observe that "successful leadership is everywhere" around us, operating "without titles or prominent positions, . . . always plural and differential in social locations." As a model of such leadership, Chadwick and her coauthors cite the leadership of Black, Indigenous, and women of color civil rights activists. Such models call upon us to focus on coalition building to learn from the social movements that advance "societal change for the greater good" (Chadwick et al. 16; see also Quinteros and Covarrubias). Chadwick and her collaborators envision leadership as an "organic" part of facilitating collaborative learning to build social-justice and anti-racist coalitions (14). For everyday examples of such "organic" leadership, Chadwick and her coauthors cite family members and community educators such as Paulo Freire.

Critical pedagogy provides a comparable point of reference for the vision of leadership set out by Anicca Cox in her chapter in this section. Cox reflects on the informal and formal leadership roles she stepped into in her first few years out of graduate school. She discusses how she worked as a writing program administrator (WPA) to support the participatory leadership of her coworkers.

Cox draws on feminist standpoint theory to reflect on how her approach to leadership was shaped by "the subjectivities of gender, race, class, and other social locations" that helped her intervene in institutional cultures that subordinated modes of collective understanding that were vital to her coalitional work. From her experiences as a leader, she reflects on the limitations of her graduate school preparation and the ways she adapted her studies to try to improve exploitative workloads, in part by intervening in the nuclei of contradictions that arise in institutions that profess to be teaching centered while exploiting those who do most of the teaching.

Such contradictions also present challenging opportunities for leaders seeking to address inequities in nonacademic institutions, as Charisse S. Iglesias discusses in the third chapter in this section. Iglesias suggests a set of heuristics that other recent PhDs can use to adapt their studies of participant-action research and other ethnographic methodologies to map organizational structures, values, and ways of thinking. She reflects on her research and leadership with "community-academic partnerships" to encourage recent PhDs to consider the engagements that they bring to their efforts to intervene in institutional and cultural systems that may hinder their growth and their collaborations with the coworkers and communities they seek to serve. From these reflections, she argues that graduate curricula need to do more to prepare the rising numbers of PhDs who are searching for jobs beyond the confines of the academy, concluding that "next-gen scholars do not have the luxury of waiting for . . . graduate programs to catch up to market demands."

Iglesias argues that graduate programs need to revise their curricula to prepare students for varied careers and not just add internships. Some programs already take a more integrated approach to preparing graduate students to administer writing programs. Such efforts can be enhanced by expanding the frame of reference from administering to leading teams, programs, and coalitions, including labor organizing. Comparable enhancements could be made to programs that attend to community and school partnerships but may not offer training in how to support coalitional leadership in local schools and communities. Two of the chapters in the next section provide positive examples of how attending to such forms of leadership can strengthen collaborations with teaching assistants and school teachers, and the third chapter offers a critique of how departments in research universities often advertise their commitments to public service while failing to invest in partnerships with local schools and communities.

Building Networks to Claim Support for Your Work as a Leader

Traditional research hierarchies are crumbling because they have failed to recognize the leaders who build and sustain the collaborations that public institutions rely on to recruit and retain students from underserved communities. In the pandemic, the first digital-native generation of faculty were pressed into service to help departments transition to online teaching and mentor students through the isolation of going to college in their bedrooms. Many early-career faculty then took on even more service commitments to develop online programs and the diversity initiatives that are being targeted by reactionary politicians. Through these commitments, recent PhDs have shared in the feelings of precarity that have been experienced by the generations who faced decreased employment opportunities as they came of age amidst the two greatest disruptions since World War II: the great recession and the global pandemic, which contributed to "the long-term precarity" faced by all the faculty who work on year-to-year and course-by-course contracts (Cox).

The first two chapters in our second set of readings are coauthored by faculty with their students and former students working through the shared challenges of confronting the microaggressions that foster feelings of precarity among faculty and students in vulnerable positions. The first chapter discusses the student-faculty coalition building that Felicita Arzu-Carmichael and Mena Hannakachl undertook as an Afro-Caribbean professor and an Arab Chaldean student who had graduated from high school and entered college in the midst of the pandemic. They discuss how their coalitional teaching and learning enabled them to reimagine what counts as leadership to include developing "action-oriented networks between faculty and students" that are sustained by "microaffirmations" that strengthen resilience and resistance (122).

The discussion of microaggressions is continued in the second chapter in the section by two teacher educators, Alice Hays and Shaylyn Marks, and two local teachers, Alexandra Chapa-Kunz and Amaradeep (Rupsy) Bajwa, who had both graduated from the teacher-educator program. Their chapter concludes with recommendations based on their collaborative experiences and those drawn from an interview study by Rita Kohli on how communities of resistance help teachers of color overcome racist obstacles to their leadership.

The disparities in service faced by women and people of color are an outgrowth of the systemic devaluation of service in higher education, as Adele Leon pointedly critiques in the third chapter in this section. Leon reflects on the lack of support she received coordinating a community-writing program that her department professed to value but failed to fund. Leon examines the contradictions that service presents to next-gen faculty who are asked to commit to work that is systematically discounted and disproportionately downloaded on women and BIPOC faculty. At the same time, such commitments can also be a means to develop the engagements that many faculty want to undertake in the work they seek to do.

Leon is one of several contributors in our collection who call for revising annual and tenure reviews to recognize the leadership of next-gen faculty with developing the sorts of community partnerships that are marginalized by the siloed conceptions of research that are currently crumbling as the Trump administration uses cuts of research funding to force universities to comply with its priorities. Early-career faculty and staff who step up to launch majors and programs often face the sort of debilitating microaggressions that Tom Hong Do discusses in chapter 9. Stories like the counternarratives that he recounts fill the pages of Cristyn Elder and Bethany Davila's edited collection *Defining, Locating, and Addressing Bullying in the WPA Workplace*.

If senior faculty do not do a better job of listening to early-career and marginalized coworkers, departments will lose the leaders on whom their futures depend. In the process of developing this collection, we lost several contributors who decided to quit academia (see, for example, Arellano). They are part of the lost generation of faculty who are quietly quitting and stepping back from all the service work they are expected to do but not recognized for having done. In "The Big Quit" and other articles in *The Chronicle of Higher Education*, Joshua Doleža examines how early-career faculty and others who have taken on disproportionate service work are becoming more strategic in focusing on the leadership commitments they care most about (see also McClure and Hicklin Fryar).

Traditional research hierarchies have limited universities' abilities to adapt to the changes in the educational and political environment that have made service and outreach so vital to the evolving mission of institutions of public learning. In "From Activism to Organizing, From Caring to Care Work," Seth Kahn and Amy Lynch-Biniek reflect on how labor activism and diversity issues have been treated as peripheral matters that are merely a concern for minorities, women, and others in precarious positions. Kahn and Lynch-Biniek argue that all faculty must share in the responsibility of organizing and caring for students and coworkers because the degradation of working conditions has left the few remaining tenured faculty with impossible service expectations, and labor organizing and caring for students cannot be left to overloaded instructors who labor without job security and free-speech protections. This argument against the unbundling of faculty work has double resonance for women and faculty and students of color because they are generally expected to be the caretakers of their department, and they often turn to peer mentors and community partners to sustain themselves in departments that do care for them or their commitments, as is discussed in Tracy Lachica Buenavista, Dimpal Jain, and María C. Ledesma's edited collection *First-Generation Faculty of Color: Reflections on Research, Teaching, and Service*.

On Not Getting Hustled

Our final set of readings examines the dynamics of care-full leadership—leadership that balances coalitional compassion, self-care, and a critical awareness of how uncaring institutions impose impossible expectations on engaged faculty and staff who care enough to step up and lead. Our discussion draws on the distinctions that Carmen Kynard draws between the lifework that sustains us and the job expectations that press us to keep hustling. Kynard argues that the job and the work are easy to confuse if one is comfortable with the "white liberal concessions" that are "the price" of advancement in the "white-masking discourse" of "professionalization" (18). As Kynard discusses, people in precarious situations "can be exploited" into thinking that adding "CV lines" will enable them to get ahead even though they are not "moving towards the work that [they] have been called to do" (18).

Like many other recent PhDs, the authors of the pieces in our last section have learned from living through the precarities of the pandemic to not get "hustled" into equating professional advancement with self-realization. Ana Ribero reflects on how parenting in the pandemic helped her understand how caregiving is treated as a personal responsibility by the male ethos of academic professionalism. Tom Hong Do examines how such emotional labor gets downloaded onto faculty of color who step up to try to make a difference, and Brad Jacobson critiques the neoliberal regimes that deny the values of caring for families and communities.

To respond to the "crisis of care" created by these regimes, Ribero presents *motherwork* as an alternative to *motherhood* to intervene in the privatized conceptions of service that treat mentoring and community engagement as part of women's duties. This patriarchal hierarchy overshadows the mutual support networks that are examined in Sonia C. Arellano, José Manuel Cortez, and Romeo García's "Shadow Work." Arellano and her coauthors look past traditional liberal pronouncements on DEI to focus on the distributed forms of leadership that are involved in the authentic work of "community building and friendship" that they cultivate as BIPOC faculty (38; see also Ribero and Arellano). Ribero concludes by outlining the sorts of institutional interventions we have touched on in previous sections of this introduction, including strategies for building coalitions of faculty, staff, and frontline administrators to revise hiring, job categories, and promotion reviews (see also Rhoades, "Working in Coalition"; Mechenbier et al.).

When the collective need to reform uncaring institutions is treated as the personal challenge of individuals who cannot meet expectations, next-gen faculty end up being depicted as unable to "fit" into the neoliberal regimes they are working to overcome. This collective struggle is examined in Brad Jacobson's chapter in our collection (chapter 8). Jacobson outlines how his institution failed to take account of the experiences and needs of parents like himself during the pandemic. As Jacobson discusses, universities have adopted corporate models that treat faculty as employees and students as customers rather than as citizens, community leaders, and life-sustaining family members. Jacobson calls for humane coalitional leadership that prioritizes faculty and student well-being and recognizes how wellness is sustained by community-engaged partnerships. Jacobson's chapter recounts how the pandemic pressed parents to come to terms with department expectations that did not respect their personal commitments and community engagements.

This misalignment has reached a tipping point as the precarities of next-gen faculty have come to align with the needs of beleaguered institutions seeking to rebuild public support and retain first-gen and new-majority students. Engaged professional organizations like the Coalition for Community Writing are providing life-sustaining resources for enacting the sorts of reforms in promotion and tenure reviews that Jacobson and others in our collection call for (see "Promotion and Tenure Resources").

The concluding chapter by Tom Hong Do documents how much departments stand to lose when they fail to listen to next-gen faculty who are attuned to the experiences and aspirations of new-majority students. His counterstory reviews the emotional labor that faculty of color have to work through to transform white-washed curricula without offending delicate white sensibilities. The inequitable service loads imposed on women and faculty of color have been carefully tracked in research studies such as "The Burden of Invisible Work in Academia," which concludes by arguing that "developing systems that link such labor with its economic value can validate faculty work and render this labor more visible" (Social Sciences Feminist Network 241). This care work "may be invisible," but "it is nonetheless essential to the functioning of institutions" (241; see also Baez). Do and many other BIPOC faculty are constantly confronted with "mismatches" between their goals and the expectations imposed on them. As Rebecca Covarrubias discusses, these mismatches often derail the careers of faculty and students from minoritized backgrounds, as was the case for Do, who left his institution to find a department with colleagues who valued his work.

As Anicca Cox details in her study of long-term, full time NTT faculty, it is easy to feel overwhelmed by long term precarity, but the chapter contributors to this collection and their allies are stepping up to leverage the nuclei of contradictions within neoliberal regimes, particularly the devaluing of vital service work. Sustaining this work against the frontal assaults that have been launched on institutions of public learning will take vision and hope. Jennifer Sano-Franchini's contribution to our collection takes on broader resonance when read against the call for proposals that she sent out for the 2024 Conference on College Composition and Communication. Sano-Franchini reminded us of the potential abundance that is masked by neoliberal claims of scarcity and the anxieties of those whose privileges have been called into question by historic transitions they cannot stop. Our collection documents the abundance of possibilities for the historical convergence of rising new-majority student populations and next-gen faculty. Sano Franchini's notion of abundance calls us to reject the rhetoric of scarcity, resist deficit models of care work, and embrace the potentials of coalitional leadership that serves anti-racist and social justice goals.

Leadership Strategies for Your Work, Your Job, and "the Hustle"

To help readers reflect on these challenging leadership opportunities, this section introduces a few suggestions on leadership development that we will follow up on in the introductions to the three sets of readings. We have framed these suggestions using Kynard's distinctions between the work we aspire to do, the job we are assigned to do, and the hustling around that can prevent us from staying centered in our lives and work. These action points draw together the leadership strategies that are set out in the readings in the sections. These suggestions are also informed by research on the experiences of early-career faculty, particularly BIPOC, women, and first-gen faculty. At the end of this section, we cite some resources to help you develop your leadership, particularly the handbooks on shared equity leadership that have been created by Adrianna

Kezar and her collaborators at the Pullias Center for Higher Education at the University of Southern California. The process model we are outlining expands upon the integrative capacities of workshop pedagogies, distributed network theories, and rhetorical analyses of institutions by beginning with reflection and brainstorming, expanding into institutional mapping to explore capacity-building opportunities, and then recursively moving back to double-loop inquiry to include further critique and strategic planning to advance collective actions aimed at equitable reforms.

In the introduction to the first section, "Leading from the Job You Have to Create More Equitable Workplaces," Charles McMartin suggests strategies to help you see yourself as a leader, even if you are not in a designated leadership position. Charles will elaborate upon these suggestions on how to work from the same growth mindset we use in facilitating workshops:

ENVISIONING YOUR LEADERSHIP: Where do you see yourself acting as a leader to enable collective action? What models and commitments guide your leadership?

WORKING FROM WHAT YOU KNOW FOR WHAT YOU VALUE: When you think about your own leadership, what are the experiences, relationships, and values that guide your collaborations with the groups you hope to serve?

CENTER ON "THE WORK," NOT "THE JOB": When you think about what you feel called to, do you think about a cause or constituency, or do you think more about the type of work you want to do? As you get centered in your life and work, you also need to do a critical analysis of your position description and the criteria for promotion and renewal. After mapping out these duties and expectations, you can then consider how to articulate what you do in reviews and mentoring discussions.

In the second section, "Building Networks to Claim Support for Your Work as a Leader," Sonia C. Arellano continues the discussion of how not to get hustled into losing sight of the work you want to do and the life you hope to have. To resist the assimilationist tendencies in professionalization, Sonia suggests these strategies for building mutual support networks to strengthen your resilience and resistance:

SEEK AND ENGAGE: As you "put yourself out there" to articulate your commitments, how can you locate peer mentors who know your institution and the communities you seek to partner with?

FOLLOW YOUR HEART AND HEAD: As you get oriented to how your institution works and where it doesn't work for you and those you seek to serve,

who are the "boundary spanners" who bridge institutional barriers and the networks you seek to engage (Purcell et al.)?
- **TAKE ON LEADERSHIP ROLES:** In addition to building cross-cutting collaborations, what formal leadership roles can help you expand your impact? How can you help create new roles that will raise collective awareness of the transformations that are needed in your institution?

In the third section, "On Not Getting Hustled," Eric A. House introduces our concluding chapters on how next-gen faculty and new-majority student leaders can take care of themselves and others to resist the Trump regime.

- **MOVING FROM MICROAFFIRMATIONS TO COALITIONAL ACTIONS:** How can you develop your collaborations into mutual support networks that recognize the contributions of your coworkers and students to empower collective action?
- **CARING ENOUGH TO LEAD:** How can you help your department slow down and attend to how they do what they do rather than treating collaborators and collaborations as a means to an end?
- **ON NOT GETTING HUSTLED:** As you continue to center on the work you aspire to do and the life you hope to live, how can you look past institutional politics and interpersonal conflicts to help your collaborators envision and enact their collective potentials?

INDIVIDUAL AND COLLECTIVE LEADERSHIP DEVELOPMENT AS A TRANSFORMATIONAL PROCESS

We will develop these points in the introductions to the sections to help you create your own leadership development plan. We hope our suggestions will help you expand upon your expertise with collaborative learning, rhetoric, and community partnerships. Supporting materials are provided by the Pullias Center for Higher Education resources on leadership:

- *Shared Equity Leadership Toolkit* by Adrianna Kezar, Elizabeth Holcombe, and Darsella Vigil.
- *Shared Equity Leadership: Making Equity Everyone's Work* by Adrianna Kezar, Elizabeth Holcombe, Darsella Vigil, and Jude Paul Mathias Dizon.
- *Leading for Equity from Where You Are: How Leaders in Different Roles Engage in Shared Equity Leadership* by Elizabeth Holcombe, Adrianna Kezar, Jordan Harper, Darsella Vigil, Natsumi Ueda, and Jude Paul Matias Dizon.
- *Capacity Building for Shared Equity Leadership: Approaches and Considerations for the Work* by Elizabeth Holcombe, Jordan Harper,

Natsumi Ueda Adrianna Kezar, Jude Paul Matias Dizon, and Darsella Vigil.
- *Emotional Labor in Shared Equity Leadership Environments: Creating Emotionally Supportive Spaces* by Darsella Vigil, Elizabeth Holcombe, Adrianna Kezar, and Natsumi Ueda.
- *Publications* by the Pullias Center for Higher Education.

Works Cited

ADE Ad Hoc Committee on English Majors' Career Preparation and Outcomes. *Report on English Majors Career Preparation and Outcomes*. Modern Language Association, 2024. https://www.maps.mla.org/content/download/191583/file/ADE-Ad-Hoc-Career-Report.pdf.

Alonso, Johanna. "The Changing Demographics of Admitted Students." *Inside Higher Education*, 11 July 2025, https://www.insidehighered.com/news/admissions/traditional-age/2025/07/11/rates-admitted-students-who-are-black-hispanic-have?utm_source=Inside+Higher+Ed&utm_campaign=6178ba4edb-DNU_2%E2%80%A6.

Arellano, Sonia. "Reflections from a Recovering Academic: Offering Guidance, Seeking Accountability, and Inspiring Leaders." *Composition Studies*, vol. 52, no. 2, 2024, pp. 166–70.

Arellano, Sonia, et al. "Shadow Work: Witnessing Latinx Crossings in Rhetoric and Composition." *Diversity Is Not Justice: Working Toward Radical Transformation and Racial Equity in the Discipline*. Special issue of *Composition Studies*. Edited by Ersula Ore, Christina Cedillo, and Kim Wieser, vol. 49, no. 2, 2021, pp. 31–52.

Baez, Benjamin. "Race-Related Service and Faculty of Color: Conceptualizing Critical Agency in Academe." *Higher Education*, vol. 39, no. 3, 2000, pp. 363–91.

Baker-Bell, April. *Linguistic Justice: Black Language, Literacy, Identity, and Pedagogy*. Routledge, 2020.

Barroso, Amanda. "Gen Z Eligible Voters Reflect the Growing Racial and Ethnic Diversity of U.S. Electorate." *Pew Research Center*, 23 Sept. 2020, www.pewresearch.org/short-reads/2020/09/23/gen-z-eligible-voters-reflect-the-growing-racial-and-ethnic-diversity-of-u-s-electorate/.

Bialik, Kristen, and Richard Fry. "Millennial Life: How Young Adulthood Today Compares with Prior Generations." *Pew Research Center*, 14 Feb. 2019, www.pewresearch.org/short-reads/2020/09/23/gen-z-eligible-voters-reflect-the-growing-racial-and-ethnic-diversity-of-u-s-electorate/.

Brown, Tessa. "What Else Do We Know? Translingualism and the History of SRTOL as Threshold Concepts in Our Field." *College Composition and Communication*, vol. 71, no. 4, June 2020, pp. 591–619.

Buenavista, Tracy Lacha, et al., eds. *First-Generation Faculty of Color: Reflections on Research, Teaching, and Service*. Rutgers UP, 2023.

Burmicky, Jorge, and Oscar E. Patrón. "How Leaders Are Keeping DEI Work Alive." *Inside Higher Education*, 8 Aug. 2025, https://www.insidehighered.com/opinion/views/2025/08/08/how-leaders-are-keeping-dei-work-alive-opinion.

Carter, Shannon, et al. *Writing Democracy: The Political Turn in and Beyond the Trump Era*. Routledge, 2020.

Chadwick, Jocelyn A., et al. "Educational Leaders Discuss the Essence of Leadership." *The English Journal*, vol. 107, no. 4, Mar. 2018, pp. 13–19.

Cole, Rose M., and Walter F. Heinecke. "Higher Education after Neoliberalism: Student Activism as a Guiding Light." *Policy Futures in Higher Education*, vol. 18, no. 1, 24 May 2018, https://doi.org/10.1177/1478210318767459.

Condon, Frankie, and Vershawn Ashanti Young. *Performing Antiracist Pedagogy in Rhetoric, Writing, and Communication*. WAC Clearinghouse, 2017.

Covarrubias, Rebecca. "Continuing Cultural Mismatches: Reflections from a First-Generation Latina Faculty Navigating the Academy." *First-Generation Faculty of Color: Reflections on Research, Teaching, and Service*. Edited by Tracy Lacha Buenavista et al., Rutgers UP, 2023, pp. 150–61.

Cox, Anicca. "Sad Math and the Weight of the Institution: Seeking Remedies for Faculty Long-Term Precarity." *College English*, vol. 86, no. 3, Jan. 2024, pp. 219–43.

Cutler, Sonel, and Alecia Taylor. "Why Scholarships for Students of Color Are Under Attack." *The Chronicle of Higher Education*, 18 Mar. 2024.

"DEI Legislation Tracker." *The Chronicle of Higher Education*. Updated 16 May 2024, www.chronicle.com/article/here-are-the-states-where-lawmakers-are-seeking-to-ban-colleges-dei-efforts.

Doleža, Joshua. "The Big Quit." *The Chronicle of Higher Education*, 27 May 2022, www.chronicle.com/article/the-big-quit.

Dryer, Dylan. "Hurry Up Please It's Time: Last Call for Writing Studies in Departments of English." *ADE Bulletin*, no. 157, 2019, pp. 71–77.

Dutton, Christa. "In Trump's First Weeks, Dozens of Colleges Have Shut Down DEI Efforts." *The Chronicle of Higher Education*, 5 Mar. 2025, www.chronicle.com/article/in-trumps-first-weeks-dozens-of-colleges-have-shut-down-dei-efforts.

Elder, Cristyn, and Bethany Davila. *Defining, Locating, and Addressing Bullying in the WPA Workplace*. Utah State UP, 2019.

Epstein, Kitty Kelly, and Bernard Stringer. "The Student Strike that Won Ethnic Studies and Black Student College Admissions." *Journal of African American Studies*, vol. 26, 28 Jan. 2023, pp. 503–13, https://doi.org/10.1007/s12111-022-09598-y.

Fry, Richard. "Millennials Overtake Baby Boomers as America's Largest Generation." *Pew Research Center*, 28 Apr. 2020, www.pewresearch.org/short-reads/2020/04/28/millennials-overtake-baby-boomers-as-americas-largest-generation/.

Gallagher, Chris. *College Made Whole: Integrative Learning for a Divided World*. John Hopkins UP, 2019.

Goldstone, Andrew. "English PhD Job Statistics, or, The Worst Is Not/So Long as We Can Say . . ." 20 Nov. 2023, andrewgoldstone.com/blog/job-market2023/. Accessed 19 May 2024.

Hill, Faith. "The Not-So-Woke Generation Z." *The Atlantic*, 14 Nov. 2024.

Holcombe, Elizabeth, et al. *Leading for Equity from Where You Are: How Leaders in Different Roles Engage in Shared Equity Leadership*. Pullias Center for Higher Education, American Council on Education, 2022, pullias.usc.edu/download/leading-for-equity-from-where-you-are-how-leaders-in-different-roles-engage-in-shared-equity-leadership.

Holcombe, Elizabeth, et al. *Capacity Building for Shared Equity Leadership: Approaches and Considerations for the Work*. Pullias Center for Higher Education, American Council on Education, 2023, pullias.usc.edu/download/capacity-building-for-shared-equity-leadership/.

House, Eric A. "Reflections on a Hip-Hop DJ Methodology." *Methods and Methodologies for Research in Digital Writing and Rhetoric Centering Positionality in Computers and Writing Scholarship*, vol. 2. Edited by Victor Del Hierro and Crystal VanKooten, WAC Clearinghouse, 2022, pp. 65–79.

Jones, Natasha N. "Coalitional Learning in the Contact Zones: Inclusion and Narrative Inquiry in Technical Communication and Composition Studies." *College English*, vol. 82, no. 5, May 2020, pp. 515–26.

Jones, Natasha N., et al. "So You Think You're Ready to Build New Social Justice Initiatives? Intentional and Coalitional Pro-Black Programmatic and Organizational Leadership in Writing Studies." *WPA: Writing Program Administration*, vol. 44, no. 3, Summer 2021, pp. 29–35.

Kahn, Seth, and Amy Lynch-Biniek. "From Activism to Organizing, From Caring to Care Work." *Labor Studies Journal*, vol. 47, no. 3, pp. 320–44.

Kannan, Vani. "Taking a Lead from Student Movements in a 'Political Turn.'" *Writing Democracy: The Political Turn in and Beyond the Trump Era*. Edited by Shannon Carter et al., Routledge, 2019, pp. 130–37.

Kezar, Adrianna, and Dan Maxey. "Collective Action on Campus Toward Student Development and Democratic Engagement." *New Directions for Higher Education*, no. 167, Fall 2014, pp. 31–41.

Kezar, Adrianna, et al. *Shared Equity Leadership Toolkit*. Pullias Center for Higher Education, American Council on Education, 2022, pullias.usc.edu/download/shared-equity-leadership-toolkit/.

Kezar, Adrianna, et al. *Shared Equity Leadership: Making Equity Everyone's Work*. Pullias Center for Higher Education, American Council on Education, 2021, pullias.usc.edu/download/shared-equity-leadership-making-equity-everyones-work/.

Knox, Liam. "What Trump's Victory Means for Higher Ed." *Inside Higher Ed*, 6 Nov. 2024, www.insidehighered.com/news/government/politics-elections/2024/11/06/what-trumps-victory-means-higher-ed.

Kohli, Rita. *Teachers of Color: Resisting Racism and Reclaiming Education*. Harvard Education Press, 2021.

Kynard, Carmen. "'All I Need Is One Mic': A Black Feminist Community Meditation on the Work, the Job, and the Hustle (and Why So Many of Yall Confuse This Stuff)." *Community Literacy Journal*, vol. 14, no. 2, 2020, pp. 5–24.

Kynard, Carmen. "Towards a Black Composition Studies: BLACK AS GRAVITAS (PART 1)." *Education, Liberation & Black Radical Traditions for the 21st Century*, 1 Sept.

2020, http://carmenkynard.org/towards-a-black-composition-studies-black-as-gravitas-part-i/.

Kynard, Carmen. *Vernacular Insurrections: Race, Black Protest, and the New Century in Composition-Literacies Studies*. SUNY, 2013.

Lusin, Natalia, and Mai Hunt. *The MLA Job List, 2020–22*. Modern Language Association, 2023, www.mla.org/content/download/191179/file/Job-List-Report-20-22.pdf.

Martin, Georgianna L., et al. "Reframing Activism as Leadership." *New Directions for Student Leadership*, no. 161, Spring 2019, pp. 9–24.

McClure, Kevin R., and Alisa Hicklin Fryar. "The Great Faculty Disengagement: Faculty Members Aren't Leaving in Droves, but They Are Increasingly Pulling Away." *The Chronicle of Higher Education*, vol. 68, no. 11, 4 Feb. 2022, chronicle.com/article/the-great-faculty-disengagement.

McMartin, Charles. "Teaching Toward Coalitions: Combatting Attacks on CRT." *Confronting Toxic Rhetoric: Writing Teachers' Experiences of Rupture, Resistance, and Resilience*. Edited by Jamie White-Farnham, Bryna Siegel Finer, and Cathryn Molloy, Peter Lang, 2025.

McMartin, Charles, and Thomas Miller. "The Challenging Opportunities Facing Next-Generation Faculty and Staff Leaders." *College English*, vol. 86, no. 3, Jan. 2024, pp. 195–218, https://doi.org/10.58680/ce2024863195.

Mechenbier, Mahli Xuan, et al. "Politics of Service." *Academic Labor: Research and Artistry*, vol. 4, "A National Snapshot of the Material Working Conditions of Contingent Faculty in Composition and Technical and Professional Communication," no. 7, 2020, https://digitalcommons.humboldt.edu/alra/vol4/iss1/7.

Ore, Ersula, et al. "Diversity Is Not Justice: Working Toward Radical Transformation and Racial Equity in the Discipline." *College Composition and Communication*, vol. 72, no. 4, 2021, pp. 601–20.

Parker, Jessica. "Writing and Unwriting Race: Using Hip-Hop in Writing and Literature Classrooms." *Performing Antiracist Pedagogy in Rhetoric, Writing, and Communication*. Edited by Frankie Condon and Vershawn Ashanti Young, WAC Clearinghouse, 2016, pp. 195–209.

Perryman-Clark, Staci. *The New Work of Writing Across the Curriculum: Diversity and Inclusion, Collaborative Partnerships, and Faculty Development*. Utah State UP, 2023.

Phillips, Rachel, and Sandra Hollingsworth. "From Curriculum to Activism: A Graduate Degree Program in Literacy to Develop Teachers as Leaders for Equity through Action Research." *Educational Action Research*, vol. 13, no. 1, 2005, pp. 85–102.

"Promotion and Tenure Resources." *Coalition for Community Writing*, https://communitywriting.org/promotion-and-tenure-resources/. Accessed 6 Mar. 2025.

Purcell, Jennifer W., et al. "Boundary Spanning Leadership Among Community-Engaged Faculty: An Exploratory Study of Faculty Participating in Higher Education Community Engagement." *Engaged Scholar Journal*, vol. 6, no. 2, Fall 2020, pp. 1–30, https://doi.org/10.15402/esj.v6i2.69398.

Quinn, Ryan. "Texas Lawmakers Create Overseer to Ensure Colleges Follow Laws." *Inside Higher Education*, 11 Aug. 2025, https://www.insidehighered.com/news/governance/state-oversight/2025/08/11/texas-lawmakers-create-overseer-make-colleges-follow.

Quinteros, Katherine, and Rebecca Covarrubias. "Reimagining Leadership Through the Everyday Resistance of Faculty of Color." *Journal of Diversity in Higher Education*, vol. 17, no. 6, 12 Jan. 2023, pp. 843–55, https://doi.org/10.1037/dhe0000471.

Read, Brock. "6 Trump Trends to Watch Closely." *The Chronicle of Higher Education*, 7 Mar. 2025, https://www.chronicle.com/article/trends-were-watching-trump-edition.

Reichert Powell, Pegeen. *Retention and Resistance: Writing Instruction and Students Who Leave*. Utah State UP, 2014.

"The Revenge of the Humanities." *College Uncovered*, Season 4, Episode 4, Hechinger Report and GBH News, 1 May 2025, https://hechingerreport.org/college-uncovered-the-revenge-of-the-humanities/#:~:text=American%20higher%20education%20is%20approaching,also%20appeared%20in%20GBH%20News.

Rhoades, Gary. "From the Margins to the Center: Negotiating a New Academy." *Contingent Faculty and the Remaking of Higher Education: A Labor History*. Edited by Eric Fure-Slocum and Claire Goldstene, U of Illinois P, 2024.

Rhoades, Gary. "Working in Coalition, and Wall-to-Wall: The New Progressive Normal." *Journal of Collective Bargaining in the Academy*, vol. 12, May 2021, https://doi.org.58188/1941-8043.1877.

Ribero, Ana Milena, and Sonia C. Arellano. "Advocating Comadrismo: A Feminist Mentoring Approach for Latinas in Rhetoric and Composition." *Peitho*, vol. 21, no. 2, 2019, pp. 334–56.

Sano-Franchini, Jennifer. "Writing Abundance: Celebrating 75 Years of Conversations about Rhetoric, Composition, Technical Communication, and Literacy." 2024 Call for Proposals, Conference on College Composition and Communication.

Social Sciences Feminist Network Research Interest Group. "The Burden of Invisible Work in Academia: Social Inequalities and Time Use in Five University Departments." *Humboldt Journal of Social Relations*, vol. 39, 2017, pp. 228–45.

Serwer, Adam. "The Great Resegregation." *The Atlantic*, 22 Feb. 2025, https://www.theatlantic.com/politics/archive/2025/02/trump-attacks-dei/681772/.

Stenberg, Shari J. *Repurposing Composition: Feminist Interventions for a Neoliberal Age*. Utah State UP, 2015.

"The Youth Vote in the 2024 Election." Center for Information & Research on Civic Learning and Engagement, 11 Nov. 2024, https://circle.tufts.edu/2024-election#youth-vote-+4-for-harris,-major-differences-by-race-and-gender.

"Truths about DEI on College Campuses: Evidence-Based Expert Responses to Politicized Misinformation." Shaun Harper, et al. University of Southern California Race and Equity Center, 2024, race.usc.edu/wp-content/uploads/2024/03/Harper-and-Associates-DEI-Truths-Report.pdf.

Vigil, Darsella, et al. *Emotional Labor in Shared Equity Leadership Environments: Creating Emotionally Supportive Spaces*. Pullias Center for Higher Education, American Council on Education, 2023, pullias.usc.edu/download/emotional-labor-in-shared-equity-leadership-environments-creating-emotionally-supportive-spaces/.

Walton, Rebecca, et al. *Technical Communication after the Social Justice Turn: Building Coalitions for Action*. Routledge, 2019.

Watson, Leah. "The Anti-'Critical Race Theory' Campaign—Classroom Censorship and Racial Backlash by Another Name." *Harvard Civil Rights-Civil Liberties Law Review*, vol. 58, Summer 2023, pp. 487–549.

Wergin, Jon F. *Leadership in Place: How Academic Professionals Can Find Their Leadership Voice*. Anker, 2007.

SECTION 1

Leading from the Job You Have to Create More Equitable Workplaces

Introduction to Section 1

CHARLES MCMARTIN

Searching for a job, any job, in the worst academic job markets in recorded history does not encourage early-career faculty to think of themselves as leaders. When interviewing thirty recent PhDs in the fall of 2021, I asked whether they saw themselves as leaders. Many paused for a while over that question. The lucky few who had been hired as writing program administrators (WPAs) and teaching assistants (TAs) supervisors responded that they had leadership responsibilities. Still, others faltered until I clarified that our study was not focusing on traditional conceptions of leaders as those who have power over others (McMartin and Miller). When I sketched out a vision of leadership as the art of building coalitions and helping people get organized to achieve their collective goals, then the conversations changed. Most respondents focused on their teaching as a place where they served as leaders—not because the classroom was where they could act as authorities, but because they saw it as a place where they did their most empowering work. In these interviews, next-gen leaders talked about how they were drawing on their studies of rhetoric, writing, critical race theory, and other paradigms to build a place where they could do the sort of work with collective empowerment that the chapters in this section discuss.

https://doi.org/10.7330/9781646428007.s001a

As early-career faculty, staff, and nonacademic professionals in an era of exceptional precarity, we face unprecedented and unpredictable challenges when stepping into new institutional roles. Our positions are often tenuous, even if we are on the tenure track, and even more unstable in other positions. We generally enter new jobs with little information about our new context's history, interpersonal conflicts, and institutional politics. These dynamics can be complicated to negotiate for those of us in faculty positions engaged in forms of scholarship concerned with equity and community work. Such scholarship can be challenging to navigate in institutional reward systems that privilege traditional forms of publishing (Baez; Kezar and Lester). Our senior colleagues often encourage us to focus on the sorts of research that made them successful rather than work on what we value. The contributors in this section offer an engaged and embodied form of scholarship that addresses the challenges of leading from where you are, whether it be working outside academe, like Charisse S. Iglesias; in lecturer positions, like Sean Moxely-Kelly and Abigail Oakely; or as a new WPA concerned with building a program that supports all the people who teach in it in the ways Anicca Cox discusses.

In each of the following chapters, the authors discuss how they have worked from the knowledge, relationships, and values that they bring to their work to create more equitable workplaces. Moxley-Kelly and Oakley introduce the GRAM model—gather, read, analyze, and make—as a method for extending labor advocacy. They examine how non-tenure track (NTT) faculty can map institutional priorities, build relationships across institutional hierarchies, navigate consensus among NTT faculty, and develop adaptive forms of leadership. Cox emphasizes the importance of preparing graduate students to work in various institutional contexts beyond research-focused universities. From her experience working outside such institutions, Iglesias outlines a dynamic toolbox of strategies for early-career PhDs entering industries outside academia. She emphasizes the need to map new contexts, negotiate personal values, and repurpose skill sets to move through the adaptive process of self-development and institutional engagement.

Adaptive leadership provides a generative frame of reference for assessing how recent PhDs in writing studies and related fields can draw upon their disciplinary expertise, life experiences, and practical skills to frame problems, work through recursive processes, critique systemic inequities, and engage collaborators in developing mutually beneficial solutions. In the first chapter in this section, Moxley-Kelly and Oakley look to John Wergin's writings on "leadership in place" for a model of adaptive leadership. Wergin looks past those in hierarchical positions of authority to examine the collective forms of agency that are exercised in collaborative networks such as the labor organizing work that Moxley-Kelly and Oakley examine. "Adaptive" leadership emerges from grassroots collaborations that extend beyond institutional boundaries to address problems that cannot be solved using established methods, technical expertise, or traditional presuppositions. Early-career PhDs like the contributors to this collection are often improvising through collaborative discovery processes without fixed goals or clear metrics to learn the leadership strategies Wergin discusses—"the art of problem framing, the art of stimulating energy for adaptive work, the art of negotiating conflict, and the art of building consensus" (Wergin 3). These coalitional learning strategies are familiar to those who have taught writing workshops, studied rhetorical analysis and learned how to use theoretical paradigms to frame and explore the workings of systems and networks.

In thinking about the case studies in adaptive leadership in this section, I return to the overall framework of our collection. We look to the leadership of scholar-activists like Carmen Kynard, particularly the need to distinguish between the work, the job, and the hustle, to stay focused on the work we value most. Kynard's heuristics are particularly useful for those of us who are concerned with the work of disrupting "the white, neoliberalist, racial-affect-sanitized ethos of the Western academy and its epistemological violence" (12). Kynard centers her scholarly work on "Black thought and Black life" as "a conduit for the higher calling of community knowledges, ancestral life-forces, and radical protest histories," and she continues to lead our profession in this work (18, 12). In contrast with that community-based work, our jobs often require us to navigate "the arbitrary neoliberalist structures of the job market, publishing, tenure, and the grind of academia" (18). Graduate students and early-career faculty are in precarious positions that can pressure them to conflate their work with their job and invest their energies in the hustle of getting "your paper / to make that money / to get tenure and promotion" and caring about "journal article rankings, university press rankings, CV lines, job market trends, hiring committees, salary negotiations, job applications, interviews, and other submissions of all kinds" (19).

The adaptive leadership strategies of the next-gen faculty contributors in this section demonstrate how to prioritize the work that matters most to us. Their chapters demonstrate how working in academic and nonacademic settings requires navigating multiple and intersecting challenges: redressing institutional structures that perpetuate racism, adapting curriculum to the lived realities of new majority students, responding to declining enrollments, revising neoliberal management models, and combatting reactionary politicians' assaults on diversity and equity initiatives. Amid all these pressures, we must pause and ask ourselves, "How can we prioritize the work that matters most to us in the midst of our institutional and professional realities?" Below, I share a few key takeaways about launching your career while prioritizing the work.

Envisioning Your Leadership

Recognizing Yourself as a Leader: Darsella Vigil and her coauthors remind us that "leaders must first turn inward and do their own personal work in order to then turn outward to transform their institutions" (1). Following this advice, reflect on where you naturally exert influence or where you aspire to make meaningful changes within your academic and professional circles. This might include mentoring students, spearheading collaborative projects, or initiating a new program or major. Remember that leadership does not mean administration or management; leadership is about change and working with others to enable collaborative action. Where do you see yourself acting as a leader? Who are the people around you that can help lead change in your context?

Creating Your Own Measures of Success: Reflect on the deeper meaning behind your work. Ask yourself what drives you beyond the responsibilities of your job title. Whether it's a commitment to social change, supporting marginalized voices, or advancing knowledge in your field, clarifying your purpose can guide your actions. As Jenna Sheffield and Paul Muhlhauser's study of tenure-track faculty in rhetoric and composition demonstrates, when we measure our work using the metrics of tenure and promotion, we will never feel like we have done enough. Remember that no matter how much of your time and energy you pour into the academy, it "does not love anyone" (Kynard 19). Remember why you were drawn to your work in the first place. Whether it was a passion for teaching, a desire to effect change through language, or a fascination with the power of rhetoric, honoring your core motivations can help you navigate challenges and stay focused on your purpose.

Working from What You Know for What You Value

Naming Your Funds of Knowledge: The authors in this first section review how they drew on their expertise in rhetoric and teaching to develop values-based leadership in a nonacademic organization, in their effort to build a faculty coalition, and in their work building a new writing program that supports the unrecognized work of instructors. When you think about your own leadership, what are "the funds of knowledge" that you draw on to consider how you collaborate with others, build relationships, and try to support the individuals and groups with which you identify (Moll et al.)? Who are your models when you think about individual leaders and the sorts of collaborative decision-making and action you want to engage in? What values are enacted in these examples, and how do they guide your collaborations? Where do those values come from, and how can you put them to work more effectively by drawing on your formal expertise and the lessons you have learned about collaboration inside and outside of classrooms?

Centering on "the WORK," Not "the JOB"

Centering the Work: Kynard centers her vision of the WORK on the teaching-life. She uses a series of questions focused on "critical moments in Black communities and classrooms to remind myself of who I am, where I come from, why I been sent, and the work I am here to do" (12). These centering questions call upon us to reflect on whom we seek to work for and how our connections with them transcend the institutional confines of the JOB. When you think about what you are here to do, do you think about a cause or constituency, or do you think more about the type of work you want to do? What questions can you ask yourself to remain centered on the WORK?

Reminding Yourself Who the Work is For: Consider the communities you come from and care most about. How can your work contribute to their needs and aspirations? How can you cultivate and maintain relationships with mentors and peers who remind you of your values and connect you to others doing the work you care about? We all need a constellation of friends, mentors, and communities in our lives to sustain and renew our resilience. It is important that we find and stay rooted in those networks of care, so that we do not get stuck in our own department or even in national networks of folks within a particular discipline or profession. How can you cultivate and maintain your relationships with the individuals and communities that will help sustain your work?

Works Cited

Baez, Benjamin. "Race-Related Service and Faculty of Color: Conceptualizing Critical Agency in Academe." *Higher Education*, vol. 39 no. 3, 2000, pp. 363–91.

Kezar, Adrianna, and Jaime Lester. "Supporting Faculty Grassroots Leadership." *Research in Higher Education*, vol. 50, no. 7, 2009, pp. 715–40, https://doi.org/10.1007/s11162-009-9139-6.

Kynard, Carmen. "'All I Need Is One Mic': A Black Feminist Community Meditation on the Work, the Job, and the Hustle (and Why So Many of Yall Confuse This Stuff)." *Community Literacy Journal*, vol. 14, no. 2, 2020, pp. 5–24, https://doi.org/10.25148/14.2.009033.

McMartin, Charles, and Thomas P. Miller. "Challenging Opportunities Facing Next-Generation Faculty." *College English*, vol. 86, no. 3, 2024, pp. 195–218.

Moll, Luis C., et al. *Funds of Knowledge: Theorizing Practices in Households and Classrooms*. Lawrence Erlbaum Associates, 2005.

Sheffield, Jenna Pack, and Paul Muhlhauser. "When Enough Isn't Enough: Rhetoric and Composition Tenure-Track Scholars' Perceptions and Feelings toward Tenure Processes." *College English*, vol. 83, no. 3, 2021, pp. 200–34.

Vigil, Darsella, et al. *Emotional Labor in Shared Equity Leadership Environments: Creating Emotionally Supportive Spaces*. American Council on Education USC Rossier Pullias Center for Higher Education, 2023, pullias.usc.edu/download/emotional-labor-in-shared-equity-leadership-environments-creating-emotionally-supportive-spaces/.

Wergin, Jon. "Leadership in Place." *The Department Chair*, vol. 14, no. 4, Spring 2004, pp. 1–3.

1
Putting the Rhetorical Expertise of NTT Faculty to Work

SEAN MOXLEY-KELLY AND ABIGAIL OAKLEY

Current research on advocacy of non-tenure track (NTT) faculty within the university tends to focus on medium- and small-sized universities. Typical advice includes to work collectively within the NTT rank, build coalitions between NTT and tenure track (TT) faculty, emphasize the valuable research and service work of NTT faculty, and maintain institutional memory, particularly of past accomplishments (see Wootton and Moomau; Lind and Mullin; Nardo and Heifferon; Norgaard). At very large universities, however, these efforts can be complicated by unwieldy administrative workings that are often mired in reams of red tape.

In this chapter, we focus on the collective strategies of NTT faculty representatives within Arizona State University (ASU). In particular, we examine the rhetorical practices of a group of NTT representatives in the department of English, each of whom volunteered for an uncompensated service role in addition to their 5/5 course load. Effecting change within the opaque bureaucracy of a large public, research-oriented university boasting one of the largest student bodies in the United States is a complex challenge. Nevertheless, these representatives successfully argued for an increase to the take-home salaries of their NTT rank during the 2021–2022 academic year. We will examine the ways

https://doi.org/10.7330/9781646428007.c001

this change came about and the implications for those—like the authors—that struggle to practice effective advocacy in NTT roles.

There are two types of full-time NTT faculty in the ASU Department of English that are distinguished by their representation structure and responsibilities: Instructors with 5/5 teaching loads, who elect representatives to vote in department meetings, and teaching professors with 4/4 teaching loads and a 20 percent service requirement, who all have departmental voting rights. In this chapter, we use the terminology used by ASU when referring to these positions and reserve the term NTT faculty for times when we are describing both groups, commenting broadly on the profession, or extrapolating our advocacy efforts to other NTT roles.

Our chapter highlights key strategies the instructor representatives engaged in to advocate for increased wages. Specifically, we discuss how they researched the conditions for instructors within the university, engaged in the affective work of listening to and commiserating with their colleagues, navigated consensus of a large body of colleagues, and productively worked with administration to articulate the shared benefits of increasing instructor wages. Based on these strategies, we suggest a method for NTT faculty to engage in workplace advocacy when facing the issues of liminal spaces and adaptive problems (Wergin, "Leadership"). In particular, we offer a complementary method to Schreiber and Melonçon's Gather, Read, Analyze, and Make (GRAM) Model for improving academic programs and working with administration. Our experience and findings suggest that NTT faculty can effectively engage in workplace advocacy by *gathering* relevant data, *reflecting* on professional narratives and our place within our work community, and *participating* when we have the time and will to do so.

Institutional Context

ASU's sprawling main campus is located in Tempe, Arizona. The arid, hot desert climate of southern Arizona lends itself to growing palm trees, easily spotted against the bright, cloudless blue sky across the campus. In addition to this main campus, there are ASU branches in Mesa, Glendale, and downtown Phoenix. In 2022, there were a total of 142,616 ASU students across all campuses, with 57,588 of those in Tempe ("Facts and Figures"). The Department of English on the Tempe campus employs seventy-six instructors and twelve teaching professors, for a total of around eighty-eight full-time NTT faculty; nearly all teach primarily or exclusively first-year writing or business writing courses through ASU writing programs. At a university that places a premium on enrollment growth, writing programs teachers are the only faculty group to see nearly every student in relatively small classes, with course caps of twenty-four. Because of this, many writing programs teachers have been told that they are the reason some students remain on campus rather than dropping out.

ASU operates under the charter for the New American University, an attempt by President Michael Crow to keep ASU at the forefront of innovation in education. The New American University exchanges exclusivity for inclusivity:

> ASU is a comprehensive public research university, measured not by whom it excludes, but by whom it includes and how they succeed; advancing research and discovery of public value; and assuming fundamental responsibility for the economic, social, cultural and overall health of the communities it serves. ("ASU Charter")

This charter serves as a unifying mission statement, rhetorical touchstone, and driving force for all the colleges and departments within Arizona State University. However, for its employees ASU remains a neoliberal institution, with the hallmark emphasis on "individualism and individual responsibility" (Stenberg 5). That is to say, at ASU it is incumbent on the individual to act in service of the larger institution, and "individuals are . . . expected to make choices that will maximize their human capital" (Stenberg 5). One instantiation of this philosophy happened about a decade ago, with an attempt by the Department of English to significantly change instructors' workload.

In 2014, the same year that President Michael Crow debuted the charter (Crow and Dabars), the ASU Department of English announced a plan to increase the instructor teaching load from what was then 4/4 with a 20 percent service responsibility, to 5/5 with no service. In addition, the department raised the course caps from nineteen to twenty-five, giving all instructors an additional forty-nine students per semester (Flaherty). This placed ASU Instructors in the top quintile of workload for full-time NTT writing faculty across the country (Mechenbier et al. 38). Administration did not plan to increase instructor pay, which was then $32,000. The explanation for this change given by Mark Lussier, the chair at the time, was simply "budgetary restraints" (qtd. in Flaherty). While there was an initial outcry by instructors, this issue was only resolved after instructors made the issue public with protests and articles in *Inside Higher Ed* and local news sources (see Flaherty; Stewart). The department eventually relented and raised instructor pay to compensate for the additional workload.

This 2014 event is a sticking point in the NTT history at ASU. Many of the current NTT faculty were present for these events, including us (Sean and Abigail). As we discuss later, trust is a crucial part of NTT faculty advocacy, and the 2014 event lost the administration of the Department of English nearly all of its goodwill from the NTT faculty. Unfortunately, the administration has never really managed to earn trust or goodwill back.

NTT advocacy was vital to the negotiations in 2014 and has continued to be important. For the past decade our advocacy has focused on working conditions, arguing for lower course caps, fewer courses per semester, higher salaries, multi-year contracts, and professional development opportunities, just as NTT faculty across the country do (see American Federation of Teachers; Culver and Kezar; Kahn; Schell; McBeth and McCormack).

We have seen some success, most notably an increase in the base salary for instructors from $49,000 to $60,000 in the fall of 2022. Concurrently, the university renamed all NTT faculty to "career faculty." These changes to salary and terminology were announced as "step one" in a plan to make improvements for NTT faculty. Despite inquiries, it was unclear what the additional steps of the plan were. At the time of writing, the only other change has been renaming the 4/4 load NTT position to teaching professor (from lecturer).

NTT faculty's reaction to these changes has been mixed. Because teaching professors did not also receive an increase in pay, they were understandably upset. Within the instructor rank, for new hires the raises represented a 22 percent increase. But long-term instructors, making close to $60,000 after years of merit increases, were also bumped to $60,000. This disparity in wage increases left senior instructors feeling administrators dramatically undervalued their years of teaching experience and service to the institution, and these feelings of frustration have only compounded the loss of trust in administrators after the 2014 events. Additionally, the decision-making process for these changes has seemed opaque, and they are widely considered inadequate to address the concerns of the NTT teaching population.

Adaptive Work in Liminal Spaces

In a 2020 special issue of *Academic Labor: Research and Artistry*, Lisa Melonçon, Mahli Mechenbier, and Laura Wilson report on their work on contingent faculty in writing programs. They provide and analyze the largest data set on the working conditions and perspectives of contingent faculty in order to reveal "what it really means to work off the tenure track" (Melonçon et al.,

"Introduction" 5). In the conclusion to the issue, they advise that "we need to be more aware of how changes are being implemented and how—in specific details—small victories were gained. These sorts of examples, when placed alongside field-wide data and information, can provide powerful exigence to instigate change at all levels and locales" (Melonçon et al., "Looking Forward" 129). Despite the mixed response, the 22 percent raise we received seemed to count as a "small victory" worthy of analysis. As Seth Kahn points out, not all forms of "valuing" NTT faculty are made equal, and compensation is the most important ("We Value"). But as with many things at ASU, how this small victory was gained was not readily visible to us. To understand why, we must first reflect on our positionality.

We find the metaphor of liminality useful as we conceptualize our position in the university. Tracy Whalen explains liminality as "a threshold (or *limen*), caught between practices, cultures, frames for knowing the world, and modes of communication . . . an interstitial place, the place of in-between" (1, emphasis in original). The liminal space applies to nearly any administrative or advocacy-based role in the university. The writing program administrator (WPA), for example, sits in a place of "middle management," having "a degree of authority over one group (the writing faculty and consequently the students) while simultaneously requiring subservience to another (English department chairs and larger institutional authorities)" (Rose et al. 45). The department head exists in a similar manner, reporting to higher-level administrators and other institutional authorities, while being responsible to those in charge of departmental programs and teachers within the department. In each case, taking on a role of authority often means an individual gains access to additional knowledge, but lacks the power to make changes based on that knowledge. So elected instructor representatives and administration alike exist in a liminal space of knowledge, power, and the lack thereof—as do instructors, like the two of us as we began this chapter, who want to contribute to improving the working conditions of our rank.

We see liminality as a shared challenge for NTT leaders and administration, but other challenges differentiate us from administration. Leadership scholar Jon Wergin discusses the distinction between technical and adaptive leadership work. While technical solutions may be challenging to implement, the solutions themselves are familiar from past experience. In contrast, "when problem definitions are not clear cut and technical solutions are not available" ("Leadership in Place" 2) a more significant leadership challenge is presented, which requires adaptive work. Adaptive work depends on learning by all stakeholders, who "must recognize that their existing perspectives won't lead them to a resolution" (Wergin, *Leadership in Place* 15). While department chairs and NTT leaders both operate in liminal spaces, chairs have the advantage of tenure and systems of university support; as a result, their problems can be solved with a mix of technical and adaptive work. In contrast, for the instructors at ASU, there are few systems of structural support for our advocacy. Our knowledge and experience are distributed widely across 76 individuals. With no service responsibility, only small amounts of that expertise can be contributed to the collective work at any time. In other words, for NTT leaders our problems are nearly all adaptive, not technical; we operate with a systemic lack of preexisting solutions. We (Abigail and Sean specifically) conceptualize these struggles as a fog of war. Although neither of us is overly fond of the martial metaphor, we continue to use it, and will return to it throughout this chapter, because it reflects the complexity of the systems in which we operate and the ways a systemic lack of information complicates our ability to act (as well as the history of conflict between NTT and administration).

We are particularly attuned to these challenges because they represent a stark contrast to our experiences as graduate students, a time when we both felt confident in our ability to navigate the complexities of our departments. Then, we each took on multiple leadership roles and projects. I (Sean) worked as a graduate assistant to the writing program administrator and was research fellow for a grant-funded graduate student professional development program. My dissertation examined career stories of pioneering women in engineering, looking especially into how they represented their work and crafted professional identities through narrative. During my (Abigail's) graduate career, I spearheaded reform to department online teacher training. For my dissertation, I performed an institutional ethnography focusing on graduate teaching associates' experiences learning to teach online and triangulated that with administration's experiences and the impact of public-facing statements including ASU's Charter.

However, translating this valuable experience into leadership roles post–graduate school has been challenging. Both of us accepted positions as instructors at Arizona State University and found opportunities to apply our organizational expertise highly limited. Some of our challenges were motivational as new PhDs burnt out from graduate school, managing 115 or more students per semester and then confronting a pandemic. It was difficult to do more than survive the quotidian aspects of the job. But other challenges were structural. As instructors, few formal leadership opportunities are available because administration avoids asking us to do more than our 100 percent teaching contract requires. Nevertheless, seven instructor representatives are required for departmental procedures, so these roles are filled by elected volunteers each year. Although Wergin argues that adaptive leadership "does not have to reside with people having formal authority," he also acknowledges that "designated leaders can make leadership in place more likely" (*Leadership in Place* 15–17). So, it was to the role of English department instructor representative that we turned our attention.

Methods

In order to better understand our recent "small victories" we decided to interview those who were involved and to participate in leadership ourselves. First, we crafted our research questions as:

- How have we, as a rank, advocated for ourselves during a time of pandemic? And how can we, or someone in a situation like ours, contribute to these efforts despite the challenges, both structural and individual, of understanding our own agenda?

We requested interviews with all seven instructors who served as English department instructor representatives for the Fall 2021–Spring 2022 year and contacted the chair of the English Department and head of writing programs. Five instructor representatives and the head of writing programs agreed to participate. We conducted thirty-to-sixty-minute interviews with each participant. Our questions focused on eliciting recollections of past advocacy efforts, reflections on the effectiveness of those approaches, and recommendations for current and future advocacy. Our recruitment and interview protocols were institutional review board–approved.

During the course of this project we (Abigail and Sean) were elected as instructor representatives, and we served in this role as we analyzed our interview data and wrote this chapter. As we work to situate this research within a theoretical methodology that encompasses our own advocacy, we find that there isn't quite a single participatory research framework that fits our role. We are not quite the researcher as participant that Barbara Probst describes in "Both/and: Researcher as Participant in Qualitative Inquiry," nor do we neatly fit into a participatory action research (PAR) methodology. Parts of our research strongly align with PAR, a methodology that "combines theory and practice, action and reflection with the participation of stakeholders who seek practical solutions to concerns and issues" (Jacobs 48), and we are in alignment with the "commitment to radical social change" that Mary Brydon-Miller and Patricia Macguire center in their explanation of PAR methodology. However, PAR typically has a greater degree of collaboration between participants and researchers during data collection and analysis than we have. We are practicing the activism we write about rather than bringing the colleagues we interviewed into the research process. In this way, we are situated as *activist*-researchers rather than *participant*-researchers.

Our activist-research positionality requires us to practice *critical imagination*, a method of considering the data and its context deeply (Royster and Kirsch). Critical imagination also necessitates a reflexive praxis in which researchers consider their place within the research paradigm as they interpret data (Royster and Kirsch). As activist-researchers, we worked to tack[1] back and forth between the data and the literature, listening and thinking reflexively about our data and the similar situation we were simultaneously living. To process the interview data, we collaboratively developed "process codes" (Saldaña), which we applied to the interview transcriptions in two rounds of coding using the coding software Dedoose. Finally, our participants were given pseudonyms.

Results: Research and Listening, Doing Affective Work, Navigating Consensus, and Working with Administration

Our analysis of the interview data and our own experiences revealed four themes: research and listening, doing affective work, navigating consensus, and working with administration. We discuss each theme as a type of action that participants take; at the same time, we'll tell the story of how, over the course of the 2021–2022 academic year, participants advocated for improved conditions and (at least in part) effected a change for higher pay. Again, we want to clarify that we use instructor to refer to the 5/5 load position, teaching professor for the 4/4 load position, and NTT faculty to encompass both or refer to these kinds of positions across academia.

As we processed, reflected, and wrote, we found the GRAM model helped us conceptualize the work we saw our participants doing. Many scholars note that academic programs have their own particular exigencies, challenges that necessitate their own appropriate responses. The GRAM model, as articulated by Schreiber and Melonçon, adapts change management processes developed for business contexts into a four step, recursive process for improving academic

---

1. We borrow the term tacking from Royster and Kirsch, who explain that feminist rhetorical researchers tack in to established research methods and tack out to incorporate a more global view of the data and related

programs. In their November 2023 *Academic Labor* special issue, Melonçon et al. further position GRAM as a way to encourage the re-professionalization of teaching and improve NTT working conditions; specifically, they argue GRAM can be a tool to "convince" administrators to recognize their agency and take actions that change "patterns ... programs, processes, and professional development opportunities" (Melonçon et al., "Looking Forward" 135). The four steps of GRAM are *gather* data, *read* institutional landscapes, *analyze* information, and *make* changes to "curricula or processes" (Schreiber and Melonçon 262–63). The approaches our participants describe reflect many elements of Schreiber and Melonçon's work and offer support for the effectiveness of their model. In the final section, we reflect on what these themes mean for us, as Instructors occupying a liminal space and advocating for NTT faculty.

Research and Listening

> I really feel like when I got in the Instructor Representative position that all it was about was survey. Find out what our people want. We had response rates that were over 90 [percent], which I think is incredible. And, you know, all they need to do is be asked. (Tony)

Collecting data was a central concern for the instructor representatives we interviewed, but participants struggled to find the data they needed to make the claim for higher wages. There is a paucity of data-driven research on contingent faculty issues in the rhetoric and writing and technical writing fields (Melonçon et al., "Introduction" 9); moreover, instructor representatives saw the need for collecting data specific to their institution. In place of scholarly research, they instead practiced listening to their constituents, to each other, and to administrators. Listening to this range of stakeholders helped the representatives realize that there was not a strong consensus among NTT faculty about how to argue for improved working conditions.

Mary explained that the instructor representatives started their appointment in the 2021–2022 school year by distributing a "survey to the Instructor rank to find out, kind of, what our priorities were." In addition, the representatives had the results of a similar survey of the teaching professors. The survey results, according to one instructor representative, Tony, revealed that "one of the biggest concerns was not the 5/5 teaching load, it was the pay. . . . There were comments that they, we had learned the tools to teach the 5/5 and survive it, but what we couldn't have survived was not having enough money to pay rent. So that shifted our focus."

Still, debates continued within the representative group about how to proceed, debates which were settled by listening to administration. One participant felt the representatives should argue for both higher pay and lower course load, but in an early meeting the representatives received messaging that "we couldn't have both" and decided to focus on salary issues. Listening also provided perspective about how little upper administration knew about the material working conditions of instructors and emphasized the steep challenge of delivering appeals that bridged that knowledge gap. John reported that in meetings, "we had one administrator that was like, 'Is rent high for you guys right now?' And then we had another one say something like, 'Is it inflation?'" In fact, in the year leading up to these meetings Phoenix-area rents increased nearly 30 percent, more than double the national average (Reagor), which was widely reported in local and national news. John reflected on this experience in saying "how out of touch the administrators were with what people [in the] lower middle class are going through, or even just their own people, I think is what was so striking." The representatives were justly surprised by how little administration knew about these macroeconomic changes and the impact of those changes on their employees. Efforts to appeal for change would have to make explicit context which representatives took for granted as part of their lived experience.

The representatives considered it rhetorically important to be able to represent the workload and financial situation of the majority of NTT faculty, so they gathered data to illustrate both these challenges to administrators. The results of the survey from the beginning of the year, which the representatives shared with administration in their initial meetings, were "like personal stories and experiences related to this issue" of low pay. The representatives realized this emphasis on qualitative data wasn't working, rhetorically. As Anne says, "We're English teachers, so we do a lot of anecdotes and we tell stories and all of that, but the admin needs tended to be more data driven." Our participants recognized the need for a shift to quantitative data, but it took time for the instructor representatives to figure out how to meet this need. Due to the fog of war in which they operate, the representatives did not have a good sense of what specific data they needed or what resources were available to properly collect, analyze, and present that data.

Finding ways to collect quantitative data on NTT faculty was a pivotal strategy as instructor representatives argued for increased wages. Some of this data was readily available, such as the number of students and pages of student work we read, salary data, and inflation trends, but other data required more creative work to collect. Tony, for example, "looked at the average cost of rent here in the Phoenix metropolitan area . . . the instructors, most of them, still were paying off student loans . . . so I thought we should only be putting out 25 percent of our monthly take home for rental expense and calculated that out and that came up to a number of $65,000." Gertrude explains that presenting the results of Tony's work "was when a light came on" for administration. The quantitative data, Gertrude expounds, "presented a message that the more personalized, individualized, still very significant sort of testimonial evidence, wasn't quite getting . . . across." Unfortunately, as Tony's description of his research process indicates, the quantitative data was collected from public sources and involved a lot of educated guesswork. There are ways in which the data used did not reflect the specific situation of the instructors because the shift to quantitative data came after the surveying was completed. For instance, although they could present data on average rents, they did not have data on how many of our faculty rent versus own.

This cycle of data gathering with a focus on administration's interests is often repeated with new instructor representatives taking part in the conversation. The cycle of new representatives each year and a break during the summer, during which most instructors do not work for ASU, contributes to the fog of war around research and listening. At the time of writing, we are working to gather more data regarding how Instructors want to improve their working conditions. We have learned we cannot gather financial data through approved channels at the university, for example, surveys distributed by the department. Anything gathered via unapproved means would probably not be acceptable to administration. So, despite much repeated effort, this objective remains unachieved—an illustration of the challenges of navigating the fog of war in our positions.

DOING AFFECTIVE WORK

> I'm weary. I'm tired because I know it's a lot there's a lot of fighting, you know . . . I really wish there was a more relational term I could put it into, but pugilistic terms because you're constantly fighting with yourself, fighting with others to change the dialogue towards something that moves in the direction of income equality and a livable wage. (John)

It is difficult to overstate the importance of emotional labor that instructor representatives engage in. Over the course of our interviews with the representatives, we found that the affective work they engaged in included feeling a sense of duty to the work of being a representative and on managing tough emotions like anger, frustration, and fear in both them and their coworkers. Wilson et al. would call this "affective investment," which they define as commitment to organizational and institutional interactions including "between material bodies, ... institutional and organizational infrastructures, ... and the political and social aspects of decision making" (93). Each representative, in various ways, talked about their affective investment in their roles.

Instructor representatives take on that role because they are motivated by not only their work conditions, but also their sense of continual, persistent responsibility to and solidarity with their peers. It's this feeling that drives them into the most institutionally recognized service role available. As Gertrude put it, "when I first got involved it was out of a sense of duty that it was my turn," and other participants similarly express that "I feel like somebody's got to do something here" and "I think it's important." This 'sense of duty' was not participants' only reason for stepping into their role as a representative. They believed their experiences and abilities as educators prepared them to communicate effectively with administration and advocate for their NTT colleagues. Some participants also noted that they had the time and flexibility to attend extra meetings and invest extra labor. Their sense of duty illustrates the representative's embodied, affective connection to the priorities of the entire rank.

In the Department of English, NTT faculty afford administration little, if any, benefit of the doubt in communications and in conversations about the job and administration. Conversations between colleagues in our rank are often laced with anger, resentment, and, at times, despair. Many instructors work two jobs or take on additional classes to make ends meet, resulting in heavy burnout, as Tony expressed: "I think we're just so burnt out, we're burnt out with the fight that we had for salary, the continuation of the 5/5. And I think everyone now just goes in, teaches their 5/5, and walks out the door as fast as they can. . . . I think we've all swallowed the poison and . . . I think that no one really gives a shit anymore." Adding the work of a representative, being responsible for and advocating for a better quality of life, only adds stress to an underpaid, overworked instructor, which can have significant consequences. John described that "I had kind of a stress breakdown in one of the meetings where I was getting so much pushback from other people in our rank and then so much pushback from administrators, just denying the problem." Affective investment in both the job of teaching and the work of advocacy compounds and exacerbates hard feelings in our work environment.

It is tempting to get lost in the frustration of the "uphill battle" for better working conditions, but we must keep in mind our own boundaries both in terms of workload and things that are outside of our control. For instructor representatives, that also means being a sounding board for our colleagues and balancing our affective investment in both our colleagues and the university with empathetic yet professional responses to these instances. Gertrude explained: "Venting is significant. Hearing other people's concerns is important. Being there for other people is significant. But then recognizing, you know, the things I cannot change, the things I can, is something that I think that all of us in interacting with each other need to be pragmatic about." In Gertrude's view, emotional conversations and reactions are an important part of the instructor representative role, but it is also within the role of the representative to maintain a pragmatic perspective on NTT advocacy both in terms of what goals are achievable and the best method to achieve those goals.

It would not be fair, however, to characterize affective investment as always draining; it can also have the opposite effect. I (Sean) had never served as an instructor representative before starting this research project. I found the process of conducting interviews with the representatives, hearing about their affective work and the results they produced, very invigorating. Their affective investment led me to volunteer for the role myself, with the intention of continuing and building on their work. After three years of full-time teaching, I (Abigail) finally felt that I was able to move past the burnout from my PhD program, and I also ran for a representative position for the first time. My first three years were fairly insular, as I was focused on surviving a significantly increased teaching load and managing my symptoms of burnout. My motivation for advocacy was less of a "calling," and more of a desire to again be an active participant in the bettering of my workplace.

NAVIGATING CONSENSUS

> I know there were plenty of people who would have been ready to take further steps beyond just conversation. But with such a large rank, and people in so many different positions and with different levels of precarity, even that is really hard to put together. So as much as they think, you know, "maybe more aggressive tactics could be useful in some situations," getting enough people to work with that is definitely a challenge. (Mary)

Whatever challenges we face, NTT faculty in ASU's English Department have an undeniable strength: there are nearly one hundred of us, working full-time to provide necessary classes to over ten thousand students a semester. Our participants recognize the importance of "designated leaders" (Wergin 17) and describe the instructor representative role as a valuable asset to our advocacy efforts because representatives can focus and deliver the full weight of the instructor rank. Anne described the existence of the position as "an advantage" because everything is "sort of funneled into a smaller group" which provides a "core" that other NTT on campus lack, while Mary points out that the representative position means advocacy can happen without the majority having to "stick their neck out." However, to realize this purpose requires developing a consensus among the elected representatives and between representatives and the instructor group.

An event that occurred at the end of the 2021–2022 school year illustrates the challenges of navigating consensus as an instructor representative. After an academic year of meetings with administrators after which the representatives heard that a pay increase might be on the table for further discussion in the following year, one of the representatives took dramatic individual action. This representative sent an impassioned email to the dean, provost, and entire instructor group arguing for our wage increase. The representative quoted responses from the early-semester surveys in which NTT faculty vividly described their own financial precarity, such as not being able to run their air conditioner during the hot Arizona summer for fear of the high utility bill.

Sean and Abigail responded to these events differently. I (Abigail) believe that this email was detrimental to the message that the instructor representatives had been trying to send to the higher administration: that we are reasonable, and there are legitimate reasons behind asking for increased pay. As our interviews revealed, the representatives spent time negotiating the data they collected and practiced the most rhetorically effective ways to present arguments to administrators. Data-driven communications punctuated with personal accounts made sense for an administrator audience. These are all intentional and purposeful actions taken by the Representatives together as a unified front, and, as Wootton and Moomau point out, faculty reputation is an important aspect of changing one's working conditions within the university. So, for a single representative to go rogue and email an impassioned message to upper administrators directly seemed to tear down much of the ethos-building work the representatives had done. I found that several other instructors and representatives shared my perspective.

However, I (Sean) was more inclined to see the email as an attempt to ensure NTT voices were appropriately heard. When confronted with dramatically out-of-touch administrative comments, followed by slow-playing actual action, the representatives had reason to doubt the stories they were telling mattered. Distributing the survey responses widely and publicly can be read as a way to ensure those stories were heard by amplifying their volume. In addition, I initially saw the move as an individual action with individual repercussions; this aligns with how the representative who sent the email saw his actions. He expressed fearing "I'm going to get fired" but "I don't care." He saw the consequences as personal, and he accepted them because he knew his position (a partner with a stable job) freed him to take risks others could not.

Reflecting on our initial disagreements about this event led us to consider our respective positions. Both of us are scholars of inequalities, particularly gendered inequalities, in workplaces. But I (Sean) have the privilege of researching those inequalities largely from the outside. I was much more willing to accept frustration, an emotion that is rooted in anger, as a justification for taking individual action; I less readily considered the way these actions reflected on the community. But Abigail provided an alternative perspective. I (Abigail) argue that what Sean describes here is part of the work of being in the oppressing class and applying the theory of the marginalized group. Reflection and reflexivity are necessary components to this kind of advocacy work because instructor representatives speak on behalf of others. Being an instructor representative is not the work of an individual but rather the work of a speaker on behalf of a collective. We (both Sean and Abigail) agree that this incident highlights how the fog of war can make us reactive rather than reflective in moments of stress or crisis.

Participants also described engaging in alternative ways of consensus-building that combined individual priorities with group action in ways that we both agreed represented more respectful and productive ways of managing consensus. For instance, Mary discussed her opposition to course overloads, which pay a low per-course rate. Mary believes that "as long as we keep taking them, they're going to keep offering us . . . overloads at really poor pay." Indeed, overloads can represent a "shadow economy" (Norgaard) that obscures the realities of course staffing and potential instructor negotiation power, another expression of the fog of war. Although this is not a cause that instructors have tackled as a group, Mary chooses not to take overloads herself and once unsuccessfully attempted to negotiate for higher pay for an overload. Despite the lack of collective commitment, she believes in this action and tries to move other people towards her position with what she characterizes as "quietly advocating" through conversations. While her individual attempt to negotiate a pay raise was unsuccessful, the department later increased the instructor overload pay rate—though it is still not commensurate with our full salaries.

WORKING WITH ADMINISTRATION

> We highlighted how, when we have had to shift our methods for instruction because of how much more time it takes to process paperwork, maybe, the individual attention gets lost with the students. And so by being able to focus both on the numerical data but also the impact on students, I think that's where we gave a really meaningful message to the provost, and she was really receptive of the message that we delivered. . . . We weren't just thinking about ourselves, we were thinking about the larger ASU community. (Gertrude)

Over the course of the 2021–2022 school year, the instructor representatives organized meetings with the chair of the Department of English, the dean of humanities in the College of Liberal Arts and Sciences, and finally, late in the spring semester, the university provost. In these meetings, instructor representatives presented the quantitative data and survey results they had gathered to motivate administrators to advocate or (if they had the power) act to improve working conditions for NTT faculty. In their work with administration, several participants emphasized the importance of audience awareness. Gertrude, for example, argues understanding and speaking to administration is where activists should shine:

> If we do take ourselves seriously as not only teachers of writing but specifically teachers of arguments, we need to absorb our own lessons and we need to make sure that when we are presenting information—especially to administrators—that we're doing so in a way that establishes our ethos, that we are presenting data driven claims, and that we are recognizing ourselves as stakeholders. And if we can't take that lesson out of our classrooms and apply it to our advocacy, then I don't know how seriously you take yourself as a teacher and a professional.

This approach and these meetings, particularly the final meeting with the provost, represented the culmination of the instructor representatives' efforts to listen, affectively invest, and develop consensus throughout the year. We do not want to overstate the impact of the instructor representatives' work, and multiple participants noted that our pay increase was likely in progress before the final meeting with the provost. Still, all participants felt their work had made a difference. Their meetings and advocacy throughout the academic year meant that, as Anne says, "the provost was aware of the issue and was talking with admin in various departments at various levels." Notably, the representatives were told by the provost in their final meeting to not expect any information until the following academic year, which the representatives strongly pushed back on. Ultimately, per Mary, "shortly after that meeting... they made an announcement that they were going to increase our pay." According to John, even ASU administration "acknowledged the impacts we've made."

A key component of instructor representative rhetorical awareness was presenting their arguments during the kariotic moment of a new provost's first year in the position. Such "transitions in a key position of power" can serve to "amplify individual agency at a crucial moment" (Norgaard 147). Anne saw that "new people stepping into those roles" brought "kind of an openness," and Mary saw that NTT faculty's working conditions were "already on the radar of our new provost" because we had "been pushing for improvements." The representatives took advantage, immediately responding to the provost's messaging that she was available for conversations with faculty about working conditions. The arrival of the pandemic also presented a kairotic moment for instructor representatives to negotiate. Mary noted that, "Our students have greater needs because of the pandemic.... We definitely tied in those issues to our arguments, you know, our mission in the university to work with every student." Teaching through the pandemic was a challenge for NTT faculty at ASU, but our close proximity to students helped the instructor representatives see our students' struggles and incorporate that valuable perspective into their rhetorical appeals in the moment.

This openness to conversations produced needed trust between the instructor representatives and the provost. Research on strategies for changing contingent faculty working conditions frequently emphasizes that building such professional trust between NTT and administrative allies can pay dividends (Lind and Mullin; Nardo and Heifferon). Unfortunately, in our case, NTT faculty members are hesitant to trust in the good will of administration because they remembered how they had been mistreated in 2014. Other challenges to trust are structural. In a conversation we (Abigail and Sean) had with a TT ally, they pointed out that administrative roles are as much "managing up" as "managing down," and administrators may be more or less capable with each skillset. The ability of our departmental administrators to "manage up" is hard for NTT faculty to assess (and thus build trust in) because the work is often invisible in process and because the results that are visible come out of a very large and complex administrative bureaucracy. In addition, NTT faculty often have not participated in administrative roles and have limited knowledge of the inner workings of the department. As a result, the liminal nature of departmental administration obscures the department's decision-making process for NTT faculty. Unfortunately, it is much simpler and easier for NTT faculty to direct their frustrations toward those administrators who are visible to them—in our case, the WPA and department chair.

But without trust between NTT faculty and administration, it is difficult to work with administration to achieve NTT faculty advocacy goals. Our participants navigate these challenges with care. As Anne said, "we have to work with admin to whatever degree is possible, but we also have to push back." Instructor representatives must balance trusting middle-management administrators to advocate for NTT faculty to upper-level administrators with holding those same administrators accountable for their actions and promises to NTT faculty. As representatives now, we (Abigail and Sean) are continuing this openness to trust, although not without occasional complications. Early in our tenure, we were told by a knowledgeable coworker that upper administration regularly sends out information or instructions that have bearing for our rank, but insists that it be delivered verbally *only*, not put in writing. Needless to say, this minor revelation did not breed trust.

Conclusion: Action Items: Gather, Reflect, and Participate

In the work leading up to the 2022 raises and title changes, the ASU instructor representatives gathered data about our program, considered their own experiences, assessed the needs and wants of administration, negotiated their findings amongst themselves, and developed and delivered arguments for program changes, effectively enacting the GRAM model. Their process is a testament to the abilities of trained scholars of English, even when they are weighed down by a 5/5 workload and uncompensated additional service work during a time of pandemic. We set out in this study not only to learn about the rhetorical choices made by NTT leaders, but also to figure out an entry point into workplace activism for other NTT faculty members, ways that we can act as individuals who feel ourselves to be perpetual occupants of multiple liminal spaces. Having learned from our participants, colleagues, administration, and our own advocacy efforts, we offer the following ways for NTT faculty to engage with advocacy work for their rank.

ACTION: GATHER

Making rhetorically effective choices requires piercing the institutional fog of war and developing an understanding of institutional structures and interests. At ASU, the charter is ever-present in university communications, and, as President Crow has intended, a guiding factor in how we discuss ASU and the work we do here. But this is perhaps an unusual situation. While other universities may have mission statements, they may not be as pervasive as ASU's Charter. It is rhetorically important, then, that NTT faculty make a concerted effort to acquaint themselves with the professed priorities and values of their institutions. These priorities provide rhetorical vernacular to frame the value NTT faculty bring to their respective institutions. In turn, this rhetorical vernacular can provide more secure positioning from which to argue for better working conditions, salary, and benefits.

At ASU, an effective way to learn about administrative structure and institutional values (beyond the charter) is to attend open departmental and university meetings. Anne argued that "more people could show up to the department's meetings. Even though we have representatives, instructors aren't banned from going to the department meetings." Anne also argued for NTT faculty to read the notes that are distributed after meetings because "there's a lot of information there that's really important." In the sea of emails, it is tempting to ignore things like minutes from meetings, but staying informed about departmental issues can generate trust between NTT faculty and administrators. Our research and experiences indicate that NTT faculty can more effectively advocate for improved working conditions when they engage with the information available to them about the workings of their departments. We also recommend that NTT faculty work with administrators to collect data annually that assesses NTT advocacy priorities and working conditions.

One way we can apply this lesson from a liminal space is to make one-on-one conversations between NTT representatives and NTT faculty a more focused priority. Feeling heard, even just by each other, contributes to a culture of inclusivity, and feelings of inclusivity can improve contingent faculty morale (Melonçon et al., "Looking Forward" 143). These conversations require affective and emotional labor, so instructor representatives at ASU have strategically met with other instructors during office hours over Zoom to reduce the time commitment. At the time of writing this chapter, Abigail, Sean, and the other instructor representatives are trying to make check-ins a part of the representative-instructor relationships. Non-representative NTT faculty can help by being available for these conversations and proactively sharing their views.

ACTION: REFLECT

Requiring approval of every action that one takes on committees (or with fellow instructor representatives) is one of the best ways to ensure nothing is actually completed. However, it remains important that an individual does not make a rash decision that can affect the entire group—such as angrily addressing upper administrators on behalf of those in your position. Effective advocacy requires a shared governance process, clearly articulated advocacy goals, and a plan for how best to present those goals to administrators.

As activist-researchers reflecting on this interview study, we have reimagined our own experiences as a resource rather than as a burden. Homegrown NTT faculty are often dismissed by TT faculty as those who failed to launch. While preparing for this project, I (Sean) thought my "homegrown" status at ASU was a burden. I am frequently reminded that I used to feel like I belonged in the department, a feeling that faded correspondingly with my odds of becoming a tenure-track professor. I (Abigail) still have a lingering sense of bitterness after applying to over sixty TT positions during my final year of graduate studies and only being offered a FT-NTT position at my alma mater. However, career stories are created in retrospect, as inchoate experience is shaped retroactively into a coherent narrative (Ibarra); thus, finding career satisfaction can be a process of finding the right story to tell about past professional experience. Such a retelling can be particularly difficult in an academic environment, where only one career outcome—joining the tenure track—is considered a success. But, for us, those experiences could be imagined as a strength, one that prepares us to maximize our contributions in formal or informal roles and assist with navigating the fog of war. Reconciling desire and reality is difficult, personal work. Without completing this work, we believe it is too easy to slip into distrust and anger over one's academic career.

ACTION: PARTICIPATE

We began this project asking what we could do from our liminal position to advocate for ourselves. From these interviews, we see value in participating in the formal structures of power available to us. We hope we have shown that changes can be affected from these positions. Participation in these kinds of "shared governance" roles can draw NTT faculty "out of their classrooms and departments into a wider arena, where they [can] attain a greater understanding of the structure and functioning of the university and a broader perspective on the role of instructional staff in the larger picture" (Love 135). The benefits of participating in these roles can be invigorating, even amidst the challenging affective aspects of the work. These roles also present an opportunity for those of us trained in rhetoric and writing to apply our rhetorical expertise. All of these types of shared governance roles take time and should be distributed among NTT faculty as much as possible, but our study has shown that one of the best outlets for NTT faculty hoping to engage in advocacy is to participate in these formalized shared-governance roles.

Ultimately, it's important for NTT faculty to act upon their motivation for advocacy. Depending on NTT faculty's workload and working conditions, not every NTT faculty member will have the motivation to always advocate on behalf of their rank. For this reason, we need NTT faculty to act upon that motivation when they have it. Acting upon this motivation when we have the energy allows folks serving in an advocacy position to step down when their motivation subsides. Such rotations can foster collaborations among NTT faculty advocates with institutional knowledge of administrative workings and those with fresh perspectives ready to help push past the fog of war. Participate in the ways you can and support others working in advocacy positions—by talking to them, gathering data, or reflecting together whenever possible.

Works Cited

American Federation of Teachers. *Reversing Course: The Troubled State of Academic Staffing and a Path Forward*. ERIC Clearinghouse, 2008.

"ASU Charter." *Arizona State University Office of the President*, president.asu.edu/asu-mission-goals. Accessed 21 Feb. 2025.

Brydon-Miller, Mary, and Patricia Macguire. "Participatory Action Research: Contributions to the Development of Practitioner Inquiry in Education." *Educational Action Research*, vol. 17, no. 1, Mar. 2009, pp. 79–93, https://doi.org/10.1080/09650790802667469.

Crow, Michael M., and William B. Dabars. *Designing the New American University*. Johns Hopkins UP, 2015.

Culver, K. C., and Adrianna Kezar. *Designing Accessible and Inclusive Professional Development for NTTF*. Pullias Center for Higher Education, University of Southern California, 2021, pullias.usc.edu/wp-content/uploads/2023/10/Designing_Accessible_and_Inclusive_PD_Aug21_final3.pdf.

"Facts and Figures." *Arizona State University*, n.d., www.asu.edu/about/facts-and-figures. Accessed 23 Aug. 2023.

Flaherty, Colleen. "One Course Without Pay." *Inside Higher Ed*, 16 Dec. 2014, www.insidehighered.com/news/2014/12/16/arizona-state-tells-non-tenure-track-writing-Instructors-teach-extra-course-each. Accessed 21 Feb. 2025.

Ibarra, Herminia. *Working Identity: Unconventional Strategies for Reinventing Your Career*. Harvard Business School Press, 2003.

Jacobs, Steven. "The Use of Participatory Action Research within Education-Benefits to Stakeholders." *World Journal of Education*, vol. 6, no. 3, 2016, pp. 48–55, https://doi.org/10.5430/wje.v6n3p48.

Kahn, Seth. "We Value Teaching Too Much to Keep Devaluing It." *College English*, vol. 82, no. 6, 2020, pp. 591–611.

Kahn, Seth, et al., eds. *Contingency, Exploitation, and Solidarity: Labor and Action in English Composition*. WAC Clearinghouse and UP of Colorado, 2017.

Lind, Carol, and Joan Mullin. "Chapter 1: Silent Subversion, Quiet Competence, and Patient Persistence." *Contingency, Exploitation, and Solidarity: Labor and Action in English Composition*. Edited by Seth Kahn, William B. Lalicker, and Amy Lynch-Biniek, WAC Clearinghouse and UP of Colorado, 2017, pp. 13–26.

Love, Carla. "Non-Tenure-Track Faculty and Shared Governance." *Profession*, 2000, pp. 132–37, www.jstor.org/stable/25595711.

Mechenbier, Mahli Xuan, et al. "Results and Findings of the Survey." *Academic Labor: Research and Artistry*, vol. 4, no. 3, 2020, pp. 22–59, digitalcommons.humboldt.edu/alra/vol4/iss1/3.

Melonçon, Lisa, et al. "Introduction to 'A National Snapshot of the Material Working Conditions of Contingent Faculty in Composition and Technical and Professional Communication.'" *Academic Labor: Research and Artistry*, vol. 4, article 3, 2020, pp. 1–21, digitalcommons.humboldt.edu/alra/vol4/iss1/3.

Melonçon, Lisa, et al. "Looking Forward: Considering the Next Steps for Contingent Labor Material Work Conditions." *Academic Labor: Research and Artistry*, vol. 4, article 8, 2020, pp. 127–51, digitalcommons.humboldt.edu/cgi/viewcontent.cgi?article=1075&context=alra.

McBeth, Mark, and Tim McCormack. "An Apologia and a Way Forward: In Defense of the Lecturer Line in Writing Programs." *Contingency, Exploitation, and Solidarity: Labor and Action in English Composition*. Edited by Seth Kahn, William B. Lalicker, and Amy Lynch-Biniek, WAC Clearinghouse and UP of Colorado, 2017, pp. 41–55.

Nardo, Anna K., and Barbara Heifferon. "Chapter 2: Despair Is Not a Strategy." *Contingency, Exploitation, and Solidarity: Labor and Action in English Composition*. Edited by Seth Kahn, William B. Lalicker, and Amy Lynch-Biniek, WAC Clearinghouse and UP of Colorado, 2017, pp. 27–40.

Norgaard, Rolf. "Chapter 9: The Uncertain Future of Past Success: Memory, Narrative, and the Dynamics of Institutional Change." *Contingency, Exploitation, and Solidarity: Labor and Action in English Composition*. Edited by Seth Kahn, William B. Lalicker, and Amy Lynch-Biniek, WAC Clearinghouse and UP of Colorado, 2017, pp. 133–50.

Probst, Barbara. "Both/and: Researcher as Participant in Qualitative Inquiry." *Qualitative Research Journal*, vol. 16, no. 2, 2016, pp. 85–102, https://doi.org/10.1108/QRJ-06-2015-0038.

Reagor, Catherine. "'We Have a Problem': $800 Rent Hikes Squeezing Metro Phoenix Tenants." *Arizona Republic*, 15 Mar. 2022, www.azcentral.com/story/money/real-estate/2022/03/15/metro-phoenix-families-face-us-biggest-rent-increases/6886155001/. Accessed 21 Feb. 2025.

Rose, Shirley K., et al. "Directing First-Year Writing: The New Limits of Authority." *College Composition and Communication*, vol. 65, no. 1, 2013, pp. 43–66.

Royster, Jacqueline Jones, and Gesa E. Kirsch. *Feminist Rhetorical Practices: New Horizons for Rhetoric, Composition, and Literacy Studies*. Southern Illinois UP, 2012.

Saldaña, Johnny. *The Coding Manual for Qualitative Researchers*. Sage, 2021.

Schell, Eileen E. "The New Faculty Majority in Writing Programs: Organizing for Change." *Contingency, Exploitation, and Solidarity: Labor and Action in English Composition*. Edited by Seth Kahn, William B. Lalicker, and Amy Lynch-Biniek, WAC Clearinghouse and UP of Colorado, 2017, pp. 102–18.

Schreiber, Joanna, and Lisa Melonçon. "Creating a Continuous Improvement Model for Sustaining Programs in Technical and Professional Communication." *Journal of Technical Writing and Communication*, vol. 49, no. 3, 2019, pp. 252–78, https://doi.org/10.1177/0047281618759916.

Stenberg, Shari J. *Repurposing Composition: Feminist Interventions for a Neoliberal Age*. Utah State UP, 2015.

Stewart, Elizabeth. "ASU Writing Instructors Balk Over Pay Cuts." *Phoenix New Times*, 10 June 2015, www.phoenixnewtimes.com/news/asu-writing-Instructors-balk-over-pay-cuts-7401614. Accessed 21 Feb. 2025.

Wergin, Jon. "Leadership in Place." *The Department Chair*, vol. 14, no. 4, Spring 2004, pp. 1–3.

Wergin, Jon. *Leadership in Place: How Academic Professionals Can Find Their Leadership Voice*. Ankor Publishing, 2007.

Whalen, Tracy. "Introduction: Rhetoric as Liminal Practice." *Rhetor*, vol. 1, no. 1, 2004, pp. 1–11.

Wilson, Laura, et al. "Affective Investment." *Academic Labor: Research and Artistry*, vol. 4, no. 1, 2020, pp. 83–107.

Wootton, Lacey, and Glenn Moomau. "Building Our Own Bridges: A Case Study in Contingent Faculty Self-Advocacy." *Contingency, Exploitation, and Solidarity: Labor and Action in English Composition*. Edited by Seth Kahn, William B. Lalicker, and Amy Lynch-Biniek, WAC Clearinghouse and UP of Colorado, 2017, pp. 199–211.

2
Crossing Over

Transitioning to Early-Career Leadership with Labor Equity in Mind

ANICCA COX

In the mornings, I walk along the ditches by my sister's house in the early part of the day before the heat comes in the fallow time between one tenure track job and the next. Under the cathedral of cottonwoods and willows, I remember those generations of people who made these ditches together, these acequias, who still work them together to share the precious resource of water and preserve the holy lineage of land-based relationships. When I step out on top of the ditch corridor I am confronted with the beauty of the Sandia Mountains—the watermelons—as the Spaniard colonizers called them because at sunset, they turn rosy like the sweet interior of summer fruit off the vine. All through June and July this walking is most of what I do, almost all I can do. Maybe we don't talk enough about rage. Maybe we don't talk enough about disappointment. Maybe we forget, it hurts the most when we care.

I write this story at a moment of sense making. This sense making seeks to parse the difficulty of having been fully immersed in a project of institutional change and then leaving that work with unfinished business, a terrifying level of burnout, and feelings of failure. For me, that moment was magnified by a professional period of "becoming," immediately post graduate school in my first tenure track job. I was left feeling like a part of my own trajectory was severed even as it had just begun. Simultaneously, I experienced a "running towards" sensation as I left the institution to return to my geographical home and my

https://doi.org/10.7330/9781646428007.c002

community connections in the Southwestern United States, followed by a fallow, exhausted period of recovery and retreat from my own academic life.

This story began in the fall of 2021, when I took a job as an assistant professor at a small, private, undergraduate-serving institution in the Southeastern United States after completing a degree in a large, Midwestern R1 rhetoric and writing program. I was hired in a cohort of four, and together we were charged with building a first year writing program and eventually rebuilding a communications degree. My colleagues and I each brought unique experiences and backgrounds as teachers and as scholars, but we all shared a strong focus on student mentorship and innovative, equity-based classroom practices. We were eager to integrate into the institution and effect positive changes there. We each had expertise in areas of curriculum, research, administration and leadership practice. We also had significant support in the form of a university provost who hired us expressly to begin to transform university conversations on several fronts from equity-based approaches to instruction to curriculum, policy, and assessment. And, we were ready!

In the first semester I was appointed chair of a writing task force. Using a "charge" document written by myself, the provost, and associate provost, we set forth to build our first-year writing program. The process was an integrative and expansive one that included writing new learning outcomes and course descriptions, building a two-semester FYW sequence, coordinating with state articulation and transfer standards, devising placement and assessment processes, revising supplemental instruction, and collaborating with a wide range of other faculty, staff, and administrators on our campus. These collaborations were to build "cultures of writing" in our own division with part-time faculty and then expand outward through faculty development workshops across campus. This process both harnessed my narrower areas of specialization from my graduate training and went far beyond them as my administrative work became a holistic practice over time.

In the two years that followed, we were able to accomplish much of this work. We operated collaboratively with one another as we made our way through the task force's charge and learned how to support our students (and each other) through the second half of the acute pandemic years in a new institutional setting—one so different from our graduate program experiences. In that time, I stepped into a more formalized leadership role as the writing program administrator (WPA) and as a division head. That division would include our cohort of four tenure-track (TT) faculty, two senior faculty from communication fields, and around six non-tenure-track (NTT) writing instructors. Yet, at the end of those two years, all four of my cohort would leave the institution, much of our work undone. In addition, one senior faculty member would also leave the institution over conflicts with our revision to the degree plan. The other would migrate much of his appointment to another program for similar reasons, leaving the division in a near total turnover at the TT level. So, while I was largely proud of our efforts, I also left profoundly disappointed that we were unable to fully develop our vision in a collaborative and sustained way. For me, the impacts of that rupture in turn resulted in an affective and embodied sense of burnout and failure, some of which I will detail in this chapter.

In the months after my departure, I worked to make sense of how my experience may mirror some of the pain points other early-career faculty face as they cross over from graduate training to faculty life and to consider how we might develop adaptive, resilient ways of being in our leadership roles. Here, I highlight Chris Gallagher's concept of "institutional literacies" as a way of thinking about institutional leadership through participatory practices that contribute to positive change (79). I devote my discussion in this chapter to my own institutional story. Using a narrative approach, I work to highlight some of the salient experiences of my leadership work and the ways that work was grounded in labor issues, specifically an understanding of the challenges and problems of academic labor and their impacts on classroom and institutional conditions.

Using the "charge" document for our task force as a point of analysis, I seek to tell stories of institutional change work informed by that understanding. I additionally intersperse moments of affective and embodied experience, like the epigraph that begins this chapter, to mark the lasting impacts of our/my relationship(s) with institutional structures. In my case, that experience ended in exhaustion, burnout, and disengagement with some aspects of my professional life. I do so to demonstrate what I believe is a real value in considering our work through both intellectual *and* personal/political lenses. Much of that impulse is grounded in the foundational theories that support my research, namely materialist feminisms and feminist standpoint theory. According to Sandra Harding, standpoint theory, emerged as a vehicle for feminists to take up a politics of understanding the "relations between the production of knowledge and the practices of power" (1). Such a critical orientation, she argues, may be useful to the production of knowledge even as scientific communities have so often eschewed the intersection of those two activities. Broadly conceived, standpoint theory asks researchers to consider how knowledge produced from outside dominant perspectives, produces "distinctive kinds of knowledge" that are bound up in the subjectivities of gender, race, class, and other social locations to intervene in those structures (1). Or, as bell hooks, writing about standpoint, argues, there is political and personal power in the discursive, in "Speaking from margins. Speaking in resistance" (159). Here, I consider my own standpoint as a valuable way to speak back, through leadership, to institutional cultures that continue to be dominated by hierarchical views of our shared work.

Ultimately, this chapter is meant to "be of use" to those who are curious about what leadership looks like for those of us just entering our faculty careers from our graduate training—under the constraints of an ever-shrinking or less viable set of professional conditions for the professorate—and how we are adapting to current conditions. In the following sections, I first describe the work my cohort and I were asked to do at our new institution and some of the features of that context. Second, I consider how my graduate training informed, intersected and/or diverged from the necessary institutional work I was tasked with, highlighting the need for "institutional literacies" for pre-tenure faculty. Finally, I map a heuristic approach to how we crafted measures of success inside specific institutional conditions aimed at "leaving the university better than we found it," and ultimately what it meant to leave that context after working so hard to improve it.

I hope to demonstrate how collaborative curricular and programmatic work with equity-based labor practices in mind can provide locations for sustainable change for early-career faculty even in the face of the perils and pitfalls of hostile institutional cultures. I argue that in fact, to advance the long-term change our institutions need, we should focus on building systems for collaboration and solidarity that work to improve teaching and learning conditions.

Cautions and Contexts for Change

In the fall of 2022, in my second year as pre-tenure faculty member, I was asked to take on the role of WPA and division head in our newly formed Composition, Communication and Rhetoric division. I did so as someone who felt that the dire conditions I saw negatively impacting both colleagues and students well outweighed my concerns for my own safety, security, or tenure process. Disciplinary lore and advice from mentors often include a caution against pre-tenure faculty crossing over into WPA roles for several reasons. Primary among them is the reality that writing program administration so often involves pushing back against a range of problems, from simple inertia to composition's sometimes subordinated role within departments, to encountering acts of resistance against curricular work that prioritizes equity, fairness, and transformation within traditional models of writing instruction in the humanities. That work can make WPAs vulnerable and subject to any number of hostilities from the institution itself. For me personally, a central concern of this role is that in any program that includes the labor of faculty working off the tenure line, there will be ethical disappointments that occur between needing to staff courses with qualified, student-centered instructors, and asking those instructors to do so at the expense of their own material and affective well-being.

And yet, under the right conditions, WPA work can help transform universities from the ground up, instilling values of fairness, solidarity, and relational growth amongst colleagues. As Shari Stenberg and Debbie Minter's interview study with veteran WPAs demonstrate, WPA work by its nature is a "being up against," but they see this work as productive, not hopeless. The results of their study show that the resiliency required to do WPA work successfully can in fact be accomplished by "connecting with others, approaching administration as a dynamic, nonlinear process, and finding ways to act, even amid constraints" (646).

A few things aided me in my efforts. First, I did so in close collaboration with my three colleagues in a kind of cohort; I was not alone. Our grouping was specifically engineered by the provost who was well aware of the dangers faced by a single rhetoric and composition scholar tasked with building a writing program. Second, I was supported in my work by my orientation to leadership work, which is broadly grounded in my firsthand experience and study of issues related to academic labor equity. Briefly, that study and experience included employment as an adjunct post-master's degree, five years as a junior WPA in a writing program staffed wholly by part-time lecturers, a dissertation study on the standpoints of NTT instructors, several other shorter studies of labor equity in writing studies, and years of union organizing at the graduate student level. Cumulatively, my past work taught me how labor-centered leadership practice demands both individual critical resistance to oppressive structures *and* coalition and solidarity building amongst colleagues, students, and administrators.

The Charge

On a sunny September afternoon, I sat outside the campus ministry center with my provost and associate provost. For two hours, we engaged in a wide-ranging conversation about what the work of our new division would look like, what we would do and what resources and time frames we would need to complete it. Broadly, it began with a three-to-four-year vision in a phased approach beginning with first-year writing—writing outcomes, curriculum, assessment and incorporating professional development and training for our part-time faculty—and culminating with building a potential writing minor and developing writing across the curriculum (WAC) and writing in the disciplines (WID) initiatives on our campus.

Collaborating and building solidarity with my administrative counterparts as we wrote was valuable work because it accomplished the following:

- It built relationships that we could draw on again and again as a stronghold in our work;
- I drew on my expertise in WPA work and rhetoric and composition theory and praxis;
- It illuminated the institution specific conditions and constraints I would be operating under including sites of resistance to change and allies with whom I would need to build further relationships;
- It helped integrate my own vision with a larger institutional mission of change and improvement spearheaded by our provost;
- It outlined the labor that I and my closest colleagues would need to navigate together;
- And I certified my leadership role.

This process also revealed the near invisibility of NTT labor concerns. As we wrote, I added a number of items that I viewed as integral to thinking about WPA work with labor equity in mind. Those included considering retention and persistence of first-year students as a direct result of instructional and curricular landscapes. Those landscapes are shaped by *who* the teachers of first year writing (FYW) are (rank) and what conditions they work under (material, discursive, social). The more precarious a teacher, the more precarious a program and its students. We articulated that understanding in our charge document to achieve the following purposes:

- Ensure consistency across multiple sections of FYW courses;
- Increase persistence by designing curriculum to support student success;
- Develop curriculum that can be shared broadly across departments and that serves the needs of disciplinary writing;
- And offer/design professional development opportunities for FYW faculty, departmental faculty, and later, across campus.

We framed our deliverables with a series of guiding questions:

- How can the writing program act as a resource for TT and NTT instructors both within the department and beyond it?
- How can we find resources to support NTT faculty development?
- How can we best partner with the writing center on campus for all our initiatives?

However, in some ways, even as I insisted on a consideration of the labor of my colleagues as a guide for our shared work, much of what I knew as "best" from my previous scholarship and experience, was difficult. Our instructors, more commonly just referred to as "adjuncts," were without even a rank designation. They had no semblance of renewable contracts, no avenues to shared governance, or promotion, or permanency, etc. Worst of all, their pay was unreasonably low even in a region with a low cost of living.

To my best understanding, the institution had only minimally responded to these conditions prior to our arrival. Adjuncts were not invited to meetings; there was no shared or developed curriculum; there were no meaningful or legible assessment practices; and no one had offered to remunerate adjuncts for professional development work let alone offer that at the institutional level. In addition, course materials were not aligned to any meaningful assessment process, nor were they rooted in the disciplinary expertise needed to successfully teach college level writing.

Indeed, as readers will see in the list above, NTT faculty are notably absent as full partners in this work. This was in part because in our first year we were not put into any *departmental* leadership roles. Instead, we worked extradepartmentally with the provost in the absence of the department's capacity to support us. Though my first concern in any curricular work is related to the labor of *all* faculty I also was unsure of how, without any real authority over scheduling or pay, to build the first iteration of the program without further exploiting NTT for their unpaid labor.

Instead, I worked first to contribute to the stability of NTT material conditions before asking those colleagues to contribute to curricular design. This is an imperfect approach but one that was guided by my desire to improve institutional structures in the long term.

When I was formally put in the role of WPA and division head at the end of my second semester (meaning I had authority over hiring, contracts, and personnel issues), I began to intervene in those material conditions in a phased approach. First, I secured funds for program development (PD) for our part-time instructors directly from the provost. With this support, we held a two-day workshop where we could collaborate closely with NTT faculty on building semester plans and where we offered meals and stipends for attendance. Next, we set up paid program PD meetings four times each semester to support teaching in our newly developed curriculum and to have conversations about how we each would adapt that curriculum to our own teaching practices. For per course pay, I took the provost up on her offer of higher pay on a "case by case basis" for instructors (all the board of trustees would allow). This approach ensured that we effectively increased their per-course pay by 25 percent. Next, I advocated for full-time positions in our program and got one approved within my first year of the division head role and began to plan for a second.

I advocate this approach as a first step for new faculty leaders building program sustainability and for those considering how to build labor equity, particularly in small institutions that are often un-unionized with small numbers of faculty. This approach considers structures and systems first. I feel that asking teachers to participate in programmatic design without increasing material security undermines both teacher and student conditions in the long run. In addition, attention to the documents that guide policy are one place that new faculty can take a leadership role. The writing of those documents provides an opportunity to collaborate, learn, and build programs based on shared aims.

Finally, as we began to develop assessment practices within our TT cohort, we gathered with our NTT counterparts in a series of pilot assessment meetings where we were able to discuss values associated with writing, to answer questions about curriculum, and offer instructors a place to discuss their classroom practices, challenges, and needs. Our framework for this assessment process was informed by "dynamic criteria mapping" that Bob Broad refers to as a "home gardening approach to learning and evaluation" (2). This approach fosters the sort of collaborative, locally contextualized assessment, programmatic practices, and teaching improvements that are often desperately needed in small institutions.

Many of us early-career faculty leaders who work in small undergraduate institutions find that they differ from the large university experience where we received our graduate training. I encountered, for example, a staggering dearth of systems to support the daily functioning of our program. I learned that we needed to design a writing program that could be responsive to, and also innovative, within parameters both quotidian and epistemological. Stenberg and Minter discuss how such "rhetorical responsiveness" includes "analyzing institutional context; being mindful of what, or who, is the priority; and being willing to revise and rethink a plan or position" (653).

Our successes were based in that responsiveness, they were achieved through collaboration—I asked my colleagues to take on aspects of our charge based on their expertise and affinity—and persistence, repeatedly reminding my dean and provost: "we cannot achieve our institutional goals if we don't have full time faculty *and* without reassigned time for our tenure-stream faculty to build this program." I was lucky to have their agreement. We were also supported by a mutual understanding of institutions with our provost, and in some ways, a desperate need on the part of the institution itself to rapidly improve or fail and collapse. New faculty leaders like me can attune in this way to institutional priorities and needs with great success: pay attention to institutional cultures and exigencies while collaboratively visioning new pathways.

However, as we built, the institutional conditions continued to be dire. That meant that we had to work to include faculty across ranks at the ground-floor level while participating in shared governance to advocate for better working conditions at the policy level of the institution where a focus on labor equity was not always shared by my other tenure-stream counterparts.

In my work life there, I had difficulty building a collaborative teaching community in those shifting conditions. For example, staffing challenges were far more extreme than my experience at previous institutions. When I stepped into the WPA role, we had around six NTT faculty colleagues teaching FYW. One week before the semester, three of those faculty left. This, I would learn, was the sort of staffing constraint that we regularly faced. I had little to no guidance on hiring protocols and had to spend days of emails to correct avoidable mistakes with human resources and move faculty through the process of hiring as swiftly as possible. Accordingly, a significant portion of my work was spent on getting someone, anyone, to teach courses on short notice for low pay and to then support them in any way possible. It meant that we faced severe challenges in building collaborative programs across institutional ranks, and we also faced difficulties with demonstrating to the university that the labor conditions of our part-time faculty were integral to the function of our program and university mission.

When thinking critically about my own choices in leadership, I understand now that I was working to balance the ideal with the material. Having full participation from all faculty ranks is the ideal. Doing so in collaborative and supportive ways was the goal. However, these goals meant asking people who just entered the institution and who had no real institutional support to contribute to curriculum design and programmatic governance. We were asking people to take on these challenges while getting paid $1,500 dollars per course with no benefits and no guarantee of continuation. These conflicted ideals are why it was exceedingly important to offer $500 more a semester for PD and to work toward full-time employment for our teachers in the long term. New faculty leaders need to make such inequities visible across their institutions even if like me, they are unable to remain in the institution to see the problems resolved. Increasing the visibility of NTT labor makes it possible to have difficult conversations and to make apparent the working conditions of all faculty from the ground up.

Contexts Matter

> The role of task force chair: Serve as project manager for goals and time frames; manage progress updates and communication to chairpersons, dean, and provost; request resources for task force as needed; and designate sub-group teams (including with support from faculty across campus). (Task Force Charge 1)

I started my job with two maxims handed down from mentors in graduate school as models. The first was to "leave a place better than you found it." The second was, "You can do good work in any institution and any place." My mentors emphasized that my training at an intensive research institution and established rhetoric and composition doctoral program would allow me to work, contribute, and thrive in a range of contexts outside the R1 setting. However, my leadership role taught me that practicing these maxims is difficult. I had to reframe how R1 institutions measure success and adopt my own metrics for recognizing progress in my context. My focus expanded from centering publication to working with the people around me to make my institution better than when I arrived—articulating these new measures of success required that I learn as much as possible about my context. To move forward, I had to expand the story of who I am.

The context I stepped into as an early-career administrator was one of a number of constraints, some material, others not. Materially, we were in a small, undergraduate serving institution that was driven by tuition (read: student loan) and neither publicly funded nor endowed. This meant that students were largely exploited financially and largely under-supported academically, a situation upper administration was working diligently to address. However, the less movable parts of the instructional context were harder to make sense of and far less porous and, I believe, based in a longstanding institutional culture, proliferated by some tenure stream faculty who saw their roles as sacrosanct.

That culture, despite the innovative activities of those in administration and new faculty, was rooted in exceptionalism, conservatism, and a resistance to change. The resistance was somewhat understandable. The changes demanded of the faculty and their work were wide ranging. Retention and persistence were low, assessment was nearly non-existent, and there was almost no oversight of any faculty activity until the provost (our strongest supporter) was hired. Many systems and structures had to be built and rebuilt. Others were being dismantled rapidly. As I previously mentioned, the university was in a kind of change-or-disappear paradigm, one faced by many small, private colleges (Mintz). Such precarity is speculated to be a result of declining enrollments coupled with the rising cost of tuition, which is usually very high at small, private, undergraduate serving institutions (Rosenberg).

For us, that meant programs and whole divisions were being merged, curricula needed updates, and there was a reliance on the development of online programs for revenue. Nearly every system, from registration to advising and placement, needed overhaul or was being built from the ground up.

Those changes brought a mix of resentment and incredulity. Our cohort emerged as upstarts—worse, upstarts on a time clock. We had to move fast to alleviate the painful conditions of first-year students, but that allowed us almost no time to build the sustainable collegial relationships we would need to nurture our innovations. It is very difficult to build a thing without buy-in even with upper administration clearing the path. Those tensions surfaced in moments like these: A colleague came to my office and noted both that our (my cohort's) hires were a real "feather in the cap" of this place and simultaneously vehemently opposed any conversation about meaningful faculty evaluation to improve collegiality, recognition of effort, and teaching. Using Marxist terminology, he let me know he saw my need for faculty evaluation within my own program and division as merely a tool for alienating people from their labor. Interactions like these and others let me know that we were a part-but-not-a-part of the institutional space. Patricia Hill Collins's "outsider within" framework from standpoint theory is useful here, in the way she describes the conditions of social-institutional locations that both offer critical perspectives others do not have, and how groups are treated with resistance when they seek to make change based on those insights (104).[1]

---

1. Hill Collins' work refers specifically to Black Feminist perspectives and Black women's roles in systems of power. Rather than co-opting her important work, I note it here because she also places the framework of "outsider within" and analysis of it in a larger political context of power that anyone might experience at some time, specifically in academic realms.

This kind of tension between enthusiasm and resistance—manifest in one conversation with a colleague—was pervasive. As a specific and kind of extended example, below I describe one salient instantiation of the tension that I came to call the "we are a teaching-focused institution" paradigm/refrain.

I heard the refrain repeatedly across campus: "we are teaching-focused." On a faculty affairs committee where we were tasked with delineating promotion standards for lecturers vs. TT faculty, the refrain was used to argue that rank doesn't matter because "we are all teachers," and should ignore difference in pay by rank. It surfaced again when we met with the tenure and promotion committee accompanied by blame leveled at upper administration that they simply hadn't "hired people into the correct rank," ignoring differences in credentials. Besides, they argued, there weren't enough NTT faculty to make the policy decision matter.

Given the prominence of the refrain, I was confused when I noted to other division heads, the limitations to my ability to accurately assess my colleagues on their teaching in our annual review process (because they produced no teaching materials for that assessment), but I was met with silence and anger. When I began conversations about course observation at our divisional level—a critical practice in writing programs—I was told to wait until a campus-wide observation protocol was designed for tenure-stream faculty. The reason being that my own efforts would present a perceived threat to other divisions. This directly hampered my ability to scaffold peer observation for NTT instructors and their access to focused, one-on-one conversations about classroom practice.

I by no means intend this as a leveling of abject criticism at my former institution because I know that, underneath the discourses graduate school presents to so many of us—a research focused, visible, opportunity-rich academic life—resides a wide range of institutional experiences where what I detail is in fact commonplace. In addition, the "we are a teaching institution" paradigm belied a sense of injustice that the TT faculty held about their own work, work that had historically been underresourced, underpaid, and ignored. In response, they turned their sights on academic freedom as a tenet of recognition for their work through a newly organized faculty senate and used that body to publicly air grievances with upper administration. They did not, however, as far as I could discern, turn to solidarity, coalition, and labor organizing. This is not uncommon. In scholarship, I and others have discussed and critiqued how the notion of the professorate as a class of professionals with elevated social status subsumes the reality that the professorate is a class of workers who need to organize. That paradigm can limit opportunities for creating institutional labor equity (Cox et al.).

Ultimately, I began to wonder, could we call ourselves a teaching-focused institution if we had little to no idea what that meant to us? The indicators I knew to look for seemed elusive: observations were underutilized; our class sizes were relatively small and so numerically, student evaluations were of little significance, and teachers produced no pedagogical materials for regular reviews. NTT faculty were the most undersupported and underresourced group on campus, though they were tasked with a significant amount of teaching labor. I noted, too, a dearth of pedagogically focused professional development on campus and teaching materials were infrequently shared between colleagues. One of my graduating senior students informed me that she was incredibly relieved to be leaving given the racism and xenophobia she had experienced that had been directly ignored by administration when she reported it, an indication of the cause of the appalling retention rates. Her choice to stay and graduate was accompanied by institutional harm.

This student's experience is unsurprising; it is commonplace in university settings. However, I saw it also intersecting directly with the work of our writing program as a part of the institutional matrix of student well-being, general education, transfer requirements, and retention and persistence rates. A salient example of this connection was that before I started teaching, our provost warned me about the "dirty dozen." The dirty dozen was a framework for error correction for students, featuring common writing "mistakes." Any Google search will yield multiple permutations of it. This list appeared in posters across campus, accompanied by the visual image of white, Western outlaws. The list appeared on sample syllabi in our department and was frequently used by the writing center, appearing on their website as a suggested resource.

What this meant for me was that this list became the de facto visible articulation of what writing instruction was and how it was conducted on our campus. In fact, it was the only shared document I could find beyond our department that addressed writing instruction on campus. Composition has widely critiqued the reliance on error correction and rote grammar instruction as ineffective foundations of writing pedagogy. Education scholar April Baker-Bell, drawing on lineages of Black rhetoric and composition scholars adeptly encapsulates the deeper racialized implications of an exclusive focus on "White Mainstream English." Her research demonstrates the importance of studying "how linguistic hierarchies and racial hierarchies are interconnected. That is, people's language experiences are not separate from their racial experiences"

(2). Those racial experiences are so often connected to the political contexts of writing instruction. Carmen Kynard traces the lineage of Black Power movements and struggles against linguistic oppression and how they have "functioned conterminously for college composition" (78). In her historical work, Kynard additionally illuminates the Black Marxist tradition that considers the interrelationships of both class and race as integral to liberation struggles (78). As someone attuned to institutional hierarchies and the implications of normative practices, I saw the seemingly innocuous document as a clear indication of the work to be done.

Where did this document intersect with labor equity on our campus? I believe it is deeply intertwined. As an indicator of that relationality, one of our instructors had the Dirty Dozen on her syllabus and asked me for feedback as she transitioned to our new curriculum. I began a conversation with her about how students interpret our values as instructors. If error and grade penalties come first on our syllabi, we are signaling to students that we prioritize that approach to writing instruction. She responded that this was all based on a syllabus she was given, and so she, as someone who had little access to departmental or curricular conversations previously, assumed that she must include these items and that they were departmentally sanctioned or mandated. Given her own marginalized position within the institution, it could hardly be a surprise that she was unmotivated to make changes to existing materials. We cannot simply uproot something without nurturing the thing that will grow in its place.

In these kinds of moments, I began to ask, what does it *mean* to be a teaching focused institution? Here, I turned to my primary research methodology. Rooted in materialist feminism and standpoint theory, I began to look at the paradigm as a kind of "problematic" (Smith). A problematic, as articulated by institutional ethnographer Dorothy Smith, refers to a kind of tool that uncovers "an actual property of the social relations of an organization of our/people's ordinary doings into a topic for ethnographic research" (39). It can act as a kind of heuristic for understanding what may lie underneath dominant institutional discourses or how people's doings are "hooked into a larger fabric not directly observable within the everyday" (39). A problematic can indicate difficulties in both the material and ideological function of workplaces.

So, in understanding how and when the refrain appeared, I began as a researcher to better understand some of the discursive and material conditions there. As a WPA, I used this notable slippage and disjuncture to consider how I might act within these conditions to synthesize the work of labor equity and writing program administration to larger institutional change work. A heuristic question that emerged from an attention to this problematic could be phrased as "what institutional practices best call attention to and build on teacher identity and shared governance?" Or "what practices would we have to build in order to connect teacher identity and shared governance to support our institutional (teaching focused) mission?" Such heuristics are located in understandings of labor, both teaching and institutional, and can help focus actions in that matrix.

Fortunately, what we encountered as we worked more closely with our NTT colleagues was a genuine warmth and receptiveness to our work. These faculty, subject to the worst material and social conditions of the institution, knew full well how important positive institution-wide changes could be. One of my colleagues remarked, "there was never really anything to help me teach here before, and I just had to kind of figure it out." Others, who were perhaps intimidated by the new curricular design we proposed, took us up on every opportunity to discuss materials and began to reach out for assistance and with questions. In settings like a TT faculty governing body, colleagues would openly deny the existence of systemic racism or refuse any accountability for equity work in their classrooms, but in our FYW program we discussed these issues directly. Parts of our charge guided us here:

- How do we build anti-racism/equity-based models from the start (baked in) not retrofitted later? What models will we work from?
- What does support for multilingual writers and translanguaging look like in our first-year writing sequence? (Task Force Charge 1)

Together, we examined the relationships of assessment to legacies of racism, pushed each other to think of ways to better care for our students, designed activities aligned with anti-oppressive teaching practices to be shared and adapted, and engaged scholarship from writing studies, mapping ways to implement those theories in our classes. For me, this was a positive indication of the value of collaborative curricular practice as a foundational leadership strategy that can support both instructors and students while raising awareness of the material conditions of teaching. Equity-based approaches to curriculum and collaboration are important facets of this work for new faculty leaders to consider, and as new faculty leaders, we are well positioned to offer this kind of orientation to our writing programs because most graduate programs have shifted toward centering social justice in their curriculums and trained their students in these discourses.

What Did You Prepare Me For? Looking Forward and Looking Back to Consider Graduate Education

> What relationships do we have to build to support that work? Who are our stakeholders? (Task Force Charge 2)

In Laura Micciche's 2002 "More Than a Feeling: Disappointment and WPA Work," she names "an exacting bitterness, or disappointed hope, in what the academy has become and failed to become" (433). She links such a phenomenon to a number of causes including a shrinking job market with ever fewer footholds for material security. Twenty years on, my own generation of scholars continues to be trained to enter the profession under these conditions and, disappointingly, under ever more extreme austerity conditions like the ones that unfolded at West Virginia University during the 2021–2022 academic year (CCCC Statement in Response). In my own doctoral dissertation, I wrote about the need for graduate programs to train students in "institutional literacy" (Gallagher), which I imagined should include knowledge of the institutional workings of universities to "make good" on our ideological stances of change, social justice, and equity. Gallagher teaches us that to be institutionally literate means to participate in the revision of institutional structures rather than simply be in opposition to them (79). These practices involve stepping in, relying on collaboration, and focusing on building networks.

The long-term labor equity landscape in our field would be improved if graduates were trained in these institutional literacies and better prepared to be effective leaders who are more realistic about the work of university faculty. This requires knowledge of commonplace institutional genres and practices (like annual reviews, budgets, bylaws, promotion standards, accreditation, etc.) that are infrequently examined in our graduate seminars. Given how hierarchy so often resides in and stems from textual genres and institutional policies, they deserve our full intellectual attention. If we view the work of our discipline as institutionally bound and centered in improving oppressive conditions, institutional literacies can offer tools for intervention. This framework, of understanding structurally located oppression, comes from radical traditions, both anti-capitalist and feminist (Combahee River Collective). For me, it is an effective framework for institutional adaptation and intervention.

Teaching institutional literacy can also help graduate students connect with the NTT faculty who are frequently the ones staffing writing programs. In my own program, our regular interactions were typically limited to tenure track graduate faculty. Association with those faculty came with a kind of "prestige" bonus that engendered competitive individualism in graduate students and their mentoring relationships. I was fortunate that my dissertation work led me in a different direction.

I am not entirely alone in these feelings of an incompleteness in my training. Studies such as the annual job market survey from the Consortium of Doctoral Programs in Rhetoric and Composition indicate a sense of overall precarity in moments of professionalization and certification (Leverenz and Micciche). The survey acts as a real time indicator for graduate programs on the subjective experiences of those they are mentoring and training and is a valuable, authentic data point for writing studies scholars as we consider what graduate education is and isn't preparing us for. In addition, our discipline has begun to think more concretely about how graduate-level training can help scholar-teachers prepare for a shifting employment landscape. The 2019 "CCCC Position Statement of Professional Guidance for Mentoring Graduate Students," in fact, recommends the following:

> **AVOID MYTHS:** Mentors should not invoke or imply damaging and unrealistic myths about what success on the (academic) job market must look like (e.g., that only R1 academic positions are desirable, that a national academic job search is the only way to secure satisfactory employment). Instead, faculty should work with graduate students to imagine myriad post degree options and follow students' leads on working to meet their goals.

What this indicates to me is that our field sometimes knows more about the material conditions of our work than graduate training lets on. From my own experience and observing my cohort colleagues, I found that though we were somewhat aware of these conditions, we were encouraged by our mentors to be highly visible scholars first, to focus our service efforts at the disciplinary level, and to hope that that level of visibility might lead to better institutional positions under better conditions. In some ways, that strategy is effective. Out of my cohort of four, three of us left after our second year to go work at R1 institutions with lower course loads, access to teaching graduate students and colleagues who were also more engaged at the disciplinary level.

However, when taken from the perspective of labor equity, programmatic continuity, and the building of sustainable and better conditions for those off the tenure line, our departures left a rift in the institutional landscape itself. We were only beginning to build a nascent community and the relationships needed to staff our courses with full-time, ranked instructors with benefits.

Our institution needed these reforms to have faculty who could make students feel welcomed in the institution, and thereby to improve retention and persistence rates. However, I hoped that the relational community of NTT faculty, the design of the WPA position in documents and practice, and our strong alliance with upper administration provided good starting points toward building labor-minded institutional practice after our departures. Notably, this challenges the trope of the solitary WPA who imposes a personal vision on a curriculum they "own," while managing others' labor invisibly and under ethically fraught conditions. Instead, we aimed to create opportunities for institutional participation across ranks, fostering coalitional practices to address the university's labor conditions. New faculty leaders should think relationally to build sustainable systems that support labor equity and other equity concerns. Identifying early on the most pressing concerns and then building practices to address them is one way to work effectively.

Taking Stock, Measuring Impacts Over Time

In the two years that I worked there, I continued to dialogue with my dissertation mentor about pathways for scholarship and my administrative practice. Together, we began to imagine a framework for measuring impacts of institutional change and how I might gain perspective on what I linked, over time, to my own failures. This became a kind of heuristic that was helpful to me and may be helpful to others who are seeking to do this work. He noted that there are two good indicators. One is of course positive feedback. Another, he noted, is negative feedback. Negative feedback, he explained, indicates discomfort with the necessary changes we made at the university and that the seeking of attenuation to those changes was in fact an indicator of progress. Horizontally with our TT colleagues, this reality was clear to me. Unfortunately, but unsurprisingly, much of this resistance appeared in gendered relations where help was directly refused, or our work was consistently undermined by senior male colleagues. However, we also received enormous support and encouragement from those we were in coalition with—our NTT colleagues, the writing center director, and administrators across campus.

Ultimately, my feelings of burnout coincided with professional opportunities beyond my institutional context. Overwhelmingly, I desired to return to the land, water, and cultural landscape of my home community and family, as the epigraph to this chapter describes. This desire was in conflict with my instinct to "complete" the project of our work at the university.

In a journal entry from that summer, I wrote:

> After a few weeks of free fall, I finally reach out to my mentor, kind of almost on accident. I am glad we use a messenger app because he doesn't have to see me, sitting in front of my computer sobbing uncontrollably when he tells me that the first step to recovering is naming the harms themselves, and then telling other people and then figuring out what is particular to location and what is ongoing in all institutional locations and then making some decisions about how to mitigate those harms for myself.

In order to recalibrate, I reconsidered the intersection of my own approach to institutional work, and the on the ground conditions of institutions themselves. Much of this had to do with time frames for change. Given our time bound, rapid charge, leaving the work undone seemed catastrophic. Worse, leaving with a sense that the work was undervalued, left me with many unanswered questions about its importance over time. However, what I can see now are a few indicators of success that I think are valuable to consider emerging from my own institutional story. All are tied into the labor configurations of the institution because they improve the material conditions of teaching and learning for faculty and students. Here, I tell those stories by focusing on our successes, rather than our challenges.

We successfully accomplished some of the following:

- An intact institutionally grounded and specific FYW curriculum complete with assessment, placement, and supplemental instructional models that were based in disciplinary best practices;
- A nascent yes, but cohering programmatic community that could provide resources for NTT teachers and an awareness on the part of administration of the importance of this community;
- Staffing with full-time faculty with disciplinary training;
- Expanded conversations about writing on campus in anti-oppressive frameworks;
- Strong relationships with the university writing center.

I was, nonetheless, concerned with the continuity of our work. Luckily, we were able to run four searches to replace our cohort and one to hire a full-time lecturer in the division. To strengthen our emerging coalition, we enlisted the writing center director and selected four candidates who aligned with the institution's future needs—those who could navigate administration, teaching, and research seamlessly.

Small institutions often require that kind of dexterity and as my colleague, Bernice Olivas, explained to me years ago in one of our many conversations about coalitions and solidarity, you often work toward a shared set of goals with people you generally dislike. In my years there, I learned that though many faculty were initially resistant to the changes we were tasked with making, but once the positive impacts of those changes began to surface, we were greeted with more acceptance. A few acknowledged the difficult work we were tasked with and retrospectively expressed gratitude for it. It was my hope that slow cultural change might continue as our curriculum and departmental community coalesced and improved learning conditions for students.

In many ways, I learned in my early-career leadership role that durable change work includes both Kairos *and* Chronos, as other scholars have noted (Lindquist; DeVoss et al.). How do we create those opportune moments for change? How do we do so collaboratively and relationally with our colleagues, even as we know that the stakes are high when material conditions impact every part of our work? How do we assess things in the glacial scales of time that institutions sometimes work inside of? These are questions I found useful to ask as a new faculty leader.

In seeking to "leave it better than we found it" we met our charge to a great degree under our available time frames. However, in reconsidering, amidst my own embodied sense of unfinished work, burnout, and failure, it may have been useful if we had foreseen additional frames for our work—ones that could help us better understand our own and others' expectations for progress. Two heuristic questions might guide that kind of frame for others—administrators who are collaborating with new faculty leaders for change work and graduate program mentors who are hoping to guide students successfully into their professional careers:

- What are the recognizable and shared aspects of progress and achievement for this kind of work over time—pacing and indicators of success?
- How can we calibrate time frames for institutional change work in ways that do not outpace faculty bandwidths, inputs, and remuneration?

University leaders can help new faculty make these kinds of shared assessments. This may be particularly important in the face of large-scale institutional reform efforts and, in my experience, can make or break faculty retention. In turn, mentors can guide graduate students to define these work expectations as conditions of their acceptance of faculty positions ahead of time. For my cohort, due to its rapid pace, we often referred to it as a search for the "minimum viable product," a term taken from user experience modalities. In essence, all was prototype. The benefit of our approach was that we were able to quickly interrupt some of the most difficult conditions of teaching and learning. The challenge was to come in behind the urgent "fixes" and to imagine sturdy, networked systems that might help sustain those changes, which is harder, longer work. That labor requires an actual or rhetorical "staying in place," that is, constant, long-term coalition building both in affinity and across discord, and a long-term view of change processes with systems for assessing progress and maintaining momentum in sustainable, human-centered time frames.

This staying in place, however, may be a "wicked problem," because it discourages faculty from pursuing improved working conditions at other institutions and reflects the kind of complex, systemic challenge that resists straightforward solutions (Garskie). Graduate training offers us the tools to "trade up" when our working conditions no longer suit us or become hostile. This is important and necessary for many, particularly those who have been historically and currently excluded from positions of power in universities, namely, our BIPOC, disabled, and 2SLGBTQIA+ colleagues. It must be said, as we navigate a Trump 2.0 administration that we must remain vigilant about protecting each other, *now*. Even so, we are on the precipice of enormous losses within our institutional cultures. As a scholar who takes heart in histories of radical resistance, it is my ongoing hope that leadership with labor equity in mind can help us cross over in our thinking and doing in our relations with institutions. In my own experience, whether we stay or go, we can advance some of the long-term change needed in our institutions by building systems for collaboration and solidarity to improve material teaching and learning conditions. We will need those relational capacities in the days to come, more than ever, as we come under attack. As Stenberg and Minter note, "relationality is interwoven with agency," and WPA work lives at the interstices of these two practices (652). Changes that build relationships to harness agency can make and keep our institutions more hospitable and safer, and begin to transform the too common, long-seated cultures of disappointment and despair we encounter in them.

I dedicate this writing to Bill Hart-Davidson, my mentor, whose grace, generosity of spirit, and bountiful kindness live on in all of us who were lucky enough to learn from him. Thank you for showing me the way.

Works Cited

Baker-Bell, April. *Linguistic Justice: Black Language, Literacy, Identity, and Pedagogy*. Routledge, 2020.

Broad, Bob. "Organic Matters: In Praise of Locally Grown Writing Assessment." *Organic Writing Assessment: Dynamic Criteria Mapping in Action*. Edited by Bob Broad, Linda Adler-Kassner, Barry Alford, Jane Detweiler, Heidi Estrem, Susan Marie Harrington, Maureen McBride, Eric Stalions, and Scott Weeden. Utah State UP, 2009. JSTOR, https://doi.org/10.2307/j.ctt4cgpzr. Accessed 5 Oct. 2023.

"CCCC Statement in Response to Proposed Cuts at WVW and Academic Austerity in Higher Education." Conference on College Composition and Communication, National Council of Teachers of English, Sept. 2023, cccc.ncte.org/cccc/response-to-proposed-cuts-at-wvu-and-academic-austerity-in-higher-education/.

"CCCC Statement of Professional Guidance for Mentoring Graduate Students." Conference on College Composition and Communication, Nov. 2019, National Council of Teachers of English, cccc.ncte.org/cccc/resources/positions/professional-guidance-for-mentoring-graduate-students/.

Combahee River Collective. *Combahee River Collective Statement: Black Feminist Organizing in the Seventies and Eighties*. Kitchen Table: Women of Color Press, 1986.

Cox, Anicca, Timothy R. Dougherty, Seth Kahn, Michelle LaFrance, and Amy Lynch-Biniek. "The Indianapolis Resolution: Responding to Twenty-First-Century Exigencies/Political Economies of Composition Labor." *College Composition and Communication*, vol. 68, no. 1, Sept. 2016, pp. 38–67.

DeVoss, Dànielle Nicole, et al. "Infrastructure and Composing: The When of New-Media Writing." *College Composition and Communication*, vol. 57, no. 1, 2005, pp. 14–44. JSTOR, www.jstor.org/stable/30037897. Accessed 5 Oct. 2023.

Gallagher, Chris W. *Radical Departures: Composition and Progressive Pedagogy*. NCTE, 2002.

Garskie, Lauren. "Wicked Problems." *Keywords in Design Thinking: A Lexical Primer for Technical Communicators & Designers*. Edited by Jason C. K. Tham, WAC Clearinghouse and UP of Colorado, 2022, pp. 155–59.

Harding, Sandra, ed. *Feminist Standpoint Theory Reader*. Routledge, 2003.

Hill Collins, Patricia. "Learning from the Outsider Within: The Sociological Significance of Black Feminist Thought." *Feminist Standpoint Theory Reader*. Edited by Sandra Harding, Routledge, 2003, pp. 103–31.

hooks, bell. "Choosing the Margin as a Space of Radical Openness." *Feminist Standpoint Theory Reader*. Edited by Sandra Harding, Routledge, 2003, pp. 153–61.

Kynard, Carmen. *Vernacular Insurrections: Race, Black Protest, and the New Century in Composition-Literacies Studies*. SUNY P, 2013.

Leverenz, Carrie, and Laura R. Micciche. "Report on the 2020 Job Market Survey Conducted by the Consortium on Doctoral Programs in Rhetoric and Composition." Doctoral Consortium in Rhetoric and Composition, cccdoctoralconsortium.org/.

Lindquist, Julie. "Time to Grow Them: Practicing Slow Research in a Fast Field." *JAC*, vol. 32, no. 3/4, 2012, pp. 645–66. JSTOR, www.jstor.org/stable/41709847.

Micciche, Laura R. "More than a Feeling: Disappointment and WPA Work." *College English*, vol. 64, no. 4, 2002, pp. 432–58.

Mintz, Steven. "Can These Colleges Be Saved? How to Secure the Future of the Small Liberal Arts College." *Inside Higher Ed*, 11 Nov. 2021, www.insidehighered.com/blogs/higher-ed-gamma/can-these-colleges-be-saved-0. Accessed 5 Oct. 2023.

Rosenberg, Brian. "Will Coronavirus Kill Liberal Arts Colleges?" *Times Higher Education*, 10 Apr. 2020, www.timeshighereducation.com/opinion/will-coronavirus-kill-liberal-arts-colleges. Accessed 5 Oct. 2023.

Smith, Dorothy E. *Institutional Ethnography: A Sociology for the People*. Rowman and Littlefield, 2006.

Stenberg, Shari J., and Debbie Minter. "'Always Up Against': A Study of Veteran WPAs and Social Resilience." *College Composition and Communication*, vol. 69, no. 4, 2018, pp. 642–68. JSTOR, www.jstor.org/stable/44870979. Accessed 5 Oct. 2023.

3
Navigating Industry Careers through Cultural Integration

CHARISSE S. IGLESIAS

This chapter is a story of adapting and translating, of discovering yourself in different contexts and applying your existing skill sets to navigate and potentially improve the set standards of industries outside of academia. This chapter does not explicitly advocate for leaving academia, but instead, to follow a story led by your values in directions you may not expect. The way that I follow my story is inspired by the way feminist writer and scholar Sara Ahmed follows her words in *Living a Feminist Life* and turns them "this way and that, like an object that catches a different light every time it is turned; attending to the same words across different contexts, allowing them to create ripples or new patterns like texture on a ground" (12). All life paths take turns in (un)expected directions, allowing you to choose how you will position yourself in that new turn. My departure from academia was less a critique of what I perceived to be a systemic obsession with tying personal identity to the overproduction of grant proposals, conference presentations, academic publications, etc., and more of a passion for direct action *with* people and the wonderful generative insights that come from those interactions.

I have taken the lessons from the turns of my story as a way to strengthen my passion for conducting institutional transformation across fields, sectors, and disciplines through coalitional building and intersectional leadership. From

FIGURE 3.1. PANEL 1: a ball is thrown from a large tower (ivory tower) into a body of water; PANEL 2: as the ball moves underwater, it grows fins; PANEL 3: the ball gets taken out of the water with a hook; PANEL 4: as the ball moves through the air, the fins transform into wings; PANEL 5: the ball hides behind a cloud, looking suspiciously at something; PANEL 6: the ball flies toward the ground behind a line of balls with wheels.

my time as a Peace Corps volunteer in Indonesia to a community-engaged practitioner and researcher both inside and outside the academy, I explored pathways that better aligned with my values and personal mission and helped me critically embrace my lived experiences and develop my own style of intersectional leadership.

For example, I like teaching and learning complex ideas by drawing comics (Iglesias and Irving), as shown in figure 3.1. Drawing comics helps me translate complex ideas I may not fully understand (McNicol) through the seemingly simplified world of icons (McCloud). When I rely on icons to move a story forward, I (un)intentionally slow down to "consider the power of [my] rhetorical productions" (Sealey-Morris 48). An icon such as wings can mean a few things depending on the context in which the reader grew up, views, and creates the world. Figure 3.1 is a comic I drew to explore my feelings when exiting and entering new contexts.

The comic in figure 3.1 tells the story of a ball being thrown (or gently tossed) out of the ivory tower of academia. It grows to adapt to different environments like the ocean and sky. When it meets other balls, it sees that they have also adapted to their respective environments. As I continued my career outside academia, I adapted to different environments by integrating and learning new skills and lingo, trying to sprout wings or wheels in my attempts. However, the ball never strays away from who it inherently is: a ball. I am still me. My personal mission has stayed fairly consistent, but it has manifested differently depending on my environment and needs.

In the next section, I share my story of leaving academia and explain how I meaningfully pursued a career trajectory that fulfilled my intellectual, geographical, and financial needs. Then, I share strategies of cultural integration that I learned from my community-engaged practice and research to transition outside of academia and find a career-path that aligned with my values.

Departure from Academia

As an intersectional feminist woman of color, I am strengthened by feminist theory, which informs my daily life and ongoing reflective practice. I value research and ways of knowing that do not represent traditional, top-down, colonial, hierarchical forms of knowledge production. My commitment to feminist theory incites a rethinking of how I position myself in the academy and, furthermore, how my authentic potential may possibly exist outside of it.

One of the most common questions I hear from PhDs about leaving academia is: How do I transfer my academic expertise to industry careers, a.k.a. alternative academic or alt ac? Figuring out how your theoretical upbringing and frameworks fit into a new industry can be challenging to conceptualize and execute. This is especially true because the tenure track professorship is the typically expected journey for PhDs. As I pursued my graduate career attempting to fit into the expected mold, I was disenchanted, realizing that there are more PhDs produced than tenure-track positions available (Larson et al.; "Market Comparison"). I was already prepared for tight competition, but this kind of competition seemed unreasonable and misaligned with how I wanted to live my life pledged to systems change, community-centered, and culturally responsive practice. These values guided my job search—whether that existed for me in the ivory tower or outside of it.

After I decided to make the switch out of academia, it took me six months to prepare applications and feel ready to apply for jobs. Those six months were spent translating my CV to resume format, talking about my abilities on LinkedIn, adopting industry lingo, and interpreting job descriptions (@ashleyruba_phd; @academic_exit)—on top of handling my regular academic responsibilities.

I began my search by looking at the UC Berkeley Rhetoric Careers page and Modern Language Association's *Profession*. These resources recommended trajectories beyond the tenure track, including careers as community college instructors, research associates, grant writers, higher education administrators, instructional designers, publishers, and more ("Beyond Tenure Track"; Lanchart and Hartman). Informally, I followed several insightful career coaches and individuals who had left academia to support this transition, including @fromphdtolife, @ashleyruba_phd, @academic_exit, @cjcornthwaite, @lifeaftermyphd, @altacchats, @academicfemale, and @clcaterine. Formally, I attended Beyond Academia webinars and the annual conferences hosted by UC Berkeley graduate students with the goal of expanding career options beyond the traditional academic track. I also relied heavily on my institution's Graduate Center industry career workshops that focus on tailoring appropriate application materials, choosing an appropriate industry, and deciphering job descriptions. I am grateful for these programs and resources so I could find my path outside of academia; however, searching for these resources takes extensive labor that could be streamlined and incorporated within graduate programs.

Call for More Internal Support

Graduate programs can pull from a plethora of external expertise to prepare graduate students for the shifting job market. For example, my program hosted alt ac workshops and invited alumni in industry positions to speak about their experiences. As already stated, however, this focus on adapting our academic expertise to various industry careers should be embedded into graduate curricula as opposed to treated as a supplemental skill that can be covered in an optional workshop or professional development event. As the academic job market evolves, graduate programs must appropriately manage the expectations for PhD students and provide early and proactive discussions of industry careers, including how to (re)frame and build the necessary capacity to articulate research values into industry goals. This speaks to the timely discussion on the revision of institutional structures in chapter 2 by Anicca Cox that encourages a collaboration with the institution to iterate and recreate structures that evolve with the changing needs of faculty, staff, and students.

Outside of graduate programs in English departments, there is a growing trend of connecting PhD programs with industry needs. According to Andrew Stapleton from *Academia Insider*, universities are developing industrial PhD programs that connect university research and industry needs through collaborative academic-industry partnerships and goal setting ("What is an Industrial PhD?"). These industrial PhD programs are gaining popularity because they are responding to PhD students' demands for expansive job training. Stapleton's YouTube video on the different types of PhDs notes two or three PhD programs in Australia that are growing in popularity. Because of their novelty, Stapleton encourages prospective PhD students to be critical of these initiatives. Universities are often obsessed with innovation but, at the same time, "very bad at implementing brand new things because they're just a big bureaucracy kind of nightmare" ("The New and Different Types of PhD"). Along with these Australian programs, Northeastern University is currently offering industry partnerships for all their PhD programs, arguing that "the future of research will be collaborative" ("Experiential PhD").

Innovations like the industrial PhD may take time to integrate into graduate programs of rhetoric and writing studies because they require faculty to partner with industry leaders—relationships that take time to curate. However, next-gen scholars do not have the luxury of waiting for the bureaucratic systems of graduate programs to catch up to market demands. For those unwilling and unable to wait, the next section describes cultural integration as an adaptive process from my practice and research in community engagement that may support those looking to transition outside academia.

Applying My Research to Industry

As Professor of Marketing Margaret Echelbarger has discussed, it is important to note that academia, itself, is an industry (@tweetsbymidge), so I encourage readers to stop labeling everything outside of academia as "industry." I assume that most readers will agree that coming into the academic industry as a newcomer is like coming into a new culture with its own set of rules, expectations, norms, and language. For me, that initial experience was all-encompassing and overwhelming. Coming into any new industry—any new context—invites newcomers to engage in a process of cultural integration. This process takes time, reflection, and intentionality all while holding yourself accountable to your core values.

So, when people ask, "How do I transfer my academic expertise to industry careers, a.k.a. alternative academic or alt ac?" they are asking, "How do I culturally integrate into my priority industry?"

I came to the study of cultural integration as a practitioner and researcher of community engagement. My skill set is in developing strategies, framing practices, and stories to promote equitable and sustainable projects, typically between historically marginalized communities and universities. This work has grounded my ambitions and values for the past decade. I first explored this line of thinking as a Peace Corps volunteer in Indonesia and later as the graduate director of a community writing pathways program in Tucson, Arizona. Both of these experiences shaped my values and informed my career ambitions. Culturally integrating into my current industry of a public health nonprofit demanded that I reflect on my expertise and experiences in fresh ways. I model that reflective process here before offering insights that can help others engage in their own reflective process.

The first lesson I recognized through my reflective process was a critical awareness of my positionality and how it impacts work with historically marginalized communities. As a Peace Corps volunteer in Indonesia, I loved interacting with the local universities, Islamic middle schools, and surrounding communities of Kediri, East Java. I even embraced struggling to understand cultural differences, but I wish I had come to the Peace Corps with concrete skill sets that the local communities needed and wanted rather than my mere post-college, idealistic, unbridled enthusiasm. I could have been more critical and versed in modern forms of colonialism, the savior complex, and the deep mistrust that historically marginalized communities harbor toward researchers, universities, the Global North, and Western populations in general.

After completing some community projects, I realized I needed to be more critical of the real and perceived power dynamics that existed between me and my Indonesian counterparts. I had not successfully integrated into the culture to combat some of those dynamics. However, I was lucky to continue this line of thinking as a PhD student through which I was graced with a progressive advisor, Stephanie Troutman Robbins, who helped me understand my own positionality and how it influenced my community-engaged research with historically marginalized communities.

The second lesson I recognized was my ability to build reciprocal and equitable community–academic partnerships. Equitable community engagement requires effective cultural integration strategies like practicing patience, self-awareness, and the ability to assess new organizational contexts and systems. This work also requires establishing transparent and authentic relationships between community and university partners. At the core of building those relationships is clarifying where both partners stand regarding communication strategies, intentions, research goals, accountability, data sharing, analysis, and other legal aspects. The same can be said for any lengthy partnership in your life: set the stage equitably, integrate into each other's cultures, and iterate as needed. While reflecting on my experience building these equitable relationships and engaging in community–academic partnerships, I recognized my strength and articulated these experiences so that other recent PhDs can navigate a range of industries.

Cultural Integration as a Lens

When I found career paths that aligned with my skill sets and values, the process of cultural integration served as a valuable lens for reframing my perspective of what it meant to exit one industry and enter another. Most importantly—just like the ball in the comic in figure 3.1—I remained myself in each environment I entered. My lived experiences and whole self-informed how I perceived and interacted with the world in front of me. Cultural integration is a generous and generative lens for negotiating the tension of maintaining your values while exploring, adapting, and accepting the norms of new industries.

As alt ac industry careers become an increasingly more common trajectory for PhDs (Digital Pedagogy), readers should expect to examine how skill sets learned in graduate school can transfer across industries but also be critical of how they integrate into established systems. PhDs exploring careers outside the academic industry should be mindful and critical of the traditions and norms of their priority industry. Any outsider to a new industry is afforded the opportunity to observe and assess the established system. Because PhDs are trained to learn at an expert level, I argue that PhDs can use the frame of cultural integration to revise, surpass, and improve inequitable industry norms rather than simply assimilate. The next sections discuss four adaptive strategies for cultural integration. Each section will define the strategy, provide examples of how I practiced it, and offer discussion questions for readers about how they might apply each strategy in their unique contexts.

OBSERVE THE CONTEXT

All good stories start by setting the scene. As a rhetoric and composition doctoral student, I taught composition to undergraduate students. I trained students how to set the scene in their writing by slowing down, defining terms, and contextualizing concepts to the overall theme. The students are bringing the readers into their stories through these techniques. The same applies when entering new industry settings. Observing the context means slowing down, noticing power dynamics, and forming connections among roles and people.

This part of my story describes how I came to and observed my new context outside the academic industry. After graduating with my PhD, I took a job at a public health nonprofit, Community–Campus Partnerships for Health (CCPH), that I had been following for years—observing my future context before I entered it. I was inspired by CCPH's nuanced perspective on community engagement and their equity frame called the Principles of Partnership. This equity frame promoted three main components: structure (organizational policies and practices), process (relational and group dynamics), and meaningful outcomes (short term and intermediate) (CCPH Board of Directors). These interconnected components work together to cultivate an equitable community–academic partnership.

Notice that the first thing I observed about my new context was their core mission and the frame they used to articulate the value of their work. As PhD students engage with their disciplinary specific research, I recommend that they identify and follow the organizations and businesses that speak to their values. Not only could they be observing their future contexts before entering them, but also the work of those organizations and businesses could propel their own research development as CCPH propelled mine.

My process of observing my context also included some prior experience dabbling in interdisciplinary research with public health scholars. As a doctoral student, I explored dissertation sites and began a partnership with my university's college of public health. I co-authored an article evaluating a service-learning program (Lohr et al.) that brought me into the public health world.

Initially, I misunderstood a lot of aspects regarding research methods and writing style and even authorship order.[1] There was a lot of discomfort and awkward maneuvering just from this brief incident, but it helped shape my

---

1. I did not have much of a stake in the research article we co-authored, so I offered to be the last author and was corrected that the last author spot was reserved for the supervisor or principal investigator. Usually research articles in rhetoric and composition are single-authored, so I lacked the institutional awareness of these logistical nuances.

awareness of a new field. When I accepted a position at the public health nonprofit where I work now, I knew I was entering a field and industry with a drastically different approach compared to the methods I used. There were new rules to learn and gatekeepers to get to know. Exploring a different field while I was still studying was helpful in facilitating this transition. As awkward as interdisciplinary work can be, I gained and still gain insight into community-engaged research that overall strengthens my own practice. In broad terms, rhetoric and public health have similar frameworks to conduct community engagement; but of course, the execution differs based on context, researcher positionalities, and field priorities. A lot of public health research I read comes from a more quantitative and mixed methods-based perspective and rhetoric from a qualitative, exploratory-based perspective, so I am observing community engagement from many diverse perspectives. Other PhD students would benefit from exploring outside their disciplinary silos so they can grasp a holistic and varied approach to their research study.

I want to acknowledge how awkward interdisciplinary work can be for graduate students at first. As Anu Taranath, a leader in racial equity and social change, wrote in her book *Beyond Guilt Trips: Mindful Travel in an Unequal World*: "Discomfort, without a productive valve to release it or a venue to talk it out, often manifests in less-than-productive-ways" (65).

I love being an interdisciplinary scholar, but it did not happen overnight, and honestly, it is an ongoing process. I know much more about community engagement now than when I first started, and it cannot be overstated that coming into a new industry is like entering conversations midway through. As such, bringing assumptions to this space may not be generative to your integration, and these experiences can help graduate students practice the cultural integration skills they will need when adapting to new industries.

The most essential skill interdisciplinary experiences offer graduate students is listening. Just as each discipline contains ongoing scholarly conversations, each industry has its own set of critical conversations that will continue after you leave, so listen to understand rather than to react. Please be kind to yourself for not understanding everything immediately. You are learning what the conversation is about, where it has been, and where it is headed. The purpose of observing as the first step in entering a new industry is to see how people operate within their given activity system. How do they communicate with each other? How do they resolve conflict? How do they bring in outsiders? Observing the scene, asking questions, and checking in were daily activities for me at my new nonprofit job so that I could participate productively.

Also, observing could help you identify their initiation process for outsiders. I was grateful to have welcoming mentors and managers who valued transparency in their processes and open communication. One of my new colleagues even made an acronym sheet for easy reference that facilitated my onboarding process. The acronym sheet was a simple but extremely loud expression of valuing and practicing openness in the workplace culture. They wanted me to join the conversation, so they developed the resources to support my integration. I was lucky that the workplace culture actively invited newcomers, and this made it easier to join the new conversations so that I could define the context on my own terms.

As an outsider, you are expected to ask questions and seek counsel. Outside of the general onboarding you may receive, set up meetings with people in your team, make connections with those who make acronym sheets for you, and attend as many social functions as possible to become aware of the workplace culture.

The following are questions to support observing your new context and how you can check your assumptions as you integrate into new contexts.

Reflection Questions
- Who are the gatekeepers of the new conversations?
- What assumptions have you brought to the new context?
- Where can you observe respectfully and productively?
- When do you seek clarification if you are confused or uncomfortable?
- Why are you listening to new conversations? To learn or to respond?
- How are you keeping record of the social norms? Are you referring to and updating that record?

NEGOTIATE VALUES

After observing for a time, the next step in the process of culturally integrating into a new industry is creating and negotiating your values. This step requires figuring out how to integrate into a new context without letting go of past lessons and experiences that have informed your whole self. This step also prompts you to consistently evaluate and reflect on your values so you can strategically decide how you adopt the new norms of your industry. As explained in chapter 1 by Sean Moxley-Kelly and Abigail Oakley, consistent and sustainable growth requires you to set and respect your own boundaries to avoid losing yourself in a new context.

It is difficult and impractical to fully adopt the norms of any new context. For example, as a Peace Corps volunteer, I was encouraged to meaningfully integrate into the cultural and social norms of the communities in which I worked. While I attended all the religious and cultural events, I knew that I would not adopt the Islamic faith or find the same connection to Southeast Asian village culture despite being ethnically Southeast Asian. At the same time, it was difficult to maintain my individuality. For example, when I would talk with family and friends in the US, I did not sound like myself. I would behave or say certain things that were perceived as off-putting because they did not match the social norms to whom I was speaking. Culturally, when passing by people, a common practice in my Indonesian village is to bow as you pass and make yourself as small as possible to avoid disturbing conversations.[2] I wanted to be an effective volunteer, but I also needed to be myself, so negotiating my values and identity was initially a difficult challenge, especially in a deeply religious and traditional space.

Fortunately, I found a balance between maintaining my values and adapting to my new context by focusing on building authentic and reciprocal relationships. I spent the first year of service making connections, drinking coffee with neighbors, and getting to know the local landscape. The second year I acted on those connections, co-developing initiatives that responded to authentic needs and attempting to set up plans for sustainability. It was my job to take the time to connect with the local communities, knowing full well that the intention to develop intimacy and authenticity came from the relationships I cultivated over time. In the same way that I strategically adopted the norms of my context in Indonesia, I had to negotiate my values and identity in my new industry. Unquestioned and uncritical devotion to the norms of a new context can harm both you and the new context. For the most part, organizations are hiring people for their unique expertise, and that includes their diverse intersectional identities and lived experiences.

As a community-engaged researcher, I was ready to bring critical perspectives to a productivity-obsessed capitalist work environment and help interrogate the intentions, purpose, and methods behind product development and organization-wide initiatives. I recognize that creating for the sake of creating can be (self-)destructive. Rather, I have used my graduate training to advocate for creating innovative products while also establishing systems to hold my organization accountable to the communities we serve through self and community evaluation.

Self-evaluation looks like examining your positionality within the context of the product and the communities you attempt to represent. Strategies to

---

2. I still do this many years later.

adopt to accomplish this could include reflecting on your feelings and behavior as you create the product; having regular conversations with friends and colleagues from the different phases of your life to see if your thought process has changed drastically; and being mindful about grounding your work to your positionality.

Community evaluation looks like asking stakeholders to evaluate the influence of products created for the community. Strategies to adopt to accomplish this could include discussing the product with trusted members of the community, consistently aligning the product with the values of the community, and having real users test the product to check for usability issues.

Consistently conducting self and community evaluation in new contexts can be a struggle to navigate, so I turn to Mia Birdsong's reflections on accountability in *How We Show Up: Reclaiming Family, Friendship, and Community*. Birdsong writes that accountability is "seeing the ways we cause hurt or harm as actions that indicate we are not living in alignment with values that recognize our own humanity or the humanity of others. It's about recognizing when our behavior is out of alignment with our best selves" (18). Birdsong's words have grounded me as I pursue environments outside my comfort zone.

There were also key ways that recent PhDs need to adapt when entering new industries. For example, I was often called in to check the tone and readability of my written reports and other products. When I was in my PhD program, I thought I was adept at using plain language. I never tried to mimic the convoluted prose that the academic industry traditionally promotes, and my colleagues often praised my accessible language. However, my prose style did not meet the needs of the audience in my new context. My assumption of what constituted plain language was, in fact, not plain. After receiving that feedback, I reflected on my assumptions and iterated my thought process for considering the role of language in my job and how I wanted to present it while still holding on to my values.

The following are questions to support negotiating your values and how you can check if your products align with the values of both you and the new context. The next section takes this positioning a step forward by building connections across organizational contexts.

Questions to Negotiate Values
- Who are you, and what do your identities bring to this new context?
- What are new context norms that seem foreign or off-putting to you, and are you willing to embrace that discomfort?

- Where can you practice holding yourself accountable through self and community evaluation?
- When are you willing to question your assumptions toward a certain topic or community to improve how you conduct your work?
- Why is maintaining your values and identity important when integrating into new contexts?
- How often can you commit to conducting self and community evaluation?

REPURPOSE ESTABLISHED SKILL SETS

The previous sections focused on understanding your new environment and strategically adopting new social norms. The next two sections look at how to repurpose your academic skill set and intersectional identities to potentially effect change in new industry settings. This work requires reframing established skill sets and (re)aligning them to effect change once you have established a secure position in your new context.

One of the best pieces of advice I received from my graduate school mentors was to repurpose my research. One dataset in a research article could be used to build a conference presentation that could prompt a grant application that could be translated to a new unit inside the classroom. Repurposing materials and research could occur for a couple reasons:

- Academia (and many industries) exploit their workers and leave them very little opportunity for a work-life balance; therefore, repurposing is seen as a survival tactic to fulfill the many expectations of a PhD student.
- Regardless of industry, work and innovation should flow organically. What is used effectively in one context could be translated to another if successfully contextualized.

As a graduate student, repurposing materials and past research was a key strategy while completing my dissertation. Through the COVID-19 in-person restrictions, I had to think creatively about how to conduct research and gather data. My initial dissertation plan was to observe and examine the framing of community partners in a public health service-learning program; instead, I reflected on how I believed community engagement should be implemented and evaluated. I repurposed a seminar paper that examined language and cultural inclusion of one of my in-service Peace Corps trainings and used the community writing course I was already teaching as research sites for my dissertation that created a framework triangulating community engagement through administration, training, and teaching.

As I repurposed my research, it caught "new light" and created "new ripples and patterns" (Ahmed 12). My research portfolio contained important insights that simply needed to be expanded, pulled, and prodded to yield new findings. By repurposing established and emerging skills and data sets, I could see old data in new ways, and by collaborating with colleagues and perspectives in different settings, I familiarized myself with the nuances of the different contexts within my dissertation project.

When I felt I had adequately observed my current organization and strategically adapted to the norms of its social ecosystem, I applied the repurposing skills I had developed during my dissertation to my new work. In my current context, I often draw from the same data set in multiple ways and for multiple purposes. For example, I created a report that inspired the creation of a health equity guidebook for healthcare providers. That guidebook then catalyzed a process manuscript detailing the influence of organizational principles and frameworks of equitable community–academic partnerships. Repurposing can be used in various contexts and through different industries. Changing perspectives and recognizing new patterns and ripples can support recent PhDs as they become fluent in the nuances of their new context.

Recent PhDs also have valuable skill sets that do not need repurposing. One of the key assets I brought to my current organization—which I argue should be a central concern for graduate programs that work with local communities—is expertise in enacting reciprocal community–academic partnerships. My understanding of reciprocity draws from Katrina Powell and Pamela Takayoshi's argument that "authentic reciprocity involves researchers and participants constructing roles for one another and negotiating those roles both within and outside the context of the research project" (401). I have translated this relational and participatory understanding of reciprocity into my current context as a training director by promoting the practices of establishing productive, interpersonal relationships with community partners inside and outside community–academic research projects.

The first two steps I detailed on cultural integration focused on how recent PhDs can situate themselves in their new contexts. Effectively repurposing past research and academic skill sets occurs through careful observation and strategic adoption of industry norms. My repurposing advice to recent PhDs is to examine their research portfolio and note the organic connections between projects. What inspired a piece of one project to be utilized in another? Are projects related by topic, theme, value, and/or access? After tracing the discernable connections, they can create a clear process or protocol that leverages this skill to achieve two goals: (1) build upon their amazing work and (2) effect positive change in a new context.

The following are questions to support repurposing established skill sets and how you can check your awareness of different organizational contexts.

Questions to Repurpose Established Skill Sets
- Who can you rely on as a mentor to support your reading of the different contexts?
- What nuances do you notice regarding rules, expectations, and language differences in the different contexts?
- Where would you like to start exploring the nuances of different organizational contexts?
- In what ways could your expertise and research improve your industry?
- Why is it just as important to learn how to turn a seminar paper into a dissertation chapter as it is to turn a newsletter post into a process manuscript?
- How often are you changing your perspective to notice new patterns and ripples?

(RE)ALIGN

There is no final step to cultural integration as it is an iterative process. We are constantly invited to new situations where observing, adapting, and repurposing established practices may support our professional lives. As we consider new contexts, I offer (re)alignment as another step within this ongoing process. Integrating into our new industries and building meaningful relationships with our colleagues allows us to naturally recognize ways our contexts change and, in turn, recognize ways that we are changed. With those changes, we need to (re)align.

In my context, after reshaping existing systems and creating new systems to ensure our community partners could tailor and, in some cases, co-create our products, checking my alignment looked like checking in on myself and my work and personal relationships. Self and community evaluation played central roles in confirming that my own work ethic and the products I made authentically responded to evolving organizational and community partner needs.

While initiating conversations about these system challenges, I drew from my experiences as a Peace Corps volunteer to demonstrate the harm that can occur from creating products without aligning with community partners. In many instances, I failed to involve the Indonesian community partners and their evolving needs in product development. Situations may change and affect what our needs are at the moment, but without that ongoing communication and collaboration, products that we claim are *co-created* may not reach target goals. That experience taught me to avoid one-off interventions that serve only my resume. I noticed similar motivations within my organization and wanted to ensure that the effectiveness of our products were regularly measured by the communities we claimed to serve.

As we are in the process of transforming our environments and ourselves, we should engage this change work cautiously and note when our organizations attempt to appropriate these types of equity initiatives. Sara Ahmed emphasizes that social justice and diversity work focused on transforming institutions is often "used by institutions as evidence that they have been transformed" (103). Creating for the sake of creating is dangerous. As I sought to enact change in my context, I focused on the impact my work would have on the communities I cared about. Creating without implementing systems of community accountability is performative and risks gaslighting both the workers and the community partners that change was being enacted when nothing was actually happening. One-off interventions do not work, and performative work is a waste of time and talent.

At the time of writing this chapter, I am revamping my organization's three-month onboarding curriculum and training workbook. We are a quickly growing nonprofit, and we need to build infrastructure that can sustain and retain our valuable team members. Research shows that longer onboarding and training increase retention because they make company culture, expectations, and roles more transparent to team members (Perucci). This onboarding and training workbook is relational and collaborative, where team members are expected to rely on their colleagues to learn and grow within the organization.

In an attempt to align the organization with my current needs, I first decided to create the workbook as a way to fill the gaps of my own onboarding and training process. While I greatly appreciate and admire the team that hired and onboarded me, I needed more context into the workplace culture, especially as this was my first job after graduating. My organization already had models for practicing community–academic partnerships that promote equity, so I adapted those same models to practice equity *within* our organization. In the initial internal training introducing the new onboarding policy, I showed a clip of an *I Love Lucy* episode where Lucy and Ethel work at a conveyor belt in a chocolate factory. The chocolates arrive too quickly onto the conveyor belt, and the pair gets overwhelmed and panic. Inattentive to Lucy and Ethel's struggles, the supervisor demands faster production. Readers, I felt like Lucy and Ethel during my first few months in this job because priorities were communicated differently, and I failed to communicate my struggles, which proved to be an opportunity for me to align either myself to the organization or the other way around. In this way, alignment can happen in a multitude of ways and directions. I opted to align the organization to more reasonable work practices.

The products that we create are only as strong as how we work with each other within the organization. The panic and stress that the clip presents are avoidable through transparent, proactive, and constructive communication within the work environment. That type of communication needs to be fostered from the very beginning. Therefore, the onboarding and training workbook is meant to set up systems for each new hire to feel successful and grow in their roles within a team. I created this workbook as a way for new hires to slowly integrate into the workplace culture. Integration, as I have stated, does not occur overnight. Instead, approaching the phase of integration where you are positioned to eventually effect change in the organization takes intentional and strategic moves into every corner of the organization. Just as dabbling in public health as I was earning my PhD helped me gain a greater understanding of community engagement, observing and participating in the organization in many different directions could support recent PhDs to have a fuller understanding of how the organization operates so that they can influence how it operates. Again, this means observing conversations, mapping out connections among roles and people, repurposing your skill sets, and (re)aligning yourself in your new context.

The following questions are meant to help recent PhDs generate ideas for how to (re)align in their new industry settings. Although this is the last step in the cultural integration process, there is no last step. There will always be new factors and challenges to consider and confront. As you finish reading this section, be mindful that integration is iterative.

Questions to (Re)Align
- Who can you call on to hold you accountable to your actions?
- What aspects of your work life feel unaligned?
- Where can you start aligning your workplace environment to your values?
- When do you feel the most out of control in your new context?

- Why is the *I Love Lucy* clip so relatable and why do we allow ourselves to continue in those kinds of environments?
- How can you support your own onboarding into a new context?

Position Yourself in Your New Turn

PhDs should be mindful and intentional about how they want to proceed if the academic industry may not be the direction for them. There is a whole world outside of the ivory tower, and I am grateful that I can still actively join scholarly conversations despite not taking an expected role in the community. Regardless of the career trajectory, positioning yourself in your new turn, maintaining your values, and adapting to new contexts will serve your career and mission.

For those of you exploring alt ac careers, know you are not alone or without resources. You are more than the role you have. Seeing how your abilities can be transferred to different contexts may bring you closer to what you actually want. Seeing beyond boundaries and silos and experimenting in other settings has strengthened how I think of and practice community engagement. It has made me appreciate my wonderful mentors and colleagues who continue to push me to align my work with my best self.

One of my colleagues asked about my transition to the nonprofit industry. Was I being intellectually challenged? Was I being held accountable to my values? In many ways, I am held more accountable because my work is direct action. My work contributes to how medical schools train their students on the structural racism inherent in patient pain treatment (Hoffman et al.) and medical devices ("Fight"). My work contributes to how international scholars collect human samples from rural communities in culturally responsive ways and avoid perpetuating historical mistrust toward researchers and institutions. The stakes are high, and I am interested in sharing this approach to community engagement and cultural integration across industries. More importantly, I hold myself more accountable to my values in this industry because it better aligns with my best self.

I encourage all recent PhDs to reflect on their positionality and look for new light, new ripples, and new patterns. Your research, lived experiences, and intersectional identities could enhance any industry—academic or not. Discover yourself in different contexts and seek out organizations and industries that best align with your values and mission. My advice is to go where your values lead.

Works Cited

Ahmed, Sara. *Living a Feminist Life*. Duke UP, 2017.

@academic_exit. "PhDs: when you're reading an industry job description, it may look like a foreign language. Here are a few key terms to look out for that can help you if you're not yet corpspeak-fluent." *X*, 26 Oct. 2023, 12:40 a.m., twitter.com/academic_exit/status/1717627229964734487?t=qJSJGHceAVvBk5Sb690GeA&s=03.

@ashleyruba_phd. "Ever read a job ad and think, 'what does this mean??' It's because you don't understand business jargon. Here are five common terms, translated for academics:" *X*, 25 Oct. 2023, 8:21 a.m., twitter.com/ashleyruba_phd/status/17171 99601118429593?t=IWtvvCyRLpVfksKV4vlS8g&s=03.

"Beyond Tenure Track." *UC Berkeley Rhetoric Careers*, rhetoric.berkeley.edu/graduate-program/careers.

Birdsong, Mia. *How We Show Up*. Hachette Books, 2020.

CCPH Board of Directors. Position Statement on Authentic Partnerships. Community-Campus Partnerships for Health, 2013.

Digital Pedagogy. "The Truth About the Academic Job Market + Alt-Ac Careers." *YouTube*, uploaded by Digital Pedagogy, 14 Jan. 2022, www.youtube.com/watch?v=48ZHfa8ZJr4.

"Experiential PhD." *Northeastern University*, catalog.northeastern.edu/graduate/phd programs/experiential-phd/#overviewtext.

"The Fight to Fix a Racist Medical Gadget." *Science Vs.* From Spotify, 22 Sept. 2022, open.spotify.com/episode/2UbfqpaUDKUsU2DdvyiKSx?si=a6259752b9bb4f5f.

Hoffman, Kelly M., et al. "Racial Bias in Pain Assessment and Treatment Recommendations, and False Beliefs about Biological Differences Between Blacks and Whites." *Proceedings of the National Academy of Sciences*, vol. 113, no. 16, 2016, pp. 4296–4301.

Iglesias, Charisse S., and Maxwell Irving. "Composing Reciprocity with Comics: Composing the Labor in Community-University Partnerships." *The Journal of Multimodal Rhetorics*, vol. 5, no. 1, 2021, pp. 3–17.

Lanchart, Michelle, and Stacy Hartman. "Ten Jobs Where You Can Use Your PhD." *MLA Profession*, profession.mla.org/ten-jobs-where-you-can-use-your-phd/.

Larson, Richard C., et al. "Too Many PhD Graduates or Two Few Academic Job Openings: The Basic Reproductive Number R0 in Academia." *Systems Research and Behavioral Science*, vol. 31, no. 6, 2014, pp. 745–50.

Lohr, Abby M., et al. "Service Learning on the U.S./Mexico Border: Transforming Student Paradigms." *Pedagogy in Health Promotion*, 2022.

"Market Comparison." *Rhet Map*, http://rhetmap.org/market-comparison/.

McCloud, Scott. *Understanding Comics: The Invisible Art*. HarperCollins, 1993.

McNicol, Sarah. "Using Participant-Centered Comics as a Research Method." *Qualitative Research Journal*, vol. 19, no. 3, 2019, pp. 236–47.

Perucci, Darren. "How Long Should Onboarding Take? (10 Factors to Consider)." *BambooHR*, www.bamboohr.com/blog/how-long-should-onboarding-take/.

Powell, Katrina M., and Pamela Takayoshi. "Accepting Roles Created for Us: The Ethics of Reciprocity." *College Composition and Communication*, vol. 54, no. 3, 2003, pp. 394–422.

Sealey-Morris, Gabriel. "The Rhetoric of the Paneled Page: Comics and Composition Pedagogy." *Composition Studies*, vol. 43, no. 1, 2015, pp. 31–50.

Stapleton, Andy. "Hidden Aspects of Unconventional PhD Types." *YouTube*, uploaded by Andy Stapleton, 15 Nov. 2021, www.youtube.com/watch?v=FBiICHs5Kpg.

Stapleton, Andrew. "What Is an Industrial PhD? Can Academics Move to Industry?" *Academia Insider*, 8 June 2023, academiainsider.com/industry-phds/.

Taranath, Anu. *Beyond Guilt Trips: Mindful Travel in an Unequal World*. Between the Lines, 2019.

@tweetsbymidge. "On this point, I probably should have gone to therapy to expedite this process, but it wasn't in the cards (pandemic, etc.). Also, keep in mind that academia IS an industry. It is not special . . . it is an industry like any other industry (with some unique affordances ofc)." *X*, 22 Oct. 2022, 8:40 a.m., twitter.com/tweetsbymidge/status/1582758682269429761?t=vN288Bg5jfiz2ylFxa-CUg&s=03.

Section 1 Response

Mapping Core Leadership Competencies through Next-Gen Stories

Learning from Cultural Integration and Labor Advocacy Across Institutional Roles

Jennifer Sano-Franchini

Over the last several decades, US higher education has undergone profound changes. On one hand, access to higher education has increased as a result of factors such as the 1944 GI Bill, the civil rights movement, and the push for affirmative action, upheld by the 2003 *Grutter v. Bollinger* decision. At the same time, as neoliberal rationality has taken hold in higher education, many universities and colleges have turned to privatized services including third-party educational consultants and contractors to guide strategic vision, implement new budget models, and provide enrollment and learning management systems, as well as infrastructural support and student services. The corporatization of higher education has broadly ushered in staffing models that rely increasingly on personnel cuts as well as a turn to adjunct and non-tenure-track labor in lieu of tenure-track faculty positions. This trend was exacerbated during the COVID-19 pandemic; as Jim Ridolfo observed based on rhetmap.org job data, academic positions in rhetoric and composition that had already been on a slow decline prior to COVID, saw a steep drop in numbers after the onset of the pandemic (Lindgren, see: "'Racing' bar chart: Comparing each year's job postings per week until week 17/January 1").

As the numbers of available academic positions in rhetoric and composition have decreased at the same time that working conditions and job security have worsened in a number of different ways, more and more academics have been looking to other industries as well as "alt ac" positions as means of employment. This trend, sometimes referred to as the "Great Resignation" (Gewin "Has"; Gewin "How") is documented in published stories of folks leaving academia—at times referred to as academic "quit lit" (Arellano; Arellano et al.; Ball; Estrem; Kurlinkus; Madden). With fewer faculty available to do the important work of service needed to keep programs and units running, those who remain are often saddled to do more, often with no increase in pay nor the lightening of other responsibilities. Some have coped by being more discerning about how and where they are willing to spend their time and energies, as reflected in articles about "quiet quitting" (Forrester) or a "peer review crisis," (Flaherty; Horta and Jung; Parrish; Tropini et al.). Quite reasonably and for a number of different reasons, it seems to have become increasingly challenging to find people who will take on service roles including leadership positions, particularly when these positions do not come with a pay increase or other material perks that are commensurate with the expanded responsibilities.

How does this multifaceted, complex, and tumultuous time of intense uncertainty, political and cultural attacks on higher education, austerity measures impacting higher education, and the reevaluation of life goals and work-life balance amongst workers require a rethinking of academic norms—including how we understand the work of leadership in higher education? This very concern is taken up in McMartin and Miller's "The Challenging Opportunities Facing Next-Generation Faculty and Staff Leaders," where the authors "reframed leadership as a collaborative process of enabling collective action" (196). That is, rather than conceptualizing leadership narrowly—as determined on the basis of a formal title or position within an institutionally-recognized governance structure that authorizes a person with the ability to move an organization in a particular direction, McMartin and Miller offer "a distributed conception of leadership that focuses on building grassroots coalitions to advance social and institutional reforms" (196). In other words, McMartin and Miller advocate for understanding leadership as (1) dispersed throughout organizations and (2) in terms of outcomes, including impacts for students as well as college and university employees.

The essays included in this first section by Sean Moxley-Kelly and Abigail Oakley, Anicca Cox, and Charisse Iglesias offer valuable insights for what such a "distributed conception of leadership" looks like in practice. Whereas Moxley-Kelly, Oakley, and Cox discussed the experiences of those in more formal leadership positions—of elected non-tenure-track faculty representatives and as a writing program administrator, respectively, Iglesias describes the work she did in a more informal leadership role. In addition, Moxley-Kelly and Oakley highlight the collective strategies and rhetorical expertise of non-tenure track faculty in uncompensated service positions, and they offer a gather-reflect-participate method for non-tenure-track faculty broadly to take part in workplace advocacy. As I read through the chapters and considered what core issues bind them together, I began to wonder what it would look like to map the leadership competencies that emerge from these next-gen stories. Inspired by the work of Bill Hart-Davidson that mapped the work patterns and core competencies of technical communicators ("On Writing"; "What Are"), I identified four interrelated and overlapping core leadership competencies as reflected in these three chapters:

1. feeling institutional structures,
2. sensing positionality,
3. discerning possibility, and
4. taking action for collective change.

Taken together, these core leadership competencies offer a way of thinking about how we can adapt and develop as leaders in uncertain, unprecedented, and challenging times. They can also be understood as a set of skills that comprise the kinds of rhetorical expertise that are essential for effective leadership.

The sections that follow elaborate upon the four core leadership competencies identified above, including how each of the three chapters exemplified them.

Feeling Institutional Structures

> "Maybe we don't talk enough about rage. Maybe we don't talk enough about disappointment. Maybe we forget, it hurts the most when you care." (Cox 56)

As reflected in the above quotation by Anicca Cox, *feeling institutional structures* is not just a matter of learning conceptually how institutions are structured including their procedures, processes, constraints, and flows of governance; it is also a matter of meaningfully attending to how it feels to exist and persist in institutions in an emotional and embodied sense, and to reflect on what specific features of the institution contribute to those feelings. That is, *feeling institutional structures* as it emerged across these next-gen stories is an embodied approach to recursively (re)-interpreting always-changing institutional contexts by feeling one's affective location within it. Moreover, I understand *feeling institutional structures* as a core leadership competency given that leaders must often quickly acquaint themselves with new and changing institutional contexts as they determine a strategic way forward that improves outcomes—outcomes that generally include the effects of institutional actions on peoples and communities. Together, these three chapters provide a glimpse of the various affective attunements that next-gen scholars experience and work through as they transition into new institutional arrangements.

The experience of being a new faculty member is oftentimes one of excitement, energy, and anticipation, especially for those who have, by many accounts, successfully come out of a long and grueling academic job search experience. Anicca Cox describes the cyclical set of emotions that frequently come with doing academic work in current times, where one oscillates between feelings of hope and excitement ("we were ready!"), to a sense of conflict about institutional constraints and outcomes, to burnout and at times, feelings of failure. This cycle of emotions may be felt all the more deeply by those who take on administrative roles, and I wonder if Cox's description of this affective cycle is a reflection of how institutions are notoriously both in states of perpetual transformation at the same time as they tend to be slow to meaningful change. In this way, I found Cox's attunement to these sensibilities to be rhetorically meaningful.

Another example of *feeling institutional structures* is reflected in both the chapters by Sean Moxley-Kelly and Abigail Oakley and Anicca Cox, as each describe their deeply felt vulnerabilities that came with doing leadership work as non-tenure-track and untenured early-career faculty, respectively. In the case of Moxley-Kelly and Oakley, the authors reflect on the experiences of those engaged in labor advocacy as elected representatives of the instructor rank at their institution. Moxley-Kelly and Oakley report that as non-tenure-track faculty in these elected positions, many described feeling a sense of duty and responsibility to their peers in the Instructor rank, and we can see how this sense of responsibility is meaningful for pushing advocacy efforts forward. In this way, although there may have been a sense of vulnerability among the authors by virtue of their employment status as non-tenure track faculty members, they were attuned to other pressing factors that ultimately influenced their willingness to take on risk in their leadership roles. Meanwhile, Anicca Cox discusses her experience moving into an early-career leadership position while keeping labor equity issues in mind. In her case, Cox describes how she was willing to take on the risk of labor advocacy as an untenured faculty member in part because of how she was positioned in relation to others at the university—she was not alone but worked in collaboration with three other colleagues and with the support of their provost.

Moving beyond academia, Charisse Iglesias draws on her experiences transitioning from academia to a public health nonprofit organization to offer what she refers to as a "cultural integration" approach for moving across industries. As she does so, Iglesias describes her six-month process of figuring out how to reframe her work for nonacademic industry positions. During this time, she reflected on her past experiences, including how her experiences within academia are both limited and situated within a much broader context (understanding as she does that academia, too, is an industry). From this process, Iglesias identified lessons for cultural integration that may be helpful to others who are also moving across industries. At the same time, Iglesias takes care to keep in mind that others' experiences, contexts and goals may well differ from her own. Keeping this sense of perspective in mind is key to Iglesias' approach. She demonstrates how she engaged in *feeling institutional structures* as she took a step back to identify academic norms and disciplinary conventions as they are—as contextual and not universal, and even potentially damaging when inappropriately imposed onto other contexts.

Sensing Positionality

> "I encourage all recent PhDs to reflect on their positionality and look for new light, new ripples, and new patterns." (Iglesias 96)

The above-mentioned sense of perspective via cultural integration that was central to Iglesias's approach to *feeling institutional structures* is also important grounding for the second core leadership competency that I observed in all three next-gen narratives in this section—*sensing positionality*. I understand sensing positionality as being attuned to the varied and at times conflicting ways in which one is positioned within and across institutions and systems, whether in relation to people, identities, access to resources, access to information, or other modes by which power is circulated. This second core competency requires a nuanced understanding of how one's complicated and multidimensional positionalities may afford them certain privileges in particular contexts at the same time that they may be precluded from other privileges—even in that same context. Together, the chapters in this section offer several examples of how the authors considered their positionality within and in relation to a number of different sociopolitical and institutional contexts, as well as how that positioning has implications for the sorts of work that they would be best situated to do. In other words, all three narratives provide insights into how sensing positionality is a core leadership competency and form of rhetorical expertise that enables leaders to understand the affordances of their social location for not only identifying what approaches they are best situated to employ, but also to concretize the motivations that may be underlying any given action. As a result, the ability to sense positionality equips leaders to effectively identify appropriate strategies and paths forward for meaningful institutional change from where they stand.

Iglesias speaks to the competency of sensing positionality by framing leadership as requiring a learner's disposition. She explains, "All life paths take turns in (un)expected directions, allowing you to choose how you will position yourself in that new turn" (79). This understanding of life paths as constantly dynamic, in flux, and always changing makes clear why it is important that those in leadership roles are readily able to sense positionality within a given historical and spatiotemporal context. For example, this understanding is reflected in her suggestion that we need to make changes to how we prepare PhD students for a range of career tracks and how we speak with them about post-graduation outcomes, given how job availability and working conditions have changed over time. The core leadership competency of sensing positionality was also present in the chapter by Moxley-Kelly and Oakley, as they wrote explicitly about their positionalities as authors and in reference to their institutional location. That is, they describe how they occupied a "liminal space of knowledge, power, and lack thereof" as elected representatives for the Instructor rank and as administrators (37). Moreover, they explain how this sense of positionality informs their sense of responsibility and desire "to contribute to improving the working conditions of [their] rank" at the same time that it also both enables and constrains what they are able to accomplish (37).

For Cox, sensing positionality is articulated through a focus on Sandra Harding's foundational standpoint theory in combination with labor as a critical frame for thoughtfully and strategically navigating new institutional contexts. Cox explains, "labor-centered leadership practice demands both individual critical resistance to oppressive structures *and* coalition and solidarity building amongst colleagues, students, and administrators" (60). In this way, Cox highlights how those in leadership positions—and particularly leaders invested in labor issues—benefit from the ability to recognize the multiple, intersecting ways in which they are positioned in a given context—both in an individual sense as well as in terms of how one exists in relation to the various, at times conflicting, systems and collectives among which one may be located. Importantly, Cox's chapter reminds me of how an effective leader is one who is deft at drawing on their sense of positionality in efforts to recognize possibilities for coalition and solidarity building.

In addition to being able to sense one's positionality within always-shifting spatiotemporal and organizational contexts, Iglesias's chapter teaches us how another important element of *sensing positionality* as a leadership competency involves being able to recognize capacity—not only of oneself but also of others. In Iglesias's systematic approach for transferring academic expertise to other industry contexts, Iglesias engages in an important leadership activity—helping others to recognize their capacities, even—or especially—when it might not be immediately apparent. Iglesias encourages, "Because PhDs are trained to learn at an expert level, I argue that PhDs can use the frame of cultural integration to revise, surpass, and improve inequitable industry norms rather than simply assimilate" (87). From Iglesias's account, it becomes noticeable how effective leaders are often able to reframe context so that others might understand their own locations within them anew. For example, Iglesias says, "coming into a new industry is like entering conversations midway through" (87). This point is useful as it can be easy for people to enter into new workplace contexts ready to make change without sufficiently learning about the existing conversation and the unique organizational culture and ways of knowing and communicating that may be important to those who occupy that space. It is not uncommon for enthusiastic new employees to enter into new institutional contexts not realizing the depth of institutional history that existed before they arrived. Yet understanding this context is essential for actually identifying and enacting ways that institutions can be improved in ways that are both sustainable and effective. We might consider what we could glean from understanding Iglesias's framework for transferring expertise across industries as a useful approach for leadership. How might this framework be a way of reading the stories that follow?

Discerning Possibility

The third core leadership competency that emerged through the chapters included in this section is the ability to *discern possibility* in challenging circumstances, even at times when it may seem like there are none. Discerning possibility in many ways builds on the prior two competencies as one's ability to feel institutional structures and to sense positionality can helpfully contribute to discerning possibility. More likely, these competencies intermingle in a recursive process where discerning possibility can become a way of re-feeling institutional structures and re-sensing one's positionality within those structures. Moreover, discerning possibility often requires the ability to look beyond the options provided to identify alternative courses of action that meet the needs and interests of constituents. In other words, one's ability to discern possibility is contingent on the ability to not simply allow others to determine the terms of engagement. At times, this means working to proactively reshape the terms of the conversation. At others, it might mean acknowledging and then looking beyond a point of impasse. For example, Iglesias demonstrates the core leadership competency of discerning possibility when she thought expansively beyond traditional, narrow academic trajectories for post-doctoral employment in considering her own path forward.

Likewise, Moxley-Kelly and Oakley's narrative is a strong example where non-tenure track faculty found—and enacted—possibility after experiencing a kind of impasse. Perhaps even more importantly, they did so through something akin to what Natasha Jones has referred to as coalitional learning (517). Although Jones focuses on coalitional learning as it occurs across disciplines, I would suggest that there is some similarity to how Moxley-Kelly and Oakley learned and attended to the needs and concerns of the constituents they were elected to serve. Many of us who work in neoliberalized institutions "that [place] a premium on enrollment growth" know what it's like to be stretched thin, underpaid, and told that the criteria for obtaining resources has changed and expectations increased. In their case, Moxley-Kelly and Oakley were presented with a choice to either argue against a higher teaching load (going from 4/4 to 5/5) and larger class sizes or for increased pay for members of their rank "to compensate for the additional workload" (35). Ultimately, they argued for—and received—an increase in take-home salaries. This outcome is one that would not have resulted had they continued to focus on the thing that had recently changed—an outrageous increase in workload. Yet to discern possibility, leaders must be able to look beyond the thing right in front of them or that might be drawing the most attention at the time, as so often happens in crisis capitalist situations. As Moxley-Kelly and Oakley's story reflects, leaders must also be able to listen with care to people working in difficult and often frustrating circumstances who may just need to vent and understand how cultivating trust is so important for expanding what is possible. They additionally maintain a practical—yet not overly conservative—perspective about what is achievable in their context.

In similar ways, Cox furthers this point and expands our understanding of discerning possibility as a core leadership competency in her discussion of Chris Gallagher's concept of "institutional literacy." She explains, "Gallagher teaches us that to be institutionally literate means we participate in the revision of institutional structures rather than simply be in opposition to them" (71). This point speaks to the ways in which leaders in particular are those who are called to participate in making institutional change, as opposed to merely identifying problems, and how this change often requires institutional literacy. As a result, Cox's chapter outlines specific ideas for revising graduate training in ways that will enhance students' ability to discern possibility. These ideas include increased education about "commonplace institutional genres and practices like annual review, budgets, bylaws, promotion standards, accreditation, etc." (71). I would argue that it would additionally be useful for graduate students to learn about things like the rhetorics of institutions as well as the nuts and bolts of insurance, retirement accounts, labor unions, and working with graduate students in addition to undergraduate students. In short, doing so would help students cultivate the ability to be "attuned to institutional hierarchies and the implications of normative practices" in ways that can prepare them to engage in the core leadership competency of discerning possibility (69). As Cox puts it, "Given how hierarchy so often resides in and stems from textual genres and institutional policies, they deserve our full intellectual attention" (71). In this way, Cox's chapter teaches us that if we look expansively at the different pieces that make up institutional structures and that enable them to function, we are more likely to be able to discern possibilities, even where it might initially seem like there are none.

Taking Action for Collective Change

The fourth and final core leadership competency that I noticed across the chapters in this section is *taking action for collective change*. Taking action for collective change makes explicit how leaders always act on behalf of a collective and not just themselves, whether they mean to do so or not. That is, it makes transparent how even leaders who are motivated by their own self-interests alone nevertheless inevitably take actions that affect collectives beyond themselves. Moreover, in many cases it is not enough for those in leadership positions to sit on their feelings, reflections, and observations; an effective leader must be able to take those observations and make them actionable in ways that can actually have a positive impact on the lives of those around them. The ability to take action for collective change is likewise co-constitutive with the other three core leadership competencies of feeling institutional structures, sensing positionality, and discerning possibility, which provide important groundwork that enables the ability to take action. In addition, there is a similar recursive process across these competencies as taking action might happen after one has discerned viable possibilities within a given situation and identified the most effective course of action. Yet taking action for collective change and the aftereffects one experiences as a result of those actions can likewise become a way of feeling institutional structures, re-sensing positionality, or further discerning possibilities.

Indeed, all three chapters highlight how the authors took coalitional action in different ways, oftentimes through advocacy as in the cases of Moxley-Kelly and Oakley as well as Cox. For instance, Moxley-Kelly and Oakley described how they advocated for higher take-home pay through a community-focused approach to managing disagreement and dissensus that allowed for multiple perspectives. Furthermore, they highlighted the need to cultivate quantitative data literacy for advocacy purposes—a strategy that tends to be more effective in institutions governed by neoliberal values. On the other hand, Cox was able to draw on the support of her provost in efforts to develop the writing program with attention to labor equity through coalitional work on a university task force. This work would lead to several outcomes, including but not limited to the development of a first-year writing curriculum grounded in disciplinary best practices; increased attention to the importance and working conditions of non-tenure-track faculty and the development of a programmatic community that could provide support for these faculty members; and "expanded conversations about writing on campus in anti-oppressive frameworks" (74).

As I read through these chapters, one question I had was whether leaders should necessarily focus on enacting *sustainable* changes as opposed to temporary ones. On one hand, Iglesias's chapter seems to suggest that it is essential that we attend to sustainability, given that sustain is the fourth step in her cultural integration framework. At the same time, Cox speaks to some of the many challenges of enacting sustainable change in what are oftentimes transient academic work lives. That is, the fact that Cox reflects on how her decision to eventually leave the institution is a factor that makes long term sustainable change difficult to see through. People rotate in and out of academic institutions quite frequently, and perhaps even more so post-COVID-19. How should those in leadership positions respond when these movements happen? What structures can or should be put into place so that effective changes are maintained and ineffective ones revised or undone? Can temporary changes at times be the best option within a given situation, and if so, when? And how might we account for the less apparent impacts of change beyond how long an initiative lasted on record versus whether small scale efforts may have spurred other meaningful efforts or initiatives?

Conclusion

Thinking back to the broader context for this work, I have to admit that this was an incredibly difficult piece for me to write for a whole host of reasons, many of which have to do with the contextual factors of privatization and austerity cuts in higher education that I described at the start of this response. In Fall 2023, my own employer made national news as the senior administration declared widespread layoffs and budget cuts under the guise of what was euphemistically referred to as "Academic Transformation." In the case of my own department, we've lost more than a third of our faculty as some fourteen tenure track faculty members were either "non-renewed," took early retirement, or resigned on their own accord for a number of reasons mostly related to Academic Transformation and its aftermath. Beyond indicating to those of us who remain that tenure is no protection from academic austerity, we have been given higher teaching loads with no reduction in our research expectations, at the same time that we have fewer faculty members to serve on committees and to take on administrative responsibilities. What I find especially troubling about these trends is how such conditions make equity and social justice based institutional reform even more difficult than they already were. Nearly all of the women of color faculty I've met in the short time I've been here have now departed the institution. And how do the temporal demands of neoliberal institutions contrast with the time needed "to build the [kinds of] sustainable collegial relationships" (Cox 68) required to bring about meaningful change?

As I read through the chapters in this section that focuses on understanding and reconceptualizing leadership from "where we are" while going through all of this, I began to wonder whether a broader understanding of leadership might simply be necessary as a result of the temporal demands and labor conditions that have been placed upon so many of us. In other words, neoliberal austerity in higher education has often meant that universities have merged programs and departments in their quest to seek out all "efficiencies," as doing so can mean needing only one mid-level administrator as opposed to two or three, thus reducing expenditures on course reassignments or summer salaries for administrative work. Yet when there are fewer people in institutionally-recognized positions of leadership on which we can lean, perhaps we are forced to look to more distributive forms of "leadership" to make change happen. And what are the affordances and challenges of such models? It seems that there is an increasing need for grassroots interventions and leadership at a time when senior administrators who are institutionally empowered with the most decision-making authority are oftentimes either hamstrung or driven to enact changes on the basis of neoliberal marketing principles and higher education consulting companies that are apparently unconcerned with any sense of a public and social good, or principles of community care. And these conditions have only exacerbated with the onset of the most recent US presidential administration as federal funding and research grants have been slashed in the name of "government efficiency." Yet as we look for leadership as it occurs beyond institutionally-sanctioned and authorized roles, there are challenging questions about labor compensation that need to be considered. For instance, what are we to make of the tension between grassroots participation above and beyond one's regular work responsibilities while trying not to fall into the neoliberal grind, getting sucked into doing work far beyond one's regular responsibilities or above one's pay grade without reasonable compensation?

Another challenge that I had when it came to this response was that it raised, for me, difficult questions about leadership that I've needed time to grapple with. That is, I wondered about the affordances of "leadership" as an organizing episteme for this collection. As I read through these chapters, I began to wonder: What *is* leadership? What activities count as leadership and who are acknowledged as leaders? What contexts are often associated as being places where we can observe leadership at work? Are there examples of collaboration and collective work that exist outside of "leadership" and if so, why and what are they? What are the affordances of naming particular activities as "leadership"? That is, what are the material stakes of shifting our understanding of leadership? Does "leadership" necessarily suggest an individualistic worldview? What does it mean to understand leadership as collective or distributive work? Might more expansive understandings of leadership make it easier to recognize contributions by minoritized peoples that too often go overlooked? Are there ways that interrogation into "leadership" in rhetoric and composition can help us move toward more equitable practices for understanding and compensating labor? And, on the other hand, what challenges might it pose for this goal? How might understanding leadership as distributed raise compelling questions about unequal compensation and exploitation? I suppose I don't have conclusive answers to these questions, but I believe that this collection productively brings them to the surface for continued consideration and interrogation.

Finally, as our discipline has been re-examining the purposes and paths of graduate training in rhetoric, writing, and composition studies, we might consider the implications of this book for graduate student training. For instance, how might framing certain activities we do in terms of leadership help graduates translate their work for other industries? How do writing programs already equip students to do leadership? How might the discourse of leadership be brought into writing curricula, and what are the affordances of such a shift? I'm hopeful that this collection will help further our thinking about these questions and more.

Works Cited

Arellano, Sonia. "Reflections from a Recovering Academic: Offering Guidance, Seeking Accountability, and Inspiring Leaders." *Composition Studies*, vol. 52, no. 2, 2024, pp. 166–70.

Arellano, Sonia, Will Kurlinkus, Caitlan Spronk, and Alexandra Hidalgo. "The Mass Exodus: Why People Are Leaving Academia and What We Can Learn from Their Stories." *Constellations*, vol. 7, 2024, https://constell8cr.com/issue-7/the-mass-exodus-why-people-are-leaving-academia-and-what-we-can-learn-from-their-stories/.

Ball, Cheryl E. "Recognizing Your Values." *Composition Studies*, vol. 52, no. 2, 2024, pp. 149–53.

Estrem, Heidi. "From On-Campus to Behind-the-Capitol: Transitioning from Academia to State Educational Policy Work." *Composition Studies*, vol. 52, no. 2, 2024, pp. 145–48.

Flaherty, Colleen. "The Peer-Review Crisis." *Inside Higher Education*, 12 June 2022, https://www.rcdocconsortium.org/reports-statements-research.

Forrester, Nikki. "Fed Up and Burnt Out: 'Quiet Quitting' Hits Academia." *Nature*, 2023, https://www.nature.com/articles/d41586-023-00633-w.

Gewin, Virginia. "Has the 'Great Resignation' Hit Academia?" *Nature*, 2022, https://www.nature.com/articles/d41586-022-01512-6.

Gewin, Virginia. "How Five Researchers Fared after Their 'Great Resignation' from Academia." *Nature*, 2023, https://www.nature.com/articles/d41586-023-03484-7.

Hart-Davidson, William. "On Writing, Technical Communication, and Information Technology: The Core Competencies of Technical Communication." *Technical Communication*, vol. 48, no. 2, 2001, pp. 145–55.

Hart-Davidson, William. "What Are the Work Patterns of Technical Communication?" *Solving Problems in Technical Communication*. Edited by Johndan Johnson-Eilola and Stuart A. Selber, U of Chicago P, 2013, pp. 50–74.

Horta, Hugo, and Jisun Jung. "The Crisis of Peer Review: Part of the Evolution of Science." *Higher Education Quarterly*, vol. 78, no. 4, 2024, pp. 1–14.

Jones, Natasha N. "Coalitional Learning in the Contact Zones: Inclusion and Narrative Inquiry in Technical Communication and Composition Studies." *College English*, vol. 82, no. 5, 2020, pp. 515–26.

Kurlinkus, Will. "Ungrateful: The Affective Calculus of Leaving the Tenure Track." *Composition Studies*, vol. 52, no. 2, 2024, pp. 154–59.

Lindgren, Chris. "Rhetoric, Composition, and Technical Communication Job Postings per Year." *rhetmap.org*, https://lingeringcode.github.io/rhetmap-time-series/. Accessed 6 Mar. 2025.

Madden, Shannon. "Fear, Self-Loathing, and Stress for Breakfast: Escaping Toxicity and Dysfunction in Academia." *Composition Studies*, vol. 52, no. 2, 2024, pp. 160–65.

McMartin, Charles, and Thomas Miller. "The Challenging Opportunities Facing Next-Generation Faculty and Staff Leaders." *College English*, vol. 86, no. 3, 2024, pp. 195–218.

Parrish, Danielle E. "The Peer Review Crisis Continues: What Comes Next?" *Journal of Social Work Education*, vol. 60, no. 2, 2024, pp. 171–73.

Tropini, Carolina, et al. "Time to Rethink Academic Publishing: The Peer Reviewer Crisis." *mBio*, vol. 14, no. 6, 2023, pp. 1–7.

SECTION 2

Building Networks of Resistance to Claim Support for Your Work as a Leader

Introduction to Section 2

SONIA C. ARELLANO

Since we started this book project a few years ago, I have experienced incredible life changes. When Charlie interviewed me for the study he and Tom conducted, I would never have guessed that the inadequate leadership I discussed in that interview would be the catalyst for my departure. Leaving my academic career was not easy, but I know it was necessary for my life and my health. When people ask why I left, the answers are layered and complex, and some may think I simply did not "fit." The reality is I exercised agency, and I made a difficult choice to no longer accept the ethos imposed upon me.

The ways I was asked to abandon myself for the job, for the students, for the university were too much. I was no longer able or willing to work under the conditions of my job. And let me be clear, I was in an incredibly privileged position. I was a tenure-track professor; I was not raising children as discussed by colleagues in this collection; I had generally nice colleagues in my department; my research and publications were successful and supported. However, my negative experiences (which are published elsewhere) outweighed the positive ones. Ultimately, the values of the university did not align with my values as a human, and I had to come to terms with that reality. While next-gen faculty and students may find themselves facing a similar conundrum, each person's strategic response to exercise agency can take different shapes.

One of the inescapable realities of higher education is that its institutional origin and infrastructure reproduce social inequalities that privilege a white-middle-class professional ethos. The university at its inception was a colonial project. Because "[t]he university cannot solve the colonial problem to which it was already tethered," DEI initiatives (when they were in place) could not actually address social inequities in academia (Arellano et al.). With the recent elimination of DEI and other programs, next-gen faculty and students continue to struggle to figure out how to endure and survive, dare I say thrive, with increased constraints and a larger impetus. The authors in this section developed various types of coalitional leadership in their efforts to build networks of resistance, including coalitions between students and faculty and between faculty and communities. These chapters chronicle how next-gen faculty and students resisted oppressive professionalization processes to assert their leadership.

The authors in this section built the sorts of networks of resistance that have been examined in Juan Carlos González's study of the academic socialization of Latina PhD students. The students interviewed by González faced considerable "opportunities and challenges" in their efforts to mix Latina and academic cultures (348). He found that some students had positive experiences and support systems while others had negative experiences and challenges, with various factors contributing to the varied experiences.

González studied a very specific group, but his concept of academic socialization processes is helpful in assessing the challenging opportunities faced by the next-gen faculty included in this collection, most of whom not only come from marginalized backgrounds but are also part of a generation seeking more equitable institutions. According to González, academic socialization processes systematically replace students' foundational cultural norms with white middle-class norms in ways that make it difficult for them to successfully exercise agency without acculturating into the professional norms (348). In the following chapters we hear from next-gen faculty and students who were discouraged from challenging the institutional norms that they were being socialized into.

Although "advice" against challenging institutional norms is often well-meaning and couched as care for the success of early-career faculty and students, it is also detrimental to their cultural identity and sense of value, as Felicita Arzu-Carmichael and Mena Hannakachl discuss in the fourth chapter in our collection. In the fifth chapter by Alice Hays, Shaylyn Marks, Alexandra Chapa-Kunz, and Amardeep (Rupsy) Bajwa, we hear from early-career K–12 teachers of color who are challenged for revising their classrooms and curriculum even though they were sought out to diversify the curriculum. In the sixth chapter, Adele Leon reflects on how she challenged traditional research hierarchies that devalued her work with local communities. Each of the authors in the following chapters had a negative experience with academic socialization as their own cultural norms were challenged or devalued. However, each of these authors chose to assert their agency in distinctive ways.

In his study González found that the students who had "the most positive doctoral experiences" had "opportunities to build communities with similarly thinking students and faculty of color across their institutions, in their departments, and in the local community" (357). Throughout these chapters, readers will find the stories of next-gen faculty and students who sought out such opportunities to build communities—between students and teachers and between professors and their communities. González also found that Latina PhD students often resisted academic socialization in ways that "helped them survive the academy from within and allowed them to create networks with other academics that had similar feelings about doctoral socialization conflicting with their culture and academic purpose" (359).

The authors of the chapters in this section also leaned on the communities they built, their networks of resistance, to find their voice—a common result of successful resistance to academic socialization (360). In chapter 5, Felicita Arzu-Carmichael and Mena Hannakachl demonstrate how microaffirmations can create opportunities to build networks of resistance between students and faculty. In chapter 6 two faculty of teacher training programs, Alice Hays and Shaylyn Marks, partnered with former students of their program, Alexandra Chapa-Kunz and Amardeep (Rupsy) Bajwa, to address the challenges teachers of color face when serving diverse students and establishing autonomy in their schools. In both chapters five and six, faculty and students had opportunities to work together to build their networks and resist academic socialization. In the process, all involved exercised their voice and leveraged their agency, demonstrating the leadership potential in such collaborations. Collaboratively writing these chapters is beautiful proof of finding their voices together on the page.

In chapter 7, Adele Leon shares how she honed important leadership qualities during an undervalued administrative experience working with community partnerships and went on to create another beautiful community partnership program as an early-career faculty. Leon's struggles with community building shaped her leadership by reinforcing her commitment to equity, resistance, and accountability through the support of her faculty mentor and the guidance of the scholarship of bell hooks, who helped her to understand how "service is devalued" in "an imperialist white-supremacist capitalist patriarchal culture . . . as a way of maintaining subordination" (hooks 83). These critiques strengthened Leon's solidarity with the communities she sought to serve by helping her resist the research hierarchies that attempted to bend her leadership to serve "on behalf of the institution, not on behalf of students and colleagues" (hooks 83).

Not all next-gen faculty and students are as successful with building communities of resistance as the authors of the chapters in this section. The following contributors offer innovative and transformational strategies to help faculty and students carefully and conscientiously build such networks together. Others, like me, chose to resist the academic socialization process by leaving the academy with the support of my networks of resistance. I found my voice outside the walls of academe, similar to some of the other contributors to this collection who have left professor positions since writing their chapters. Like rising numbers of next-gen graduates and faculty, colleagues are exercising agency by choosing to leave, not because they failed, but because they knew they would be happier and healthier elsewhere. We hope this section provides readers with some ways to strategically develop their collective agency to determine the best path forward for themselves.

Before reading this section, we want to share some general takeaways about creating networks of resistance to consider while reading:

Seek and Engage
- Put yourself out there: When building communities, you often must put yourself out there. Seek out like-minded and equity-driven people. Sometimes such people can be found in your existing communities (think about colleagues, organizations on campus, collaborations at conferences). Other times you'll have to put a bit more effort into finding such communities.
- Follow up: When you do connect with others, be sure to follow up. People are busy, so don't hesitate to offer a slight nudge to connect, especially when it's an invaluable connection.
- Look to existing resources: Talk with established scholars or administrators for advice and look to existing frameworks or successful models.

Follow Your Heart and Head
- Follow your heart, feelings, and gut: Focus on the positive in situations (when you can) because these will provide more opportunities than focusing on the negative. For example, seek connection when you

experience microaffirmations. Additionally, stay committed to causes, organizations, writing genres, and communities that are important to you, no matter if others support it. When you are following what calls to you, you are often doing important work.

- Listen to your head and logic: Don't make assumptions about who may or may not align with your values and have your best interest at heart. Remember, as Zora Neale Hurston famously said, "all my skin folk ain't kinfolk." More experienced colleagues will always have advice on what's best. You have your own specific context, so take what is useful and leave the rest. Additionally, let people show you who they are because your biggest supporters may surprise you.

Take on Leadership Roles

- Traditional administration: One way to engage in networks of resistance is by taking on traditional administration and leadership roles within institutions. Although your ability to make change may be limited, you cannot discount the potential of even small changes within institutions. As demonstrated through these chapters, often the visibility of next-gen, diverse folks in such positions can be powerful.
- Create new roles: An apparent way to build networks of resistance is by creating new roles to support resistance. For example, creating new support groups for minoritized folks, or new classes that incorporate DEI work, or new community engagement opportunities that align with your commitments. Throughout these chapters, you'll see how many people saw an opportunity to create something new and bravely did so.
- Accountability and reciprocity: As highlighted in chapter 7, engaging in leadership roles that are guided by principles of accountability and reciprocity are key to empowering all people involved. As Leon claims, "resistance leads to transformation." Therefore, in building networks of resistance, the faculty and students in these chapters are ultimately inspired by the potential of transformation. When you ensure accountability for the work you do and reciprocity for all involved, empowerment and transformation become more likely.

Works Cited

Arellano, Sonia, et al. "Shadow Work: Witnessing Latinx Crossings in Rhetoric and Composition." *Diversity Is Not Justice: Working Toward Radical Transformation and Racial Equity in the Discipline*. Special issue of *Composition Studies*. Edited by Ersula Ore, Christina Cedillo, and Kim Wieser, vol. 49, no. 2, 2021, pp. 31–52.

González, Juan Carlos. "Academic Socialization Experiences of Latina Doctoral Students: A Qualitative Understanding of Support Systems That Aid and Challenges That Hinder the Process." *Journal of Hispanic Higher Education*, vol. 5 no. 4, 2006, pp. 347–65, https://doi.org/10.1177/1538192706291141.

hooks, bell. *Teaching Community: A Pedagogy of Hope*. Routledge, 2003.

4
Student-Faculty Coalition Building

Autoethnographic Perspectives on Leadership and Empowerment

FELICITA ARZU-CARMICHAEL AND MENA HANNAKACHL

> "Black feminism is a practice; it's about what you do."
> *Carmen Kynard*

It became apparent in fall of 2021 during a writing course I taught and in which Mena was enrolled, that we had intersecting experiences and interests related to racial microaggressions. Making sense of these troubling experiences and their material consequences proved challenging yet productive. Our experiences with racial microaggressions during the pandemic occurred in the face of growing diversity, equity, and inclusion initiatives at our institution and across the country. As a junior faculty of color and an undergraduate student of color, we recognized that the retention and success of racially diverse faculty and students seem to be important issues for educational institutions. In fact, our academic home has these factors as part of its strategic goals. However, Sara Ahmed reminds us that "a commitment does not necessarily commit the institution to anything or to doing anything" (116), as evidenced by the recent dismantling of diversity, equity, and inclusion efforts across many institutions in response to anti-DEI political pressures (Gretzinger et al.). Thus, the experiences of historically minoritized faculty and students are often still fraught with challenges; these challenges reflect the "macro-pictures of political life in

American universities" (Kynard "Teaching" 1). From fall 2021 up until the time we wrote this chapter, we worked to respond to the racial microaggressions we experienced with microaffirmations we found to be impactful. Through coalitional teaching and learning, these microaffirmations also allowed us to develop a renewed understanding of how leadership and a sense of empowerment can lead to enacting change. The guiding question contributors in this edited collection were asked to answer is: What has the pandemic taught us about collective leadership? The pandemic has taught us that microaffirmations create opportunities for coalition building between faculty and students, allowing us to "work together to imagine new, justice-driven approaches to institutional leadership structures" (Jones et al. 30). The pandemic also taught us that it is important for academic institutions to change how they think about what counts as leadership: leadership must entail creating and sustaining action-oriented networks between faculty and students.

In this intergenerational autoethnography, we—Felicita Arzu-Carmichael, an early-career Afro-Caribbean faculty and Mena Hannakachl, a recently graduated Arab Chaldean student—take up a Black feminist articulation of leadership and empowerment to demonstrate how microaffirmations, "subtle verbal and nonverbal strategies Peoples of Color consciously engage (with other Peoples of Color) that affirm each other's value, integrity, and shared humanity" (Solórzano et al., "Theorizing Racial Microaffirmations" 185), grounded in social justice, might lead to coalition building among faculty and students. Moreover, Black feminist thinking invites us to understand empowerment as a process grounded in "self-conscious struggle" (Hill Collins) and as an analysis of the experiences, perspectives, and cultural norms of peoples of color. In terms of leadership, "Black feminism is a practice; it's about what you do" (Kynard, "Racial Memory" 322). This involves creating a critical awareness of how our bodies inhabit spaces, including the "assumptions, stereotypes, and misrecognitions people place on it" (Williams 74) that impacts the work we do, how we do it and how we understand its impact in wider contexts.

In our chapter, we first tell of when our racialized bodies have experienced microaggressions in a variety of academic spaces, especially online spaces. We follow Solórzano et al. arguing that "the practice of naming racial microaggressions disrupts the normalized existence of racism and white supremacy in everyday life and calls attention to the structural inequities and individual pain they cause" ("Theorizing Racial Microaffirmations" 207). We recognize, as Diab et al. puts it, that the "collective interpretation of narratives ... is crucial to collective recognition of our problems, our commitments to counter them, and our efforts toward making commitments actionable" (3). Thus, in making our commitments actionable, we then analyze these overt and covert racial microaggressions, as they emerge in sites such as the writing classroom and on feedback to student papers. Our goal is to demonstrate how sites of learning and community building are also political sites of trauma and tension that place early-career faculty and undergraduate students of color at risk. To demonstrate this, we draw on Walton et al.'s four R's heuristic (recognize, reveal, reject, and replace) that advocate for change and the development of coalition-led policies and procedures. Finally, we conclude by sharing how microaffirmations led to building coalitions that create opportunities for renewed perspectives on leadership and empowerment.

***

Felicita's Autoethnography

CHANGING TIMES

January 6, 2020, marked the start of the winter semester at our institution. That semester, I taught my newly designed special topics course, Rhetoric(s) of Race and Ethnicity. The class was underenrolled, but the few students in the class and I engaged in rich conversations about race, ethnicity, and racial oppression in various contexts. I was thankful to my department chair and college dean for allowing the class to run since underenrolled classes are typically cut before the start of the semester. I designed the class as a hybrid course, whereby for the first week of the semester, students and I met in-person three days a week (Monday, Wednesday, and Friday) so that I can orient them to the class and the ideologies in which it is grounded. During the second week, I moved our Friday sessions to online and students began working more independently, engaging with and reflecting on major ideas and concepts we would have discussed collaboratively on Mondays and Wednesdays. The impetus for this class came from my desire to intentionally center race and racial analysis in the work I would do with students, especially since departmental records show that there hadn't yet been a class offered that centered on race. Lisa A. Flores persuasively argues that "race is foundational to the work of rhetorical criticism and that any criticism void of this consideration is incomplete, partial, if not irresponsible" (6). The events that would unfold as that semester progressed proved Flores's point about the importance of race in the rhetorical work we do.

On March 3, 2020, I began receiving university emails regarding COVID-19. At that time, there were no confirmed cases of COVID-19 in the state. By

9 a.m. on March 11, 2020, our department began conversations about moving our classes to fully online, should the necessity arise, due to the rapid spread of COVID-19. By 4 p.m. that same day (March 11, 2020), the university sent an email notifying the campus community that all in-person classes would be suspended at 5 p.m. and that faculty should move all instruction to online effective Monday, March 16, 2020. Naturally my primary and only concern at that time was the health and well-being of my students, my family, and myself. Although I worked to maintain the integrity of the first race course in my department, I also recognized that my students' engagement in this course would not be as I had hoped because their lives and the lives of people they love could be in jeopardy. It didn't take long into our now fully online course that I started to read about and see intersections between significant health inequities surrounding COVID-19 and many of the key issues we had discussed in Rhetoric(s) of Race and Ethnicity. There were so many important conversations I wanted to have with my students about what we were all learning via news outlets, and what a few of them were experiencing firsthand, but I struggled with doing this meaningfully in an asynchronous online course that was not meant to be one. Yet, I improvised. I made changes to the course content to accommodate the rapidly shifting circumstances of some students in the class and the growing conversations surrounding race and COVID-19.

That semester ended April 2020, only a few weeks before the nation was rocked by the senseless and brutal racially motivated murder of George Floyd in May 2020. During this time in May 2020, I was now teaching an online summer first-year writing course. Later that summer, I also worked to support faculty in my department in pivoting to online teaching for fall. I co-led a professional development workshop that summer, and I would continue to lead a number of other workshops as the semester progressed. While supporting faculty's professional development, I was also still struggling to come to terms with how Rhetoric(s) of Race and Ethnicity unfolded. I was now faced with another difficult question "How do I as a teacher-scholar committed to racial equity and justice continue to guide my students in achieving course learning outcomes while also recognizing that many of these same students are witnessing and being impacted by the devastating effects of violence against communities of color during a global health crisis?" To respond to this question, below I share the work that unfolded during the pandemic and that continues to this day. This work was possible in coalition with faculty and students and taking up leadership roles within my department and institution.

WRITING INSTRUCTION AND RACIAL MICROAGGRESSION

My identity as a Black woman, an immigrant scholar, and multilingual speaker is central to my pedagogy. Christina D. Shelton reminds us of how our bodies matter as texts in our classrooms, and in the fall of 2020, I experienced firsthand the risks associated with my Black body as a text in the writing classroom. That semester I taught my first core course as a tenure-track faculty. This fully online asynchronous course, Issues in Writing and Rhetoric, was a course designed to introduce students to "important past and present issues in the field of writing and rhetoric" and that provides students with "a theoretical and historical foundation for understanding current issues, changes, and challenges for the discipline." When I was preparing to teach this course, I thought what better way to introduce students to key issues than through the lens of our field's major conference, the Conference on College Composition and Communication, where key issues, past and present, are addressed. Recognizing that there are "racialized politics, histories, and ideologies that inform the crafting and instituting of core curricula in rhetorical studies" (Martinez 402) and that "core curriculum is by and large the domain of white Euro-Western perspectives and ways of knowing" (Martinez 403), I was mindful of the course's objectives and course description, cognizant of how the course had been taught in the past by senior faculty based on my review of existing course syllabi, and intentional about how I would enact a Black feminist pedagogy to help my own students meet these goals. I sought the support and collaboration of more established teacher-scholars in the field, who graciously agreed to be guest speakers in my course.

Throughout that semester in Issues in Writing and Rhetoric, one student was very resistant to completing reading responses when the readings were either authored by scholars of color and/or when the readings were evidently about issues impacting marginalized peoples, particularly immigrants and Black or Latinx folx. In these reading responses, I ask students to, among other things, identify the author's assertion and the means by which the author has developed and supported that assertion. The student repeatedly failed to engage these two areas when it came to certain readings despite the detailed comments and questions I would leave on their papers and a request to meet and discuss what seemed to be a gross "misunderstanding" of the assignment instructions. The student's avoidance of the issues seemed intentional; on discussion forums, they would likewise either avoid the topics altogether or make heaping generalizations about "people who come here" needing to "follow the rules" and about problems faced in society because people insist on talking about "color stuff." I felt personally attacked by this student, and I struggled with how to productively address the situation in an asynchronous online course; I was also concerned for the embodied experiences of my other students and about how they were reading and engaging in this online writing course. As Abby Knoblauch and Marie Moeller remind us, embodiment involves the "experience of orienting one's body in space and among others" (8), and my orientation to this class, to the one particular student, and to my other students in class, was complex. My students and I were experiencing material consequences and effects to the teaching and learning that was occurring in my virtual classroom, and each week I grew concerned about how those consequences would impact the work we were striving to do together. Moreover, the classroom is a political space and faculty of color, especially those of us who are early-career, experience trauma in the classroom when we are faced with racial microaggressions such as these. Notably, I am the only Black junior faculty in my department, and these experiences I describe are not unique. Instead, they paint a "macro-picture of political life in American universities" (Kynard, "Teaching while Black" 1).

As the semester progressed, I began getting emails from other students in class who recognized the hostility and racism in the student's online forum posts. I was thankful for these emails because while I assumed my other students were uncomfortable, now I knew for certain they were paying attention. I reached out to a senior faculty member to ask their advice on whether I should continue to communicate with this student privately (via my comments on their assignments, private replies on forum posts and emails), address them publicly (reply to their forums publicly so that my other students in class could see that I was not ignoring the issue), or something else. Perhaps this was a conversation I should have had with an administrator because I was becoming increasingly concerned about my safety and the safety of my other students. The senior faculty member advised me to keep my conversations with the student private. I ignored that advice. I felt a public response was an opportunity to move beyond the common statement about the class being a "safe environment" that appears on most course syllabi, and toward what Jones et al. call a "coalitional Pro-Black praxis" (29) that redresses anti-Blackness. Moreover, it is necessary to speak out against oppressive language comments publicly (Jones and Walton). I recognized that this student's resistance to the work I was asking them to do was because they did not see the relevance of race or inclusion to writing. As Kynard reminds us, "racial violence is deeply entrenched and propagated by our colleges, the intellectual traditions and methods of the entire arc of English studies, and the processes and politics of college writing/ college classrooms" ("Racial Memory" 318), so I should not have been surprised when this senior faculty member not only discouraged me from addressing the issue publicly, but they also showed resistance to this race-conscious work I pursued (more on this later).

During that fall 2020 in Issues in Writing and Rhetoric, I made two choices based on the experiences my students and I were having. First, I focused more of my attention on building coalitions with students by recognizing those in the course who were doing the work and who demonstrated a clear interest in grappling with issues in the field. In fact, I subsequently invited two of these students to collaborate with me for a presentation at the 2021 NCTE conference held online and under the theme "Equity, Justice, and Anti-Racist Teaching." I felt it important that these students continued to participate in important conversations we were having in class and that they saw firsthand how the issues that mattered to them were also foundational to changes occurring in our field. Moreover, Laura Adler explains that "[COVID] has negatively impacted students' ability to translate education into work opportunities, with the disappearance of internships and summer jobs" (8). Thus, I also aimed for these students to see themselves as leaders amongst their peers and for my course to help them achieve any professional goals they might have. After all, "the classroom, with all its limitations, remains a location of possibility" (hooks, *Teaching to Transgress* 207). Thus, faculty and students must remain open-minded to these possibilities. Undergraduate students are typically not expected to present at national conferences or publish academic papers, and understandably so. But times are changing, and the way academics think about what matters to an undergraduate education and what counts as leadership are also shifting.

Second, I spent the next year designing and proposing an upper-level writing course that centers race and social justice. While the structure for this new course was informed by Issues in Writing and Rhetoric from fall 2020, I had recognized the need for this course in winter 2020 while teaching Rhetoric(s) of Race and Ethnicity. As I mentioned, Rhetoric(s) of Race and Ethnicity was a special topics course, and it was under enrolled. Notably, Aja Y. Martinez unapologetically argues that "ethnocentric white students only tolerate the work of POC when it comes in the forms of electives—so they can elect not to take these courses" (403). While there could be any number of reasons why this course was underenrolled (it being a new class could be a factor), the fact that it was an elective should also be considered. Thus, I aimed for a new course that would improve on Rhetoric(s) of Race and Ethnicity and be a standing course in the department. When I mentioned to a senior faculty member back in winter 2020 that I was considering this new project and asked for their input, they advised me not to do so because it "wasn't the time for that!" and there were "other more pressing matters" that I should focus on (this was the same senior faculty member who had advised me not to publicly address the student in class). This faculty member claimed that because things were so uncertain in 2020, as a junior faculty member, I should not be prioritizing a new course. While I agreed that matters such as retaining our current majors and minors was a priority, I did not see this as a separate matter from creating a course that centers race for these same students.

The pandemic taught academics that the inequities in education and health were primarily based on race. Even today, the immediate political agenda of the current administration is a racial one, as Nikole Hannah-Jones observed (MSNBC). Students at my institution deserved to participate in the ongoing conversations that reveal how these issues are rooted in historic injustices. What's more, they needed to identify how their training in rhetoric and their own identities and positionalities are central to advocating for social change. A Black feminist pedagogy enabled me to do this work because it offers "a critique of traditional curricula and pedagogy" (Henry 89). I also had tremendous support from my department chair and other colleagues who did recognize that it was in fact "the time for that!" So, I pressed on. I follow scholars such as Lisa A. Flores and Aja Y. Martinez in recognizing race as foundational to rhetorical criticism. What's more, teaching courses that center race allow me to bring myself, my experiences, and the histories and experiences of historically marginalized peoples to the forefront. Moreover, as I have argued elsewhere (Arzu Carmichael), teaching classes that center race and social justice allow faculty to educate students who are unaware of how they benefit from racist systems but also empower those who bear the negative effects of these same systems. As hooks reminds us "we are all subjects in history. We must return ourselves to a state of embodiment in order to deconstruct the way power has been traditionally orchestrated in the classroom, denying subjectivity to some groups and according it to others" (*Teaching to Transgress* 139). In other words, all students benefit from learning about these important issues so that change can be affected in our institutions.

At the end of fall 2021, my newly designed course, Race, Social Justice, and Professional Writing, was approved as a US-diversity, writing-intensive-in-general-education, and writing-intensive-in-the-major course. In this course, students study race in relation to corporate social justice in professional writing contexts. I create opportunities for them to select course readings that are of interest to them, draft open-ended questions for class discussions, and lead those class discussions. I limit my lectures only to the beginning of a new unit. The discussions in the rest of those units are student-led, and I contribute only when I need to clarify an idea and/or share my own perspectives on those questions and details students present. Paulo Freire refers to this as a "problem-posing" approach to education whereby students become empowered by the agency they develop (Freire 12). I taught this course for the first time in fall 2022, and my department plans to offer it every year. The department has also moved to make Race, Social Justice, and Professional Writing a core course in our Professional and Digital Writing major. Also, the Communications and Journalism Department at my institution approved adding Race, Social Justice, and Professional Writing to their Communications, Social Justice, and Advocacy Minor. These moves demonstrate a commitment to make learning about race foundational to degree programs and to "divesting from the impulse to center the white, patriarchal, cisgender, male experience (and all the other oppressions and -isms that come with marginalization) so others' voices can be realized and acknowledged as always having been and continuing to be a part of TPC" (Mckoy et al. 227).

MICROAFFIRMATIONS, SOWING SEEDS OF LEADERSHIP AND EMPOWERMENT

Brittney Cooper asserts that "'empowerment' is a tricky word. It's also a decidedly neoliberal word that places the responsibility for combating systems on individuals" and that "the politics of personal empowerment suggests to us that if we simply 'free our minds then our asses will follow'" (122). My own understanding of and experiences with being empowered align with Cooper's perspectives. I found that my personal empowerment came to fruition when I work collaboratively with others to advance racial justice. When I started my new position as assistant professor of writing and rhetoric in fall 2018, there were many aspects of my new position that made me feel excited and like I belonged. My new colleagues in the department were smart and friendly, the student population was vibrant and earnest, and there were many courses I looked forward to teaching. Another important factor that made me anticipate my position in a new university was getting to meet and work closely with another Black faculty in my department; this faculty member almost immediately became my unofficial mentor. Her office was adjacent to mine, so each day when I came to work, we would greet each other before going about our days. This greeting often involved catching up on recent global news, discussing departmental business, sharing teaching experiences, and complaining about the cold Michigan weather! Aside from these typical chit chats, this colleague and I would also talk about our families and cultural experiences. Like me, this faculty member is a Black woman and an immigrant. Although we came from different parts of the world, our shared ancestry united us in ways that I had never experienced in my academic life. Our daily chit chats would involve talking about our mothers and how they raised us, our ancestral lands that we missed so dearly because of the earthly cultural foods that emerged from them, our local communities with people riding bikes and roaming the streets selling fruits and vegetables, etc. We found in each other a connection that was truly unique, and this connection was a constant microaffirmation that was empowering. Microaffirmations are experiences that affirm and validate one's racial identity (Solórzano et al., "Critical Race Theory"). Importantly, these racial microaffirmations can cause people from racially minority populations to "feel that their inclusion, well-being or success is promoted" (Rolón-Dow and Davison 1). Not only did this faculty member orient me to my new department and role as assistant professor, but she also helped embed me in the community of Black faculty at my institution through the Black Faculty Association (BFA).

Since joining the faculty at my institution, I've been an active member of the BFA, a group designed to explore ways of recruiting and retaining Black faculty and establishing a sense of place and belonging among Black faculty. My membership in BFA is how I came to know other Black women faculty and have since created a bond and sisterhood with them. I remember the first time I attended a BFA meeting. The room was filled with Black professionals from all over the African diaspora. I had never experienced anything like this before during my time living in the US; the racial, ethnic, cultural, and linguistic diversity of BFA was reminiscent of my home country. Moreover, this microrecognition that Rolón-Dow and Davison describe as a form of microaffirmation that "illustrate moments when whiteness as an institutional norm is disrupted," (7) highlights the importance of visibility in one's empowerment. During this first meeting, I met another colleague from another department, and she and I quickly gravitated toward each other. This colleague was from the Caribbean, so she and I bonded over being able to talk in our native Creole languages, and she told me where the best spot nearby was to get oxtails that I had been craving since moving to the area. In the years to come we would visit each other's homes and with our families, attend Caribbean events together, and discuss ways of navigating working as Black women at an institution where we were the minority. This counterspace BFA provided allowed me and other Black faculty to work in coalition to affirm our value and shared humanity (Solórzano et al., "Theorizing Racial Microaffirmations") through providing resources, mentorship and opportunities that build community. As a Black woman and immigrant, the coalition building I was able to do in BFA allowed me to be resilient and resistant in the face of racial microaggression in other spaces (Solórzano et al., "Theorizing Racial Microaffirmations") because I received support and from a culturally relevant perspective (Acevedo-Gil and Madrigal-Garcia qtd. in Acevedo and Solórzano). This culturally relevant perspective was foundational in helping me transition from graduate student to assistant professor. It was also a key factor in developing my own leadership and mentoring practices, which proved helpful as I contributed toward filling leadership gaps within my department.

As the research shows, higher education institutions have been dealing with faculty departures that occur for a variety of reasons (White-Lewis et al.; Flaherty). My own department has not been exempted. When the opportunity arose to take up a leadership position due to faculty departures, I stepped up to ensure continuity of a valuable program. As Mena discusses below, she worked as an embedded writing specialist (EWS). I directed the EWS program during the 2022–2023 academic year, and Mena was one of fifteen student employees whose unique perspectives on writing and inclusive peer mentorship were foundational to the programmatic choices I made during this time. To ensure that these perspectives would show up in EWS work, I recruited and hired students whose identities and backgrounds reflect the growing diversity among students at my institution. These brilliant, advanced student writers participated with me in weekly workshops about topics such as language politics, cross-cultural diversity, modeling peer reviews, linguistic justice, and rhetorical approaches to grammar, to name a few. They then drew on these workshops, most of which were led by the EWSs themselves, and applied that knowledge to mentoring first-year students one-on-one and in small groups. EWSs and I wrote literacy narratives together, gave each other feedback on our narratives, and discussed ways these narratives might be used as artifacts in the first-year writing classrooms. They also gave key insights into revising the EWS handbook that guides the entire program. This coalitional action extended beyond our on-campus work when, for example, I collaborated with Mena and another faculty member to present the EWS program at the 2023 Wayne State's Teaching of Writing Conference in Detroit. Due to our various coalitional-led work, Mena and I were invited to contribute to a series that highlights scholarly teaching with the Center for Excellence in Teaching and Learning at my institution. During this series, Mena and I highlighted the importance of coalition-building between faculty and students, and we discussed our own experiences engaging in this work.

The pandemic has created opportunities for us (faculty and program administrators) to listen more attentively to the expertise that students bring with them to the academic spaces they occupy. Moving forward, it will be vital that this form of coalitional leadership among students and faculty continue to be instrumental in informing major programmatic changes.

***

Mena's Autoethnography

"PUTTING MYSELF ASIDE": HOW MICROAGGRESSIONS HURT

My transition from high school to college occurred amidst the height of the COVID-19 pandemic. The last semester of my senior year in 2020 was fully remote and so was the beginning of my college experience. I completed my college writing foundations requirement in fall 2020 remotely that brought on its own challenges since my academic and social interactions with classmates and professors were limited. My orientation to college was also remote, and like many other students, I was dismayed that my first college experience would be via a screen. Yet, it became apparent that virtual learning was going to be the "new norm" and a significant factor in how I would later shape my sense of belonging to my courses and my campus community. This sense of belonging and what leads to it is something I was very aware of as a high school student. My language and culture have always intersected in rich ways with my identity as a student, but as I began my college career, I was beginning to see these intersections and embodied experiences unfold differently in the virtual learning space. This reality manifested in complex ways and is further demonstrated in the analysis of my experiences below.

I believe that my identity as a woman, immigrant, Chaldean, Arab, and multilingual is my biggest asset. These intersecting identities constantly enable me to challenge and question the dominant discourses and ideologies of the world and classroom. Having been an English as a second language (ESL) student in high school, I understood that the ESL categorization meant I had no other choice but to learn White Mainstream English (WME)—it was the only version of English expected of me. I thought any other way of using language was "improper." I instinctively brought this attitude to college. There was even a time when I enforced and conformed to these standards because it was what I knew and what I understood would please my instructors. However, as I advanced in my studies, I became intrigued to question the ideologies behind this version of English. When I switched my major from communication to writing and rhetoric during my sophomore year of college, I started receiving many racial microaggressions that were "subtle, innocuous, preconscious, or unconscious degradations, and putdowns" (Pierce, qtd. in Acevedo and Solórzano 2): "You speak English well." "Good for you for pursuing a writing major when it's not in your native language." "Your accent is not bad." I found a pattern of being appraised and commended for speaking in WME. These unsettling comments ignited my interest in how language works. Yet, the microaggressions I experienced were not limited to verbal comments but also actions. These are called "non-verbal microaggressions, [that] can be kinesic (body language)" (Solórzano et al., "Theorizing Racial Microaffirmations" 201).

Meanwhile, I had the pleasure of getting hired as an EWS (which is similar to the role of a teaching assistant) in first-year writing classes. My role and responsibilities as an EWS involved tutoring students one-on-one about their writing, leading class activities, developing resource materials, and working closely with the course professor and EWS director to provide support to students. I was deeply fulfilled and honored to help students think critically about their different writing situations. However, my own observations and subsequent analyses of the kinds of assignment descriptions, rubrics, and syllabi students were referring to invited me to pose a variety of questions. In a class, how can one single rubric have the power to rank all first-year writing students against one another when they all have different linguistic backgrounds? This experience helped me identify how writing instructors are knowingly or unknowingly complicit in WME. I was inspired to further research it.

These instances of microaggressions would persist and manifest on a larger scale, as I soon came to learn when interacting with a professor. This specific interaction was remote due to the pandemic. It had been roughly two years since the start of the pandemic, which implies that my professor and I have been perhaps adaptive to the nature of remote spaces and conferences. Unsurprisingly, remote spaces can feel impersonal since they lack authentic connections or contact like fully observing one's body language and many other factors one would get in an in-person setting as was evident in a virtual conference with my professor. I had expressed excitement about seeking publication on an academic paper I had recently written analyzing the complicity of writing instructors in enacting and enforcing WME. However, the feelings were not reciprocated: there was an abrupt sense of defensiveness and frustration in their response. They replied with comments like, "Do you know how difficult it is to get published? In fact, you would be immediately rejected if they found a misplaced comma!"

"How is a misplaced comma relevant to this conversation," I thought, "considering you have not even read my paper?" The professor automatically assumed that the language choices I made in my paper would not align with the expectations of the academic journal that would result in my paper getting rejected. It is widely known that gatekeeping practices exist in academic publishing (Horning), yet scholars in the field have spoken out against the exclusionary nature of some of these practices. For example, in addressing gatekeeping practices in academia, Mich Ciurria points out "maybe you have a good idea, but you didn't present it in the conventional academic style.... You didn't write in precise white mainstream English. These are all discriminatory forms of academic gatekeeping" (para. 2). Thus, for a professor to make such remarks about my writing suggests that my variety of English was not worthy of academic publishing. Moreover, editors in the field have acknowledged the importance of mentoring young and emerging writers (Pemberton), a reality that this professor failed to acknowledge. Instead, they chose to belittle my accomplishments and, by extension, my version of English.

When I further expressed interest in linguistic justice because this topic deeply affects me as a multilingual student of color, they proceeded to exclaim, "do you want to eat and get a job?" to convey the necessity of following WME in order to thrive in the real world. I was taken off guard. It seemed like my future and survival needs were dependent on following and conforming to WME and the histories from which it stems. This assumption consistently showed up in other spaces, like in my work as an EWS and in casual conversations with colleagues outside of work. I constantly discussed the implications of WME and the importance of language diversity with the professors I closely worked with that would lead me to the same dead end. I experienced a professor explicitly referring to the works of scholars of color as a "paradox" implying that their work is too difficult to understand and make sense of. In another instance, the same attitude was displayed by a colleague. They noted that this work seemed too abstract, that it was just "too controversial" to get us anywhere. But this is the rhetoric that is motivating anti-DEI legislation today and that is used against advocates for change: it is too much work (especially said by people who believe they are not affected by these issues).

Ironically, my interactions with the professor who discouraged me from seeking publication about a paper arguing against WME validated the same argument I made in that paper. Indeed, as my research showed and my experience confirmed, many instructors are not only complicit in WME, but their complicity is intentional and blatant. As Vershawn Ashanti Young persuasively puts it, "Don't nobody's language, dialect, or style make them 'vulnerable to prejudice.' It's ATTITUDES. It be the way folks with some power perceive other people's language" (110). Thus, I believed that my work ethic alone wouldn't impact change because it's people's attitudes that made me vulnerable.

At the end of the conversation, this professor left no room for ambiguity: "I am not asking you to abandon who you are, but I ask you to put it aside," they remarked in a condescending tone, which is exactly what dominant language ideology (like WME) also claims: "Peeps can speak whateva the heck way they want to—BUT AT HOME!" (Young 111). I left the meeting wondering how in the world could I contribute to class without bringing my unique immigrant experiences and perspectives? How could I show up to class by putting myself—*aside*? "Is this even possible?" I wondered. My perspectives, style of writing, and the issues I care deeply about stem from my memories of the experiences I have had. In other words, my writing is an extension of who I am, the places I have occupied, and the memories I have created in them as a student, an immigrant, a woman, etc. These are the aspects that have enabled me to feel connected to places such as my classes and establish an innate "sense of place," as bell hooks asserts. After all, "we are born and have our being in a place of memory. We chart our lives by everything we remember from the mundane moment to the majestic. We know ourselves through the art and act of remembering" (hooks, *Belonging* 5). It is only natural for one to bring their memories, their experiences, their perspectives when presenting themselves to the world (or in this case—the classroom). My perspectives, my attitudes, my *life* is shaped by my diverse and immigrant background; it's impossible to separate myself from my past, my memories.

What the pandemic taught me about this interaction is while the virtual classroom does not create microaggressions, it allows microaggressions to thrive. Tasha Souza recognizes that students in online classes already have fears about contributing to class and these fears are magnified when students are also coming to terms with any trauma associated with the global pandemic. My professor was blatant and insensitive in their remarks because they simply could be, and the absence of a physical classroom space fostered their insensitivity. I wondered how this interaction might have been different if it occurred in the face-to-face classroom?

It's fair to pose the question: where did the professor's preconceived assumptions come from? Why was I not given the chance to prove myself? Ironically, my experiences with the professor suggest to me that *I* should have been the one who felt insulted, being denied the right to freely and rhetorically use language. It's worth noting that it was our first interaction. They *had not* read anything I had ever written; they *never* had me in a previous class; they did not *know* me! So, how could they *know* I was going to fail? Although the experiences I had with this particular professor may seem individualized, they are depictions of how "individualism enables us to deny that racism is structured into the fabric of our society . . . the focus on individual incidences prevents the analysis that is necessary in order to challenge this larger system" (DiAngelo 2–3). In other words, the professor's racially motivated remarks showcase the institutional racism that nurtures their kind of thinking. Their thinking is due to a broader institutional culture that supports and reinforces it. The preconceived assumptions the professor made about me and my abilities reflect the "peculiar linguistic manners and rhetorical strategies (or race talk)" many whites engage in that is used to "avoid direct racist language to express their racial views, employ 'semantic moves' to avoid discussions, project their own views to implicate the minority party, and become close to incoherent when discussing forbidden issues or racially sensitive matters" (Bonilla-Silva 1365). Unfortunately, their ways of acting and responding to the works of students and scholars of color and our informed perspectives at least suggest to them that they are enacting what is right because it is the mere history of our field, which makes the problem bigger than one incident or person.

BRINGING MYSELF FORWARD: HOW MICROAFFIRMATIONS HELP

The instances of microaggressions I endured had a significant, negative impact on my self-esteem as an emerging writer, EWS, and contributor to the field. One particular type of action that helped me overcome the residual effects was "micro affirmations" that "allow for an opportunity to repair and heal from microaggressions through everyday acts of acknowledgment, support, and recognition" (Huber et al. 8). As a way to combat the forms of oppression against me and to protect me against microaggressions amidst and after these encounters had occurred, I specifically engaged in experiences that empowered me. I intentionally wrote papers and conducted research on issues affecting students of color that I was able to identify with. I took a literature class, particularly literature of ethnic America, that centered around immigrant stories, since I was yearning to belong to a place that would accept me without asking me to "abandon" any parts of who I am. During the class, my voice was reclaimed, celebrated, and recognized by my professor and classmates, which was empowering. The aspects of my identity that I was encouraged to put aside in one space were amplified and validated in another. The fact that these conflicting experiences occurred in academia was confusing yet unsurprising.

One of the ways I responded to my negative experiences during the pandemic was by first finding a community that could support me. Building a coalition with faculty and students within my major program would help me create a sense of community, so I started by connecting with some of my former professors who I already had a positive and established relationship with. I needed their support and encouragement in regard to responding to the microaggressions I was experiencing. These talks tremendously strengthened my sense of positive informal mentorship because they occurred outside of the classroom and extended my relationship with them beyond the classroom. The pandemic taught me the importance of coalition building through relying on mentorship and support from my college community.

In addition to connecting with faculty, I also connected with some of my colleagues and classmates outside of the classroom for lunch or coffee. My hope was to continue having conversations surrounding the intersection of race, social justice, and writing and address the unacceptable behaviors that were quietly accepted by others and often by my colleagues. However, I recognized that in order to effectively respond to the challenges the pandemic posed, advocacy and coalition building were critical in addressing and making sense of these systemic and institutional issues. By deciding to pursue dialogue to build coalitions to address behavior instead of shutting out my colleagues and classmates, I strived to foster a more intentional and supportive community.

Moreover, I enrolled in the literature class after I experienced many racial microaggressions about my identity. I was unaware that the course readings included literature that was specific to my culture and background until the reading list was assigned. The fictional work was by an Arab American writer about another Arab American woman. I recall tearing up after reading the amazing fictional work because it was my first time ever seeing myself, my experiences, my background, my intersectional identities all represented in a text assigned by a white professor. Representation in course readings has the power to move and inspire students, but it also has the potential to powerfully validate and empower us. This act is another type of microaffirmation called, "microtransformations," that "describe actions, verbal remarks or environmental cues that lead the recipient to feel that they, as a member of a particular social identity group(s), or the group they belong to are further integrated into the university; or that their capacity for success or some facet of social or academic life is enabled, enhanced or increased" (Rolón-Dow and Davison 254). And no surprise, microtransformations are even more effective when students have teachers who look like them. Moreover, when I had Dr. Arzu-Carmichael as my professor for the first time, I vividly remember relating to her in some way since we are both multilingual, immigrant women of color. As noted in the introduction, we quickly came to learn that we had many mutual experiences and shared commitments. The mere fact that I was able to identify with my professor was in itself a microtransformation and one prime example of our coalitional work on this chapter.

Importantly, I slowly came to the realization that I alone could not carry the weight of institutional and systemic inequalities and should not have attempted to solve it—by myself. After all, it does not take one person to fix the damage; it is a collective fight. Through alliance and coalition building, the collective fight and action would be much more effective. Moreover, I felt a sense of empowerment when, with my consent, my white classmate recognized the racial microaggression I was experiencing and chose to center my experience in her paper. She knew that it could possibly put her at risk since our professor did not align with those ideas and values, but she included it anyway. This act is a type of microaffirmation called "microprotections" that "occur when actions, verbal remarks or environmental cues lead the recipient to feel shielded or protected from harmful or derogatory behaviors, practices and policies tied to their identity . . . when others advocated for them when they experienced duress related to their identity" (Rolón-Dow and Davison 255–56). For my classmate to be willing to advocate on my behalf in a manner that was both subtle yet impactful emphasized to me the empowerment that can come from having a co-conspirator who is willing to advocate for equality (Mckoy et al.). She took the metaphorical bullet for me; she shared my story when I could not yet that made me feel so incredibly supported and emboldened. These moments are not only prime examples of microaffirmations but also important testaments to the impact of coalition building. Such acts of advocacy reshaped my concept of student empowerment and leadership. I now deem the concept of student empowerment as a reciprocal and transactional act that emerges through coalition building and leadership. Sharing our lived experiences is crucial to solving the problem because we get to identify them and educate each other, but once again—we need each other to seek a solution and support each other.

A raging sense of resistance grew out of me by having been oppressed and empowered like that. Some common racial microaggression responses as Solórzano et al. point out are "denial, self-policing, proving aggressors wrong, resistance, establishing counter spaces, creating art, micro affirmations" ("Theorizing Racial Microaffirmations" 201). The immense feelings of oppression made me rebel against those practices in my own EWS work. Now, I had the agency and authority. But, instead of having it conflict with the way I worked with the students I tutor, I made it my mission to demonstrate my leadership skills by valuing their experiences and languages and reminding them that who they are matters without them ever having to tell me that. Reading their work and giving feedback was my way of empowering them while also being a leader within my department and the EWS program. In my role as an EWS, I worked with one particular Black student that would always apologize to me for not writing in WME since they have been policed for it in the past by other instructors. However, I used that opportunity to employ the framework of microaffirmations; to help them embrace their language and recognize that their language matters in their writing (Alvarez et al.). Another way I rebelled against these practices was by intentionally sharing samples of my essays about my immigrant experiences to both take space as an EWS of color and to create representation in the classroom. My intention was to ensure that they were prepared to advocate for themselves, their story, and their language.

I wish I never had to have these conversations with the students I tutor because they should not experience what I experienced, but unfortunately, I know they will. This begs the question: When does the cycle of exclusion, gatekeeping, oppression, and abuse stop in our field? While I cannot exactly provide an answer, I can encourage some pieces of advice to my own fellow students of color, colleagues, and classmates. Regardless of how often you have to bring attention to these issues—do not stop. It can feel exhausting, repetitive, and often unproductive; however, this is how change slowly happens—by forcing these dialogues, listening, and working in collaboration with faculty and other students with whom you have shared values. These acts allow us to empower each other, especially through building coalitions.

My coalitional work extends beyond my leadership roles and scholarly work. During my junior year of college in 2022, I won a prestigious "Keeper of the

Dream" scholarship, an award given to university students who honor the legacy of Dr. Martin Luther King Jr. through their work to promote interracial understanding and equity. Through this recognition, I received the opportunity to work with our campus's Center for Multicultural Initiatives (CMI), an office committed to supporting underrepresented students. As a peer mentor with CMI, I support first year students through their college experience by providing personal, social, and academic support. For example, I was asked to offer individualized writing support for a group of sixty incoming freshmen who lived on campus for a week to experience the university. I shared my knowledge on linguistic justice in a presentation on how language, identity, and culture strongly intersect. Importantly, my work with CMI mirrors the work I do as an EWS. My goal in both programs was to invite students, especially incoming students, to start the academic year with a strong sense of self and an open dialogue about the value of the cultural and linguistic diversity they are bringing to their new campus community. In the CMI program, I did this work in collaboration with CMI professional coordinators and student ambassadors all working toward the goal of preparing incoming students for college life. My coalitional work with CMI also allows me to be a voice in the selection process for the 2024 Keeper of the Dream. In this capacity I have the opportunity to identify other young leaders on campus and continue the legacy of Dr. Martin Luther King Jr.

Becoming Change Agents by Applying the 4R's

In "some home truths on the contemporary black feminist movement," Barbara Smith shared that a major contribution to Black feminist struggle is "a commitment to principled coalitions, based not upon expediency, but upon our actual need for each other" (9). Our commitment to principled coalitions led us to not only identify racial microaggressions we were both experiencing but also to reveal these injustices in ways that will lead to a sense of empowerment for us both and to systemic changes within our institution. Moreover, because our field is rooted in monolingual norms and principles (Sánchez-Martín), students and faculty of color from immigrant backgrounds, such as Mena and me, are repeatedly faced with such racial microaggressions that further marginalize us. As a result, we aimed to understand our margin of maneuverability to fully recognize the work that was possible individually and collectively. Walton et al. assert that one's margin of maneuverability refers to the "limited moves any single person might make in response to inequities" (4). Enacting change includes recognizing injustices, revealing these injustices, rejecting the injustices, and replacing the unjust practices with intersectional, coalition-led practices. In what follows, we share examples of how we applied this framework to our own coalitional actions.

RECOGNIZE THE INJUSTICE

During the 2020 academic year, we recognized our collective experiences with racial microaggressions in and out of the classroom. As discussed in our narratives above, these included dismissiveness when we centered DEI-related issues in our work; explicit lack of cooperation or engagement with questions in class; and an expectation to conform to white ways of teaching, learning, and knowing, among others. We recognized that while these expectations that were imposed upon us were presented as harmless or even well-intentioned, they were in fact harmful as they were rooted in white supremacy.

REVEAL THE INJUSTICE

We revealed those injustices to a trusted senior faculty member, who we believed would support us and advocate with us for change. This co-conspirator listened deeply and affirmed our experiences. Given their own margin of maneuverability and power to act, they then worked with us to determine actions that needed to be taken.

REJECT THE INJUSTICES

The injustices we were facing occurred at multiple levels given our different positionalities as faculty and student. Yet, in coalition, we purposefully continued centering race and inclusion issues in our work while, with our co-conspirator, we continued revealing the injustices we were facing. Our work to reject the injustices is evident even through acts such as proposing a standing course that centers race, enacting anti-racist teaching and mentoring practices, and collaborating on this chapter.

REPLACE THE INJUSTICE

Moving from reject to replace requires multiple plans, as Walton et al. affirm. While we are still working through these plans, including additional reveals, we have been fortunate to engage in coalitional-led work through the EWS program. This work has subsequently informed programmatic changes in our department, including changes within the First-Year Writing Program, of which Felicita is the associate director.

In our intergenerational autoethnography, we drew on a Black feminist articulation of leadership and empowerment to demonstrate how microaffirmations might lead to faculty and students of color building sustainable and action-oriented coalitions. We drew on our experiences as an early-career Afro-Caribbean faculty and an undergraduate Arab Chaldean student to show how our racialized bodies have experienced racial microaggressions in a variety of academic spaces, and we analyzed those overt and covert racial microaggressions. Then using Walton et al.'s 4 R's, we demonstrated what we believe to be our most actionable insights for building coalitions of action between faculty and students. We hope that our collective experiences with and analysis of racial microaggressions and microaffirmations can provide ideas of how leadership and mentorship can be understood in order to create opportunities for coalitional-led actions among faculty and students. As Hill Collins reminds us, "neither empowerment nor social justice can be achieved without some sense of what one is trying to change" (xii). The global pandemic has shifted how academics recognize and understand leadership, and we hope that our stories as women academics of color can contribute to the existing dialogue surrounding the performative advocacy of DEI initiatives and creating sustainable infrastructures for coalition building between faculty and students.

Works Cited

Acevedo, Nancy, and Daniel G. Solórzano. "An Overview of Community Cultural Wealth: Toward a Protective Factor Against Racism." *Urban Education*, vol. 58, no. 7, 2023, pp. 1470–88.

Adler, Laura. "The 'Long Covid' of American Higher Education." *Society for the Advancement of SocioEconomics*. July 1, 2021, sase.org/blog/the-long-covid-of-american-higher-education/. Accessed Feb. 2022.

Ahmed, Sara. *On Being Included: Racism and Diversity in Institutional Life*. Duke UP, 2020, pp. 1–18.

Alvarez, Sara P., Amy J. Wan, and Eunjeong Lee. "Workin' Languages: Who We Are Matters in Our Writing." *Writing Spaces: Readings on Writing*, Volume 4. Edited by Dana Driscoll, Megan Heise, Mary Stewart, and Matthew Vetter, Parlor P, 2022, pp. 1–18.

Arzu Carmichael, Felicita. "Teaching Anti-Racist Reading Practices in First-Year Writing." *Writing Program Administration*. Special Issue: *Black Lives Matter and Anti-Racist Projects in Writing Program Administration*. Edited by Sheila Carter-Todd and Jennifer Sano-Franchini, 2021, pp. 138–45.

Bonilla-Silva, Eduardo. "The Structure of Racism in Color-Blind, 'Post-Racial' America." *American Behavioral Scientist*, vol. 59, no. 11, 2015, pp. 1358–76.

Ciurria, Mich. "Academic Gatekeeping Is Killing Me." *BiopoliticalPhilosophy*, 27 Jan. 2022, biopoliticalphilosophy.com/2022/01/27/academic-gatekeeping-is-killing-me%EF%BF%BC/. Accessed 30 May 2022.

Cooper, Brittney. *Eloquent Rage: A Black Feminist Discovers her Superpower*. St. Martin's P, 2018.

Diab, Rasha, Thomas Ferrel, Beth Godbee, and Neil Simpkins. "Making Commitments to Racial Justice Actionable." *Across the Disciplines*, vol. 10, no. 3, 2013.

DiAngelo, Robin. "White Fragility: Why It's So Hard to Talk to White People about Racism." *The Good Men Project*, vol. 9, 2015, pp. 1–4.

Flaherty, Colleen. "Calling it Quits." *Inside Higher Ed*. 4 July 2022, www.insidehighered.com/news/2022/07/05/professors-are-leaving-academe-during-great-resignation. 14 Dec. 2022.

Flores, Lisa A. "Between Abundance and Marginalization: The Imperative of Racial Rhetorical Criticism." *Review of Communication*, vol. 16, no. 1, 2016, pp. 4–24.

Freire, Paulo. *Pedagogy of the Oppressed*. 30th anniversary edition, Continuum, 2005.

Gretzinger, Erin, Hicks, Maggie, Dutton, Christa, and Smith Jasper. "Tracking Higher Ed's Dismantling of DEI." *The Chronicle of Higher Education*, 14 Feb. 2025, www.chronicle.com/article/tracking-higher-eds-dismantling-of-dei. Accessed 17 Feb. 2025.

Henry, Annette. "Chapter 4: Black Feminist Pedagogy: Critiques and Contributions." *Counterpoints*, no. 237, 2005, pp. 89–105.

Hill Collins, Patricia. *Black Feminist Thought: Knowledge, Consciousness, and the Politics of Empowerment*. Routledge, 2008.

hooks, bell. *Belonging: A Culture of Place*. Routledge, 2009.

hooks, bell. *Teaching to Transgress: Education as the Practice of Freedom*. Routledge, 1994.

Horning, Alice. "Getting up from a Fall: Five Years as Editor of *WPA: Writing Program Administration*." *Behind the Curtain of Scholarly Publishing: Editors in Writing Studies*. Edited by Greg Giberson, Megan Schoen, and Christian Weisser, Utah State UP, 2022, pp. 139–52.

Huber, Lindsay Pérez, Tamara Gonzalez, Gabriela Robles, and Daniel G. Solórzano. "Racial Microaffirmations as a Response to Racial Microaggressions: Exploring Risk and Protective Factors." *New Ideas in Psychology*, vol. 63, 2021, https://doi.org/10.1016/j.newideapsych.2021.100880.

Jones, Natasha N., Laura Gonzales, and Angela M. Haas. "So You Think You're Ready to Build New Social Justice Initiatives? Intentional and Coalitional Pro-Black Programmatic and Organizational Leadership in Writing Studies." *WPA: Writing Program Administration*, vol. 44, no. 3, Summer 2021, pp. 29–35.

Jones, Natasha N., and R. Walton. "Social Justice." *Keywords in Technical and Professional Communication*. Edited by Yu Han and Jonathan Buehl, WAC Clearinghouse and UP of Colorado, 2023, pp. 267–72, https://doi.org/10.37514/TPC-B.2023.1923.2.32.

Knoblauch, A. Abby, and Marie E. Moeller, eds. *Bodies of Knowledge: Embodied Rhetorics in Theory and Practice*. Utah State UP, 2022.

Kynard, Carmen. "'Oh No She Did NOT Bring Her Ass Up in Here with That!' Racial Memory, Radical Reparative Justice, and Black Feminist Pedagogical Futures." *College English*, vol. 85, no. 4, 2023, pp. 318–45.

Kynard, Carmen. "Teaching While Black: Witnessing and Countering Disciplinary Whiteness, Racial Violence, and University Race-Management." *Literacy in Composition Studies*, vol. 3, no. 1, Mar. 2015, pp. 1–20, https://doi.org/10.21623/1.3.1.16.

Martinez, Aja Y. "Core-coursing Counterstory: On Master Narrative Histories of Rhetorical Studies Curricula." *Rhetoric Review*, vol. 38, no. 4, 2019, pp. 402–16.

McKoy, Temptaous, Christina D. Shelton, Donnie Johnson Sackey, Natasha N. Jones, Cecilia Haywood, Jasmine Wourman, and Keshia C. Harper. "Introduction to Special Issue: Black Technical and Professional Communication." *Technical Communication Quarterly*, vol. 31, no. 3, 2022, pp. 221–28, https://doi.org/10.1080/10572252.2022.2077455.

MSNBC. "Nikole Hannah-Jones: Trump Came Right 'Out the Gate' with a Racial Agenda—Not an Economic One." *YouTube*, uploaded by MSNBC, 2 Feb. 2025, www.youtube.com/watch?v=0rUk1FNe7ac.

Pemberton, Michael A. "Gatekeeper, Guardian, Or Guide?" *Behind the Curtain of Scholarly Publishing: Editors in Writing Studies*. Edited by Greg Giberson, Megan Schoen, and Christian Weisser, Utah State UP, 2022.

Rolón-Dow, Rosalie, and April Davison. "Theorizing Racial Microaffirmations: A Critical Race/Latcrit Approach." *Race Ethnicity and Education*, vol. 24, no. 2, 2021, pp. 245–61.

Sánchez-Martín, Cristina. "'The Power of Many' (Counter)Stories: Materializing Spaces of Belonging for (Im)migrants in Rhetoric and Composition." *College English*, vol. 85, no. 2, 2022, pp. 167–84.

Sensoy, Özlem, and Robin DiAngelo. *Is Everyone Really Equal? An Introduction to Key Concepts in Social Justice Education*. Teachers College P, 2017.

Smith, Barbara. "Some Home Truths on the Contemporary Black Feminist Movement." *The Black Scholar*, vol. 16, no. 2, 1985, pp. 4–13.

Solórzano, Daniel, Miguel Ceja, and Tara Yosso. "Critical Race Theory, Racial Microaggressions, and Campus Racial Climate: The Experiences of African American College Students." *The Journal of Negro Education*, vol. 69, no. 1/2, 2000, pp. 60–73.

Solórzano, Daniel, Lindsay Pérez Huber, and Layla Huber-Verjan. "Theorizing Racial Microaffirmations as a Response to Racial Microaggressions: Counterstories Across Three Generations of Critical Race Scholars." *Seattle Journal for Social Justice*, vol. 18, no. 2, 2020.

Souza, Tasha. "Responding to Microaggressions in Online Learning Environments during a Pandemic." *Academic Impressions*, 1 June 2020, www.academicimpressions.com/microaggressions-online-learning/.

Walton, Rebecca, Kristen Moore, and Natasha Jones. *Technical Communication after the Social Justice Turn: Building Coalitions for Action*. Routledge, 2019.

White-Lewis, Damani K., KerryAnn O'Meara, Kiernan Mathews, and Nicholas Havey. "Leaving the Institution or Leaving the Academy? Analyzing the Factors That Faculty Weigh in Actual Departure Decisions." *Research in Higher Education*, vol. 64, 2023, pp. 473–94. https://doi.org/10.1007/s11162-022-09712-9.

Williams, Bianca C. "Radical Honesty: Truth-telling as Pedagogy for Working through Shame in Academic Spaces." *Race, Equity, and the Learning Environment*. Routledge, 2016, pp. 71–82.

Young, Vershawn Ashanti. "Should Writers Use Their Own English?" *Iowa Journal of Cultural Studies*, vol. 12, no. 1, 2010, pp. 110–17.

5
Challenges and Opportunities for Teacher Leaders in K–12 Schools

Lessons Learned from Teachers of Color in K–12 Schools

ALICE HAYS, SHAYLYN MARKS, ALEXANDRA CHAPA-KUNZ, AND AMARDEEP (RUPSY) BAJWA

Prior to the second Trump administration, pressure has been increasing to respond to reports of achievement gaps between students of color and their white peers since the 1980s, and these pressures have been intensified by federal court mandates to diversify district staff (Madkins). In *Teachers of Color: Resisting Racism and Reclaiming Education*, Rita Kohli examines how the "pressure to address 'minority teacher shortages' began to mount" in the 1980s (Kohli 10). In response to these trends, the educational community has attempted to recruit more teachers of color to better support the rising numbers of students of color, who are now the majority in American public schools according to the National Center for Educational Statistics (Kohli). While ethnically diverse college students are enrolling in rising numbers, educator demographics continue to remain stagnant and predominately white. As Kohli discusses, "the need to diversify the teaching force has become an urgent topic of concern among educational researchers, teacher educators, school leadership, and policy makers alike" as educators have come to understand "how integral Teachers of Color are to the success of Students of Color and the educational experiences of all students" (3–4).

Given the overwhelming whiteness of teacher education programs, Marcelle Haddix argues that teacher candidates of color often experience "their racial and linguistic identities being marginalized, undermined, and silenced" throughout their credential experience (3). Unfortunately, these experiences persist when teachers of color enter the workforce. Despite being able to offer a great deal in providing culturally sustaining and humanizing curriculum and pedagogy, teachers of color "have attested to experiencing racial *microaggressions*, being forced to serve as racial experts, being stereotyped and limited to particular professional roles, and feeling triggered as they witness students experience racism that they themselves endured in their own education" (Kohli 12).

Additionally, teachers of color often feel the "undue burden" of the invisible labor tasks requested of them, especially being responsible for diversity, inclusion, and equity work (Flaherty). Research suggests that teachers of color can help raise expectations for students of color by using their cultural knowledge to build bridges to learning with those students (Villegas and Davis). Insofar as teachers' curricular and intellectual decisions play a critical part in students' academic success, schools must provide these teachers with opportunities to structure their teaching in a way that increases student achievement. This freedom is especially important because high teacher turnover is "strongly associated with a lack of classroom autonomy and school influence" (Carver-Thomas 14). In an effort to better support and sustain a diverse teaching force, Kohli asserts that "teacher education programs, schools, and districts must first acknowledge the entrenched systems of oppression that make school a hostile place for people of color—students and educators alike" (28).

Acknowledging the unique challenges teachers of color face when entering the field of education, this chapter explores the experiences of next-gen teachers of color as they navigate resistance to integrating social justice themes in their Common Core centered curricula and the strategies they use to reimagine their curriculum and pedagogy in culturally sustaining ways to best meet the needs of the diverse students they serve (Kohli; Paris). The stories and experiences shared within this chapter serve as counterstories, inviting readers to reflect on the ways teacher education programs and departments can adjust their curriculum and pedagogy to better prepare and support teacher leaders who understand the institutional and political forces that often shape curricula.

The goal of our work is to reflect upon our experiences in preparing preservice educators through our teacher residency program. As we continue to refine our own pedagogical practices and programmatic structures to be more inclusive and responsive to the needs of our diverse credential candidates, we became particularly interested in the ways our candidates were internalizing these approaches and taking charge to implement culturally responsive and sustaining pedagogies. Our residency program graduates were primarily hired into our local high school district that, along with our local community, has politically conservative values that align with political attempts to maintain the status quo. Because this alignment creates considerable difficulties for teachers seeking to advance change, especially novice teachers, we became curious about the ways that our former residents were continuing to develop their teaching ideologies to implement culturally responsive and sustaining pedagogies and navigate collaborative relationships in their new settings. Given the oppressive political climate educators face today, in which space has been created for educators to receive critiques from a multitude of forces, we find now more than ever that teacher preparation programs have an obligation to develop the leadership and collaborative skills of preservice educators to better equip novice educators with the necessary tools to become independently skilled teacher leaders in their respective spaces.

As we explored the broad challenges that teachers of color face, especially in the conservative districts and communities where many serve, we became particularly interested in how our former candidates of color navigated these spaces to develop culturally responsive and sustaining pedagogical practices, collaborative relationships with veteran teachers, and interactions and relationships with administrators and other campus leaders. Thus, we attempt to better understand the unique, and largely unspoken, challenges faced by teachers of color as they strive to establish autonomy in their decision making to best serve their diverse students.

Building on Gholdy Muhammad's call to prepare preservice teachers to be disruptors of oppressive curriculum choices and pedagogical strategies, we (Alice and Shaylyn) began by questioning the ways that our own graduates had been prepared, and how these experiences work to inform their current practices in their respective classrooms and school settings. To engage in this work, we collaborated with two of our residency graduates, Rupsy (a Punjabi female with five years of secondary experience) and Alex (a Latina female with four years of secondary experience) in writing this chapter, and we use their voices to share their stories and address the following questions:

- What were the daily decisions that these teachers had to make to connect their curriculums with the lived realities of their students?

- What leadership challenges did these teachers face when attempting to implement social justice approaches and methods into standardized curriculums?
- What kinds of "invisible labor" did these teachers take on when advocating for curricular changes in K–12 contexts as faculty of color?
- How can English-education programs and English departments more generally prepare future teachers for the leadership challenges associated with implementing social justice approaches into standardized curriculums?

Methods

PARTICIPANTS

Rupsy and Alex both participated in a teacher residency program that consists of a partnership between a mid-sized university and a single, local high school district that serves 42,000 students. California teacher candidates must have a bachelor's degree in their desired content area prior to beginning their credential program that offers several pathways towards certification, one being the residency. The design of the residency program is to provide an apprenticeship structure where credential-candidates are paired with a veteran, mentor teacher to work alongside for the full duration of their residency year. In addition to the mentor support that residents receive throughout their residency year, the residency program offers monthly support for both residents and their respective mentors through professional development summits. The additional time spent in the classroom combined with additional layers of support from both the university and district make residency programs a highly effective model for teacher credentialing.

Rupsy was a member of the first cohort, and Alex was a member of the second cohort. Currently, Rupsy is in her sixth year of teaching, and Alex is in her fifth year of teaching. They were both hired by the school district where they completed their residency program. In the few years that Rupsy and Alex have been independently teaching at their respective school sites, they have encountered firsthand experiences with politically conservative ideals filtering into the school environment, which include policy restructuring based on the belief that the Gay Straight Alliance is "a radical leftist group filled with predators," (Torrez) exclusionary practices for students identifying as LGBTQ+, and consistently high expulsion rates for Hispanic and Black students (Pierce).

These "encounters" highlight the need for culturally responsive and sustaining practices combined with highly skilled educators who have developed the confidence, collaborative leadership skills, and assertiveness to become disruptors (Muhammad) of the status quo that currently works to disenfranchise historically marginalized populations of students.

STUDY DESIGN

Our qualitative study sought to better understand the unique challenges teachers of color face entering the education profession. In particular, we sought to better understand the obstacles and difficulties that novice teachers of color faced when working collaboratively with professional learning communities to implement culturally responsive and sustaining pedagogical practices and develop a sense of autonomy and leadership within their respective school communities. To gain a better understanding of these complexities and challenges, former credential candidates who taught locally were interviewed using a semi-structured interview format that addressed the aforementioned research questions. Upon the completion of the interview process, interviews were transcribed and coded to identify three key themes: student considerations, challenges from leadership and administration, and invisible labor and/or additional expectations.

Findings

To better understand the unique issues teachers of color face as they enter the profession, we interviewed former credential candidates from our residency program who are currently working for a local school district. Through semi-structured interviews, these former residents shared their stories and experiences as they reflected on their first few years in the teaching profession. These stories largely hinged on their unique experiences as teachers of color in conservative districts. Alex stated the challenges most succinctly during our interview conversation: "There is no room to not be excellent!" Both Rupsy and Alex demonstrated feelings of an external pressure to go above and beyond in their work to meet the needs of all their partners in education, including their students, the parents, and their administration. Themes of student considerations, challenges from leadership and administration, and invisible labor and/or additional expectations consistently emerged throughout the interview conversations. To best capture the authentic voices and stories, both interviewees have provided written documentation of their experiences, which is shared below.

STUDENT CONSIDERATIONS

Culturally responsive and sustaining pedagogy demands that teachers consider student identity while developing curriculum (Muhammad; Gay) This consideration is particularly important when we think about students of color as they rarely see themselves reflected in the curriculum they receive (Muhammad; Haddix). Rudine Sims Bishop is frequently lauded for identifying the need for students to see themselves reflected in the texts they read, as well as being able to see others through a window of a text or even walk through the door of someone else's world through texts. Rupsy and Alex both discuss the challenges of providing students with the sorts of accessible "windows, mirrors, and sliding glass doors" that Bishop so eloquently defined in ways that they themselves did not experience.

Alex: When adjusting for student considerations, it can be challenging to balance the needs of my students with the requirements of the curriculum. While there has been a push toward more skills-based instruction supported by state standards, there also remains a heavy focus on "classic" texts that may not be as relevant to today's students. Having been a student who never saw myself reflected in the texts I read in my K–12 journey, I know the struggle of feeling the classwork I do has nothing to do with my life. This is why I start my school year off heavily focused on getting to know my students' likes, dislikes, and cultural experiences through writing and discussion activities. By having them complete assignments that show me their personalities, I start to see a pattern of which topics are more interesting than others and how to create connections with units that may have older texts that are not reflective of my students' life experiences.

My own experience fuels my adaptability in my classroom. Many professional developments focus on student engagement because "if you are not interested in the content the students will also be bored," but I have found this ignores the diverse perspectives students can bring to texts that often do not reflect their experiences. There may be content I know I have to teach that I see as outdated, but I take time to find connections between those texts and students' lives that help them buy into the work we are doing in that unit. For a single lesson, I may modify from one period to the next based on the students in the room.

I must balance the needs of my students with the designated curricular requirements of my *professional learning community* (PLC), which is the acronym that is commonly used to designate the team and department groups who make curricular decisions in the schools. Sometimes that means being the only teacher to switch out content for something more relevant knowing it may cause some friction with my colleagues. In any given ninth-grade class, I can have reading levels that range from a first-grade level all the way up to an eleventh-grade level. Therefore, whatever class I'm teaching, I must make accommodations for the students who are reading at and above grade level by attempting to use grade level texts while also providing scaffolding for my students who have significantly lower reading abilities. My approach contrasts with the growing norm of lowering text levels to meet underserved students' needs that I feel views student ability from a deficit perspective and disproportionately affects students of color. The last couple of years I have been continually developing my instructional design that often feels like a bit of trial and error. This last year, I tried to focus on adding rigor and support to my classroom, meaning that in every unit I added in a text that was either at grade level or slightly above grade level and then implemented larger supports and scaffolding to work with that text. My goal with this decision has been to raise the bar back to grade level and give all my students equal opportunities for a rigorous learning environment. Rupsy also tries to navigate the demands of her professional learning community, as discussed next.

Rupsy: I had to make the decision to either follow what my PLC wanted me to do, which was more analysis type of writing or, what I wanted to do, which was narrative writing. Although the ninth grade PLC is well intended, the pacing guide overwhelmed me as a new teacher. I couldn't make the connections to what I learned in the credential program with what I was tasked to do using the pacing guide. In the credential program, I was taught to use backwards mapping and the common core standards to plan curriculum. Additionally, the program included lessons that supported student's abilities to critically engage in the content with a civically oriented approach as well as improve literacy skills through creativity and diverse books.

In our ninth-grade class, we are supposed to be using *Of Mice and Men* by John Steinbeck and have the students write a literature response. I was struggling to teach this skill because I didn't understand how it connected with the standard it was supposed to be addressing, nor did I agree with teaching the text for ninth grade. I felt the kids were disconnected from the text, and I also believed that my students' authentic voices were missing in the response to literature writing tasks. Many of our students already write below grade level, and writing about literature that is disconnected from one's own experiences adds another barrier to being able to write well. Ultimately, I decided to use a young adult novel and focus on narrative writing in my class. I wanted my students to be able to explore their identities in meaningful ways that felt as if it was missing in the approved curriculum. It was important to me that my students saw mirrors and windows through the texts they read because it allowed them to find the joy in reading and the ability to critically think about the conflicts the story presented.

CURRICULUM CHALLENGES FROM LEADERSHIP AND ADMINISTRATION

Many teachers face challenges when they attempt to bring in new texts for their courses or when they attempt to develop a new curriculum. These challenges are complicated by the lack of distinction in schools and PLC groups between *leadership* and *administration*, which makes it confusing for novice educators to know whom to ask for support and guidance with tasks and decision making. Alex shares her experience below:

Alex: For example, while attempting to implement more diverse curriculum options that introduce students to the topic of social justice, there are a myriad of steps that I must follow to get approval to make changes. These steps include potential barriers or challenges within the school site and district leadership. Some districts require changes go through a tiered vetting system, from grade level teams to department heads, to site level admin, and then finally to district leadership. The process is time consuming, and the burden of work is placed on the teacher proposing the changes to curriculum. This causes new teachers like me to feel as if we need to walk a very thin line in terms of figuring out what might meet approval, often with little to no support in creating the lessons we wish to implement. It can often feel isolating because I may be the only voice advocating for content that allows students to think about social justice topics. Resistance to curriculum changes focused on representing students of color and the challenges they face is common and accepted. There is often a fear that teachers will be targeted by parents, staff, and/or leadership for teaching "challenging" content, and when I advocate for changes, I am battling the fear of repercussions [for myself] along with a resistance to change. The system as it is can have more obstacles than supports in place for teachers who want to design a curriculum that is more representative of their students' backgrounds while still supporting equity within grade level and content area alignment.

Like Rupsy, many new teachers of color trying to connect curriculum to the students of color often fear for their own reputation, career loss, and potentially even their own safety. Rupsy explains her fears around teaching any kind of social justice in the classroom.

Rupsy: I think that my fear stems from the divisive social climate we live in. The current (forty-fifth/forty-seventh) presidency has only made the racial tension among people more prevalent and dangerous. I often wonder if I will get in trouble if we talk about what is going on in America right now, whether that's the unjust murders of Black men or the Supreme Court banning abortion rights, for example. Another question I often have is what if students in the classroom don't know how to handle the topic of racism and I don't know how to effectively facilitate complex ideas of racism because I wasn't taught how to in the credential program? What if a fight breaks out in my classroom because of this? It is made more difficult knowing that my peers and other adults may judge me for trying to bring up potentially polarizing topics. For example, I had my co-teacher walk out of the classroom when I shared a story from a podcast episode that talked about two men from the LGBTQ+ community sharing stories about obstacles they faced.

I've also heard teachers go against another teacher of color and say things like "I would never talk about racism, or any topics related to social justice, and I can't believe that teacher does that in her classroom." Parents also push back—during COVID year, a student's mom contacted me and asked why her child had to write about police brutality. I informed her that the open prompt allowed students to write about any type of activism and that her child could write about Blue Lives Matter. The overwhelming fear is always there, and I'm constantly thinking about how I can avoid upsetting everyone around me.

Of interest, both Alex and Rupsy take note of the fact that in their fairly conservative school sites, colleagues and parents accept being openly non-inclusive (e.g., as shown through pronoun discussions), but there is fear of being too inclusive (e.g., as shown through a reluctance to hang pro-LGBTQ+ posters).

INVISIBLE LABOR

Many teachers of color often take on "more than their fair share of responsibility but are not recognized or compensated for the work that they do" (Dixon and Griffin 2). Dixon and Griffin discuss the ways that they were either directly or indirectly pushed to agree to do tasks that may be beyond their scope as new teachers. Additionally, when one educator wanted to take on explicitly named and compensated leadership roles, she was not provided with the same opportunities as other teachers at her experience level.

Alex: One of the most challenging invisible labor effects that I have dealt with as a teacher of color when addressing the need for curricular changes is the need to share my own history as a student of color in environments where my perspective is in the minority. Every interaction is different, but each one does take an emotional toll on me. Often, I feel I must navigate my feelings around my own experience and share my stories in a way that is palatable to my audience to better support my students. There seems to be an unspoken rule that I need to share my cultural and personal educational experiences to validate the ideas I present and why they are in the best interest of the students of color I serve. There is an unspoken pressure to ground my ideas in sharing my own cultural and personal educational experiences because when I don't, the ideas presented are easily dismissed. This added pressure feeds into a strive for perfectionism. As a woman of color, I have lived my life with this perfectionism that has helped me in every job I have ever worked because there is no room to not be excellent. That excellence demands an understanding of how the education system works and how I can maintain that excellence within a broken system.

When hoping to make changes to curriculum there is a large amount of preparation needed to overcome obstacles in place from the education system. As discussed earlier, the district often requires multiple levels of approval for any curriculum changes. This can require a great deal of independent preparation before the pitch to make a change. The invisible labor can include research, lesson design, and development of an implementation plan before presenting a new idea, all with the understanding that the request can be quickly denied. It takes very little time for a person to derail a curriculum idea because they see it as an incomplete pitch. That "labor" of saying no is often easier and more widely accepted than the battle to develop a curriculum that represents my students of color. My experience as a student fuels my passion for advocating for change but comes with the price of feeling significantly more drained as I navigate the expectations of a system that struggles to adapt to the diverse needs of its students and faculty of color. There are times when this invisible labor feels like an impenetrable wall and has at times led to cycling through stages of imposter syndrome as I attempt to chip away at that barrier.

Rupsy: My invisible labor comes more from the roles I am expected to fill on my campus, but also the ones I am not encouraged to fill. I am very excited about the idea of becoming a leader in my school, and education is my passion. I am not afraid to do the extra work it might take to become a leader on my campus, although my previous administration expressed doubts about my ability to take on leadership roles. I was selected as a mentor for our local teacher residency program, and I was excited to have an amazing resident, although I learned later that my administration had expressed concerns that I was not experienced enough to be a mentor. This was particularly frustrating as there was another white mentor who had the same years of experience as I did and was never questioned about his skill set. Ironically, I was later told to act as a mentor for my new special education co-teacher who was placed in my classroom. I was even told that if I did not agree to mentor him, they would pull my resident from me. I found this very frustrating, as this was someone who openly disagreed with the values I brought to my classroom, in addition to technically being my peer, which made any sort of mentorship very difficult.

Another role I was asked to fill based solely on my assumed second language pedagogy was when I was asked to become the English Language Development (ELD) chair. I do not have the training to teach ELD courses, but it was assumed that because I also speak Punjabi, I would be able to support ELD students. Specifically, I was told that I would be able to provide social and emotional support for those students because I could connect with them. I don't even write or read in Punjabi. However, when I wanted to attend professional development to improve as a teacher and potentially add on the skills to teach a specialty senior level course, I was lectured for signing up for the course because I had already "done too much." At one point, in expressing my concerns to my principal, I was told that I was "just too passionate for a teacher." I am still curious about how I am supposed to take this comment, and I can't help but wonder if I would have had the same experience if I were not a teacher of color. At times it can feel exhausting.

Implications and Future Directions

A budding body of research is starting to collectively paint a picture of the unique obstacles and struggles that teachers of color face while in their teacher credential programs and/or when they go out into the field. While student demographics continue to shift and diversify at exponential rates, educator demographics have largely remained stagnant. With such a small presence of teachers of color in the field of education, it is very likely that incoming teachers of color are the sole representation of nonwhite educators or are one of a few teachers of color. In the same way that research has indicated the harm potentially caused to students from the overwhelming presence of whiteness in the curriculum, policies, and procedures, and those in "power," the same can be true for teachers of color. Being in an environment void of cultural affirmation and representation has the potential to cause adverse effects such as feelings of exclusion and isolation. As such, our goal is to bring awareness to the complex and unique difficulties that many teachers of color face when entering education. It is our intention to pull from our own experiences and the experiences of the small sample size, combined with current research in the field, to make some preliminary recommendations as to how teacher education programs and school leaders can better support the teachers of color they serve. The recommendations provided here are based on the trends that we have collectively seen and/or experienced.

PROVIDE A SAFE SPACE TO CHALLENGE CURRICULUM

As mentioned previously, teachers of color have been widely sought out to better meet the needs of diverse students in classrooms today. Research has supported the demands for a more diverse teaching workforce as teachers of color "are more likely to have cultural match, serve as cultural brokers with the community, and see students of color as capable learners. Additionally, teachers of color have been shown to have insight into the racialized experiences of students of color and stand as their supports and advocates" (Kohli 11). While we recognize the benefits that teachers of color have in classrooms with diverse students, teachers of color cite having difficulty being able to implement culturally responsive and sustaining practices—the very thing they are being heavily recruited to do. As we saw through Alex's shared experiences, there is a challenge to balance the needs of students with the required, established curriculum. While she noted that her students' needs differed from what the set curriculum dictated, she struggled to find support in advocating for her students. Drawing from her own experiences as a student of color, she noted "having been a student who never saw myself reflected in the texts I read in my K–12 journey, I know the struggle of feeling the work I do in the classroom has nothing to do with my life."

Both the implementation of the Common Core State Standards (CCSS), as well as the lack of cultural representation and affirmation present challenges for teachers like Alex to make curricular changes. The implementation of the CCSS resulted in a curriculum for many districts that seemed rigid, and non-inclusive. Many educators felt, and still feel, as though there is little autonomy in curriculum design. This is exacerbated by school adoptions of scripted curriculums and lock-step PLCs.

The second driver in this complex issue is the lack of cultural representation, affirmation, and understanding of minority groups of students and educators. The lack of understanding and awareness as to how these cultural affirmations need to be reflected in the school environment, curriculum, and pedagogical practices creates a sense of resistance from fellow educators, education leaders, and (at times) the community at large. Both educators interviewed cited an attempt to explicitly address set curriculum standards as the reason for not being responsive to cultural inclusions in their curriculum. Additionally, they perceived a lack of understanding, empathy, and awareness from their colleagues and administrators as to why such cultural inclusions are important for minority students. While our sample size may be small, it directly aligns with the research and additional stories provided by other teachers of color.

As such, teacher preparation programs can explicitly discuss the struggles that practicing educators have adjusting curriculum and instruction based on the needs of their students and address the ways this can be uniquely challenging for teachers of color. Providing the space to discuss complex issues that arise out in the field and to practice problem solving skills and strategies directly correlating to this issue is one way to better prepare preservice teachers to feel confident in their pursuit of autonomy in the curriculum and pedagogical practices they want to implement with their students. In addition to exposing preservice educators to issues such as these, we also recommend that teacher preparation programs provide space and models for how to navigate these obstacles. Through discussion and simulated practice, preservice educators can develop the leadership skills of identifying student needs, adjusting curriculum to meet student needs, and navigating challenges that might occur when trying to implement and/or advocate for such changes. Practice with this problem-solving and articulation process provides preservice educators with experience in anticipating the challenges that frequently occur in conservative educational spaces.

PROVIDE COMMUNITIES OF RESISTANCE TO EMPOWER LEADERS

Throughout the interview process, Alex expressed feelings of despondence when discussing her experiences with her PLC group. She stated that "the problem is that I found other teachers that were there for me and willing to listen to the issues I was facing, but most of them are too comfortable to speak up or make systematic changes. They don't see a problem with the standardized way we teach English. I wish there was some sort of coalition within teachers who wanted to make these changes and then be able to advocate for one another." Rupsy shared similar sentiments about the struggles she had working with her PLC group. She stated, "I had to make the decision to either follow what my PLC wanted me to do or what I wanted to do... the pacing guide overwhelmed me as a new teacher. I couldn't make the connections to what I learned in the credential program with what I was tasked to do using the pacing guide." These sentiments and frustrations are not uncommon for novice teachers, and unfortunately, are intensified for teachers of color who want to be more culturally responsive to their diverse students and are met with resistance.

What we find is that this closely correlates with what Kohli discusses regarding teachers of color. After studying a considerable sample size of teachers of color, Kohli found that one of the shared characteristics for teachers of color who remained in the field was that they sought out or constructed a community or *communities of resistance*. Through her interviews with teachers of color, she found that the ones who remained in the profession over a duration of time were the ones who created or found small communities of resistance with like-minded individuals. Through these relationships, educators became less isolated and more confident in the work that they were doing. Novice teachers can be encouraged to create their own communities, as entering the teaching profession can prove to be daunting. In addition to this recommendation, we provide additional recommendations for teacher preparation programs and school leaders below.

Closely related to our first recommendation is the suggestion to model and provide space to practice problem solving skills. Whether it be within the context of navigating departments or PLCs, preservice educators should have some exposure to not only working collaboratively towards a common goal but also negotiating and justifying pedagogical decisions within these spaces. In the interviews conducted, we saw both educators mention difficulties in having voice and space within their respective PLCs. This is not uncommon for novice educators, and being the only, or one of a small percentage of teachers of color intensifies these struggles. Having exposure to and experience in collaborative working groups to practice problem solving and justification of decision making through simulated and practical experiences would largely benefit preservice educators. Ultimately, we find that while educator preparation programs are largely designed to prepare preservice educators to work with diverse students, problem solve in classroom spaces, and interact with students and parents, the exposure and practice applying these skills to work with colleagues is largely absent. In essence, the bulk of the preparation that is traditionally done in teacher education programs is limited to what happens within classroom spaces rather than the profession at large.

In a similar sense, we find that the mentoring process for novice teachers again heavily emphasizes the decision making, curriculum development, and support for students yet tends to avoid or negate the obstacles that novice teachers face in the professional space at large. We suggest that school leaders assist with supporting novice educators' leadership in problem solving and collaboratively working in groups and committees on campus by making this an integral part of the mentoring process with novice educators. While these collaborations can be time consuming, the time and effort to provide this type of mentorship for novice teachers can yield a positive outcome in that it would help prepare them to be more independent and autonomous in less time, strengthen their abilities to make decisions, and potentially become a leader in their respective educational setting.

Additionally, it is essential that, when our novice educators are making decisions or pitching ideas that they believe are in the best interest of their students, we as colleagues and mentors must listen. While it is easy to see pitfalls and flaws in decisions and/or the reasoning of a novice educator, having their thoughts and decisions validated and providing them with rationalized feedback will yield a more positive result than not validating their thoughts and opinions at all. In the same way that we as teacher educators must allow our preservice teachers to learn from their mistakes, we as veteran educators must allow the same space. That is not to say that we cannot give our thoughts and opinions, or question their choices and decisions, but that we need to listen and validate the suggestions, provide feedback, and rationalize the decision we are making, and then allow space for them to explore their wonderings with their respective students.

TALK INTENTIONALLY ABOUT RACE

Through our interview sessions, we found the following sentiments to be a recurring theme that aligns with the research in the field regarding the difficulties teachers of color face (see Gay). Both interviewees mentioned that they witnessed leadership or educators enacting microaggressions, making assumptions about a diverse population, or making racist comments that made them feel uncomfortable. Both interviewees navigated these situations differently: Rupsy remembers laughing them off in the moment, while Alex considers whether the person in question is someone she can "teach" or if that person now needs to be avoided entirely. Both acutely remember these uncomfortable moments that made them feel overseen and without power to challenge or address these concerns. Alex commented, "we both struggle with how to respond in moments like this and really don't know how to respond—still. It bothers us, but we are not sure how the education system can go from a place of ignorance to a place of understanding. Literature teaches us to have more empathy and perspective, and race is part of our identity that needs to be addressed but currently is not being addressed effectively."

As such, we recommend both teacher preparation programs and school leaders talk about race. Through these interviews and the research done in the field, we see a common thread of teachers of color navigating subliminal and overt racialized obstacles and experiences. We must get more comfortable discussing issues of race, not only in the context of our students, but also as educators and community members. While we recognize that navigating discussions about race can be tricky and potentially destructive if not handled appropriately, we also recognize that the avoidance of these discussions is just as destructive and harmful to those who feel silenced and/or ignored. We recognize again that many of the skills and practice-based opportunities that preservice educators receive during their programs are based on what they will do with students and how they will interact with students and are devoid of how to navigate difficult conversations with faculty members, school leadership, and community members. We recommend that formalized training and simulated practice become an integral element in teacher education programs and reinforced through professional development and other training opportunities by school leaders. Having intentional discussion and direction about these complex conversations would better equip preservice and novice educators to address these issues and conversations more readily and confidently.

Conclusion

While this chapter focuses on a small population of teachers of color, research in this area has demonstrated that these interactions feed into large, shared patterns of experience among teachers of color. As such, we call for a larger focus and understanding of the lifeways of students and teachers of color with the intent to understand, learn, and empower both students and teachers of color alike. We can't merely recruit teachers of color to fill a quota; we must honor the funds of knowledge and unique perspectives that they bring into the classroom for the betterment of our students, particularly our students of color. Additionally, we cannot simply seek to increase numbers of teachers of color without also looking at the ways where we prepare them to become educators and the where we work to validate and affirm these teachers to retain them.

Preparing our teachers of color to become educational leaders will also be critical to furthering the much-needed changes within our institutions. Some of this leadership training may include providing national professional development opportunities, such as participation in organizations such as the National Council of Teachers of English, where they may find connections with similarly situated early-career teachers in addition to established educational professionals. Additionally, supporting students through affinity groups may help to bolster students when they are feeling isolated in their push to enact change in their teaching placements. Providing training in negotiating skills may be helpful for early-career teachers facing well-intentioned, but fearful administrators as well. Ultimately, it is critical that education programs and schools consider the ways where we both prepare and receive our teachers of color to enhance attrition rates amongst this population of educators.

Works Cited

Bishop, Rudine Sims. "Windows and Mirrors: Children's Books and Parallel Cultures." *Illinois English Bulletin*, vol. 78, no. 1, 1990, pp. 3–12.

Carver-Thomas, Desiree. *Diversifying the Field Learning Policy Institute, for the IDRA EAC-South*. IDRA EAC South, 2017, www.idra.org/wp-content/uploads/2017/11/Diversifying-the-Field-Lit-Review-IDRA-EAC-South-2017.pdf.

Dixon, Davis, and Ashley Griffin. *If You Listen, We Will Stay: Why Teachers of Color Leave and How to Disrupt Teacher Turnover*. The Education Trust and Teach Plus, 2019.

Flaherty, Colleen. "Who's Doing the Heavy Lifting in Terms of Diversity and Inclusion Work." *Inside Higher Ed.*, 4 June 2019.

Gay, Geneva. *Culturally Responsive Teaching*. 2nd ed., Teacher's College Press, 2010.

Haddix, Marcelle M. *Cultivating Racial and Linguistic Diversity in Literacy Teacher Education*. Routledge, 2015, https://doi.org/10.4324/9781315850665.

Kohli, R. *Teachers of Color: Resisting Racism and Reclaiming Education*. Harvard Education Press, 2021.

Madkins, T. "The Black Teacher Shortage: A Literature Review of Historical and Contemporary Trends." *The Journal of Negro Education*, vol. 80, no. 3, 2011, pp. 417–27.

Muhammad, Gholdy. *Cultivating Genius: An Equity Framework for Culturally and Historically Responsive Literacy*. Scholastic Teaching Resources, 2020.

Paris, Django. "Culturally Sustaining Pedagogies and Our Futures." *The Educational Forum*, vol. 85, no. 4, Oct. 2021, pp. 364–76, https://doi.org/10.1080/00131725.2021.1957634.

Pierce, Harold. "KHSD to Pay $670,000, Train Staff, to Settle Suit Alleging Minorities Targeted for Suspension and Expulsion." *The Californian*, 27 July 2017.

Torrez, Marco. "Group Demands Del Oro HS Teacher Be Fired for 'Going Behind Parents' Backs' About Gender Transitioning." *KGET*, Feb. 2023, www.kget.com/news/local-news/community-discusses-gender-identity-at-khsd-board-meeting/.

Villegas, Ana Maria, and Danne E. Davis. "Preparing Teachers of Color to Confront Racial/Ethnic Disparities in Educational Outcomes." *Handbook of Research on Teacher Education*, 2008, pp. 583–605.

6
From Perfunctory to Practice

Creating an Administrative Identity as Early-Career Faculty through Community Partnerships

ADELE LEON

During my last pre-COVID-19 required annual meeting with the director of my PhD program in rhetoric and composition, I was asked how I was doing. My response was snarky and intended to critique the program's undervaluing of service and our award-winning community partnership program: "Well, thank God for Wildcat Writers because it's the one thing keeping me motivated and happy." Naively, I had hoped that our conversation would develop into a discussion about how beneficial Wildcat Writers was to graduate students' administrative development, especially given the opportunities afforded to us at a tier 1 research institution; instead, the subject was changed to reformatting my CV.

I first learned about Wildcat Writers during my graduate orientation. Through this program, graduate students and lecturers teaching composition would partner with Title I high school teachers to create collaborative projects and meaningful learning experiences for both classes' students. These partnerships would also serve as college-access pathways for our local high school students who didn't always believe that they could be successful in college. Wildcat Writers was the only community-involved outreach program in our college, and I hoped to bolster my education through working with the local community that we—both the university and the community partnership program—claimed to serve. With this interest, and by mid-semester, I was attending events to find my first teacher-partner and designing projects for our students. Dr. Stephanie Troutman Robbins led this program, emphasizing lived experiences, social justice, and collaborative mentorship as the tenants of reciprocity for our program's values. In an interview with Dr. Troutman Robbins, bell hooks stated that the primary lesson schooling and education need to learn from critical pedagogy is "to promote self-actualization that enables people to discover who they are and find their voice" (qtd. in Troutman 307). My advancement through Wildcat Writers alongside my specialization classes on diversity, equity, and inclusion (DEI), critical pedagogies, and feminist theory transformed me into the liberatory next-gen leader that I have become. It is my goal in this chapter to show early-career and upcoming next-gen academics that service work and community partnerships are valuable spaces for learning and actualizing oneself as a leader whose values and experiences are both relevant and sought-after when establishing a career.

Like many of my peers in my PhD program, I began noticing glaring instances of disconnect between the department's stated and claimed goals of support for DEI initiatives and their actual practices in supporting such endeavors. For example, as a doctoral student, I took on the role of interim director of Wildcat Writers—an unprecedented position in the program's then seventeen-year history. While in that position, I was not granted the administrative access that I needed to most successfully direct and support the program. Rather than validating my anomalous experience and acknowledging the unique opportunities for professionalization that stemmed from this service work, faculty would give only cursory support to our community writing program, offering perfunctory lip-service to graduate students whose budding research and scholarship more frequently aligned with critical, feminist, and community-engaged values of disrupting systemic hierarchies and resisting the elitist exclusionary practices of higher education.

While these instances of oversight and negligence regarding support seemed so obvious to those of us who were negatively impacted by them, these faculty were not intentionally giving preference to students who better fit the mold of the traditional, hierarchical structure of the American higher education system. Rather, these faculty were living in a system built from the exclusionary practices that critical and anti-racist scholars and practitioners have been working to dismantle. These faculty were victims of the system that they have only learned to uphold, therefore it became a personal goal of mine to unequivocally support the systematically marginalized and non-conforming constituents whose lived experiences were being passively overlooked. I hope that other early-career faculty and graduate students who have also been put into leadership roles without being given the institutional and collaborative support they need can learn from this chapter, especially those who also feel that professional statements on collaborative and anti-racist leadership are "out-of-reach." I have outlined ways of reimagining the professional skills early-career PhDs have gained through service activities as transferable skills that have helped mold their future administrative identities.

Throughout my doctoral education, I found that much research on organizational restructuring is situated in Education Leadership scholarship focused on frameworks for equity (Colorado; Dugan) and anti-racist practice (Crenshaw et al.; Emdin; Safir et al.). The crossover between this research and rhetoric, composition, and writing studies (RCWS) scholarship was rarer than anticipated, considering our field's commitment to pedagogical best practices. However, more recently, writing programs and RCWS literature have seen a sharp uptick in discussions concerning these topics. In writing program literature, directors, scholars, and practitioners have discussed restructuring programs in ways that involve collaborative leadership models (Perryman-Clark; Rougeau-Vanderford et al.), anti-racist administration (*Anti-racist*; Beavers; Carter-Tod and Sano-Franchini; Jones et al.), inclusive and equitable teaching (CCCC "Disability"; Del Col et al.; Voss et al.), assessment practices (Craig; Inoue), and various statements and addresses on inclusion and anti-racist initiatives (CCCC Black; CWPA, "Antiracist" and "CWPA Statement"; Hassel) to enhance their more socially just and progressive goals; however, these potential solutions and endeavors seem out-of-reach for junior faculty or graduate students whose leadership positions have been limited or non-existent. Thus, the best way I saw to effect change from within was through the "service" aspects of higher education so often misunderstood and undervalued by those same faculty who offered perfunctory support of, but did not engage with, such community partnerships. My current position as an assistant professor and founding director of a new community writing program has proven to me that some institutions do not impose barriers or disregard service work.

After graduating from that institution with my PhD in August 2021, I was immediately hired on as a full-time lecturer at a community college where I'd been adjuncting to supplement my meager graduate student stipend—a role I regrettably ended after only one semester. I next accepted a postdoctoral researcher position for a College of Education at another R1 university in another state. While working as a postdoc, I received a request for an interview from a private, not-for-profit, R2 university that I had applied to just prior to my dissertation defense date. That position had a flexible start date of January or August 2022, and after my initial and second round of Zoom interviews, I accepted my current position as assistant professor of rhetoric and composition with a start date of August 2022. During my appointment negotiations, I asked for and received funding to start either a new community writing partnership program or a new National Writing Project (NWP) site. Based on my advancement through the various roles of Wildcat Writers and the valuable experience I gained through the challenges and adversity related to that leadership experience, my hiring committee and department chair worked with my [now current] dean to secure an initial $3,000 start-up budget to establish a new, local NWP site. By the end of my first academic year as a next-gen leader and early-career faculty member, I founded a new NWP site. The NWP is the longest-running professional development program for English teachers in the country and the only one that focuses on the teaching of writing. It began in 1974 at the University of California, Berkeley. Since then, this grassroots model that values teacher expertise and elevates teacher voice, spread rapidly across the country and sponsors over 175 local sites nationwide. By valuing those same community voices, knowledges, and experiences, my leadership style is built from an action-oriented philosophy of anti-racist leadership that is concerned with reflecting to consider equity in every situation, stepping up to resist institutional racism, and holding oneself accountable to such. Thus, my local site in Florida specifically works to uphold the values preached and practiced by anti-racist, critical, and feminist scholars, thus allowing me the opportunity and support to cultivate my administrative identity as a next-gen leader.

While developing my NWP site and my leadership positionality, I found that the Colorado Department of Education Office of Language, Culture and Equity's *Equity Toolkit for Administrators* offered three valuable traits for leaders who consider equity in their positions of power: equitable leadership is "inclusive of all involved rather than direct authority"; it "facilitates acknowledging barriers and inequities"; and it "is about changing a current system that produces racial disparities" (Colorado 14). These principles resonated for me because I see anti-racism to be actionable and inclusive. I use an inclusive approach to "center voices from the margins" (Safir et al. 22), and I hold myself accountable to the community I intend to serve by not only drafting policies and seeking feedback from my own team, but also by seeking feedback from community members on how I can use my position of power within the university to push back against initiatives that marginalize local community stakeholders. I agree with Rachael Shah that "community members have the knowledges—and the ethical right—to hold community writing initiatives accountable" (130). To hold myself accountable to working *with* those stakeholders to co-create this new community writing program, I imagine an outcome mirroring Jaclyn Wells' take on community engagement: "When community participants enjoy tangible benefits from research, such as improved resources or access to services, their involvement is time better spent" (53). In chapter 5 of this collection, Alice Hays, Shaylyn Marks, Alexandra Chapa-Kunz, and Rupsy Bajwa explain that teacher preparation programs are obligated to develop leadership and collaborative skills of their pre-service educators so they can become independently skilled teacher leaders. This mentality helps next-gen leaders critically reflect on how institutional expectations and challenges impact opportunities for professionals that emphasizes the importance of mentorship and support networks that create opportunities for accountability. These liberatory and anti-racist practices highlight the fundamental issues that I attempt to address through my inclusive administrative identity.

Terminology

Interlacing liberatory pedagogies and anti-racist rhetorics can offer a framework for developing inclusive practices that can help shape a responsible and inclusive programmatic identity. Today's next-gen leaders have encountered and engaged in anti-racist scholarship and activism, sometimes without naming it as such. While more senior scholars likely engaged in less explicit non-racist movements, their tenure in academia has surely presented them with encounters of the anti-racism that present-day critical scholars advocate. Ibram X. Kendi identifies a key difference between being "not racist" and "anti-racist": being not racist signifies the passivity and neutrality that endorses and allows for racial injustice to continue, while being anti-racist more actively confronts racial injustice. Kendi goes on to explain that "the only way to undo what is racist is to consistently identify and describe it—and then dismantle it" (11). This dismantling necessitates action in ways that do not leave space for passivity in leadership and that intertwine with the resistance often discussed in critical and feminist scholarship on liberatory pedagogies.

Pedagogically, RCWS has built models for anti-racist teacher preparation and inclusive classroom practice (Condon and Ashanti Young; Jones; Kynard; Martinez; Poe; Sicari). These models build from foundational theorists and practitioners whose core teachings stem from liberation and critical pedagogy

(Freire; hooks, *Transgress*). The editors of *Black Women's Liberatory Pedagogies* present an anthology of experiences, pedagogies, and theories authored almost solely by Black women educators to introduce readers to the concept of liberatory pedagogy and its inherent connections to resistance. Liberatory work embodies resistance in that it "challenges the Western intellectual tradition of white and male superiority, of socially constructed knowledge and exclusivity" (Perlow et al. viii). Such work is "purposefully designed to transmit oppositional knowledge to counter white supremacist and patriarchal hegemony, and to create positive, deep structural shifts in the ways of being, worldviews, and actions of those under their tutelage" (Perlow et al. 1–2). This necessity for intentional change and resistance demonstrates the reality that in most systematic structures, passivity is a root cause of inequity.

Perlow et al. explain that resistance is what constitutes leadership. Leadership is a quality relegated to those who call themselves leaders or to those who are in leadership positions; rather, leadership in the context presented here is attributed to those who actively oppose inequitable power structures that reproduce systematic discrimination, who commit to anti-racist work *in spite of* institutional and professional norms and expectations, and who conscientiously seek out opportunities to generate change that enriches and empowers those who have been marginalized by the status quo. To enact such changes, it is often necessary to be in a position of power, and a liberatory leader would implement these practices of resistance not only in their classrooms, but also in their professional commitments to anti-racism both inside and outside of the institution. Kendi provides a definition of an anti-racist as "one who is expressing an idea of racial equality, or is actively supporting a policy that leads to racial equity or justice" (15). Together, liberation and resistance disrupt tradition in ways that can support next-gen leaders and help shape an inclusive administrative identity that works to reconstruct programmatic organization, implement anti-racist practices, and better enact the expectations for diversity, equity, and inclusion.

Positionality

As Paula Mathieu reflected on her personal history and her relationship to community writing programs, she offers advice to white people who seek this type of accountability: "The first part of the work for white people is to start to see it, recognize it, name it, name the times we cash in on privilege or don't see the racial script we are acting out" ("Contemplative" 42). As a white woman in a new position of power, I am responsible for this reflection and awareness. Feeling discomfort when reflecting on my [un]conscious and learned racism does not make me guilty of upholding the racism present within and around the programs I work; however, without seeing my privilege, recognizing it, naming it aloud, and reflecting on it to subvert the elitism and exclusion of academia, I become guilty of supporting those racist traditions.

My privilege also extends to my current position at a private university in Florida. With that designation, I am not prohibited by state or local government—nor by my institution, for which I am extremely grateful—from teaching, openly discussing, and pursuing critical, feminist, and DEI work. The lessons I learned through my coursework have become regular practices of critical reflection as I develop feasible goals with stated values and practice reciprocity through collaborative leadership and stakeholder feedback. Toni Morrison's advice is especially important for me as a next-gen leader: "I tell my students, 'When you get these jobs that you have been so brilliantly trained for, just remember that your real job is that if you are free, you need to free somebody else. If you have some power, then your job is to empower somebody else'" (qtd. in Houston 4). I am guided by liberatory and anti-racist practices in my own efforts to transfer these practices to my leadership and service work throughout graduate school. I am now in a position that allows and supports my ability to empower the community of teachers and writers around me, and it is my responsibility to be accountable to them and their needs.

Throughout my formative years in graduate school, I observed the conflict between the perfunctory lip-service about service work opportunities in my program and the reality of most of our faculty's general aversion to actually supporting either it or the graduate students who were interested in gaining research experience and leadership development through service work. I may have been naive to expect senior faculty to see the same value in service that I did, but nevertheless, this realization shaped my personal non-negotiables for community practice. In my own act of resistance, I began intentionally engaging in coursework that primarily focused on building communities of writing through liberating the spaces typically dominated by the university. Through my deliberate focus on service work and with the mentorship of our program's only Black feminist scholar, my doctoral education extended beyond preparing me for academe and ultimately equipped me to become a liberatory, anti-racist leader in my career.

Leadership Development through Service and Resistance

Coming into a PhD program, I had heard the same commonplaces about teaching, research, and service—that research was the most important thing to prioritize, that teaching is *only part* of the job, and that everyone complained about service. I concluded that I was there to learn how to publish through my coursework. I already had experience teaching and designing my own courses during my master's, and my assistantship contract only stipulated teaching requirements. Simply, the idea of service work was not considered necessary or productive for research or teaching. This chapter identifies that undervaluing of service as problematic and suggests ways to resist and reconsider how service work inherently complements both research and teaching. For me, the idea of resistance plays into my leadership development because it promotes resistance to the traditional hierarchies that value research and administration over service and that separate teaching from service-learning. In spite of the stress, exploitation, and preferential treatment that my peers and I commiserated over, it was the "service" work of partnering with the community that consistently and effortlessly brought us both the joy and motivation to complete our program. Acknowledging the joy and motivation that service work brings also resists the traditional values of higher education by leading to a transformation in higher education. Resistance leads to transformation and transformation is an active process that works to disrupt passivity, to challenge compliance, and to subvert submission by centering systematically marginalized voices, identities, and experiences.

bell hooks' account of how service is viewed in higher education illuminates the systemic devaluing of service work and highlights the need for liberation from and resistance to those imposed beliefs:

> In an imperialist white-supremacist capitalist patriarchal culture, service is devalued. Dominator culture pointedly degrades service as a way of maintaining subordination. Those who serve tend to be regarded as unworthy and inferior. In the academic world of colleges and universities the notion of service is linked to working on behalf of the institution, not on behalf of students and colleagues. (*Community* 83)

For next-gen leaders, service is linked to working on behalf of the students and colleagues being served. This perspective has led me to design service-learning classes with students who were invested in community engagement that has then given them more opportunities to learn in new ways within the community neighboring their institution. It is through these service-oriented courses that I have honed my administrative leadership style in ways that not only qualified me for my first assistant professor position, but that are also valued at my current institution. Had I ignored my proclivity for service work and instead complied with the perpetuation of exclusionary practices, my administrative skillset would not have developed into a deeper understanding of strategically incorporating diversity, equity, and inclusion practices on a programmatic scale. Felicita Arzu-Carmichael and Mena Hannakachl's insights into building student-faculty coalitions provide strong, reciprocity-based foundations for developing next-gen leadership identities that can shape new institutional roles and continue to challenge the hierarchical structures that prevent collaborative growth.

During my tenure with Wildcat Writers, the lack of faculty support for our community writing program translated into a lack of support for graduate students who chose to participate in its leadership structure. This disinterest led me to believe that the program was seen exclusively as service work by faculty in positions of power, and as a result of their misguided perception, those faculty would not consider our workload to qualify for administrative assistantships or other benefits related to the responsibilities we took on. They appeared oblivious to the natural connections between community-engaged work, real-world experience, and the academic prestige of publishing. While this disconnect might not hold true for some faculty across higher education institutions, I was surprised to learn the extent to which it existed for us at that time. In a meeting with a new administrator, I learned that Wildcat Writers was being intentionally underfunded. Apparently, an endowment of $16,000 had been left to our department to fund community writing programs, and the previous administrator who oversaw and distributed the budget withheld that information from even the faculty member directing our program. I couldn't understand why someone who outwardly claimed such support for graduate students and DEI would willfully prevent us from succeeding by withholding—funding that would have greatly benefitted Wildcat Writers. I was mad, but I was also motivated. This contempt anchored my commitment to service, and through my consistently advancing roles in our community writing program, my abstract values translated into my most marketable skills.

Practical Strategies, Lessons Learned, and Implications for Program Development

The following outlines my positions in Wildcat Writers and makes direct connections to the skills and administrative knowledge I gained through my commitment to service. I hope to highlight that this experience not only positioned me for my career in academia, but also shaped my administrative style as a next-gen leader, and it is because of these strategies and lessons learned that I am developing a new NWP site with full support from my new department and college. In recognizing that the experience, knowledge, and practical skills gained through commitments to service are directly transferrable to project and program management in higher education, current and future next-gen leaders can reimagine their own service work as professional leadership expertise that will help them strategize new ways of developing their own community writing programs. To simplify and extrapolate these valuable skills, I have ordered the following sections hierarchically, beginning with my starting position or title within our community writing program, offering a brief description of each role's expectations and following with listing the practical and transferable skills I gained through said position. In some later descriptions, I elaborate on circumstances that I believe strongly contributed to my unique identity as a next-gen leader.

COLLABORATING TEACHER

Collaborating teachers are recruited from the university and local Title I school districts to participate in a teaching partnership connecting high school classes with college writing classes through collaborative, community-engaged projects. The teachers link their curricula to meet college-level learning outcomes and incorporate social justice into community-based themes, and each partnership is assigned a partnership mentor for guidance, training, and support. Each partnership is expected to include three "field trips"—one to the high school, one to the college, and one in the community—with the objective of learning to co-create and achieve shared goals. For the Title I high school students, these partnerships are intended to serve as access pathways to college for prospective students who might have doubted their abilities to succeed; and for the college students, partnerships serve as collaborative learning experiences that allow them to learn about the local community from students whose lived experiences often taught a new perspective.

Transferable Skills

1. Critical thinking and problem solving to serve diverse populations from contrasting institutional types. As a collaborating teacher, my stakeholders included university and school district administrators, and my constituents included Title I high school students from the local community and university students from primarily out of state districts with higher socio-economic status. For example, projects needed to blend multi-level classroom learning objectives to meet incoming and matriculating students' needs and abilities.

2. Grant proposal writing to compensate for our program's minimal departmental funding support. Our program's limited funding prevented our partnerships from engaging in learning opportunities that would exceed fees beyond parking and transportation from high schools. As a first-year graduate student, being a collaborating teacher gave me earlier opportunities to develop valuable knowledge for gaining and finding both internal and external funding to support projects and ranged from community immersion to student and faculty interaction.

ADVISORY BOARD MEMBER

The advisory board is a study and action group comprised of high school and college teachers who collaboratively lead the program, mentor teacher partnerships, and design professional development workshops and events. Advisory board members report to the executive committee during monthly meetings, and as needed, to the graduate assistant director (described below) throughout the time between meetings. Historically, the advisory board would plan three professional development events per year with associated professional development certificates given to teachers and instructors. These workshops cover curriculum and trends at the high school and college level, strategies for team-teaching and linking courses, distance education tools, and the importance of focusing on the assets of underserved students. All board members must have also served as a collaborating teacher for a full academic year prior to being invited to join the board.

Transferable Skills

1. Develop and execute a strategy to support proactive and continued stakeholder engagement. When discussing the wants and needs of our collaborating teachers and their students, a consistent priority was

continuing professional development opportunities covering various topics on writing pedagogy and praxis. Because each professional development workshop was designed and facilitated by the advisory board, members were able to take information gained from partnerships and respond to teachers' needs. For example, when the pandemic hit and high school teachers abruptly shifted to distance learning, the advisory board was able to deliver a series of professional development workshops on how to use and integrate new education technology designed for hybrid and online classrooms.

2. Contribute to the evaluation of program progress and create deliverables to ensure activities, products, and partnerships meet organizational needs are in-line with both school district and university missions. After each professional development workshop, the board met to complete a SWOT (strengths, weaknesses, opportunities, and threats) analysis, reflect on the development of the program, and problem-solve issues. These discussions would, for example, lead to yearly updates and revisions to the teacher handbook, which is given to each teacher partnership at the beginning of their collaborative planning.

PARTNERSHIP MENTOR

The partnership mentor role dealt with accountability, community, and reciprocity by providing pedagogical, technical, emotional, and interpersonal support for all partnership stakeholders. In my opinion, this role was one of the best parts of this community writing program because of its depth of involvement and seemingly endless learning opportunities. Mentor training entails teaching new mentors how to foster successful teacher partnerships. The partnership mentor guides collaborating teachers with the planning stage, the organized events, and the debrief protocol. Mentors are often prompted to reflect on their own lived experiences as a former (or sometimes, still current) collaborating teacher, and were expected to maintain detailed meeting notes, agendas, and budgetary items for planning meetings and partnership events, and help plan and attend three partnership events—one on each school campus and one in the community. All partnership mentors must have also served on the advisory committee for a full academic year prior to mentoring a partnership.

Transferable Skills
1. Adaptability and flexibility to receive and apply information and enforce limitations to help collaborating teachers and their students

overcome barriers and close educational gaps. Because the high school classes we partnered with often taught English language arts as opposed to composition, and because our college instructors had more flexibility in designing their curriculum, partnership mentors would frequently work with their mentees to remix college projects in ways that would meet the learning outcomes for both classes.
2. Provide targeted support to meet the interpersonal, emotional, and pedagogical needs of collaborating teachers. With every professional relationship, there are risks and expectations for disagreement. To best support our program's mission, values, and sustainability, partnership mentors became skilled at de-escalation and conflict resolution, and when needed, could fall back on other advisory board members for advice or support.

GRADUATE ASSISTANT DIRECTOR

The graduate assistant director's (GAD) responsibilities focused primarily on gaining administrative experience and insight through taking on leadership roles. Due to the GAD's primary location on the university campus, they would coordinate with appropriate faculty and administrators to deliver Wildcat Writers recruitment talks at graduate student orientations and preceptorship classes and offer regular unscheduled support for university instructors and graduate assistant teachers who were participating in or curious about Wildcat Writers. The GAD was also responsible for managing the undergraduate intern(s), onboarding the incoming GAD, and designing and delivering professional development workshops with associated certificates of completion. To ensure reciprocity for participating district teachers, the GAD schedules principal visits to ensure that participation in Wildcat Writers constituted mandatory professional development for district teachers. This position offers a plethora of transferable skills for any graduating PhD or early-career faculty member, but the opportunities for practical, hands-on leadership learning this position offered seem exclusive to community-based programs.

Transferable Skills
1. Prepare summaries, reports, and correspondence to show program sustainability, monetary value, and measurable impacts. From this data collection and analysis of the program's success, the GAD would present various data in program reports, recruitment flyers, and professional development workshops. For example, at the close of each semester when partnerships ended, the GAD would compile a repository of

student contact information to build a network for past, present, and future Wildcat Writers students.
2. Coordinate logistics and financials for all events related to the program. In addition to the monthly advisory board meetings and professional development workshops, partnership campus and community visits also required reserving rooms, securing visitor parking, catering, finding and writing grants to support our program, and managing a budget to ensure these events could be funded. Graduate students who gain this experience through program management are instilling in themselves threshold concepts that can transfer to and are needed in both industry and academia.

EXECUTIVE COMMITTEE MEMBER

This committee of three senior members collectively decides who should be invited to join the advisory board, who should take on the role of GAD once the current GAD leaves the position, and when new policies or practices need to be established for the program. The executive team would meet after each advisory board meeting to debrief and discuss any issues, problem solve and make plans for addressing any anticipated challenges or changes. We were expected to drop in on nearby partnership events and act as support to the teacher partners when needed that gave us the insight to most accurately award a partnership with the university's yearly Wildcat Writers Service-Learning Award.

Transferable Skills
1. Strategic planning and decision-making to uphold the mission, vision, and values of the program. Because this community writing program so highly values the time, skills, and labor volunteered by the advisory board, the executive committee prioritizes board members' emotional and vocational health. To ensure we could systematically build in monitoring and evaluation procedures that would give board members an opportunity to take a leave without feeling guilty, we developed bylaws for the advisory board that included a yearly check-in with the option to select a semesterly or yearly sabbatical. This new process more actively supported board members who were less likely to request a break.
2. Identify critical issues affecting districts and develop resources to meet targeted needs. It was vital that our executive committee included a community coordinator who had been a part of the local community in multiple capacities—she was a retired public school teacher who had spent her career working with local Title I schools and was born

and raised in the city that our program called home. Through her district connections, we could prepare for upcoming legislative changes and events like forthcoming book bans and the Red for Ed movement. Building a leadership team that is representative of the constituents who our program impacted allowed us to listen and act through reciprocity and collaboration.

PROGRAM DIRECTOR

Historically, this position was never meant to be occupied by a graduate student, and my learning curve was unfortunately exacerbated by the COVID-19 pandemic. The most immediate increase in labor came when the faculty advisor was promoted to chair of a different department that happened alongside the exit of our community coordinator. As a PhD candidate, writing my dissertation during a pandemic and teaching two classes, I became the first and only graduate student program director of Wildcat Writers.

In addition to performing the relevant duties listed above as GAD and a member of the executive committee, I was in a whirlwind of onboarding two graduate assistant co-directors, a new faculty advisor, and a new senior representative for high schools, all while transitioning to online and hybrid board meetings, mentoring partnerships, and responding to our high school teachers' urgent needs for distance technology and teaching materials. Articulating transferable skills from this fiasco of a situation would be next to impossible for me, as I still feel reverberations from that year. That said, my final year with Wildcat Writers revealed what I am capable of when it comes to leadership within a community.

So, while pursuing extra-curricular activities that weren't actively supported by the faculty who were in administrative positions of power did me no favors, I can honestly say that I would have never found my home in graduate school without the community I had in Wildcat Writers. Knowing what I know now, I recognize that the "service" work I pursued in graduate school through community partnership programs consistently offered me a space where my ideas and beliefs were appreciated and challenged, and I have come to envision them as sites of liberation and resistance that realize my values.

Building My Inclusive Administrative Identity

My experiences addressing administrative lip-service helped solidify my views about what constitutes inclusive practice, and I suggest that upcoming next-gen leaders follow my process of reflecting on and inventorying the transferable skills they have learned from their various positions to create their own administrative values. Committing myself to service work led to actualizing my values through a series of principles that I believe can and should be adapted to programmatic restructuring and design. Learning to lead through an administrative positionality that succeeded through collaborative leadership and reciprocity shaped my administrative identity into one that reinforces acts of critical reflection, transparency, and accountability. Articulating my values into actionable principles has helped me not only begin my academic career in a position that actively supports DEI-centric structural change but also situate myself in a way that granted additional, unplanned funding for me to direct and design a new National Writing Project site.

Because I am guided by liberatory and anti-racist strategies that define leadership as a model and expectation for accountability, it is my belief that leaders need to develop programs with their constituents to best serve students, faculty, and the surrounding community. It has been my experience that this process can enable leaders to adequately and meaningfully reshape their identity to be inclusive and representative of a program's constituents through a reciprocal approach that enacts collaborative leadership in ways that create sustainable change. Reflective and responsive community writing leadership resists the idea that universities are knowledge makers and communities are knowledge recipients and instead places the value of the program on the sum of its parts. These parts are built through inclusivity and representation that are foundational to building an equitable program that speaks *with* and not *for* the community it claims to serve. This reciprocity-centric approach could also positively reposition the university within the community as a site for collaborative change.

When next-gen administrators—or any leader motivated by reciprocity and accountability—take on the task of building a community partnership program, they hold the responsibility and position of power that can reinforce the diverse programmatic identity that so many institutions are attempting to embody. These leaders can restructure or build new programmatic identities that are founded on liberatory and anti-racist strategies and structures to both show and embody the commitments to diversity, equity, and inclusion that many mission and value statements so frequently boast. With the essential focus on sustainability and reciprocity that community partnership and DEI models require serving as a foundation for programmatic design, our future administrative leaders can contribute significantly to the positive shift toward the next-gen future that this collection is anticipating. Paul Feigenbaum draws from both Stephen Parks' ("Texts") and Paula Mathieu's (*Tactics*) discussions of strategies and tactics for being engaged community scholars to address the common lack of institutional support: "The objective should be not to avoid the institution but to make it more conducive to the ethical visions that guide us" (56). Early-career faculty and staff are in precarious positions as both new leaders and new faculty; however, next-gen leaders are taking these positions as opportunities to restructure their programs or create new ones to be more inclusive. And while the risk of disruption can lead to personal discomfort, we can remember that "victimization does not constitute leadership. Resistance does" (Perlow et al. x). I am not advocating that new faculty risk their employment or job security by taking drastic action. I am speaking to those next-gen leaders who have positioned themselves to enact DEI work, and who were offered positions that include expectations for structural change.

White program directors might be uncomfortable with the challenges of remaining conscious of the implicit and explicit racism that exists in every program and department in higher education, but that discomfort does not compare to the impact of structural racism on the constituents of those programs. Most importantly, though, is to take action, and practice critical reflection despite the discomfort it might bring, whether that discomfort stems from reading radically honest anonymous feedback, conducting exit interviews, stopping privileged colleagues from discounting or ignoring Black or woman-identifying colleagues; all of whom should be regular practice for any person in a position of power.

Principles for Actionable Leadership

As graduate students continue to gain experience through community-engaged programs, they need to remember that the "service" they are practicing is training them in substantial and meaningful ways that other types of assistantships and fellowships might not offer. For example, I have been told time and time again by my colleagues who interviewed me that the single most impactful asset I bring to my new department is that my commitment to DEI work is actually practical and not performative. I was one of two people interviewed out of over one hundred who applied. This success was due in part to how I threaded my knowledge and experience with DEI work throughout all elements of my portfolio. My administrative experience connected my DEI work with higher-order organizational and management skills that the department was seeking. I can guarantee that these traits were most substantially developed for me only through my "service" work with community partnerships. Further, this service work taught me practical and transferrable skills that honed my action-oriented philosophy of anti-racist leadership by helping me learn how to consider equity in every situation, step up to resist institutional racism, and hold oneself accountable to such reflections in action.

My core values are grounded in the principles of actionable leadership that is enacted in conscientious, ethical service-learning and community partnership programs: equity, resistance, and accountability. While current scholarship is not necessarily in alignment with singular definitions or applications of these traits, next-gen leaders can help further RCWS's understanding and application of such actionable leadership. In my own work and personal understanding and application, I found the following scholars and practitioners' work to be the most helpful in establishing more concrete definitions.

EQUITY. Jamila Dugan explains that part of practicing equity means to "consistently examine personal identity, bias, and both personal and collective contributions to the creation and/or reproduction of inequitable practices" (36). This practice leads to critical reflection and transparency as a practice for building a strong, equitable, and inclusive administrative identity. To bolster opportunities for equity, we need also remember that "critical reflection is the necessary component of the process that, as with all forms of experiential education, enables learning or making meaning from experience" (Harrison and Clayton 30). Working toward equity is constant, and that work can and will be recognized.

RESISTANCE. Zoe Spencer explains in *Black Women's Liberatory Pedagogies* that "revolutionary praxis means 'getting dirty,' challenging the discomfort and filth of white supremacist and patriarchal oppression, engaging in forms of activism where there is *the risk* that comfort, respect, freedom, stability, and even life might be disrupted" (qtd. in Perlow et al. 59–60, my emphasis). Discomfort is not only rooted in, but also an indicator of progress—progress away from tradition and exclusion and toward resistance, liberation, and inclusion *in practice* over theory. Natasha Jones critiques the problem of anti-racist work in higher education: "The focus on Diversity, Equity, and Inclusion (DEI) programs and initiatives and inclusion work in the academy is not focused on resistance at all. The focus is always on complicity" (5). To me, systemic racism means even if you replace every racist in the system with a non-racist, the system will still disproportionately hinder marginalized groups and privilege the already privileged. To actively resist this systemic racism, resistance is necessary.

ACCOUNTABILITY. Just as Wright et al. explain in their chapter about how Black women academics and senior managers can resist gendered racism, next-gen leaders can realize the importance of centering marginalized voices to prioritize representation: "Bringing community networks from the margins into the center of higher education challenges the invisibility of Black workers" (qtd. in Perlow et al. 77). Emily Ronay Johnston explains that reflection could lead to program change through recognizing accountability needs: "Accountability signals a need for checking the intentions, desires, assumptions, and beliefs that inform our practices" (qtd. in Blair and Nickoson 58). A person should not be in a position of power over others if they refuse to hold themselves and their actions accountable to the people they are leading. Given all the abuses of power that they have seen, I believe that next-gen leaders will make accountability and transparency guiding tenets of their administrative work.

Although some faculty still might not value everything that can be gained and impacted from service work, graduate students and early-career faculty who have found their homes in community partnership programs can take solace in the practical skills they have learned. The collaborative leadership knowledge I gained is now benefiting the RCWS field and my new local community in Florida. I could not have gained these skills without the difficulties I faced, but in the long run, maintaining persistence and committing to the people who relied on me set me up to build another inclusive, equitable, and collaborative partnership program that can give back to the community. Reflecting on my growth and the impact that community partnership programs had on me, in hindsight, I wouldn't change a thing. Because of my mentors, hardships, and partnerships, I found that my core values are what led to my being a person with a position of power who can now enact the changes I believe should be made on a programmatic level. I am proud of what my commitment to service has resulted in. I am the founding director of a new NWP site in South Florida. I have found a department and colleagues whose support and collegiality are beyond what my PhD program allowed me to imagine existed in academia. And all of this is because I let myself find my home in community partnerships.

Works Cited

Anti-racist Scholarly Reviewing Practices: A Heuristic for Editors, Reviewers, and Authors, 2021, tinyurl.com/reviewheuristic.

Beavers, Melvin. "Reimagining the Possibilities: A Narrative Account of a Journey Toward Anti-Racist Administration." *WPA: Writing Program Administration,* vol. 44, no. 3, 2021, pp. 155–57.

Blair, Kristine L., and Lee Nickoson, eds. *Composing Feminist Interventions: Activism, Engagement, Praxis*. WAC Clearinghouse and UP of Colorado, 2018, https://doi.org/10.37514/PER-B.2018.0056.

Carter-Tod, Sheila, and Jennifer Sano-Franchini. "Black Lives Matter and Anti-Racist Projects in Writing Program Administration." *WPA: Writing Program Administration*, vol. 44, no. 3, 2021, pp. 12–22.

CCCC Black Technical and Professional Writing Task Force. "CCCC Black Technical and Professional Communication Position Statement with Resource Guide." *Conference on College Composition and Communication*, 2020, cccc.ncte.org/cccc/black-technical-professional-communication.

CCCC. "Disability Studies in Composition: Position Statement on Policy and Best Practices." *Conference on College Composition and Communication*, cccc.ncte.org/cccc/resources/positions/disabilitypolicy.

Colorado Department of Education, and Office of Language, Culture and Equity. *Equity Toolkit for Administrators*. Equity Assistance Center, 2010.

Condon, Frankie, and Vershawn Ashanti Young, eds. *Performing Antiracist Pedagogy in Rhetoric, Writing, and Communication*. WAC Clearinghouse and UP of Colorado, 2017, wac.colostate.edu/books/atd/antiracist/.

Craig, Sherri. "Your Contract Grading Ain't It." *WPA: Writing Program Administration*, vol. 44, no. 3, 2021, pp. 145–46.

Crenshaw, Kimberlé Williams, et al., eds. *Seeing Race Again: Countering Colorblindness across the Disciplines*. U of California P, 2019.

CWPA Executive Board and Officers. "Antiracist Initiatives." *CWPA*, 2020, http://wpacouncil.org/aws/CWPA/pt/sp/initiatives.

CWPA Executive Board and Officers. "CWPA Statement on Racial Injustice and Systemic Racism." *WPA: Writing Program Administration*, vol. 44, no. 1, 2020, pp. 15–16, wpacouncil.org/aws/CWPA/asset_manager/get_file/555795?ver=2.

Del Col, Lucy, et al. "Do Something! Forging Constellations of Curricular, Co-Curricular, and Community Opportunities for Anti-Racist Writing Pedagogies at Bates College in Lewiston, Maine." *WPA: Writing Program Administration*, vol. 44, no. 3, 2021, pp. 106–13.

Dugan, Jamila. "Beware of Equity Traps and Tropes." *Educational Leadership*, vol. 78, no. 6, 2021, pp. 35–40.

Emdin, Christopher. *For White Folks Who Teach in the Hood . . . and the Rest of Y'all Too: Reality Pedagogy and Urban Education*. Beacon Press, 2016.

Feigenbaum, Paul. "Tactics and Strategies of Relationship-Based Practice: Reassessing the Institutionalization of Community Literacy." *Community Literacy Journal*, vol. 5, no. 2, Apr. 2011, https://doi.org/10.25148/CLJ.6.2.009412.

Freire, Paulo. *Pedagogy of the Oppressed*. Seabury Press, 1970.

Harrison, Barbara, and Patti H. Clayton. "Reciprocity as a Threshold Concept for Faculty Who Are Learning to Teach with Service-Learning." *The Journal of Faculty Development*, vol. 26, no. 3, 2012, pp. 29–33.

Hassel, Holly. "2022 CCCC Chair's Address: Writing (Studies) and Reality: Taking Stock of Labor, Equity, and Access in the Field." *College Composition and Communication*, vol. 74, no. 2, 2022, pp. 208–28.

hooks, bell. *Teaching Community: A Pedagogy of Hope*. Routledge, 2003.
hooks, bell. *Teaching to Transgress: Education as the Practice of Freedom*. Routledge, 1994.
Houston, Pam. "The Truest Eye." *O Magazine*, 2003, www.oprah.com/omagazine/toni-morrison-talks-love.
Inoue, Asao B. *Antiracist Writing Assessment Ecologies: Teaching and Assessing Writing for a Socially Just Future*. Parlor Press, 2015.
Jones, Natasha N. "The Complicity/Complexity Problem of Anti-Racism Work in the Academy." *Community Literacy Journal*, vol. 15, no. 2, Spring 2021, pp. 4–8, https://doi.org/10.25148/CLJ.15.2.009617.
Jones, Natasha N., et al. "So You Think You're Ready to Build New Social Justice Initiatives? Intentional and Coalitional Pro-Black Programmatic and Organizational Leadership in Writing Studies." *WPA: Writing Program Administration*, vol. 44, no. 3, Summer 2021, pp. 29–35.
Kendi, Ibram X. *How to Be an Antiracist*. Random House, 2019.
Kynard, Carmen. "Where We Are: Discourses of Crisis in Rhetoric and Composition: Fakers and Takers: Disrespect, Crisis, and Inherited Whiteness in Rhetoric-Composition Studies." *Composition Studies*, vol. 50, no. 3, 2022, pp. 131–204.
Martinez, Aja. *Counterstory: The Rhetoric and Writing of Critical Race Theory*. NCTE, 2020.
Mathieu, Paula. *Tactics of Hope: The Public Turn in English Composition*. Boynton/Cook, 2005.
Mathieu, Paula. "The Contemplative Concerns of Community Engagement: What I Wish I Knew about the Work of Community Writing Twenty Years Ago." *Community Literacy Journal*, vol. 14, no. 2, Dec. 2020, https://doi.org/10.25148/14.2.009035.
Parks, Stephen. "Texts of Our Institutional Lives: Strategic Speculations on the Question of Value—The Role of Community Publishing in English Studies." *College English*, vol. 71, no. 5, 2009, pp. 506–27.
Perlow, Olivia N., et al., eds. *Black Women's Liberatory Pedagogies: Resistance, Transformation, and Healing within and beyond the Academy*. Springer International Publishing, 2018, https://doi.org/10.1007/978-3-319-65789-9.
Perryman-Clark, Staci M. *The New Work of Writing Across the Curriculum: Diversity and Inclusion, Collaborative Partnerships, and Faculty Development*. Utah State UP, 2023.
Poe, Mya. "Re-framing Race in Teaching Writing across the Curriculum." *Across the Disciplines*. Special issue on Anti-Racist Activism: Teaching Rhetoric and Writing, 2013, pp. 1–14.
Rougeau-Vanderford, R. Nichole, et al. "CARDS: A Collaborative Community Model for Faculty Development or an Institutional Case Study of Writing Program Administration." *Teaching/Writing: The Journal of Writing Teacher Education*, vol. 7, no. 1, 2019, pp. 19–52.
Safir, Shane, et al. *Street Data: A Next-Generation Model for Equity, Pedagogy, and School Transformation*. 1st ed., Corwin, 2021.
Shah, Rachael W. *Rewriting Partnerships: Community Perspectives on Community-Based Learning*. Utah State UP, 2020.
Sicari, Anna. "Hitting a Brick Wall and the Women Who Do the Work: Is This the Same Old Story?" *College Composition and Communication*, vol. 73, no. 3, 2022, pp. 562–92.

Troutman, Stephanie. "Still Teaching to Transgress: Reflecting on Critical Pedagogy with Bell Hooks." *The SAGE Handbook of Critical Pedagogies*. Edited by Shirley Steinberg and Barry Down, Sage Publications, 2020, pp. 302–39, https://doi.org/10.4135/9781526486455.

Voss, Julia, et al. "A Heuristic to Promote Inclusive and Equitable Teaching in Writing Programs." *WPA: Writing Program Administration*, vol. 44, no. 2, 2021, pp. 13–39.

Wells, Jaclyn M. "Investigating Adult Literacy Programs through Community Engagement Research: A Case Study." *Community Literacy Journal*, vol. 8, no. 2, Apr. 2014, pp. 49–66, https://doi.org/10.25148/CLJ.8.2.009310.

Section 2 Response

That's How They Get You

Christina V. Cedillo

A common adage states that there are two kinds of people: those who make others suffer because they themselves did, and those who try to make things better so others don't have to suffer, too. Those of us in the academy should recognize this supposed platitude as a reality. We know how this bears out in terms of mentorship while navigating the treacherous landscape known as meritocracy, built on that "white, neoliberalist, racial-affect-sanitized ethos of the western academy and its epistemological violence" (Kynard 12). We (especially those of us from marginalized backgrounds) are told that we must either sink or swim if we wish to belong, never making waves or drawing attention to ourselves lest we draw the ire of those with the power to decide our professional fate. "That's just how it is" goes the tired refrain, though this may be heard less frequently as subsequent generations of scholars refuse to accept such "advice."

Or, you may be encouraged to resist the violence prescribed by academia's privileged norms and help others likewise harmed as students, faculty, and administrators whose identities do not fit the traditional whitestream profile repudiate the status quo. Yet, there can be some hedging advised by cautious mentors who themselves have been burnt when trying to enact change. I know that "Just play the game until you're in a more secure position (i.e., once you have tenure) and then you can speak out all you want" is what I often heard as early-career faculty. After all, you can't be here for others if you aren't here at all. The threat of being pushed out or even fired for causing "trouble" has become all the more palpable given the current administration's attack on diversity, equity, and inclusion (DEI), education, people of color, LGBTQ folks, women, religious minorities, and immigrants. While the advice to wait for tenure and/or promotion may be well meaning, it ignores how the very presence of faculty from marginalized communities is read as threatening to the status quo. Such counsel, though well meaning, is still predicated on a view that transformation occurs through solitary rather than collective action, by ascribing to academia's dedication to individualism. This advice, too, is falling by the wayside thanks to the efforts of next-gen faculty who, as noted in the introduction to this section, understand that "networks of resistance" are key to challenging the unquestioned assumptions on which the academy is built (González 359).

Ultimately, if we want to ensure that others do not have to abide the kinds of inequity and injustice that we ourselves have faced, there can be no waiting. Others are facing those crises now. If we are loath to take action, no promise of security will encourage us; faculty further along the career track may actually be more reluctant to speak out for fear of risking all that they gained through silence. Thus, whether one is early, mid, or senior, there is no better time to be part of any change you wish to see. That is what makes this collection so important. This volume highlights "unique, innovative, and transformational strategies" offered by contributors striving to make a real difference in diverse ways at their respective institutions and by building coalitional movements.

Institutional transformation will not come from institutions themselves because the tendency towards self-preservation is built into systems at the expense of the vulnerable even as institutions claim to champion equity and justice. Arzu-Carmichael and Hannakachl state that "sites of learning and community building are also political sites of trauma and tension" (123). Hence, when Paulette A. Meikle and Lekeitha R. Morris analyzed public statements by university presidents following the 2020 murder of George Floyd, they found that overall, few of them used the words "Black, African American, systemic racism, and police brutality" (15). And, while some statements "were bold in denouncing systemic racism and invoking the principles of social justice embedded in the university intellectual roots," schools needed to do more to corroborate their dedication to promoting justice (19). Simply put, institutions speak of sympathy and community but do little to ensure they do their part to rectify systemic trauma and oppression. As Leon reminds us, "passivity [too] is a root cause of inequity" (168).

At the same time, formulating strategic plans for such work, if undertaken at all, usually falls on new and marginalized faculty, hired as embodied representation of the communities that universities purport to be aspiring to serve. Not only are underrepresented faculty hired without being provided adequate assistance to ensure that they survive, let alone thrive; they are often the only members of their communities in their departments, leaving them with little to no culturally responsive support. Hays et al. point out that educators of color experience high rates of turnover due to microaggressions on the job and expectations of additional labor despite "being able to use their cultural knowledge to build bridges to learning" for the ever-increasing number of students of color in our classrooms (147). Faculty of color may be expected to resolve decades, if not centuries, of systemic inequality on behalf of the institution, bearing the unjust responsibility of performing miracles, then taking the fall when these miracles fail to materialize. These issues take a toll, especially on Black faculty who are subject to the "Black tax," the expectation that they should provide more labor for the same—even less—recognition and capital (Griffin et al.).

Schools uphold the very conditions that they claim to be opposing in their mission reports and administrative statements that call for greater equity. Below, I outline some takeaways gleaned from the chapters in this section regarding institutions' preservation of the status quo, highlighting the schemes they deploy. While these elements emerge across the chapters, in the interest of space, I deliberately focus on the most salient ones illustrated by each chapter. Then, I briefly distill some counterstrategies from the authors' works to emphasize why coalition building within and beyond institutional boundaries proves so vital.

Strategies That Safeguard the Status Quo

Arzu-Carmichael and Hannakachl write about the problems they faced during the pandemic despite their university's DEI goals as written into its strategic plan. Working together as a junior Afro-Caribbean faculty member and an undergraduate Arab Chaldean student, they present an intergenerational autoethnography of their experiences. But theirs are also counterstories because they center the "lived experiences of People of Color by including such methods as storytelling . . . and narratives" and "analyz[ing] race and racism within . . . contemporary contexts" (Yosso 74). Presenting such stories is crucial because these experiences and perspectives are ignored or denied within dominant narratives, and these stories allow their tellers to demonstrate where their dedication lies and where they strive to make change when members of dominant cultures cannot (or refuse to) see the need for transformation.

Hays et al. also share counterstories of next-gen teachers of color confronting resistance when serving their diverse student population by incorporating social justice themes into the Common Core curriculum while working in a conservative district. The authors are interested in how these challenges combine with the unique challenges faced by educators of color. Working with two recent women graduates, Alex, a Latina teacher, and Rupsy, a Punjabi teacher, they compose a chapter that asks what decisions they made to connect curricula to students' lives, what challenges they faced incorporating social justice methods and approaches, what forms of invisible labor they had to take on, and what more English-ed programs and English departments could do to better prepare faculty to face these challenges. First, I focus on what Alex and Rupsy's experiences teach us about institutional indifference, while in the final segment, I turn to the guidance offered by Hays et al.

Likewise, Leon relates a counterstory that underscores the radical difference between the rhetoric of social justice and what departments are actually doing—and what they allow their members to do. Writing about her experiences as the graduate student interim director for the Wildcat Writers, a community outreach program, she describes how her efforts were thwarted rather than recognized as invaluable professionalization training and how she realized that she and other grad students were not supported when their work contested elitist and hierarchical academic norms. Furthermore, she found that many of the faculty were passive transmitters of these racist patterns, having assumed academia's exclusivist contours. This makes resistance all the more of a conscious, pressing need for scholars wishing to do real work in service to their communities.

MAINTAINING WHITE TIME AND SPACE

While race and social justice are always pressing matters for students and communities of color, and the time to teach and do something about them is now, academic institutions contribute to what Tamika Carey terms "temporal hegemony," conditions "where ideological and material structures converge into a culture of hostility that pushes equity for a [marginalized] group further out of reach" (270). We see how when, in Spring 2020, Arzu-Carmichael taught a special topics course, Rhetoric(s) of Race and Ethnicity; that March, COVID-19 struck, followed in May by the murder of George Floyd. Because the course had been underenrolled, Arzu-Carmichael told a senior faculty member that she was proposing a standing course on race and social justice, only to be told this "wasn't the time for that!" and there were "other more pressing matters" (128). *No time*, though Black people are three times more likely than white people to be slain by police (Mapping Police Violence). *More pressing matters*, though students of color reported increased problems related to finances, stress, and racial injustice due to COVID, meaning these struggles were already present (Molock and Parchem). Communities of color are always disproportionately affected by structural racism and ableism.

For Hannakachl, the promise of equity crumbles when she dares to question writing instructors' complicity in enforcing White Mainstream English (WME) dominance and, therefore, white supremacy. Ersula Ore reminds us that "those operating—whether conscious or not, intentional or not—under the cultural logic of whiteness articulate and perpetuate its ideology of white racial superiority and nonwhite racial inferiority" (20). When Hannakachl tells her professor that she is interested in publishing a paper on the issue, the professor says it's too difficult to get published and that papers get "immediately rejected" for something as small as misplaced commas without even having read the essay (134). The attitudes of other instructors and her peers—who compliment Hannakachl on her "good English"—clarify that this student-teacher interaction is about more than gatekeeping a paper; it's about gatekeeping discussions about WME dominance. It's also about gatekeeping people, resulting in the professor asking Hannakachl to set aside who she is, as if that were even possible. Would the professor ask other students, students who were not people of color and whose acceptance of WME went unquestioned, to set aside their identities? Would they be fed the same lie regarding a comma? Ore states those whom the white supremacist system aims to subjugate become "attuned to a frequency that privileged others are not" (20). Thus, even as the professor probably continues to believe that their offensive words were "helpful," Hannakachl locates this encounter within a broad pattern of microaggressions bolstering WME's authority and becomes further resolved to challenge its hold.

ENCOURAGING THE ILLUSION OF WHITE INNOCENCE

Institutional spacetime is built with whiteness as the default assumption, and the institution demands that it cohere by carefully regulating how space and time operate; they reify whiteness through their actions. In addition to dealing with faculty microaggressions, Arzu-Carmichael must also contend with those of students. Teaching an online asynchronous course titled Issues in

Writing and Rhetoric, she enacts a Black feminist pedagogy to counteract how the course has been taught to center white Euro-Western perspectives despite its focus on "a theoretical and historical foundation for understanding current issues, changes, and challenges for the discipline" (125). After all, a foundational aspect of both writing and rhetoric is understanding how one's embodiment affects access to rhetorical space, visibility, presence, and authority. One student refused to engage with work by Black and Latinx critics and made disparaging public (within the course) comments about im/migrants and people of color, substantiating the arguments made by many race rhetoric scholars regarding the influence that speakers' embodied identities have on ethos and reception when addressing intractable audiences.

Nevertheless, a senior faculty member discouraged her from addressing this problem in class, promoting the student's welfare over that of the professor and other students. Thus, not only was there no time for a course focused on race and social justice (see Arzu-Carmichael and Hannakachl), but even when time and space was deliberately dedicated to discussing these issues, white hostility was to be accommodated at the expense of social justice and the comfort of the entire group. In suggesting that the student not be called out or even called in for making racist and xenophobic statements that deliberately disrupted the entire classroom community, the senior faculty member centered the student's implicit view that race has no place in the study of writing and rhetoric—a view shared by Arzu-Carmichael's coworkers, given how the course had previously been taught.

In Hannakachl's case, there's a sad lack of irony in that she could provide valuable writing instruction to other students at her institution, and yet without even having read her work, the professor had already set themselves up as the all-knowing judge. And yet, as Hannakachl points out, in making such a microaggressive call while phrasing it as if they are meant to be helpful, white scholars, teachers, and peers are the ones who set their true ethoi and intentions aside to take up the mantle of guiltlessness. This move proves one of the "alibis" where white actors who enact racism establish their "innocence" to distinguish themselves from "guilty" or "real" racists. When presented with evidence that students are facing microaggressions, white teachers may frame students' experiences as mere feelings or interpretations[1] and state what they would or will plan to do to fix the issue retroactively without acknowledging or apologizing for their actions. Notably, the professor did not just preemptively determine

---

1. Basford et al. define such responses as "microinvalidations," actions that minimize or deny the experiences of people of color (341).

Hannakachl's writerly ability but asked her to set her identity aside upon further discussion. By presenting themselves as "strategic, problem-solving teachers," the use of "this alibi both exonerates white teachers from being racist, and from participating in further discussions of race" (Carlsruh and Gutiérrez 353). The professor not only refused to acknowledge that they had unfairly judged Hannakachl and why, but their "strategy" for helping her compounded their racism by pretending to make the situation identity-avoidant (i.e., asking her to "whiten" herself) to supposedly make it easier for the student.

DEMANDING "INVISIBLE" LABOR

In the chapter by Hays et al., teachers Rupsy and Alex are women of color participating in a residency program that pairs teachers with a veteran mentor for the year, provides support through monthly meetings, and involves additional time in the classroom. I recap this information to remind the reader of the additional labor that the credentialing program already entailed. However, much of the labor that Rupsy and Alex describe is also emotional and intellectual in nature, invisible labor that people of color must often take on to survive on the job; they also engage in additional invisible labor in seeing to the needs of other people, especially other people of color, including their students and their students' parents and communities. Some of that I also discuss in the next subsection, though it certainly falls under this sort of labor.

Alex notes feeling pressured to strive for perfection and needing to understand every level of educational bureaucracy, which can be burdensome for new faculty. Every proposed change to the curriculum entails engaging in detailed research to design a new lesson and explain its execution even though she knows this proposal may easily be rejected at any stage along the chain of command. Although this onerous process evokes feelings of impostor syndrome, she states that these feelings and the need to be perfect motivate her "because there is no room to not be excellent" (155). This outlook reflects how negative educational experiences can continue to affect students of color as they themselves become educators, causing them to feel a persistent academic performance burden, that sense of pressure to perform well to avoid being stereotyped by others (see Owens and Lynch).

In addition, Alex feels the added pressure to validate her curricular changes through the lens of her own prior experiences as a student of color or else risk having them discounted. White educators are not required to share subjective information when adapting their lessons; critical justification for using a culturally-sustaining curriculum will usually suffice. Yet Alex must provide an insider perspective that may conjure painful memories or violate personal boundaries. She admits that each time she must do so, she pays "an emotional toll" (155), especially since she must also ensure that she frames her story in a way that proves acceptable to her audiences. Hence, even when participating in mentoring programs intended to promote the success and retention of teachers of color, said teachers still face adverse barriers and bureaucracy and must take on significant amounts of labor that are rendered "invisible" to white peers, mentors, and administrators because they do not have to do it or do not acknowledge that they require it of people of color.

Rupsy welcomed additional labor that involved leadership but was told that she did "too much" and proved "too passionate" (156). In today's political climate that demonizes social justice and DEI, these words can be code for causing trouble in schools that want "a well-behaved and good minority" rather than someone whom they view as "inflexible and not very open to hearing other perspectives (that are more aligned with Whiteness)" (Hayes and Juárez 9). Such an environment leads to the labor of navigating invisible benchmarks and inconsistent expectations that suddenly appear for people of color but not for others. Rupsy notes that administrators never seemed to doubt the ability and experience of her white peers or whenever overlooking her supposed lack of experience proved convenient. She volunteered to support a resident and administrators expressed misgivings, but not when it came to her white male colleague. She signed up for a professional development course to improve upon her skills and was reprimanded. In contrast, administrators forced Rupsy to mentor a peer who opposed her culturally-sustaining approach and even threatened to remove her resident unless she agreed to help the openly hostile peer.

Furthermore, they asked her to serve as chair of English language development (ELD) because she speaks Punjabi, despite a lack of training in ELD and her inability to read and write in Punjabi after having already told her that she overextended herself. Thus, while Rupsy's personal goals for advancement were read as excessive, the labor she was assigned was viewed as essential because it proved indispensable to the white institution. Administrators deliberately created emotional labor for her that they didn't for others, obstructing her aspirations, forcing her to contend with a candidly hostile peer, and demanding directorial work for which she had no training.

CENTERING PRIVILEGED STAKEHOLDERS

Here, I want to emphasize this specific aspect of the section title: "within and beyond the institution." Just as educators of color aiming to make change must focus their attention on the communities that they are part of, in and outside of the academy, so too must they confront the myriad pressures they face across these locations. Fear is a constant problem, as teachers may be targeted by people both inside (staff and/or leadership) and outside of the school (parents), leading to the loss of their jobs or threats to their physical safety and certainly to isolation within the institution. Alex again cites the time-consuming process regarding curriculum change, especially as the sole advocate for a social justice-centering approach. Rupsy states that her co-teacher left the classroom when she shared a podcast featuring two men from the LGBTQ+ community, and both Alex and Rupsy note that conservative views about LGBTQ+ people led to policy restructuring within the district. Such conditions lead to LGBTQ+ students feeling unsafe at school, poor academic performance compared to straight peers, and a reluctance to report harassment (Hall and Rodgers). Concurrently, both also report higher expulsion rates among Black and Latinx students who might be assisted by culturally-affirming curricula. Meanwhile, they note that parents and fellow teachers worry about being *too* inclusive.

Their stories reveal that rather than provide a space where educators can safely teach students, institutions reify the political ideologies of more vocal community members even when those views interfere with vital instruction, including teachers and staff who do not leave their intolerant beliefs at the door. And, since school funding is tied to policy, administrators ensure that staff follow the rules, no matter how unfair or discriminatory, providing them ample rhetorical cover. When complicit in unjust action, they can simply say that they're just following the law or the wishes of parents and other community stakeholders.

INVOKING INSTITUTIONAL MEMORY

Leon points out that leadership opportunities are few and far between for junior faculty and graduate students, but for change to occur at the institutional level, leadership positions must be open to people at diverse levels of experience for several reasons. Tenure track faculty are evaluated on their research, teaching, and service, but with service weighing the least at most institutions, many prefer not to spend time and energy on an undervalued aspect of the job; non-tenure track faculty, who are evaluated on teaching and service, may prefer to dedicate time to service to the institution that proves more legible to administrators than service to the community.[2] But next-gen

---
2. Of course, not everyone makes these same kinds of decisions and thankfully, as Leon indicates, some institutions do value service and community work.

faculty poised to make change do value community service work, recognizing that the academic trappings that bring the cultural capital we're supposed to value above all else allow us to do what matters, because as Carmen Kynard reminds us, "that's the job, not the work" (19). And they have the drive and idealism to see it through—only to be told "that's not how it's done," "you don't have the experience needed," and "you don't know how things work around here yet." Using these pretexts, senior faculty refuse to mentor and make room for junior faculty who have fresh ideas and knowledges but need support.

Moreover, given the historical lack of faculty—and still dismal numbers—diverse perspectives in leadership are indispensable; otherwise, leadership based on seniority alone is likely to be monolithically white, as is institutional memory. Leon shows how things can change when supported in taking on a leadership role when hired as an assistant professor. Provided with start-up funds, she founded a new National Writing Project site that invites "the values preached and practiced by anti-racist, critical, and feminist scholars" and "community voices, knowledges, and experience" to ground her administrative identity and that of the program (166). The institutional memory that translates into "we [people in the institution] have always done it this way" must be dislodged to make way for "we [people in the institution and the community] can do things differently."

PRACTICING STRATEGIC REDIRECTION

Along with describing the devaluation of service work, Leon highlights how faculty mentors attempted to redirect her attention towards research and teaching during her PhD program without explaining how her interest in service could prove vital to both. She states that "it was the 'service' work of working with and for the community that consistently and effortlessly brought me both the joy and motivation to complete our program," and yet when she brought this up, this connection was ignored rather than encouraged (170). The general assumption is that all graduate students should wish to work at "prestigious" R1 institutions whose sole focus is producing research rather than serving their communities. However, service can provide "an alternate route by which to diversify notions of scholarship and to challenge individuals in gate-keeping roles" (Holling and Rodriguez 57). Still, faculty at Leon's graduate institution either ignored or were unaware of how community-engaged work could lead to fruitful publications. They also overlooked the valuable experience such work afforded. She emphasizes that her service commitments allowed her to hone her "most marketable skills" (171).

Additionally, had she taken the advice to redirect her focus, she would not have been able to develop her deeply DEI-centered administrative skills. The alternative, then, would have been to develop her praxis exclusively within the academy, immersed in its whitestream values, which may have ultimately proven the point of such so-called counsel—reaffirming the hard boundaries between the institution and the community it claims to serve. Corroborating this impression, Leon shares that she discovered that the upper administration overseeing the administrator of the Wildcat Writers deliberately underfunded them. Just as Leon was expected to redirect her focus off community-engaged work, her administration the faculty member redirected vital funding away from the program. Strategic redirection is a nicer way of saying stolen time and stolen money.

Counterstrategies: Learning from the Authors

The strategic moves outlined above and illustrated by the next-gen authors featured here are designed to wear out potential changemakers, to exhaust them until they surrender or become convinced that transformation is impossible. But that isn't true—the process is deliberately *made* difficult by actors dedicated to upholding the status quo, either because it proves familiar, or they have bought into the system. Nevertheless, just as the authors depict some of the strategies these actors use, the authors' works also indicate counterstrategies for defying said schemes. In doing so, they become coalitional mentors to us readers, who can glean vital wisdom from their experiences, no matter how far along in our careers we find ourselves.

FIND/FOUND A COMMUNITY OF RESISTANCE

Changemakers may find themselves isolated by circumstance or by design, and isolation makes people vulnerable. It also deprives individuals of vital mentorship, camaraderie, and support at their institution. Building a community of resistance with like-minded individuals (see Hays et al.) provides a space where people of color can have frank discussions about race and racism, engage in pedagogical problem-solving, and recommend useful frameworks for confronting microaggressions—for example, Walton et al. 4 R's (see Arzu-Carmichael and Hannakachl). These communities should include students and folks beyond the institution, countering the exclusivist time-space hegemony maintained by the academy.

INVOKE DIFFERENT MEMORY STREAMS

Institutional memory only accounts for those who have always been granted a place at the table, but community members beyond the institution also have a wealth of knowledge to share if only they were heeded. Leon explains how the local community coordinator's connections helped her organize politically in anticipation of policy changes. By building mutually beneficial coalitions with community partners, changemakers can learn from communities themselves what communities really need rather than having institutions make paternalistic assumptions.

REDEFINE "STAKEHOLDERS"

Along those lines, we must establish a relational view of community stakeholders, and we must be uncompromising in upholding that view. The institutional apathy illustrated above hinges on purportedly prioritizing the needs of the community, but who counts as community must change. When we are told that it's not the time to center our needs (Arzu-Carmichael and Hannakachl), what keeps our students safe (Hays et al.), or what brings us joy (Leon), the definition of community does not include us or the people we value.

CULTIVATE NEGOTIATION SKILLS

Negotiation is taken to mean discussion but has more to do with safely navigating difficult rhetorical circumstances. These skills can be critical for people of color, especially as we strive for change. When people are working together, disagreements may require conflict resolution based on respect and genuine listening (Leon), but these skills are also advantageous in balancing any program's aims with community members' needs and goals. They foster flexibility, needed when we must adapt our praxis to diverse institutional/service/community contexts. These skills also prove critical when attempting to disrupt the whitestream status quo by discussing race openly in teacher preparation as suggested by Hays et al. Forthright training about race, racism, and white supremacy is an absolute must to break the illusion of white innocence that asks people of color to set their real selves and safety aside to preserve white comfort (Arzu-Carmichael and Hannakachl). We are typically the ones asked to take on this work and to deal with the recalcitrant folks who don't want to hear it, so negotiation here can mean anything from taking a hard line with such people, protecting your well-being and asking the department to find someone else to do it, or asking for proper skills-based compensation.

FOLLOW THE MONEY

Learning to follow the money is important because when institutions start to call for budget cuts, community-based work and other programs deemed "not essential" to the basic curriculum are the first to go–and we know what programs they mean. Apparently, one also never knows when money is being hidden (Leon)! Becoming familiar with internal and external sources of funding and learning how to present the numbers to different stakeholders also provides community partners with valuable work experience, especially those who are returning to the workforce after a long absence.

Some may tell you that there's no changing things. Some may say that you can buy yourself time by taking on the academy's hegemonic norms even if for a time. That won't work for a lot of us, and a lot of us don't want to buy in anyway. The next-gen authors speaking out here illustrate precisely what's at stake in this struggle and why we must work together to fight for change now. Change takes hard but loving work done in community; no one person can do it alone. You need people who have your back. But change also requires cultivating careful, critical listening skills. Those of us further along the career track should remember that early-career scholars have much to teach us, too, and that we would do well to listen reciprocally.

Works Cited

Basford, Tessa E., Lynn R. Offermann, and Tara S. Behrend. "Do You See What I See? Perceptions of Gender Microaggressions in the Workplace." *Psychology of Women Quarterly*, vol. 38, no. 3, 2014, pp. 340–49.

Carey, Tamika L. "Necessary Adjustments: Black Women's Rhetorical Impatience." *Rhetoric Review*, vol. 39, no. 3, 2020, pp. 269–86.

Carlsruh, Rachel, and José F. Gutiérrez. "White Intellectual Alibies in Use: A Critical Analysis of Preservice Teachers' Rhetoric." *Exploring New Ways to Connect: Proceedings of the Eleventh International Mathematics Education and Society Conference*. Edited by D. Kollosche, Tredition, 2021, pp. 349–58.

González, Juan Carlos. "Academic Socialization Experiences of Latina Doctoral Students: A Qualitative Understanding of Support Systems That Aid and Challenges That Hinder the Process." *Journal of Hispanic Higher Education*, vol. 5, no. 4, 2006, pp. 347–65.

Griffin, Kimberly A., Jessica C. Bennett, and Jessica Harris. "Analyzing Gender Differences in Black Faculty Marginalization through a Sequential Mixed-Methods Design." *New Directions for Institutional Research*, vol. 2011, no. 151, 2011, pp. 45–61.

Hall, William J., and Grayson K. Rodgers. "Teachers' Attitudes toward Homosexuality and the Lesbian, Gay, Bisexual, and Queer Community in the United States." *Social Psychology of Education*, vol. 22, 2019, pp. 23–41.

Hayes, Cleveland, and Brenda Juárez. "There Is No Culturally Responsive Teaching Spoken Here: A Critical Race Perspective." *Democracy and Education*, vol. 20, no. 1, 2011, pp. 1–14.

Holling, Michelle A., and Amardo Rodriguez. "Negotiating Our Way through the Gates of Academe." *Journal of Latinos and Education*, vol. 5, no. 1, 2006, pp. 49–64.

Kynard, Carmen. "'All I Need Is One Mic': A Black Feminist Community Meditation on the Work, the Job, and the Hustle (and Why So Many of Yall Confuse This Stuff)." *Community Literacy Journal*, vol. 14, no. 2, 2020, pp. 5–24.

Mapping Police Violence. 2025, mappingpoliceviolence.org/.

Meikle, Paulette A., and Lekeitha R. Morris. "University Social Responsibility: Challenging Systemic Racism in the Aftermath of George Floyd's Murder." *Administrative Sciences*, vol. 12, no. 1, 2022, pp. 1–19.

Molock, Sherry Davis, and Benjamin Parchem. "The Impact of COVID-19 on College Students from Communities of Color." *Journal of American College Health*, vol. 70, no. 8, 2022, pp. 2399–2405.

Ore, Ersula. "Pushback: A Pedagogy of Care." *Pedagogy*, vol. 17, no. 1, 2016, pp. 9–33.

Owens, Jayanti, and Scott M. Lynch. "Black and Hispanic Immigrants' Resilience against Negative-Ability Racial Stereotypes at Selective Colleges and Universities in the United States." *Sociology of Education*, vol. 85, no. 4, 2012, pp. 303–25.

Yosso, Tara J. "Whose Culture Has Capital? A Critical Race Theory Discussion of Community Cultural Wealth." *Race Ethnicity and Education*, vol. 8, no. 1, 2005, pp. 69–91.

SECTION 3

On Not Getting Hustled

Introduction to Section 3

ERIC A. HOUSE

My daughter was born one week before our new graduate assistant orientation was set to begin at my institution, which itself was about a week before the start of the fall semester. America's infatuation with the unpaid family medical leave act (FMLA) made it such that both my spouse and I could not take extended leave and financially support ourselves, so I decided to not take time off for the fall and try my best to manage my new family dynamic with a new academic year. I'm sure I was there at orientation, and I'm sure I was there to start the fall semester, but I could not tell you what I said, what I presented, or what I promised to do. In fact, many of the memories from that fall semester continue to escape me. I have to take a moment to acknowledge my positionality since I was not the birthing parent and since I had the protections afforded by my position as tenure-track faculty (Ana Ribero will invite readers to think about the ways in which gendered dynamics surrounding parenting in the academy leave much to be desired; Anicca Cox's chapter in this collection invites us to consider the material conditions of NTT faculty in our institutions). So, I wasn't recovering physically in the same ways, I didn't have the same sorts of social expectations that Ribero in this collection will remind us of, I had the benefits of job security, and I wasn't navigating problematic material teaching conditions in the same easy that Cox addresses in her piece. Yet, I still struggled mightily

---

https://doi.org/10.7330/9781646428007.s003a

with work/life balance in ways that made my personal and professional spaces both seem like an impossibility since they both demanded time and energy that was need for the other. This section recognizes that the aforementioned pressures are multiplied for those who inhabit positions that are less visible. As a response to the pressures and impossibilities presented by academia's personal and professional split, this section highlights the types of people who inhabit situations and locations that have historically been neglected by the university.

An important part of this collection's argument for new perspectives on leadership in the academy is recognizing that the university's models for leadership have privileged a competitive individualist ethos, one that promotes a toxic work culture supported by a patriarchal, white, middle-class framework. The critiques of this framework are vast; apart from the previous sections in this collection that relay narratives of institutional shortcomings as well as highlight various models for resistances within and beyond, we find scholarship across the disciplines that remind us of the varied forces impacting our labor conditions. Carmen Kynard brings our attention to the white norms that set expectations and possibilities in the academic workspace, stating, "Black folk cannot readily find themselves in most university spaces (outside of the HBCUs) and non-profit funding cultures so they have to understand rather quickly where the institution ends, where their own lives and minds begin, and not expect a centering unless by way of tokenism" (19). Kynard urges us to always keep the distinction between the job and the work, between the institutions we find ourselves in and within those in which we claim community, because, as she makes clear, "the conflation of the job and the work . . . is only possible for those groups sanctioned within the terms of a default white norm and privilege. It is easy to see the job as your work when the people and the culture around you are YOU" (19).

One might also emphasize neoliberalism's emphasis of "economy" as governing rationality, where labor is defined as human capital and where competition replaces exchange as the essence of the market (Brown 36). As Wendy Brown argues, "[human] capital's constant and ubiquitous aim, whether studying, interning, working, planning retirement, or reinventing itself in a new life, is to entrepreneurialize its endeavors, appreciate its value, and increase its rating or ranking" (36). There is no community within this frame; there is only the individual competing for market viability.

Kynard and Brown offer two moments to reflect on the forces that impact our labor conditions in the university, and while there is much more to say and cite, these two arguments might provide an adequate intro to the arguments raised in this last section. Within both Kynard and Brown's arguments is an emphasis on the impossibility of community as they both acknowledge that our institutions privilege an individualized, economized, white, patriarchal subject as the ideal participant. One must either fit within this frame or sacrifice other aspects of their lives to try to fit. Yet, those who try to sacrifice aspects of their lives aren't guaranteed success, thus placing them in a precarious situation. Chapters in this section are committed to recognizing and calling out moments where these problematic guiding logics create labor impossibilities. Wendy Hesford, Adela C. Licona, and Christa Teston remind us that such recognition by itself is not always enough, yet they do invite new speculations and open up new possibilities for becoming and belonging (15–16).

This section invites new speculations and imagines new possibilities for becoming and belonging by telling three different stories of toxic work culture in the university. In chapter 7, Ana Ribero critiques patriarchal ideologies that force academic mothers into precarious positions as she advocates for a mother-scholar frame to impact and influence university labor expectations. In chapter 8, Brad Jacobson exposes issues of labor productivity in an argument for a "slower academy." Tom Hong Do wraps up the conversation in chapter 9 as he utilizes the term "cultural taxation" to highlight the emotional labor required from BIPOC faculty as they navigate institutional racism within the academy.

While they expose different aspects of institutional toxicity, each chapter is unified through their critiques of the conditions of labor possibility and visibility in the university. One of the major issues explored is the imagined barrier that separates the personal from the professional, a point introduced and further discussed in Ribero's chapter. This imagined barrier assumes that we must spend all our energy and attention on institutional production and administration, leaving no space or possibility for life outside of our profession. It assumes that our vocation must become our whole identity, in which case we are fulfilled through our production. Either that, or we must already come to the university with an excess of time, energy, and resources to effectively have a split between the personal and professional, an idea that limits the type of person who can participate and limits the type of work that counts within the profession. While privilege has historically been a prerequisite for entering the professoriate, shifting demographics and the realization of new-majority students in universities across the nation indicate that this model is no longer sufficient. As Do's chapter warns us, the next generation of leadership must recognize these shifts and work towards transforming the overall culture of academia so that the responsibility of creating and maintaining workspaces sensitive to difference doesn't fall solely on BIPOC faculty and staff.

The chapters in this section seek to dismantle the imagined barrier between the personal and professional by arguing that effective university workspaces in this next generation must operate holistically. They argue that leaving out aspects of our home lives, ignoring the social implications of our identities, and ignoring global realities places workers in impossible and precarious situations, and forcing faculty to do so is to further the project of a white patriarchal capitalism. In fact, we cannot work effectively in these institutions when we are either forced to neglect aspects of our lives or operate from precarious positions.

Each chapter in this section asks us to rethink the impossibility (maybe even the absurdity, in some situations) of privileging individualism and demanding increased production of faculty while simultaneously refusing to support faculty work and refusing to acknowledge faculty life outside of work. As you engage with the final three chapters, consider the following takeaways centered on boundaries and community building to help you conceptualize the personal and professional dynamic.

Moving from Microaggressions to Coalitional Actions

NAME AND DEFINE ACTS OF MICROAGGRESSIONS AS YOU WITNESS OR EXPERIENCE THEM. Tom Hong Do reminds us in chapter 9 that agents of power within universities have the capacity to deny the lived experiences of those who are exposed to microaggressions. Often times, microaggressions are pushed aside by claims of ignorance or misinterpreted intentions, yet effectively naming them is an important step towards validating the experiences of those in our institutions who are the most vulnerable.

IDENTIFY POTENTIAL MENTORS AND ALLIES. Whether they be senior colleagues/peers within your home department, or whether they work in other institutional contexts, establishing a community that you can trust is critical in maintaining healthy workspaces. Do, in quoting Ore et al., notes that we have the agency "to fashion professional networks that counter the sense of isolation we often experience" (209). While it does require labor to establish those networks, such labor is imperative in creating habitable workspaces.

Caring Enough to Lead

LEADING WITH AN ABUNDANCE OF TIME AND CARE. Jacobson urges us in chapter 8 to temporally adjust our leadership practices through his calls for a "slower" academy, or an emphasis of time and care in our labor practices.

Resisting the demand for rushed production in our institutions encourages reflective and critical work while simultaneously inviting space for a variety of work-life balance options.

CREATING COMMUNITIES CARE-FULLY. In chapter 7, Ribero calls for a centering of the mother-scholar paradigm as a model that collectivizes care in order to create sustainable caregiving structures within our institutions. As the next generation moves into leadership positions, care-full practices should be an integral part of the leadership foundation, an essential intervention in reshaping the impact of academic leadership.

On Not Getting Hustled

LEARN THE HISTORIES OF YOUR INSTITUTIONAL CONTEXT. Our programs and departments are steeped in constantly shifting and evolving politics. Sometimes those politics and histories are well known, oftentimes they are implicit. As you step into new positions of leadership within your institution, try to uncover the histories and politics surrounding the position by asking questions about collaborators and stakeholders that uncover assumptions and, hopefully, potential tensions to address in your role.

DISTINGUISH BETWEEN THE WORK AND THE JOB. Carmen Kynard's words are the appropriate way to end this section's takeaways since they remind us that the work that brings many of us to the university paradoxically has little to nothing to do with our daily jobs. This is especially true if one doesn't fit in with or subscribe to the white patriarchal middle-class ethos described earlier. While the job might provide leverage, funding, and other forms of support for our work, it also shrouds the impact of those who don't fit the assumed academic identity. This collection believes the next generation of leadership can help in addressing hidden labor and institutional inequities, but until that day comes, guard yourself and your time by setting boundaries around what the job requires, and don't lose sight of the work that initially brought you here.

Works Cited

Brown, Wendy. *Undoing the Demos: Neoliberalism's Stealth Revolution*. Princeton UP, 2015.

Hesford, Wendy S., Adela C. Licona, and Christa Teston. "Introduction: Rhetorical Recalibrations and Response-abilities." *Precarious Rhetorics*. Edited by Hesford et al. Ohio State UP, 2018, pp. 1–18.

Kynard, Carmen. "'All I Need Is One Mic': A Black Feminist Community Meditation on the Work, the Job, and the Hustle (and Why So Many of Yall Confuse This Stuff)." *Community Literacy Journal*, vol. 14 no. 2, 2020, pp. 5–24.

Ore, Ersula, et al. "Symposium: Diversity Is Not Enough: Mentorship and Community-Building as Antiracist Praxis." *Rhetoric Review*, vol. 40, no. 3, 2021, pp. 207–56, https://doi.org/10.1080/07350198.2021.1935157.

7
Mothering in the Academy

Equity, Child Care, and the Tenure Clock

ANA MILENA RIBERO

I had been back to work from maternity leave for almost three months when the pandemic began, and the country shut down. During those months, I had been juggling my childcare and professional duties as a tenure-track assistant professor in the third year of her contract. On Mondays, Wednesdays, and Friday mornings, my three-year-old would go to daycare while my husband would watch the baby, and I would go to work. I was teaching two classes—a graduate seminar and a 200-level writing class. On those days, I would fit in as much work as possible—starting early, working through lunch, and scheduling all my on-campus meetings in between breaks for expressing breast milk that needed to happen every three to four hours. On Tuesdays, Thursdays, and Friday afternoons, I would care for the two boys while my husband went to work. Of course, that wasn't enough time to do all the work I had to do: I was also trying to finish my book manuscript, after all. To make up for lost time, I would work in the evenings after the boys went to sleep. I would sit at the dining room table and prepare the next day's class or review whatever reading I had assigned for my graduate seminar. I remember one night when the baby didn't want to sleep, and my husband was at work, I sat him in his bouncer next to me and read bell hooks out loud to him while he smiled at me. It was a sweet moment, but it also denoted how much the line between my duties as a mother and my work as a professor was blurring. I was either working or taking care of the children or trying to do both. I also worked on Sunday mornings while my husband took care of the kids. He and I didn't really see each other, except when handing off the children for the next shift. I was exhausted. I was afraid. I knew I wasn't doing enough work and felt guilty about it. I was behind on my research. I had extended my tenure clock by one year since having a baby, but I still felt like that wasn't enough. Like I should be doing more. The expectation that I would return to one hundred percent just a few months after giving birth was crushing. My schedule felt unsustainable, yet I was afraid to ask for more accommodations.

My situation was not unique. I realize other people live with such hurried schedules, and I understand the privilege I have as an educated, middle-class person with a partner whose job also has some flexibility, and who has access to childcare for at least one child for at least part-time (full-time childcare was beyond what we could afford at the time). I share this brief insight into my pre-pandemic life to paint a picture of what it's like to be a working parent in academia. It's like having two full-time jobs, neither of which you are doing well, while everyone else seems to be cruising.

Then the COVID-19 pandemic began. When the country went into lockdown in March 2020, my youngest son was five months old, and my oldest was almost four years old. I remember the last "normal" thing I did before the shutdown: take the boys for frozen yogurt where my oldest son proceeded to touch all the yogurt dispensers and prompted me to wonder how we would ever stay safe and healthy. In the panic that overtook the world at the beginning of the pandemic, I started seeing some interesting collective behavioral changes. As people were scrambling to move their classes online, to schedule meetings on Zoom, to deal with trying to work from home while simultaneously doing childcare, the line between home and work began to bend and then broke completely. I noticed that others were starting to experience what I had been living through as a working mother. For the first time since becoming a mother, I felt seen. As more and more people dealt with the push and pull of being an academic parent, the unsuitability of academia for parents became impossible to ignore.

The COVID-19 pandemic widely exposed the obstacles faced by working mothers[1] of young children: the devaluation of our professional labor, unequal division of childcare in the heteronormative home, and discrimination and additional barriers to professional success. While these problems predated the

---

1. While I realize that there are many ways to become a mother, I limit my discussion to issues faced by cis-gendered female mothers who give birth to their babies in order to be able to ground this essay on my own experiences as a cis-gendered female who gave birth to her babies.

pandemic, in the moment that most working parents lost their childcare and were forced to stay home, the issues became almost universal (Tugend). Discussion of the pandemic's deleterious effects on working women even made it to the mainstream, with popular media reporting on the "epidemic of loss" that academic women in particular were experiencing with regards to our professional mobility (Scheiber; Mandavilli).

Scholars have long argued that mothers receive a so-called "motherhood penalty" in hiring and wages, both in and out of academia, because evaluators see women with children as less committed to their profession and less competent in their work (anecdotally, I am one of many women I know who hid their pregnancy while on the academic job market because of the fear of this bias). Indeed, a 2007 study found evidence of hiring and wage discrimination for mothers, while fathers and childless women received no such penalty (Correll et al.). Research has also tracked the effects that lack of accessible full-time childcare has on working women with young children (Brewer et al.). Yet, this chapter approaches the conversation from the specific location of academia and argues that an academic career in particular clashes with the demands of mothering. Drawing on my personal experience and on feminist scholarship about mothering and care, I illustrate how academic mothers have long faced the stigma of the "mother track" while struggling without paid maternity leave or affordable childcare. I forward that, despite the growing attempts to close the gender gap in promotion and tenure, academia continues to assume that workers are "unencumbered" by dependents (Hallstein 3). Additionally, building on the extant literature on the subject, I explore the responsibility of academic leadership to find solutions to this form of academic sexism.

This chapter concludes by providing some possible interventions that must take place in order to make good on university leadership claims about valuing gender equity. I draw on work by women of color feminists who challenge the private/public divide and who perceive the work of mothering as part of a community's responsibility. I provide ideas for implementation, big and small, in the hopes that more people—with and without children—will join the call to restructure how academia sees women and mothers.

Mothering in Academia: The Story So Far

I submitted my monograph manuscript to my editor three days before my second son was born via a scheduled C-section in early October 2019. Reviewer responses arrived in January 2020 requiring substantial revisions that, in a letter to my editor dated January 31, 2020, I promised to complete by the end of summer 2020. On June 30, 2021, I finally sent my revised manuscript to my editor, almost a year later than what I had expected. I can say, with some certainty, that the particular effects that the pandemic had on mothers of young children kept me from being able to even think about my manuscript, especially in those early months.

Research has shown a similar trend. A study of manuscripts submitted to all Elsevier journals between February and May 2020 showed that submission rates actually increased by 30 percent over the same period in the previous year (Squazzoni et al. 7). However, the same study found that women had submitted proportionally fewer manuscripts than men during that period and that the "more junior cohorts of women" were affected the most in terms of their ability to submit manuscripts to Elsevier journals (10). The authors write, "this suggests that the pandemic could have exacerbated existing inequalities by imposing additional obstacles in terms of time and effort investment by women just as the demand for research was growing unprecedentedly" (10). In other words, the existing disproportionate expectations for women in the home with regards to childcare and home care were made worse by the pandemic that led to the lag in publications. These inequalities have long-reaching implications, as the authors note, because those who benefited from the pandemic's rush of article submissions will be the ones who experience the benefits of additional publications with regards to promotion and tenure.

While the disproportionate amount of women's (in opposite sex couples) labor in the home is a contributing factor to the gendered tenure and promotion gap, society's perception of women as mothers and workers is also a culprit. Cynthia Dewi Oka, poet and activist, describes the paradox of mothering as social practice in that being a mother is "culturally idealized (i.e., in a white supremacist way) yet lacking in any social or economic value. It is literally *priceless*" (51). In the US, cultural notions of mothering and working put women at a disadvantage, as the ideal worker is incompatible with our definitions of motherhood. Men who become fathers, on the other hand, may experience a boost in their perception as good workers, as "being a good father and a good employee are part of the 'package deal'" (Correll et al. 1307). Relatedly, Lil Brannon outlines the different expectations that academic fathers (and, I would add, fathers in general) face compared to academic mothers (and mothers in general). She writes that the behaviors of academic fathers are compared to the trope of the absent father—the bar being so low that any attention to the children is seen as exceptional (463).

Further, Brannon explains how the persistent separation between private and public spheres in society perpetuates women's status as the default parent, always relegated to the private sphere regardless of her participation in the (public) workforce. The private/public division is maintained via a silence that is rationalized under the aim of equity: discussing our home lives is seen as risking discrimination and implicit bias. However, Brannon writes, "the academic world discourages talk about our families and home responsibilities and thereby discourages women, who have historically been assigned there, from participating in full academic life" (463). Because women have been historically assigned to the private sphere, our inability to consider its effects on our professional lives creates a gendered disadvantage. Our private duties are not to be considered when we are evaluated for promotion and tenure.

Academia's definition of productivity also helps to exacerbate inequalities for academic mothers by helping to maintain the gendered division of labor in the home. Brannon writes, "notions of responsible work within the university have been based on male models that assume that one has a wife who takes care of everything—home, family, food—and that one can easily work 60-hour weeks for 6 years to create a substantial case for tenure" (464). In this model of productivity, only a scholar who is relying completely on someone else for household labor and childcare can have enough time and energy to produce a strong tenure dossier. Brannon writes this in 1993, and I would like to think that things have changed for women in academia. At least at my institution, talking about family and home responsibilities is not taboo. My department bills itself as family friendly to a fault, struggling to retain queer, childless, and unmarried scholars (an equity issue beyond the scope of this essay). Yet, I think Brannon's point about the tenure clock stands. The work that it takes to achieve tenure in many humanities fields that require the publication of a monograph or equivalent in addition to heavy teaching loads and service requirements is not conducive to the sort of parenting that is preferred in today's society: a model that demands parents to be highly involved in their children's daily activities, schools, media habits, play time, etc.[2] And because academic mothers have very often moved away from extended family and community, there is little to no help available to them in achieving the many daily duties that parenting involves. Mothers end up in the dilemma that Jean-Anne Sutherland refers to as "bad worker or bad mama"— the choice of keeping up with the children and ignoring the pace of academia or keeping up with the pace of academia and ignoring the children (216).

---

2. This sort of parenting is commonly known as intensive parenting and while it may not be the best for parent and child, it has become the norm in the US (Yerkes et al.).

While universities like my own may pay lip service to being pro-family, institutional care often doesn't extend beyond frivolous events like a "bring your child to campus day" or a table with arts and crafts activities at the department's Christmas party. On the contrary, I suggest, many of these "pro-family" events actually put more pressure on the parent (mostly on mothers who are, predominantly, the default parent in the opposite-sex couple) to make time in their schedule to attend these largely social events. Responding to the gender gap in tenure, many universities have adopted tenure-stopping policies that offer a one-year extension in the tenure clock to new parents. However, some policies that help new parents can benefit men more than women. In a study juxtaposing tenure rates in the top fifty economic departments in the US with female-only and gender-neutral tenure clock stopping policies, economists find that "men are 17 percentage points more likely to get tenure in their first job once there is an established gender-neutral clock stopping policy in place, while women are 19 percent less likely. These policies substantially increase the gender gap in tenure rates" (Antecol et al. 2422). One of the reasons behind this, the study finds, is that there are no clear guidelines for how tenure evaluators are examining the "stopped" time. The authors explain that often the stopped time is not discounted from productivity expectations (2425). Because new mothers have an additional burden when birthing and caring for babies compared to fathers (Negraria et al.), new fathers may be able to use the additional tenure clock time to publish in more prestigious journals, whereas new mothers would be unlikely to do so. Antecol et al. write, "in this case, women can even end up worse off if tenure evaluations are made using relative, rather than absolute, standards and the extra time helps fathers enough to raise the tenure bar" (2425). In addition, because it is taboo or even illegal to consider parenting roles in employment decisions, mothers who took the year extension may not have a place to note the reasons behind the extension to tenure reviewers. In a tenure dossier the documents are supposed to speak for themselves, other than the candidate statement that is traditionally no longer than three pages and must address, as per the guidelines of my institution, "the individual's contributions in areas of teaching, advising and other assignments; scholarship and creative activity; diversity, equity and inclusion; and service" ("Dossier Preparation Guidelines 2023–2024").

The discouraging effects of such policies also illustrate the gendered inequalities in academic expectations in teaching and service. In a study on academic mental health during the pandemic, Danielle Docka-Filipek and Lindsey Stone argue that "gender disparities and labor force exit are by no means reducible to the 'private' mothering and caregiving decisions women make. Instead, gender disparities in career advancement should be interpreted in the context of the ongoing gendered burdens of 'public' caregiving, which are constituted primarily by the twin pressures of extensive and intensive expectations for women's service and teaching" (2159). In other words, disproportionate caregiving obligations in the home compound with disproportionate caregiving obligations at work (e.g., teaching, mentoring, and service) to create a particularly precarious situation for academic mothers. This precarity is even more egregious for BIPOC academic mothers.

Rethinking Mothering, Rethinking Caring

I was more fortunate than most during the pandemic. My family was able to stay healthy. While many daycare centers and preschools in my community didn't survive the pandemic closures, my older son's daycare—part of my university's patchwork of early care and education services—reopened to almost-normal operations in August 2020. My university started the 2020 fall term fully remotely, and I attended classes and meetings with my baby on my lap. At that time, it wasn't unusual for someone to have a young child, a barking dog, or a nosey cat interrupt during Zoom calls. The relentless encroachment of personal life into professional life was painfully normalized.

Feminists of color have long forwarded the importance of challenging the private/public binary that devalues private work and places women in that subordinate position. In fact, Patricia Hill Collins coined the term "motherwork" to describe the ways that the mothering practices of communities of color illuminate the blurred lines between private and public. She writes, "I use the term 'motherwork' to soften the existing dichotomies in feminist theorizing about motherhood that posit rigid distinctions between private and public, family and work, the individual and the collective" (47). By arguing that mothering is work that not only influences the realm of the home, but that greatly impacts community survival, Hill Collins emphasizes that the work of mothering must be prioritized even outside of the private sphere. She defines motherwork as a way to understand mothering away from mainstream white feminist constructions that maintain the private/public binary and to account for the ways women of color have practiced mothering throughout US history. She writes, "whether under conditions of the labor exploitation of African American women during slavery and the ensuing tenant farm system, the political conquest of Native American women during European acquisition of land, or exclusionary immigration policies applied to Asian Americans and Latinos, women of color have performed motherwork that challenges social constructions of work and family as separate spheres" (47). Importantly, the concept of motherwork explains the labor that goes into mothering children from oppressed communities whose survival is not a societal priority (Hill Collins 57).

While the contexts for most academic women are different from the subordinated conditions that Hill Collins describes, I propose that the concept of motherwork is useful to challenge definitions of motherhood in academia that reproduce the private/public dichotomy. Because of these notions of motherhood, academia, as a sphere of labor, continues to prioritize patriarchal models of work and productivity that not only devalue mothering, but also conflict with the demands of the sort of motherwork that ensures community survival. This is particularly the case for the most vulnerable among us: BIPOC women faculty on and off the tenure track (Sattar).

Not only should academic communities change the way we look at mothering and the private/public dichotomy, but we also should value the work we do in the private sphere as contributing to the work we do in academia. For this, scholars Hernández-Johnson et al. propose the concept of the Mother-Scholar overlap. They write, "we use the term 'Mother-Scholar overlap' as a way to challenge traditional narratives that emphasize the necessary juggling between the mother and scholar identities, two separate and opposing forces; instead, we believe both those identities are conjoined, empowering [Mother-Scholars of color] and enriching academia and the spaces they inhabit" (129). Symonds LeBlanc et al. define Mother-Scholars as "women, mothers, and academics that intentionally blend these identities as an act of resistance to the academic institutions that often devalue and undersupport their respective maternal and professional roles" (354). Yu et al. propose that "mother-knowledge"—"the ancestral knowledge that has been passed on to [mothers] and that [we] call on, in that role"—can actually be a source of scholarly knowledge that informs our research, teaching, and service (201). When our private and public roles are no longer binary opposites, we can see how being a mother (or a caretaker, or a daughter, or a partner) can be part of what it means to be a scholar.

Evelyn Nakano Glenn locates the problem in the "privatized and gendered caring regime in which families, rather than the larger society, are responsible for caring [for children, the elderly, etc.] and in which women (and other subordinate groups) are assigned primary responsibility for caring" (84). Disrupting the neoliberal imperative for individual responsibility, she argues that care should be seen as a "collective (public) responsibility" so that it doesn't result in isolation and vulnerability for those who do the care work. She defines the vicious cycle of our current care culture, where care work is feminized and, therefore, devalued; this makes it a job left up to vulnerable populations that, in turn, contributes to its devaluation. Nakano Glenn writes, "valuing and recognizing caring would raise the status and rewards of those who engage in it and also increase the incentives for other groups to engage in caring" (94). When care work becomes a social responsibility, it is easier to recognize it as a social contribution "on a par with other activities that are valued, such as working, military service, or community service, regardless of whether caring takes place in the family or elsewhere or as paid or unpaid labor" (Nakano Glenn 88). Premilla Nadasen similarly argues that care work should be recognized for its social contribution. However, instead of calling it "care work," which connotes a level of vocational and emotional labor, she proposes the concept of "social reproduction—defined as sustaining and reproducing human life and maintaining households—a term that centers labor and capitalism" (166). Indeed, mothering and child rearing are not necessarily selfish (or selfless) endeavors: they are forms of work, whether paid or unpaid, that help to reproduce society.

Some Possible Interventions

The pandemic reminded us that administrators, faculty, staff, and students have lives outside of the university. As educators, we were asked to be flexible regarding things like assignment due dates and class attendance. As mentors, we were encouraged to care for students as whole people and to be empathetic to their emotional needs. Post-pandemic, this care model can be expanded to create a more enriching environment for academic mothers that I believe will benefit the entire academic community. In the final few pages of this chapter, I would like to provide some possible interventions that faculty and departmental administrators, as well as university leadership, can make to shape academia into a more equitable place for academic mothers. While not all universities work in the same ways or have similar funding sources, I base my suggestions on the public land-grant university model and hope that these ideas will inspire other faculty and leadership to think about what is possible in their own programs and institutions.[3]

---

3. Some of these ideas originated from a conversation with staff from Oregon State University's Family Resource Center.

COLLECTIVIZING CARE

As Mother-Scholars, we should lean on our ability to create community in order to create collective caregiving structures. Dewi Oka proposes that mothers are uniquely positioned to create these networks of care since "the ethos of mothering involves valuing *in and of itself* a commitment to the survival and thriving of other bodies. It presents a fundamental contradiction to the logic of capitalism, which unmoors us from each other" (52). Mothering involves ensuring the survival of our children above almost everything else. It is an inescapable entanglement that drives a large part of our lives. As Mother-Scholars, we can resist the neoliberalization of the university and the isolation of academic work by entangling ourselves with those around us.

The popular African proverb, "it takes a village to raise a child," simply does not apply to academic parents who for the most part have had to leave our communities and extended families to pursue our careers. This means that we need to build our own village inside and outside of higher education. Mothers' and parents' groups within the university are helpful. They can provide guidance on HR policies and information about available resources to help with the cost of childcare, etc. However, mother groups and networks outside of the university can provide spaces where we can more freely speak our minds about the challenges and joys of being a working mother. Dewi Oka writes, "mothering as revolutionary praxis involves exploring how we might reorganize ourselves to meet common needs in this historical moment, including the capacity to raise and nurture whole, resilient individuals as well as autonomous communities of resistance" (53). Leaning on our shared academic mother (or even Mother-Scholar) subjectivity, we can come together in mothering groups to help each other not only with the daily, material needs of mothering (e.g., watching the kids so we can attend a work event, picking up the children from daycare, having playdates), but also with our common political and activist goals around mothering: supporting abortion rights, demanding gun control, defending gender affirming care for our children, etc.

CHANGES TO PROMOTION AND TENURE

The COVID-19 pandemic highlighted that the private and public spheres are not two completely separate areas of life that we can juggle, and that work/life balance is inaccessible to most academics. Once we admit that what we do outside the university very much affects what we do inside it, and vice versa, we can incorporate that knowledge into how we think about promotion and tenure. Perhaps one of the simplest interventions that can help close the tenure and promotion gender gap is to provide clear guidelines for tenure evaluators to account for any stops in the tenure clock. Many universities are already including guidelines for reviewers to account for COVID-19 related productivity drops. There should be similar standardized guidelines for tenure dossiers of mothers who stopped their tenure clocks because of childbirth or adoption.

Furthermore, if as Nadasen suggests, we define care work as social reproduction work, then the university and everyone in it should be invested in that work. As such, the work of social reproduction should be made visible in promotion and tenure documents. In the candidate statement for tenure, and even in the curriculum vita, a scholar should be prompted to discuss not just what service they are doing for their department, college, university, and profession, but also what work they are doing for their community. In this category, work like childrearing could be legitimated. I gave birth to and cared for two children during my tenure clock time. Concurrently, I published a monograph, attended conferences, mentored graduate students, taught loads of courses, and did all of the other duties that are expected in my position as an assistant professor at a research university. However, that didn't affect how my dossier was evaluated because there was nowhere in my materials that allowed for my social reproduction work to be made visible.

Relatedly, the promotion and tenure process needs to incentivize care work. All university employees should be rewarded for the care work and social reproduction work they do outside the university. Care for the elderly and volunteer work in the community should receive an incentive. Perhaps social reproduction work can contribute to the service load of faculty. Of course, service to the academy is also greatly gendered, with women scholars doing a disproportionate amount of the work. Indeed, Docka-Filipek and Stone write that not only do women faculty "spend greater amounts of time on service per week," but also that the "altruistic service roles" that women take on at higher rates than men have little to no direct reward and are therefore damaging to their career advancement (2160). When we consider the intersection of gender and race, BIPOC women scholars take on an even heavier service load, as we are sought out to serve in diversity, equity, and inclusion (DEI) committees and in mentoring roles for students from underrepresented communities. This means that as we move forward to consider social reproduction work as part of the service load of tenure-track faculty, we must be intentional about how this service work will be equally distributed and highly incentivized. In my department, service is a big part of discussions on labor equity. We are careful to distribute service as equitably as possible so that it doesn't fall on those most vulnerable:

contingent and junior faculty. When service to the community is part of that service load, the conversation about equity can extend to the work of mothering and other forms of social reproduction (e.g., care for the elderly, volunteer work for the unhoused or for LGBTQIA+ youth, etc.).

PRIORITIZING EARLY CARE AND EDUCATION

Importantly, universities must continue to contribute to systems of early care and education (ECE). ECE should not be an afterthought, but instead must be incorporated into the university's strategic plan and part of its fundraising project. Quality ECE is expensive and there is simply no way to pay for it without some sort of subsidy. By quality ECE, I mean a childcare setting that invests in its teachers through fair wages and professional development and in its curricula and materials. Because many public universities are working under tight budgets, it is important that we work to advocate for increased ECE funds from the appropriate state and federal agencies as well as strengthen our foundation's efforts at fundraising for ECE.

FLEXIBLE WORK ARRANGEMENTS

Flextime is already common in many post-pandemic corporate settings, and it is something that we can adapt in universities to assuage the crisis of care. Particularly in institutions that exist in a childcare desert—defined as a community with more than three children for every childcare slot (Pratt and Sektnan)—existing childcare resources can be coordinated with flexible work hours policies to create a schedule that is manageable for parents returning to campus after parental leave. This would require a shift in how the university thinks about returning from leave, allowing returning mothers, for example, to return to campus part-time and use any available childcare, nanny share, babysitter, etc. only for that time, leaving the leftover care services available for another academic parent who also needs them. When the expectation of return shifts to part-time, there is more flexibility about when work can be done to accommodate existing childcare. Academia has always been a somewhat flexible workplace. Without being coded into policy, however, this flexibility can often create inequity, as those who are doing more service and more teaching and mentoring might be less likely to work from home or miss meetings. On the other hand, if this flexibility is extended as a pre-tenure benefit, for example, then it can serve those who need it most. Extending this work flexibility as a pre-tenure benefit would also account for the fact that the time of graduate school and the tenure clock often coincide with a woman's so-called biological clock—the phenomenon that McAlister refers to as the "competing clocks" (219). Despite statistics showing that in some disciplines women who have babies during this time are less likely to earn tenure, for many of us these are also the precious years before we enter the dreaded fertility cliff (Mason et al. 48).

PROTECTING PAID CARE WORKERS

Finally, the university must be invested in protecting paid care workers, including domestic workers who are often Black women and Latinas of precarious socioeconomic and immigration status. The growth of women in the labor force continues to be subsidized by the care work that is most often performed by Black women and Latinas. These workers are usually undercompensated and receive no employment benefits, such as health insurance and retirement planning (Mefferd and Dow). Therefore, childcare workers, particularly domestic care workers, can face financial hardship and are less able to meet basic needs, let alone build and pass down wealth. Building a system of care in academia must intentionally work towards anti-capitalist community care and away from the model of racialized exploitation that perpetuates inequality. Dewi Oka writes that "collectivizing caregiving in our communities is linked to dismantling a capitalist empire that abuses third world women's bodies as part of its infrastructure" (54). My call to assuage the precarious conditions of academic mothers comes with the unequivocal support for the lives and livelihoods of care workers. While the systems that contribute to care worker precarity are complex and numerous, a possible action university leadership can take is to ensure that care providers at all levels have a voice in decision making that affects them. At our institutions, ECE workers should be at the table when deliberations about them are being made, even when those conversations claim to have their best interests in mind. As faculty, we can also support unionizing efforts of university support staff, including care, sanitation, and facilities workers. Considering the needs of care providers along with the needs of children, parents, and universities can lead to more equitable solutions.

Conclusion

I would like to conclude by advocating for leadership to make the complex issue of academic mothering a university priority connected to institutional goals in diversity, equity, and inclusion as well as recruitment and retention. The pandemic taught us about the importance of leadership, yes, but also of allyship. Academic mothers, if we are to move beyond our precarious status in academia, need allies at the highest levels of administration.

Works Cited

Antecol, Heather, et al. "Equal but Inequitable: Who Benefits from Gender-Neutral Tenure Clock Stopping Policies?" *American Economic Review*, vol. 108, no. 9, 2018, pp. 2420–41.

Brannon, Lil. "M[other]: Lives on the Outside." *Written Communication*, vol. 10, no. 3, 1993, pp. 457–65.

Brewer, Mike, et al. "Does More Free Childcare Help Parents Work More?" *Labour Economics*, vol. 74, 2022.

Correll, Shelley J., et al. "Getting a Job: Is There a Motherhood Penalty?" *American Journal of Sociology*, vol. 112, no. 5, 2007, pp. 1297–1338.

Dewi Oka, Cynthia. "Mothering as Revolutionary Praxis." *Revolutionary Mothering: Love on the Front Lines*. Edited by Alexis Pauline Gumbs, China Martens, and Mai'a Williams, PM Press, 2016, pp. 51–58.

Docka-Filipek, Danielle, and Lindsey Stone. "Twice a 'Housewife': On Academic Precarity, 'Hysterical' Women, Faculty Mental Health, and Service as Gendered Care Work for the 'University Family' in Pandemic Times." *Gender, Work, and Organization*, vol. 28, no. 6, 2021, pp. 2158–79.

"Dossier Preparation Guidelines 2023–2024." Oregon State University, 2021, facultyaffairs.oregonstate.edu/faculty-handbook/promotion-and-tenure-guidelines#dossier. Accessed on Nov. 2023.

Hallstein, D. Lynn O'Brien. "Silences and Choice: The Legacies of White Second Wave Feminism in the New Professoriate." *Women's Studies in Communication*, vol. 31, no. 2, 2008, pp. 143–50.

Hernández-Johnson, Monica, et al. "Mothering the Academy: An Intersectional Approach to Deconstruct and Expose the Experiences of Mother-Scholars of Color in Higher Education." *The Chicana Motherwork Anthology*. Edited by Cecilia Caballero, Yvette Martínez-Vu, Judith Pérez-Torres, Michelle Téllez, and Christine X Vega, U of Arizona P, 2019, pp. 129–45.

Hill Collins, Patricia. "Shifting the Center: Race, Class, and Feminist Theorizing about Motherhood." *Mothering: Ideology, Experience, and Agency*. Edited by Evelyn Nakano Glenn, Grace Chang, and Linda Rennie Forcey, Routledge, 1994, pp. 45–66.

Mandavilli, Apoorla. "Could the Pandemic Prompt an 'Epidemic of Loss' of Women in the Sciences?" *New York Times*, 13 Apr. 2021, www.nytimes.com/2021/04/13/health/women-stem-pandemic.html. Accessed on Nov. 2023.

Mason, M. A., et al. *Do Babies Matter? Gender and Family in the Ivory Tower*. Rutgers UP, 2013.

McAlister, Joan Faber. "Lives of the Mind/Body: Alarming Notes on the Tenure and Biological Clocks." *Women's Studies in Communication*, vol. 31, no. 2, 2008, pp. 218–25.

Mefferd, Eve, and Dawn Dow. "The US Childcare System Relies on Women of Color, but Structural Barriers Systematically Disadvantage Them." *Urban Institute*, 14 June 2023, www.urban.org/urban-wire/us-child-care-system-relies-women-color-structural-barriers-systematically-disadvantage. Accessed Nov. 2023.

Nadasen, Premilla. "Rethinking Care Work: (Dis)Affection and the Politics of Caring." *Feminist Formations*, vol. 33, no. 1, 2021, pp. 165–88.

Nakano Glenn, Evelyn. "Creating a Caring Society." *Contemporary Sociology*, vol. 29, no. 1, 2000, pp. 84–94.

Negraria, Daniela Veronica, et al. "Gender Disparities in Parenting Time Across Activities, Child Ages, and Educational Groups." *Journal of Family Issues*, vol. 39, no. 11, 2018, pp. 3006–28.

Pratt, Megan, and Michaella Sektnan. *Oregon's Child Care Deserts 2020: Mapping Supply by Age Group and Percentage of Publicly Funded Slots*, Apr. 2021, health.oregonstate.edu/sites/health.oregonstate.edu/files/early-learners/pdf/research/oregons-child-care-deserts-2020.pdf. Accessed on Nov. 2023.

Sattar, Atia. "Academic Motherhood and the Unrecognized Labors of Non-tenure-Track Faculty Women of Color." *Academe*, vol. 109, no. 2, 2022.

Scheiber, Noam. "Pandemic Imperils Promotions for Women in Academia." *New York Times*, 29 Sept. 2020. www.nytimes.com/2020/09/29/business/economy/pandemic-women-tenure.html. Accessed 13 Nov. 2023.

Squazzoni, Flaminio, et al. "Gender Gap in Journal Submissions and Peer Review During the First Wave of the COVID-19 Pandemic. A Study on 2329 Elsevier Journals." *PLOS ONE*, vol. 16, no. 10, 2021, n.p.

Sutherland, Jean-Anne. "Ideal Mama, Ideal Worker: Negotiating Guilt and Shame in Academe." *Mama PhD: Women Write about Motherhood and Academic Life*. Edited by Elena Evans and Caroline Grant, Rutgers UP, 2009, pp. 213–21.

Symonds LeBlanc, Sarah, et al. "Toward a Communication Theory of Coping: COVID-19 and the MotherScholar." *Atlantic Journal of Communication*, vol. 31, no. 4, 2023, pp. 354–71.

Tugend Alina. "'On the Verge of Burnout': COVID-19's Impact on Faculty Well-Being and Career Plans." *The Chronicle of Higher Education*, 2020, connect.chronicle.com/rs/931-EKA218/images/Covid%26FacultyCareerPaths_Fidelity_ResearchBrief_v3%20%281%29.pdf. Accessed Nov. 2023.

Yerkes, Mara A., et al. "In the Best Interests of Children? The Paradox of Intensive Parenting and Children's Health." *Critical Public Health*, vol. 31, no. 3, 2021, pp. 349–60.

Yu, Min, et al. "Remember. (Re)member. Re-member: Theorizing the Process of Healing, Sustaining, and Transforming as MotherScholars." *Peabody Journal of Education*, vol. 97, no. 2, 2022, pp. 199–211.

8

(Trying to) Take It "Slow"

Navigating Productivity, Parenting, and Academic Life through COVID-19

BRAD JACOBSON

As I revise this chapter, the Trump administration (part 2) has released an executive order limiting grant funding overhead that could serve as the death knell for US higher education as we know it (Bogost). Other orders have been released seeking to close the US Department of Education and to enable immigration officers to enter schools and religious institutions, a major concern in the borderlands city where I live. Recent communication from institutional leaders has been cautious, understandably not wanting to get out ahead of any future court orders or inevitable changes that may occur. But the tone of the messages—essentially, "let's keep our heads down and get the work done"—reminds me a bit too much of my experience working through COVID-19. I am particularly reminded of an email reminding its faculty, staff, and student recipients of the values shared by our "caring, family-oriented" city, but came with a reminder: "Let's expect ourselves to get the work done." The email continued, "we have grants to administer and proposals to write, contracts to process and projects to plan. We will do it differently, but let's just cinch down and get it done."

"Let's just cinch down and get it done." The "just" in that sentence was doing some heavy lifting. Over the next eighteen months, representatives of the university would continually remind faculty and staff to think about the challenges of our times, the toll the virus and lockdown was taking on students, their families, our communities, our city. We should humanize our classes, making for maximum flexibility. But for publishing, for grant-making? "Cinch down" and get it done. This phrasing exemplifies a neoliberal discourse that "alternately coaxes and berates us to 'prove our mettle' or 'shine against all odds'" in an otherwise precarious situation (Anwer, "Academic Labor and the Global Pandemic" 6). As Megha Anwer explained, calls for resiliency ("let's expect ourselves to get the work done") serve as a reminder that regardless of personal, local, or global circumstance, our work rhythm and productivity remain the priority in the neoliberal academy. Clearly, to "cinch down" was what I needed to get that article written or finally send that book proposal during a global pandemic. And if I didn't, would it be because I didn't "cinch" enough?

In this chapter, I reflect on my experiences through COVID-19, what I learned about academic leadership in the neoliberal academy, and possibilities for change. The chapter is presented as brief anecdotes of personal and professional pandemic life paired with analysis about how choices to resist or escape the push to productivity can be reframed as "slow scholarship" or resistance to neoliberal imperatives (Gildersleeve; Mountz et al.). I focus particularly on collaboration and community engagement, two areas of educational leadership often overlooked in a system governed by productivity metrics and rankings. I argue that the next generation of faculty must work together to imagine possibilities for individual and collective action towards an academy that humanizes students and faculty.

The personal anecdotes I include serve two purposes in this piece. First, for me, parenting through COVID-19 illuminated many of the absurdities inherent to the current neoliberal paradigm that guides decision-making across US institutions of higher education. As one headline in *The Atlantic* magazine stated, "parents are not okay" (Sinker). Another: "COVID parenting has passed the point of absurdity" (Moyer). "We are broken," Melinda Wenner Moyer writes, as she navigates school closings and what used to be typical childhood illnesses alongside other parents of young children. These articles were published in 2021 and 2022, after the vaccine rollout was in full swing and many children were back in schools. These pieces and others like them remind readers that, contrary to messaging at my institution and others, we did not go "back to normal" in the fall of 2021. Many lives are still not normal years later. About an hour before writing the first draft of this introduction, I learned that one of my son's friends on his soccer team had tested positive for COVID-19; they had practiced together the night before. If our vaccinated son had contracted the virus again he would likely be ok, but at the time would not have been able to return to school for a week; we would also have been expected to keep our daughter home from daycare, even without symptoms. The potential for disruption loomed, a dark cloud in the distance ready to move in at any time.

Parenting during COVID-19 also disabused me of any neutral notion of the desired "work-life balance" that guides so many faculty workshops and online webinars. From March through August of 2020, there was no school or daycare available, and our household structure took on a peculiar rhythm. I would wake up before the sun, shuffle out of the bedroom, grab whatever leftover coffee from yesterday was awaiting me in the fridge, and try to think for even just a few minutes about doing the kind of research and writing I would need to do in order to keep the tenure-track position I had started only months prior. "I need to make these minutes count," I would tell myself, because at the first sounds of waking humans, all bets were off. After breakfast I would try to steal away for another hour or so, but once my wife's work meetings and consultations for her nine-to-five work started, I was on childcare duty, trying to keep everyone busy and happy, at least until lunch. After toddler nap time—she started walking within the first few weeks of being at home (hooray!)—we were back at it. Work was life, life was work: calling in to faculty meetings while walking a stroller; responding to email while a toddler sings herself to sleep at naptime; students Zooming in from their bedrooms.

While the call to "cinch down" in the email from the university may have come across to me as uniquely misplaced during a global pandemic, I realize my overlapping social positions and relative privilege have made me less likely to recognize the ways where similar discourses have long permeated the academy and other educational settings. Growing up white and male in a comfortable suburb in the Northeastern US undoubtedly socialized me to perform within the "white supremacy culture" of the academy that values individualism, production, and urgency (A4BL). The challenges of navigating the life-work balance of parenthood and academia are also not new concerns, and my efforts and failures to find balance will not be unfamiliar to women and faculty of color who have been making these arguments for decades. Moreover, I surely benefit from the misogyny that grants my fatherhood certain privileges and leeway that motherhood does not. Through the writing of this chapter, I remain cognizant of my various social positions as I engage with alternative discourses and commit myself to promoting a more humane and inclusive academic culture that can account for a range of personal and broader disruptions.

"Slow Scholarship" as Response to Neoliberal Imperative

The discourse encouraging individual persistence, resilience, and self-investment toward growth and productivity that I recognized in my institution's COVID-19 response is rather typical of the market-based, neoliberal discourses that govern current university structures. Neoliberal discourses and the "ranking regime" (Gonzales and Nuñez) of the modern university value individualism and standardization at the expense of collaboration and civic, democratic pursuits. Borrowing from Foucault, Ryan Evely Gildersleeve suggests that neoliberalism is not a governance structure or an organizational system, but a type of "governmentality" that aims to produce orderly subjects. As Gildersleeve writes, "Neoliberalism makes certain truths possible, certain ways of knowing knowable. It creates commonsense" (3). From a Foucauldian perspective, neoliberalism serves to guide the "possibility of conduct" (789) and "structure the possible field of action of others" (790), to frame what ordinary people feel they are able to do. For example, the ideal or successful faculty member in academe excels within the "truths" of the neoliberal university that include the normalization of individualism and relentless production regardless of social or structural conditions. Even the phrase "work-life balance" prioritizes work that "only reinstates/re-inscribes the problem rather than posing a challenge to the imbalance between work and life that most university professors experience" (Anwer, "Work-Life Balance in the Neoliberal University" 53). At a recent faculty development workshop for junior faculty I attended, work-life balance was discussed unironically within a frame of "explosive productivity."

Sean Phelan conceptualizes neoliberalism as a discursive logic that "neoliberalizes the social" by transforming previously social goods into commodities through market-based logics and practices (57). For example, the modern university neoliberalizes academic life through discursive logics of "excellence," competition, and market-based reforms, among other common-sense truths. Importantly, these social logics have material consequences. Some effects of neoliberal logics felt in academe include the corporatization of governing structures that have centralized power in administration and created an employee/employer power imbalance at the expense of shared governance (Gonzales and Nuñez; Martell), and a culture of individualism and self-servingness that exists in tension with more democratic goals. Citing examples like citation index ratings and academic awards that mark a successful academic entrepreneur in the neoliberal academy, Gildersleeve writes, "competitive entrepreneurialism fashions the ethics of our time. On our own we succeed, or we fail. And on our own we must succeed against one another or else we fail" (2). The neoliberal imperative toward individual success and production has also infiltrated university budgeting, even at public institutions, such that faculty are often responsible for deriving supplementary income from external grants and contracts. This trend toward self-promotion and personal fundraising, also known as "academic capitalism," further entrenches competition and distances next-gen faculty from civic, leadership, and equity efforts (Covarrubias and Quinteros; Kezar et al.). Again, the incentive structures of the neoliberal academy construct the ideal subject by framing the possibilities of their actions.

Because neoliberalism is a discursive phenomenon and a name for an ongoing social order, not a set of policies or a specific governing structure, Phelan suggests it must be continually recognized and acted upon, not simply critiqued. To paraphrase Foucault, neoliberal logics must be refused. The "slow" movement has emerged as one such approach to actively work against the encroachment of neoliberalism in academic life. Drawing analogs from the "slow food movement" that seeks to challenge the "frantic pace and standardization of contemporary culture" (Berg and Seeber xviii), the slow movement in academia calls for strategies and practices that resist the market-based desires of the corporate university and the feelings of competition, isolation, and anxiety that result.

Berg and Seeber use a central text of the slow food movement, "Fast Food Nation," as an example to remind readers that fast food has not only changed the way people eat, but also the way the US has structured agriculture and the landscape, the economy and workforce, and even popular culture; whether or not a person frequently hits a drive-thru, we are all living with the consequences of fast food in our lives. Berg and Seeber see similarities in university life. The corporatization of US institutions of higher learning goes beyond the "supermarket" model of research that seeks speed and standardization and "speeds up and instrumentalizes research as well as objectifies those who produce knowledge and the 'subject' studied" (58) to change the ways faculty interact with each other and the institution. In universities organized under increasingly hierarchical, corporate governance models, faculty begin to act not like community members or citizens, but as employees. The lack of community and shared purpose can impact all elements of our professional work, including research, teaching, service, and leadership. In fact, rising publication expectations and a related de-emphasis on service and leadership are two of the largest factors discouraging new faculty from taking on leadership roles and investing in campus communities (Kezar et al.). To return to Berg and Seeber's metaphor, whether or not a person interacts regularly with a US institution of higher education, we are all living with the consequences of the neoliberal academy.

While some writers have emphasized the reduction of stress and renewed joy associated with the slow professor movement (Berg and Seeber), others point out that in addition to serving as a strategy for individual benefit and personal satisfaction, slowness can function as a political philosophy and a framework for action (Martell; Mountz et al.). Mountz et al. argue that "slowing down represents both a commitment to good scholarship *and* a feminist politics of resistance to the accelerated timelines of the neoliberal university" (1238, emphasis in original). They suggest a turn toward "care-full scholarship" to counter the speed and commodification of modern academic life. For these scholars, a care-full approach is about care for our students and ourselves in institutions that devalue such practices (1239), and care in scholarship that engages in advocacy, engages different publics, and pursues personally and politically meaningful work, instead of quickly moving on to the next project. Slow, to these authors, is "about structures of power and inequality" and "about cultivating caring academic cultures and processes" (1238). Alongside practical strategies like attending to email less often, they call for more ambitious goals like collective organizing and engaging with others across levels and institutions to work toward reconceptualizing university time. An emphasis on power relations serves as a reminder that slow is not just about time and output—after all, one can work "fast" in a joyful way—but about who controls time and how. Work is not in itself a bad thing, but it is autonomy over work that can animate the slow movement in academia (Martell). Creating a more just university is thus about calling attention to not only how and how much academics work, but how we work and interact with one another and within broader systems of power relations.

Childhood Interrupted

MARCH 2020

Sitting down for breakfast. Our son tells us he had a dream. A kindergarten friend was holding the coronavirus in their hand. They gave it to him.

It's extended "spring break" as the city, university, and local K–12 schools try to adjust the plans under "safe at home" guidelines. We bring long rolls of butcher paper out to the driveway for some painting time. He makes a sign in his large kindergarten font that soon will hang from the front door: "Monsters stand here."

He makes masks out of construction paper, tells us—his mom, baby sister and I—these masks give us a special monster power. The sign out front keeps away the bad men at night, he tells us, but if they were to somehow get in the house, we'll just put on our masks and get them.

It doesn't take a psychoanalyst to figure out what's going on here. Our five-year-old is experiencing trauma at a daily pace. He doesn't go to school, where he has thrived ever since we moved him to a new city to follow my academic path. He doesn't see his friends other than via FaceTime, so he can't do the things kids do when there are no parents around: wrestle, pretend, poop jokes. Instead, he's fearful of what surrounds us.

Stories of Slowness (If Necessary and Accidental) on the Tenure Track

As I consider my experience as a faculty member on the tenure track at a research university during the long tail of the COVID-19 pandemic, I think about the choices I made to stay invested, to believe that continuing my work in writing studies could mean something while raising young children during a global pandemic. I invested in teaching. I worked on building and sustaining relationships with colleagues. Collaboration, shared goals, immediate stakes. While I see this retrospectively as a care-full approach to my work, I was worried, rightfully so, that these professional survival choices would not necessarily be "counted" in promotion and tenure review. As much as I tried to remind myself to be present with my family during this challenging time, to do the work that brought me joy and served my students and community, I would be lying if I said that guilt about not doing *enough* and falling behind on the tenure track did not keep me up some nights. As I (and many others) continue to struggle with getting "back to normal," I want to sit within this tension and ask questions about what a humanizing leadership approach might look like in higher education, and how it might encourage work with impact beyond corporatized accountability mandates. Here I return to my story of pandemic academic life and share how a nascent understanding of slow—and a leadership that encouraged slow, care-full labor—may have changed my perspective and potentially my well-being in a challenging time.

Prioritizing Collaboration

In the months before COVID-19, I had begun to discuss a research project with a new colleague I met at a grant funding presentation on campus. We bonded over our shared love of and concern for Philadelphia schools—where we both worked and unknowingly overlapped for a few years—and my colleague proposed a research project studying the effects of standardized testing on high school writing opportunities for the multilingual, multinational population of El Paso. We met a few times and began a preliminary data analysis.

When we were sent home in March of 2020 with some data gathered and only a cursory Google Sheets analysis, we had to choose whether to continue the project in our limited time or focus on our independent research activities. We decided to keep going. As parents with elementary-aged children, my colleague and I had shared text messages concerning what we knew about school closures and how we were occupying our time, and I think we both realized we would need to have accountability to others to move forward academically. We scheduled a weekly one-hour meeting, during which we planned to discuss the project, divide tasks, and set goals. In reality, on Wednesday mornings we mostly talked. We would share what shows our kids were watching, new recipes we were making, and how we were coping. As the weeks went by and we reported on what little work we were accomplishing on this project and others we needed to work on, a creeping guilt crept in. I had so little time, so little mental and emotional space, to work and write; was I "wasting" my time on this collaboration? Shouldn't I be working on the single-authored manuscript I had been struggling to revise during the fall semester? Shouldn't I be continuing that book proposal I would need to submit to earn tenure? Instead, I leaned into collaboration. My colleague and I continued our weekly meetings and, in time, made what felt like progress on our project.

Around this time, I had also received an email from my dissertation advisor asking me and another colleague, a good friend from graduate school, if we would like to propose a chapter responding to a call in *Writing Spaces*, the open access textbook for composition students and teachers. None of us had the time, of course, but we decided to schedule a Zoom meeting anyway to check in with each other and throw around some ideas. As with my other collaboration, we set up weekly meetings leading up to the proposal deadline. Then, when our proposal was accepted, we met weekly through the summer as we drafted our manuscript. These Zoom calls were working meetings and valuable relational sessions. We would spend a few minutes (or an hour) talking about life in our households and university decision-making before delving into whatever was on our writing plan for the week. We made slow and steady progress, met the deadline, and eventually published the chapter. What started as a response to an adverse situation and a reason to connect more regularly with trusted friends and colleagues in a stressful and difficult time turned into a "countable" product.

As I write this, I am aware that I may be coming off as one of *those people*. You know, the "I did so much during the lockdown" people. But I certainly did not feel that way at the time. I saw my social media feeds fill with colleagues' stories of productive writing days in the "quiet" of the pandemic, and I felt panic-stricken and inadequate. I read that this productivity talk was just "noise—denial and delusion" (Ahmad), but the competitive commonsense of tenure and promotion was ever-present: I felt like I was falling behind. Making things worse, in conversation with a supportive colleague and mentor I learned that my senior colleagues often valued single-authored publications more than collaborations. When recently completing my annual performance review—a key requirement of the neoliberal university's accountability mandate—I realized that the university asks for percentages of contribution for each collaborative endeavor, a practice that disregards the labor of collaboration that can often be more work than working individually. Again, the neoliberal logic wins out: it counts *more* if you can do it by yourself.

Slow reframes collaboration as a commitment to purpose and pleasure. Berg and Seeber write about collaboration as an approach that combines politics—a refutation of the individualist mandate of the corporate university—with the pleasure of working with and thinking with others. The emphasis on relationality in my own collaborations also placed an emphasis on self-care in a turbulent time. Mountz et al. argue that cultivating space to care for ourselves, our colleagues, and our students is "a political activity when we are situated in institutions that devalue and militate against such relations and practices" (1239). These writers encourage me to reframe my own collaborative work during the covid lockdown as care-full scholarship, rather than work that took me away from my "real" research agenda. Like Mountz and her colleagues, my collaborations were "rich, enjoyable, and rewarding rather than stressful or harmful" (1244), even if my colleagues and I did, at times, move relatively quickly to meet a deadline. By foregrounding collaborative research during a time of uncertainty and struggle, I was perhaps subconsciously focusing on myself. Looking back, I see this collaborative scholarship as much about building and maintaining interpersonal relationships as investment in the project.

Schooling Interrupted

AUGUST 2020

>It's the first day of virtual first grade. We've set up our son's room for class sessions because our toddler still doesn't have daycare and she's attracted to screens

like a moth to a flame; he'll need to close his door to do school. A kid-sized table sits in the corner of his room, with headphones, markers, pencils, a small dry-erase board. There's a small chair, but he prefers to kneel on the floor. The school provided iPads we picked up last week, masked and outdoors.

Class starts and the teacher's smiling face fills the screen. She wants to go around the "room" and do introductions. Our son is one of the first to be called on, but she doesn't know his name yet and he doesn't understand the instructions. He crawls into bed and pulls the sheets over his head.

Virtual first grade got better, surprisingly so, due to the efforts of a dedicated and talented teacher, but there was always the possibility my online teaching or my wife's meeting would be disrupted by a call from the other room: "I can't find my glue!" "I need a pencil sharpener!" "I don't understand the directions!" "Where are my markers?" Around 11 am every day I would drive to pick up a lunch tray in the pick-up lane at the school—a comfort in these times—and make sure he logged back in on time for the afternoon classes. At the end of every day, we uploaded pictures to an app that everyone was learning how to use on the fly, even the designers who seemed to be making updates three times a week. No after school activities and a full day on the computer screen made going outside at 3 p.m. a priority most days. "Back to normal," indeed.

Community Engagement as Joyful Practice

As stretched thin as we were in my household, I was determined to create a positive online learning experience for students in my English education classes. As an instructor of mostly preservice teachers, I had already felt a need to create meaningful, engaging class sessions so that the future teachers would be inspired to do the same for their students; now, in an era of online learning, I felt that pressure even more.

One way I knew to engage university students was through partnerships with local schools. As a graduate student, I had been a co-leader of a high school–university partnership program, and I wanted to build something similar in my new position. Prior to the pandemic, in the fall of 2019, a colleague connected me with a local high school teacher who seemed interested, and we got along well. I visited her class in December, and we made plans to connect our courses in the spring. We would focus on digital testimonio, a social justice–oriented genre that fit both the high school curriculum for research-based argument and the course learning outcomes for a multimodal composition and pedagogy course I would be teaching with English education majors.

The collaboration started with great promise. My class of future secondary teachers visited the high school for an observation before we introduced the project, and we had a class meeting together on campus a week before spring break in March. On the lawn outside a campus museum, high school and college students shared pizza and worked in "story circles" to offer feedback on the initial drafts, asking clarifying questions, offering encouragement, and beginning to conceive of the research and visuals that may accompany the personal narrative. We intended to meet again in April to share drafts and talk about the development of the digital video, but we also knew a closure seemed imminent due to the rapid spread of COVID-19.

As the local schools and universities shifted to improvised online learning, the collaboration sputtered but did not end. We were unable to meet again synchronously, but students posted their digital testimonios online and offered feedback to each other. My class scheduled an evening online screening and gathered in a Zoom room to watch our videos and discuss those of the high school students. Multiple students cried as we talked about what we had learned from each other, from our high school partners, and from our experiences continuing to work and learn through a traumatic time.

When my department made the decision to stay online through the entire academic year of 2020–2021, my high school partner and I committed to continuing the collaboration. We both recognized the potential for keeping students engaged when they were working at home. In the fall of 2020, students shared writing with each other and offered feedback. In spring of 2021, we endeavored for a more involved partnership, working on a podcast project where high school students would interrogate a canonical ELA text and college students would examine a pertinent issue related to English education. As part of the collaboration, we hosted a Zoom Q&A with a professor of African American literature, and we scheduled time for students to virtually interview each other. At the end of the project, students posted all their podcasts to a virtual bulletin board using the web tool, Padlet.

In an anonymous end of semester survey, students were enthusiastic about the collaboration and the course. One college student wrote that it was their "FAV PART OF THE CLASS!!!" (emphasis in original). They continued, "Working with the [high school students] genuinely got me excited to be working with students once I get into my student teaching and into my own classroom." Even in the virtual classroom environment, this student clearly valued the opportunity to collaborate across contexts. Another student's response is worth reproducing here in full:

> This was a breath of fresh air amidst a lot of mundane and serviceable courses. I appreciate it, and this coursework was a relief from the coursework of so many other classes that were merely going through the motions.

This student, like others in both the fall and spring partnerships, seemed to compare the community-engaged course with others that were "going through the motions." Broadly, there is incentive to standardize courses and assignments as class sizes rise and faculty are incentivized to place their efforts elsewhere (Mountz et al.). This trend was understandably accelerated through the stay-at-home era of COVID-19 education, as I heard from students complaining about inflexible professors and rote courses: do a reading, complete a task, get a grade, move on. In this case, a community collaboration helped to disrupt the monotony and create community across institutional contexts.

The community-engaged learning experience provides another opportunity to reflect on an unintentionally slow and care-full approach to teaching. Building and sustaining this partnership certainly took more time than if I decided to "go through the motions." My high school partner and I had to align our courses, to meet with each other's classes outside of class time, to navigate school district firewalls and create alternative assignments for students who were unable to attend a synchronous meeting. But this use of time and energy felt worthwhile.

Moreover, joyful teaching benefits everyone involved in the classroom. Drawing from scholarship connecting embodiment and affect to pedagogy, Berg and Seeber remind readers that positive emotions are motivators for teachers and students alike and that pleasure may be an important predictor of learning (34). Like my student whose "FAV" part of the class got them "excited" for their future career, the authors argue that students do not distinguish between how they feel and how they think about a course. What motivates students, they write, are the affective dimensions of learning, the positive emotions associated with learning new things or feeling a sense of affiliation or belonging. A sense of pleasure or enjoyment that emerges from doing or knowing in a classroom setting can lead to further investment, desire to learn, and identity development (Beard et al.). Both the college and high school students told us they were more engaged, and *we* were more engaged as teachers. For me, the joy of community engaged teaching and leadership provided focus and a sense of purpose in an otherwise distracted and emotionally draining academic year. Berg and Seeber (2016) suggest that a "pedagogy of pleasure" is one way to combat anxiety while also subtly challenging the corporate values of the modern academy.

Life Interrupted

AUGUST 2021

> It's summertime. I'm prepping for fall classes. Things look relatively positive as we get ready for a face-to-face semester. But the summer has been a drag. Vaccines still aren't available for kids under twelve. Even though COVID-19 numbers are down, more people are going out and about so there's more illness circulating. We heard from a pediatrician friend that illnesses more typical of winter are now raising their heads. Our toddler got knocked out with some kind of daycare bug in June just as our son's first-grade year was ending, leaving us housebound for the better part of a week. It was like a summer 2020 flashback, except with eighteen months of exhaustion built in. When will this end?

Teaching and Leadership in a Slow(er) Academy

From my first conversation with the editors of this book, all of them trusted colleagues, I struggled to decide whether to write this chapter. On the one hand, it still feels too raw, too close. My father recently got his second bivalent COVID-19 booster, an event that reminds us of the three weeks he spent in the hospital in April 2020, during which he was only able to communicate once every few days as his immunocompromised body tried to fight this novel coronavirus. With each dose of the vaccine, his immune system goes into overdrive. The first time, he awoke in the ER the morning after the vaccine, my mother having found him wandering the house confused in the middle of the night; now he gets an IV and drinks Gatorade before each booster and seems to come out okay. My four-year-old daughter who does not remember the stay home era finally completed her vaccination sequence through tears. In the car, our son talked about how they will be telling *their* kids about COVID-19 because it was such a unique event in history; I had to struggle to hold back my own tears as I thought about a recent article I had read documenting the increasing likelihood of global pandemics as climate change forces animals (and their viruses) into closer proximity to humans (Yong).

As difficult as it has been to relive elements of this challenging time in the drafting of this chapter, I believe in the value of storytelling, that our stories can help to build knowledge and create meaning in conversation with each other; stories can be central to building collective action. I also hoped that the writing of this chapter could serve as a form of "care-full" scholarship as I continue to work my way toward (hopeful) tenure and promotion. It should not have taken a global pandemic for me to reassess my values and what it means to me to be a parent, partner, scholar, teacher, and leader, yet here I am. It is a kairotic time for those of us entering faculty life—and maybe even institutional leadership—in the post-COVID-19 age to think about the kind of lives and academic institutions we want to create.

As I consider academic leadership and ways of moving forward, I am encouraged by a lineage of scholars advocating for attention to the ways that often-invisible, uncountable labor is central to a thriving educational institution. Berg and Seeber's (2016) arguments for the "slow professor" can serve as a reminder that slowness and its focus on purpose, collaboration, and joy, can exist rhetorically alongside the mission—if not the capitalist imperative—of universities. Their suggestion to seek alignment between faculty labor and university mission echoes the important work of Ernest Boyer in his attempt to reconceptualize faculty production. As O'Meara explains, Boyer's influential work, *Scholarship Reconsidered*, originally published in 1990, sought to highlight the ways a range of faculty roles and actions—including mentoring, teaching, and administration—can contribute to an institution's broader goals. Writing that "the full range of faculty talent must be more creatively assessed," Boyer called for considering factors beyond research and publication in considerations of promotion and tenure, and he introduced a language to talk about the scholarship of teaching, administration, and engagement that have been of particular benefit to composition scholars (Leverenz). But while Boyer's work initiated important conversation, O'Meara points to familiar forces when discussing why many of his arguments that have been overlooked, including ranking systems that emphasize faculty publications, citation counts, and grant expenditures, and institutional efforts to move up in said rankings that threaten to disrupt attention to teaching and learning and community engagement.

My call to slowness here is thus about more than resisting the fetishization of hard work (Martell) and the neoliberal logics of individualism and accountability by universal metrics; it is also about being reflective and purposeful about aligning my own perception of my work with the stated mission of my institution. For me, this begins with my teaching. For example, the community-engaged teaching and learning I have described in this chapter aligns with my university's strategic vision to increase community impact and benefit the learning experiences of first-generation college students through high-impact practices. Bringing a care-full approach to my teaching has also kept me from reverting to prior teaching practices in the return to in-person teaching following COVID-19. While I was certainly never an authoritarian taskmaster, I have come to value some pedagogical and administrative choices made from necessity during the pandemic—flexible attendance policies and assignment deadlines, fewer overall tasks and assignments—to be essential elements of a slow teaching practice. Perhaps textured by my own experience and living with uncertainty throughout the online and early "back to campus" semesters, I have come to recognize the necessity of acknowledging the complex lives of students and the many ways where traditional practices can and should be adapted in a care-full way. One administrative adaptation I have made is the implementation of a standing attendance makeup activity for students who need to miss class for illness or caretaking responsibilities. I utilize Pear Deck, an interactive slide deck tool, for each class period, with options for at-home students to complete otherwise in-class activities online. Afterward, they reflect narratively on their experience of the class and end with a question they still have, with the hope that I can answer it for them if it is a real point of confusion. While completing the slides at home is not a substitute for group discussion and in-class community, it does allow for multiple paths to classroom success. On a course design level, I remain committed to slow pedagogy elements of community engagement and joyful teaching. Care, engagement, and joy are needed to create sustainable institutions of public learning.

At the faculty level, a slow and care-full institution must recognize that work-life or life-work balance is not the same for everyone. As Anwer writes, there are "innumerable ways in which gender, sexuality, race, ethnicity and nationality, and physical capacities of faculty contribute to their ability to integrate their work and personal lives" ("Work-Life Balance in the Neoliberal University" 54). Continually seeking and advocating for work-life balance, Anwer argues, only perpetuates the problem rather than challenging the structures that center work in the conception of the term. To fully recognize faculty agency means allowing for multiple paths to be recognized for their various forms of labor and contributions to the academy. Boyer recognized the need decades ago to reform reward systems, so faculty members get more credit for the work they do every day that is not counted as scholarship. As O'Meara writes, "Each time a faculty member sits with a student in a coffee shop for two hours helping him or her discern a career direction, supervises a program's accreditation process, deliberates over general education requirements, or mentors other faculty members, he or she contributes to his or her institution's goals." Rewarding these activities—mentorship, effective teaching, participation in shared governance—is essential for reimagining a student-centered, community engaged system of public higher education.

What is needed going forward is less cinching, less justifying, less "counting." With attention to concerns around advancement and promotion, Mountz et al. ask readers to consider how faculty and administrators might count differently in a way that does not so narrowly constrict conceptions of both time and productivity. To build collective action toward this future, faculty at all levels, and institutional leaders like department chairs and tenure reviewers, must be active in supporting slow and care-full work. For example, Mountz et al. advocate for those serving as reviewers of tenure packets or grant proposals to "count what others don't," to value and celebrate "collective authorship, mentorship, collaboration, community building, and activist work in the germination and sharing of ideas" (1250). A recent publication by The A4BL Anti-racist Tenure Letter Working Group argues that tenure and promotion review is an opportunity to advocate for "a more holistic view of scholarly contributions" and outlines specific, practical steps for conducting anti-racist tenure reviews that align well with the ongoing discussion of slow scholarship. For example, they suggest reviewers should ask questions of the department chair to find out about departmental and institutional values. I would hope the chair can be proactive in this process, outlining in their initial request to tenure reviewers the ways the individual under review has contributed to the department and institution in less visible ways like mentoring, community engagement, and diversity, equity, and inclusion (DEI) efforts in order to shift the focus from productivity to equity (Covarrubias and Quinteros). The need to recognize mentorship is particularly important for early-career women and faculty of color who contribute a disproportionate amount of formal and informal mentoring (A4BL; Kezar et al.; Mountz et al.; Turner et al.).

Among other actions, the A4BL group advises reviewers to name *all* of the candidate's accomplishments—including leadership and service to the department, profession, and community—and to frame these contributions as scholarship rather than service, when possible. Tenure and promotion reviewers in writing studies could use position statements like the Conference on College Composition and Communication (CCCC) statements on community-engaged projects and scholarship to support claims about the value and scholarship of community engagement and collaboration, for example (CCCC "CCCC Statement" and "Scholarship"). Gonzales and Nuñez further suggest looking beyond traditional measures when recognizing community-based efforts, such as policy briefs or small action research efforts. It is this kind of collective action and attention to the full range of experiences of faculty and staff that can refuse the neoliberal logics of modern higher education and create institutions we can be proud to contribute to and represent.

I realize that much of what I have been writing here about slow-ness and care may come across as naive. Martell cautions that the slow movement tends too often to focus on individuals making changes in their own lives instead of recognizing the need for wider cultural change. Calls to "do less" (Berg and Seeger), or become a "lazy academic" who "refutes the speedy, efficient, commodification of academic activity" (Gildersleeve 6) do raise questions about for whom and for what the slow movement is for. After all, can contingent or junior faculty really "do less" and have security in their positions? I struggle to answer this question. However, I believe that slowness and a humanizing ethos are about both institutional and individual change. We, collectively, must work to change ourselves and the culture that surrounds academic life. As Berg and Seeber suggest, the language of slow can connect to a larger political and social movement. Junior faculty need to hear from others across professional positions about changes they have made as scholars and leaders. While the democratic governance of yore may never have really existed (Martell), graduate students and junior faculty need to know that there are leaders out there interested in counting differently, relating differently, and aligning the work with the democratic and civic missions of many institutions. As Anwer writes, ensuring the security of those in the most precarious positions "promotes an academic environment that is attuned to the work conditions in which everyone thrives" ("Work-Life Balance in the Neoliberal University" 55).

I am still working on creating my own sense of slow in to better situate my own life work balance, still trying to change the way I talk about time and "production," and to limit my feelings of guilt or inadequacy when I prioritize family, relationships, or teaching over institutional counting metrics. I am committed to supporting the students I work with, regardless of whether it helps my own advancement, because working with students is among the more joyful aspects of this work. I will continue to collaborate with colleagues and resist requests for research percentages for as long as I can, as the work is better and more pleasurable in conversation with others. Most importantly, I will commit to being the kind of leader who encourages slow: quality over quantity, mission over production, community over individualism. I acknowledge I have much work to do. I hope readers of this book will join me.

Works Cited

The AB4L Anti-Racist Tenure Letter Working Group. *A Guide for Writing Anti-Racist Tenure and Promotion Letters*. eLife, vol. 11, 2022, https://doi.org/10.7554/elife.79892.

Ahmad, Asad S. "Why You Should Ignore All That Coronavirus-Inspired Productivity Pressure." *The Chronicle of Higher Education*, 26 Mar. 2020, www.chronicle.com/article/why-you-should-ignore-all-that-coronavirus-inspired-productivity-pressure/.

Anwer, Meghan. "Academic Labor and the Global Pandemic: Revisiting Life-Work Balance under COVID-19." *Susan Bulkeley Butler Center for Leadership Excellence and ADVANCE Working Paper Series*, vol. 3, no. 2, 2020, pp. 5–13. www.purdue.edu/butler/documents/5-wps-2020-special.

Anwer, Meghan. "Work-Life Balance in the Neoliberal University." *Susan Bulkeley Butler Center for Leadership Excellence and ADVANCE Working Paper Series*, vol. 2, no. 2, 2019, pp. 52–58. www.purdue.edu/butler/documents/9-WPS_Fall-2019-Anwer-Work-Life-Balance_final.pdf.

Beard, Colin, et al. "Positive Emotions: Passionate Scholarship and Student Transformation." *Teaching in Higher Education*, vol. 19, no. 6, 2014, pp. 630–43. https://doi.org/10.1080/13562517.2014.901950.

Berg, Maggie, and Barbara K. Seeber. *The Slow Professor: Challenging the Culture of Speed in the Academy*. U of Toronto P, 2016.

Bogost, Ian. "The Chaos in Higher Ed Is Only Getting Started." *The Atlantic*, 24 Jan. 2025, www.theatlantic.com/science/archive/2025/01/trump-nih-pause-higher-ed/681468/.

Boyer, Ernest L., et al. *Scholarship Reconsidered: Priorities of the Professoriate*. Wiley, 2015.

Conference on College Composition and Communication. "CCCC Statement on Community-Engaged Projects in Rhetoric and Composition." Apr. 2016, cccc.ncte.org/cccc/resources/positions/community-engaged.

Conference on College Composition and Communication. "Scholarship in Rhetoric, Writing and Composition: Guidelines for Faculty, Deans, and Chairs." Mar. 2018, cccc.ncte.org/cccc/resources/positions/scholarshipincomp.

Covarrubias, Rebecca, and Karla Quinteros. "Calling Out Whiteness: Faculty of Color Redefining University Leadership." Manuscript submitted for publication, 2021.

Foucault, Michel. "The Subject and Power." *Critical Inquiry*, vol. 8, no. 4, 1982, pp. 777–95.

Gildersleeve, Ryan E. "The Neoliberal Academy of the Anthropocene and the Retaliation of the Lazy Academic." *Cultural Studies ↔ Critical Methodologies*, 2016, pp. 1–8.

Gonzales, Leslie D., and Anne-Marie Núñez. "The Ranking Regime and the Production of Knowledge: Implications for Academia." *Education Policy Analysis Archives*, vol. 22, 2014, p. 31. https://doi.org/10.14507/epaa.v22n31.2014.

Leverenz, Carrie. "Tenure and Promotion in Rhetoric and Composition." *College Composition and Communication*, vol. 52, no. 1, 2000, pp. 143–47. https://doi.org/10.2307/358549.

Kezar, Adrianna, et al. "Where Are the Faculty Leaders?" *Liberal Education*, vol. 93, no. 4, fall 2007, pp. 14–21.

Martell, Luke. "The Slow University: Inequality, Power and Alternatives." *Forum: Qualitative Social Research*, vol. 15, no. 3, 2014. https://doi.org/10.31219/osf.io/nfq4q.

Mountz, Alison, et al. "For Slow Scholarship: A Feminist Politics of Resistance through Collective Action in the Neoliberal University." *ACME: An International E-Journal for Critical Geographies*, vol. 14, no. 4, 2015, pp. 1235–59.

Moyer, Melinda Wenner. "COVID Parenting Has Passed the Point of Absurdity." *The Atlantic*. 20 Jan. 2022, www.theatlantic.com/health/archive/2022/01/covid-parenting-challenges-stress/621322/.

O'Meara, KerryAnn. "How Scholarship Reconsidered Disrupted the Promotion and Tenure System." *Scholarship Reconsidered: Priorities of the Professoriate*, by Ernest L. Boyer et al., Wiley, 2015.

Phelan, Sean. *Neoliberalism, Media and the Political*. Palgrave Macmillan, 2014. https://doi.org/10.1057/9781137308368.

Sinker, Daniel. "Parents Are Not Okay." *The Atlantic*, 22 Aug. 2021, www.theatlantic.com/ideas/archive/2021/08/parents-are-not-okay/619859/.

Turner, Jennifer D., et al. "Humanizing the Tenure Years for Faculty of Color: Reflections from STAR Mentors." *Journal of Literacy Research*, vol. 49, no. 4, 2017, pp. 582–89, https://doi.org/10.1177/1086296x17733493.

Yong, Ed. "We Created the 'Pandemicene.'" *The Atlantic*, 28 Apr. 2022, www.theatlantic.com/science/archive/2022/04/how-climate-change-impacts-pandemics/629699/.

9
Racialized Bodies Navigating White Institutional Spaces

TOM HONG DO

In a 2022 commencement speech at the University of Purdue Northwest, Chancellor Thomas Keon stood at the podium and began his speech with a mocked Asian accent. Instead of being rebuked, he was met with applause and laughter by the predominately white audience. Chancellor Keon's racist parody of an Asian accent is only one of many instances of anti-Asian racism. This racist performance at a major public event shows how university leaders often perpetuate racism because they do not even recognize it when they enact it. The relative invisibility of anti-Asian racism is systemic and even impacts higher educational research. In higher education, research on the experiences of Asian Americans has long been overlooked (Museus and Kiang), and this lack of scholarly attention has been attributed to racist stereotypes of Asians as "the 'new whites' or 'almost white'" (Chou and Feagin qtd. in Museus and Kiang 8). These stereotypes presume that Asians are shielded from the effects of racism; however, they erase the complexity of Asian American experiences and further the invisibility of anti-Asian racism, particularly in the workplace. Research on the inequitable working conditions of Black and Latinx faculty is well documented (Locher and Ropers-Huilman; Melaku and Beeman), but little is known about the racialized experiences of Asian Americans. Specifically, scholarship has paid little attention to the experiences of cultural taxation on the racialized bodies of Asian Americans precisely because Asians have long been neglected in conversations about race.

Research is needed to fill the gap in the scholarship on the racialized experiences of Asian Americans and the invisible labor they perform in navigating predominately white institutional spaces of academia. The invisible labor imposed on the bodies of BIPOC is what Amado Padilla refers to as "cultural taxation," which is the additional labor that predominately white institutions exact from racialized bodies. In this autobiographic counterstory, I argue for an understanding of microaggression and institutional intimidation as forms of cultural tax imposed on the bodies of BIPOC faculty. While cultural taxation normally refers to the additional diversity, equity, and inclusion (DEI) labor that BIPOC faculty perform, serving in unofficial roles as diversity consultants, I propose that having to navigate institutional racism is emotional labor exacted on the bodies of BIPOC in predominately white institutional spaces. To explore this further, I examine the emotional labor exacted on me while navigating my workplace conditions, focusing specifically on institutional, departmental, and interpersonal microaggression and invalidation (Kim et al.; Ore et al.). This counterstory adds a critical voice to our disciplinary concerns about labor and challenges racist assumptions that Asian Americans are immune to racism. It concludes with a call to leadership to institute structural changes that recognize the cultural taxes imposed on BIPOC faculty.

Methodology

Majoritarian narratives or "stock stories" constitute the only version of reality that the dominant racial and gendered ingroup seeks to propagate (Martinez, *Counterstory*). Construed as neutral, stock stories are circulated by the dominant ingroup to not only normalize their values, practices, and worldview but also justify their power while avoiding blame for the effects of societal inequality. The theoretical and methodological underpinnings of critical race theory (CRT) counterstory begin from a different starting point. Instead of taking stock stories for granted as objective reality, CRT counterstory is an interdisciplinary method and methodology that interrogate and expose the limitations of such narratives on the lives of people of color. It thus challenges "systems of Whiteness [that] maintain racial inequalities and oppression" (Poon et al.) by centering the experiences of racially marginalized communities as legitimate forms of knowledge in understanding the effects of racism. In doing so, it offers what Richard Delgado sees as a "counter reality" to stock stories that privilege the lives of the dominant ingroup. Aja Martinez refers to CRT counterstory as "a method of telling stories by people whose experiences are not often told. Counterstory as methodology thus serves to expose, analyze, and challenge stock stories of racial privilege and can help to strengthen traditions of social, political, and cultural survival and resistance" (Martinez, "A Plea for Critical Race Theory Counterstory" 70). In her CRT counterstory, Martinez offers two contrasting narratives of Alejandra's "fit" in the academy. She begins with the "stock story" that exposes how dominant ingroups rely on colorblind frames of merit to justify racist practices. The stock story reveals how dominant ingroups make decisions that are not predicated on any objective or merit-based measure but rather on assumptions about "fit." In contrast, Martinez's counterstory challenges this stock narrative by unpacking, analyzing, and interrogating the faulty assumptions upon which majoritarian narratives rely to justify their worldview. In this chapter, I employ CRT autobiographical counterstory to reflect on my time as a tenure-track, associate professor of English at a small liberal arts university. In doing so, I demonstrate how my embodied experiences of cultural taxation resist and contradict the model minority stereotype in order to call greater attention to the racialized experiences of Asian American faculty in predominately white institution of the academy.

Cultural Taxation and Microaggression

Research on BIPOC faculty labor has shown that predominately white institutional spaces of academia levy a cultural tax on the bodies of BIPOC. According to Padilla, cultural taxation refers to "taxes" that are imposed on BIPOC to carry out diversity, equity, and inclusion tasks simply because of one's "race/ethnicity or our presumed knowledge of cultural differences" (26). This taxation comes in myriad forms that are both explicit and subtle. Padilla identifies several explicit ways that this taxation is manifested. For instance, institutions often assume that BIPOC faculty have the "expertise in matters of diversity," and this assumption comes with the expectation that includes (a) serving as diversity educators to the majority with a lack of institutional authority; (b) serving on an affirmative action committee or task force; (C) solving problems and brokering between and among different stakeholders, to name but a few. Despite the intense labor exacted on the bodies of BIPOC faculty, the institutional reward system does not recognize such labor in tenure and promotion. In fact, such labor is not deemed as rewardable work at all but rather as a "cultural obligation" to "show good citizenship towards [the] institution by serving its needs for ethnic representation or committees or to demonstrate knowledge and commitment to a cultural group which may even bring accolades to the institution but which is not usually rewarded by the institution on whose behalf the service was performed" (Padilla 26).

Predominately white institutions exact payment not only in concrete ways but also levy a hidden tax on the bodies of BIPOC faculty. For example, research shows that racial microaggressions and discrimination are forms of cultural taxation imposed on BIPOC faculty. Kim et al. define microaggressions as "subtle behaviors or comments that often unintentionally demean or denigrate a person of color" (2). Microaggressions often go unnoticed and unchallenged because of their ubiquity that, consequently, creates a hostile work environment and negatively impacts BIPOC's workplace experience (2). Particularly for Asian Americans, the subtle racial microaggressions are often hard to detect because they come in the form of positive stereotypes, but these stereotypes erase Asian Americans by perpetuating attitudes that deny their experiences of racism and discrimination. Because such stereotypes are seen as "positive" instead of "negative," claims of anti-Asian racism can be summarily denied. Kim et al. examine three forms of microaggression: (a) microinsults, (b) microinvalidation, and (c) over-validation. Microinsults are "comments or behaviors that indirectly convey a hidden insult based on the target's race" (3). Common among Asian Americans, for instance, is the experience of being asked "where are you from?" In this context, Asian Americans are perceived as "perpetual foreigners" who exist outside the American imagination. Concomitant with this perpetual foreigner stereotype are comments made about Asian Americans' English language proficiency. Comments such as, "you speak well for an Asian," is a backhand insult that presumes all Asians speak English with a foreignized accent (Cho and Men). A second form of microaggression is microinvalidation. Microinvalidation refers to how the experiences of BIPOC are invalidated. Positive stereotypes of Asian Americans as model minorities serve as a determinant because they negate the racial realities of Asian Americans by assuming that they are somehow immune to racism. Conversely, over validation relies on excessively praising the qualities of BIPOC faculty to extract more labor. Kim et al.'s analysis reveals the hidden cultural tax, in the form of microaggression, that impacts Asian Americans' workplace experience.

These subtle forms of cultural taxation render Asian Americans invisible and perpetuate anti-Asian racism. Lynn Fujiwara, in her autoethnography, highlights both the explicit and subtle ways racism against Asians continues to go unnoticed. In her professional experiences as an assistant professor, associate professor, and department head, Fujiwara has confronted problematic behavior from her colleagues. In her efforts to address systematic patterns of marginalization and domination, she describes the feeling of being constantly invisibilized by her white colleagues who, instead of addressing the issue, would invalidate her concerns with personal attacks and public humiliation. Likewise, in a qualitative study of fourteen East Asian Americans faculty, Eunice Hong examines their experiences of navigating microaggression and racial discrimination. Hong's specific analysis reveals how subtle forms of discrimination often left her participants feeling marginalized and invisible. They were constantly being confused for other Asian American faculty or being spoken to in a foreign language of which they had no knowledge (also see Cho and Men). Collectively, the research on microaggression demonstrates the hidden cultural tax and subtle patterns of racism that extract emotional labor from the bodies of BIPOC faculty (Melaku and Beeman; Berheide et al.; Newcomb; Erickson and Ritter; Tunguz; Hartlep and Ball). In what follows, I present a counterstory of my time as an associate professor at a small, predominately white Christian university in the Midwest. In this account, I trace how those in positions of power attempted to silence and erase my social justice work through microaggressive behaviors and academic intimidation. My counterstory also provides readers with insights into the everyday forms of leadership that BIPOC faculty demonstrate while navigating the cultural taxation imposed on us at predominantly white institutions.

Silencing Discussions about Race

The incidents described in this counterstory show how institutions ensure white comfort by controlling and silencing BIPOC faculty whom administrators see as potentially divisive because they challenge the established order. At every level of leadership, from the chair of the department to the board of regents (BOR), administrators actively denied systemic racism and restricted me from exercising my academic freedom to teach and conduct research on race. Before my termination, I was a tenure track, associate professor at a small Christian university in the Midwest. Throughout my tenure there, I was warned by white allies that words such as "race," "racism," and "social justice" should not be used because these words were associated with liberal ideologies. Race had been such a fraught issue for administrators at that institution that my former dean, a white ally who assembled a meeting for new faculty to address this specific topic, warned us about the repercussions of making "white people look bad" and strongly encouraged us, in no uncertain terms, to steer clear from teaching and researching about racism. While her efforts were meant to protect us from institutional intimidation and retaliation from the BOR, such efforts were misplaced because they essentially asked faculty to remain silent. For years, the university operated quite differently than what the BOR had long desired. The disconnect between the school's daily operations and the BOR's vision was often a point of contention, and this contention played out in top-down policies that many liberal faculty members resisted. The BOR, for instance, expected faculty to center Christ in every class session to emphasize the inherent equality of every individual. While I was not averse to the theological tenet that underlies this idea, I was cognizant that such a statement tended to promote colorblind racism and gloss over systemic racism experienced by BIPOC. In my teaching, I wanted students to critically examine the impact of systemic racism on BIPOC communities' access to housing and food in our local context. However, this subject matter did not bode well with the upper administrators who perceived my work as divisive and indoctrinating impressionable young minds.

Efforts to silence and erase my social justice work became apparent during my annual faculty review (AFR) meeting with my chair. At the end of each academic calendar, I was expected to write a brief AFR report about my teaching, service, and research accomplishments and submit it to my chair. My chair would then review and comment on my AFR. Thereafter, a meeting would be scheduled to discuss the report. At my AFR meeting, my chair seemed pleased with my work, but one area of my profile concerned him: the content of my syllabus. He questioned and interrogated my decision to teach content related to racial and social justice issues in class. As a literature professor and a conservative Christian, he also often expressed skepticism about the work done in my field of rhetoric and writing studies.

"Tom, thanks for meeting with me today. I want to go over your AFR. I am sure you have taken the time to look over my comments. I commend you for taking on such big projects your first year here. I really appreciate the time and energy you have put in to revising the first-year composition sequence, but I am concerned that the sequence is too restrictive," Dan stated.

I was both surprised and confused by his concerns, since he was part of the approval process, and the department had already hammered out issues prior to pushing the composition program's revision proposal to senate for final approval. "What aspects of the comp sequence are you most concerned about? It was deliberated upon and formally approved by both the department and senate. While I am open to suggestions that will improve the assignment sequence, doing so at this point will require revision of the proposal that will need approval by both governing bodies again," I explained.

Dan attempted to articulate his dissatisfaction, but his explanation was a tangled mess. Initially, he took issue with the composition revision sequence because it was too restrictive, but then he expressed concern that it would burden adjunct faculty with more work. As Dan explained, he wanted to ensure that they could adapt what they were already teaching at other schools to our institution. He expressed further hesitation about the sequence because it required the teaching of rhetoric. I attempted to abate his concerns by explaining that teaching rhetoric is standard practice, and what we are offering is not a radical departure from other schools. In fact, I made the argument that our curriculum reflects many of the best practices that are articulated by the Council of Writing Program Administration (CWPA). To support adjunct faculty, one of my colleagues and I created an online portal with documents, handouts, and other teaching materials. We also organized a summer orientation to help adjunct faculty teach rhetoric. We led both of these initiatives without compensation. Despite my attempts to abate his concerns, Dan remained skeptical of my work and could not articulate why. His tangled critiques of what I labored to create were roundabout ways of getting to a much deeper concern he did not want to say explicitly at first.

He pulled my syllabus from underneath the stack of papers that was sitting on his desk, and he flipped through it, trying to locate a specific page for discussion. He paused at the assignment schedule and then tossed the syllabus to me. "After reviewing your syllabus, I noticed that you discuss race and racism. Will adjuncts have to change their syllabus to discuss these issues in their classes? I just want to make sure we're not indoctrinating students to a particular way of thinking. Wouldn't you agree?"

I understood this type of questioning was not an occasion for open dialogue about the merits of teaching such issues. Instead, it was a roundabout way to force my hand into agreeing with his statement. If I disagreed, I would appear insubordinate, and he would give a long-winded explanation about being objective, apolitical, and unbiased. If I agreed, I would undermine my own work and be complicit in my own silencing and invisibility. I paused, thinking about how Catherine, my white colleague who co-created the English 1100 syllabus, used the same exact syllabus, readings, and assignments but was never questioned. After taking a deep breath, I responded.

"From what I gather, there seems to be three separate issues at play here. So is this discussion really about the revision of the first-year composition sequence, adjunct faculty training, or my syllabus?" I asked.

"This," he said, pointing to my syllabus. "What you are presenting is highly problematic. We are a Christian university that fundamentally believes that all people are equal in the eyes of God."

"I'm not sure how or why my course would be considered a form of indoctrination, considering that students and I examines primary and secondary documents and conduct research on the issue. Isn't this course designed to familiarize students with whatever fundamentals we think are important for first-year writing students?" I asked.

He winced as though nagged by a persistent pain. "Examine," he stated.

"I'm sorry? What was that, Dan?" I asked.

"You said 'examines' when it is supposed to be 'examine.' It is 'students and I examine,'" he corrected me. "Anyways, I'm sure we can address these elements of writing without discussing race and racism. Some of our students are from out-of-state, so the local issues you address will be irrelevant to them. Do all students have to research about race?" Dan probed further. He wanted my agreement, which ultimately meant my silence.

However, I did not relent. During the hours-long meeting, I attempted to explain what the course is about and its requirements. "I do not require students to write their final research paper on race, racism, and housing. The theme of the class is about local community issues, of which racism is but one. I want students to find a local issue that is relevant to them and conduct research. If issues of racism happen to be a topic that engages them, that's fine. If not, that's fine, too," I explained.

He did not want to hear my explanation and continued critiquing the design of my class without knowing or understanding the content. He picked up my syllabus again and leaned back on his chair. As he flipped through the pages of my syllabus, he would pause and frown. "But the issues of race and racism are just too divisive. You have to understand that these issues will make some of our traditional students very uncomfortable," he insisted.

It was clear to me what the euphemism "traditional students" meant in this context. Dan had used it many times before when he spoke fondly of "traditional students" in his honors courses. He spoke about how they were so engaged and curious and that they reminded him of what students were like many decades ago. It is no secret that honors students were mostly white.

"I am not in the business of making learning comfortable. I'm in the business of challenging students, and addressing issues of race and racism is one way of tackling students' preconceived notions about race," I retorted.

But Dan continued to invalidate my work by dismissing my pedagogical approach.

"I just think there's another way to teach students the fundamentals."

"Sure, there are plenty of ways," I agreed. "But this is my way, just like it is equally valid to teach the fundamentals through literature. What I am hearing here is a conflation of my work as the director of the first-year composition revision coordinator and my syllabus, which are not the same. To be clear, I am not requiring any faculty member to teach about race and racism, and despite the fact that race and racism are subject matters discussed in class, I am not requiring students to do their final project on race and racism," I reiterated. I explained that my approach fostered students' personal investment and that I saw our "at-risk" students produce research projects that gained them entrance to the Conference on College Composition and Communication, the flagship conference for the field of rhetoric and writing studies.

Dan was persistent in his efforts to invalidate the work I did in class by interrogating why I was addressing issues of race. Despite the success that I had accomplished in class, he continued to dismiss my work by questioning the legitimacy of my pedagogical approach. "But what about race and racism? How do you plan to revise this syllabus so that it's politically neutral?" he asked as he glossed over my previous statement.

This silencing is a form of cultural taxation that requires faculty of color to protect whites from feeling uncomfortable by demanding that they stay silent on issues of race. What is clear from this interaction is that Dan, the senior colleague, was attempting to exert authority over me, a junior colleague, to make me comply with his demands so that "traditional students" remain comfortable in their predominantly white institution. The discomfort that whites feel about racial matters is an example of what Robin DiAngelo refers to as "White Fragility." White fragility describes "white discomfort and anxiety [that is] born of superiority and entitlement" (20). Having been insulated from racial stress as a result of separation and inequality, white people feel a great deal of discomfort, even naming themselves in racialized terms, and feel entitled to be comfortable by "reinstat[ing] white equilibrium" (20). In these ways, society is structured to maximize support for whites by providing them with "the accumulation of protective pillows of resources and/or benefits of the doubt that protects white people from racial stress" (Fujiwara 139). Because of his own white fragility, Dan attempted to exert his authority and control the curriculum in order to reinstate white comfort. His fears were borne from his sense of discomfort and anxiety around topics of race. He wanted racial issues eliminated from my syllabus, if not contained and controlled by remaining "neutral."

Ensuring white comfort requires sanitizing the histories of oppression and the experiences of those who are racially marginalized. If controversial topics cannot be avoided, the administrative arm of the institution insisted that BIPOC faculty stay politically neutral by presenting issues related to race from "both sides," free of our own political and ideological biases. As is often the case, white peoples' appeals to objectivity and neutrality derive from a shared culture and script (DiAngelo 26). These appeals to political neutrality reaffirm a central component of the white script: white people are "both objective and unique" and "just people" (26, 67). While whites may see themselves as "just people," the reality is that they, like all other racialized groups, have shared cultural ideas and practices. In this case, objectivity and neutrality are white cultural ideas meant to appear as universal truths that stand outside of time, place, culture, and race. Truth is outside the body, waiting to be discovered. Viewed from this perspective, when whites speak, they are "automatically granted universal objective reality, while [BIPOC are] positioned as the other, seen as operating out of racial intent" (Fujiwara). White faculty are seen as the purveyors of objectivity and neutrality, while BIPOC faculty who teach and research racism are too personally invested in the subject matter because of their racialized and minoritized positionality. Such attitudes reflect what Ore et al. see as "whitestream education," education that is whitewashed for the comfort of whites (207). So long as the academy operates in this vein, it "will continue to demean and exclude [BIPOC's] culturally-situated knowledge-making processes, [their] uses of language, [their] bodymindspirits [sic], and the stories [they] tell, including [their] research" (207). When Dan demanded that I sanitize my syllabus, he was demanding that I adapt to whitestream education and entertain even the most outlandish arguments to protect white fragility. Not making "white people look bad" meant that Dan wanted me to entertain arguments by "traditional students" who believe in colorblind racist ideologies (Bonilla-Silva). Because leadership demanded that I stay neutral and unbiased, I was expected to allow these cultural and colorblind racist ideologies to exist and persist for the comfort of whites.

Part of the strategy in policing and silencing faculty from teaching and speaking about race is through micro and macro invalidation. Such invalidation is represented in how Dan rhetorically framed my syllabus as if it was simply my political and personal biases, while his criticisms are supposedly neutral and objective observations. This interaction illustrates one of the many ways administrators actively sought to undermine my pedagogical approach and delegitimatize my research agenda as "mere leftist propaganda dressed in academic garb." Dan already presumed in his questioning that my teaching was a form of political indoctrination. His assumption and subsequent invalidation of my work reflect how administrators in white institutional spaces often frame the equity work of BIPOC faculty.

Iterations of Dan's microaggressions played out countless times at departmental meetings. In addition to my work as the first-year composition (FYC) director, I was in charge of creating new composition courses. With technical writing becoming increasingly important, I proposed that our department create a professional and technical writing course that included an internship component. I drafted the proposed class, had the department review and revise it, and vote on the proposed course. Throughout this entire process, I did not once encounter any resistance from my colleagues, but on the day that the department voted on the course, many of them were skeptical and resistant. My chair was particularly resistant to the proposed course, even though he had plenty of previous opportunities to voice his concerns. Whenever I spoke, he would lean forward, clasp his hands in front of his mouth in a typical corporate power pose, and squint in skepticism at each word I said. As I spoke, he produced an audible "hum." His dismissiveness made me nervous, and I began to stammer and stutter. I was visibly uncomfortable with his microaggression and looked around the room in desperate need for help. Whatever answer I gave, he seemed to be on a fault-finding mission. He would continue to doubt and probe. Following the chair's lead, other colleagues began to interrogate my work.

"Tom, I agree with what you're doing here, and I think it's a good idea. But what do you mean by 'professional writing?' Is there another term you can use to define this course? Otherwise, we can't approve it," Karen chimed in.

"Wait, so what I'm hearing is that you're more concerned about my course's proposed title and not the course itself?" I asked in disbelief.

"Well, I don't think the title really captures the purpose of the course. I think it will not be attractive to students. Plus, it's a vague term. If you keep the title, I don't think we can approve it," she argued.

"So we're arguing semantics now? How does the title of any of our courses really reflect the many topics we teach in class? What do you propose we name the course?" I asked indignantly.

"I do think we need to change the title to better reflect what students are signing up for. Otherwise, I don't see this course filling up because the proposed course needs clarification," Dan stated as a matter of fact.

At this point, I attempted to restate the purpose of the course. Their continued dismissiveness clearly frustrated one of my colleagues, Catherine—a white ally. In an attempt to rescue the proposed course from being completely discarded, she repeated what I had said verbatim. To Catherine, they expressed openness. They listened attentively, nodding agreeably and affirming her statements. At this point, I realized that the only way I could get my other colleagues to agree to my proposed ideas was to communicate with them through Catherine who would broker on my behalf. And this was a pattern: I would say something or answer their questions; they would be skeptical and dismissive; she would have to summarize my points to them. It was as though we were speaking two different languages.

Because of her brokering, I managed to get my proposal approved, but the title of the course became a point of contention.

"So, what title should we give this course?" asked Karen.

"What about 'Real World Writing'?" another white colleague proposed.

The name change was met with applause and praise. Many of my colleagues described the revised title as embodying the essence of the course and a precise and compelling title that will attract students. I was asked what I thought about it, but at that point, I was too exhausted to care. I knew that if I resisted, my proposed course would not be approved. I had to make concessions, and so I did. I agreed to the name change, although I thought the name was no more precise or compelling than the original course title. The experience, and many thereafter, left me feeling emotionally battered and invisible by the political and academic culture of the university. As the department's only person of color, I faced undue resistance, both personally and professionally, that created an additional burden in the form of emotional labor.

This particular instance demonstrates how cultural taxation, in the form of invalidation, constantly places BIPOC faculty on the defensive to justify their authority, expertise, and existence in a hostile working environment that affords little to no opportunity to make any real progress in their work. Unlike whites who are often automatically granted legitimacy, BIPOC faculty often perform additional labor to be seen as competent in the eyes of leadership. No wonder BIPOC faculty, across many disciplines in academia, often find themselves working more and harder than their white counterparts (Jimenez et al.; El-Alayli et al.). In their research on labor performed by BIPOC faculty, Miguel

F. Jimenez et al. reveal how "non-white, non-male and first-generation faculty, as well as those in associate or full professor positions, were consistently more likely to engage in diversity and inclusion activities" (1030). They also noted that BIPOC faculty engage in minority outreach and recruitment efforts and "served on diversity committees more frequently than non-Hispanic white faculty" (1030). BIPOC faculty are constantly in the position to demonstrate their competence through their labor, which are, many times, not recognized as part of retention, tenure, and promotion (RTP). While Jimenez et al.'s specific analysis addresses diversity, equity, and inclusion (DEI), their work speaks to a much broader and systemic problem in academia: the cultural tax imposed on BIPOC faculty by predominately white institutions. The cultural tax is more than physical. It impacts BIPOC faculty's social, psychological, and mental well-being. In this instance, as the chief architect of newly proposed writing courses, I experienced many forms of microaggressive behaviors that delegitimatized my authority and painted me as incompetent, even though the proposed course passed through several revision processes with my colleague's input. Although I gave them ample time to review the proposed course and make suggestions for change, no one challenged the proposal until the department meeting. I worked hard just to get shot down, and the only reason the proposed course survived is because my white colleagues were granted the legitimacy I was denied.

Having to constantly justify my work, my teaching, and my existence was an extremely exhausting experience (Berheide et al.; Newcomb; Erickson and Ritter; Hartlep and Ball; Melaku and Beeman; Ming Dariot and Yoo; Tunguz; Valverde et al.). These incidents reflect what Holley Locher and Rebecca Ropers-Huilman refer to as "racial battle fatigue" (103). Racial battle fatigue describes the condition "where people of color are emotionally, physically, and mentally distressed by their unremitting exposure to racism" (103). In my particular case, I constantly perform intense emotional labor to regulate and mediate my interactions with those in positions of authority (Erickson and Ritter; Melaku and Beeman). Efforts by leadership to restrict, control, and even silence topics about race are acts of suppressing academic freedom. Academic freedom is designed to protect teachers, students, and academic institutions to pursue knowledge without the threat of censorship. Yet, this autobiographic counterstory, and the narratives of countless scholars of color, "highlight[s] that the privilege of academic freedom is not always functioning as intended. The discrimination that [many BIPOC scholars and I] face contributed to [us] experiencing a form of racial battle fatigue that negatively impacted [our] ability and/or [...] desire to enact [our] academic freedom" (Locher and Ropers-Huilman 114).

A Way Forward: Honoring the Emotional Labor of BIPOC Faculty

This autobiographic counterstory examines how cultural taxation, in the form of microaggressive behaviors, invisibilizes BIPOC faculty. Particularly for Asian Americans who are often stereotyped for being white adjacent, such a tax takes the form of subtle slights and invalidation that devalue not only their work but also perpetuate anti-Asian racism. Microaggression, such as invalidation, places the agent in the position of power to deny the lived realities of BIPOC faculty. Insisting upon clarification when it is not needed, mischaracterizing work as political indoctrination, or withholding vital resources are just a few examples of microaggressions that seek to invalidate the work of BIPOC faculty. Addressing the cultural tax of microaggression on BIPOC faculty requires first acknowledging that it exists. More often than not, those in designated leadership positions repeatedly deny acts of microaggression, which only invalidates the experiences of those on the receiving end of such behaviors. When these behaviors are acknowledged, engaging in self-reflection is critical to understanding how microinsults, microinvalidations, and overvalidations create more work for those who are already marginalized.

Creating structural changes to academic institutions requires a different approach to how labor is characterized, assessed, and rewarded. Wendi Williams discusses how academia can rethink its labor and reward system. In her article "Lightening the Burden," Williams provides advice on how to reward emotional labor in institutions of higher education. She argues that the invisible work of emotional labor must be made visible through careful documentation of work performed. Williams, like I have suggested, begins by emphasizing the importance of acknowledging the added emotional labor that BIPOC faculty generally perform. Next, it is critical to create a "system of measurement, documentation, and compensation" (Williams). Because retention, tenure, and promotion files usually include a narrative section where instructors articulate their instructional activities, it is possible to imagine how this space offers an opportunity to document the various ways that BIPOC faculty labor emotionally to support student success. Documenting such labor includes "the amount of time faculty are spending interacting with these students through email, phone, Zoom or in-person interactions—all of which would provide a more comprehensive and accurate picture of their contributions to the well-being and ultimately retention of students made vulnerable by environmental factors" (Williams). Creating assessment protocols for emotional labor would acknowledge the dynamic and often intense work required in mentoring students, on and off campus.

When considering ways to navigate microaggression, I draw from Ore et al. about the importance of mentorship and community building. Combating macro and micro invalidation, for instance, requires sympathetic allies who not only validate one's experiences but also offer practical support. As the example of Catherine demonstrates, allies can serve as reinforcement to get policies passed. While I do not suggest that white allies necessarily speak for BIPOC faculty, they can surely work to support BIPOC faculty by *speaking with them* in meetings to create what I refer to as disruptive, strategic dialoguing. In this form of dialoguing, white allies are aware of mico- and macroaggressive behaviors in meetings and intentionally disrupt such behaviors by making direct eye contact and strategically dialoguing with BIPOC faculty to speak in an otherwise hostile environment. Dialoguing this way creates space for BIPOC faculty to speak and be heard in the room without necessarily addressing their aggressors directly or having to confront their microaggressive behavior. In strategic dialoguing, white allies intentionally serve as a sounding board, practice mirroring speech to demonstrate active listening, and reaffirm the work that BIPOC faculty do to show support and solidarity. This type of disruptive dialoguing is specifically designed to steer the conversation away from the microaggression and navigate institutional and departmental politics to rally support for the work of BIPOC faculty.

Finally, mentorship and community create and hold spaces for BIPOC faculty to combat the "feeling of disbelonging" and encourage "feelings of belonging" (Ore et al. 209). As Ore et al. note, we have the agency "to fashion professional networks that counter the sense of isolation we often experience, but also the need to independently establish a network that future generations can benefit from, build upon, and extend" (209). When trying to get new classes passed or policies changed, I would rely upon my community of more senior colleagues/allies to look over drafts of my work, get their signed approval, and submit my work along with their signed approval. I find this method most effective because I am working in a group. As a BIPOC faculty in a predominately white institution, having allies who have institutional memory is critical in combating discriminatory practices by those in leadership positions.

Works Cited

Berheide, Catherine White, et al. "Teaching College in the Time of COVID-19: Gender and Race Differences in Faculty Emotional Labor." *Sex Roles*, vol. 86, no. 7–8, 2022, pp. 441–55.

Bonilla-Silva, Edward. *Racism without Racists: Color-Blind Racism and the Persistence of Racial Inequality in America*. 5th ed., Rowman & Littlefield, 2017.

Cho, Andrew and Sopang "Pang" Men. "Navigating Weird Comments, Stereotypes, and Microaggressions as Southeast Asian American Faculty at a Predominantly White Community College." *Racial Battle Fatigue in Faculty: Perspectives and Lessons from Higher Education*. Edited by Nicholas D. Hartlep and Daisy Ball, Taylor & Francis, 2019.

Delgado, Richard. "Storytelling for Oppositionists and Others: A Plea for Narrative." *Michigan Law Review*, vol. 87, no. 8, 1989, pp. 2411–41, https://doi.org/10.2307/1289308.

DiAngelo, Robin J. *White Fragility: Why It's so Hard for White People to Talk about Racism*. Beacon Press, 2018.

El-Alayli, Amani, et al. "Dancing Backwards in High Heels: Female Professors Experience More Work Demands and Special Favor Requests, Particularly from Academically Entitled Students." *Sex Roles*, vol. 79, no. 3–4, 2018, pp. 136–50.

Erickson, Rebecca J., and Christian Ritter. "Emotional Labor, Burnout, and Inauthenticity: Does Gender Matter?" *Social Psychology Quarterly*, vol. 64, no. 2, 2001, pp. 146–63.

Fujiwara, Lynn. "Racial Harm in Predominately White 'Liberal' University: An Institutional Autoethnography of White Fragility." *Presumed Incompetent II: Race, Class, Power, and Resistance of Women in Academia*. Edited by Yolanda Flores Niemann et al., Utah State UP, 2020.

Hartlep, Nicholas Daniel, and Daisy Ball, eds. *Racial Battle Fatigue in Faculty: Perspectives and Lessons from Higher Education*. Routledge, 2020.

Hong, Eunice. "Asian American Faculty Experiences of Racism." *Journal of Research on Christian Education*, vol. 31, no. 2, 2022, pp. 169–84.

Jimenez, Miguel F., et al. "Underrepresented Faculty Play a Disproportionate Role in Advancing Diversity and Inclusion." *Nature Ecology & Evolution*, vol. 3, no. 7, 2019, pp. 1030–33, https://doi.org/10.1038/s41559-019-0911-5.

Kim, Jennifer Y., et al. "Debunking the 'Model Minority' Myth: How Positive Attitudes toward Asian Americans Influence Perceptions of Racial Microaggressions." *Journal of Vocational Behavior*, vol. 131, 2021, p. 103648.

Locher, Holley, and Rebeca Ropers-Huilman. "Wearing You Down: The Influence of Racial Battle Fatigue on Academic Freedom for Faculty of Color." *Racial Battle Fatigue in Higher Education: Exposing the Myth of Post-Racial America*. Edited by Kenneth J. Fasching-Varner et al., Rowman & Littlefield, 2015, pp. 103–14.

Martinez, Aja Y. "A Plea for Critical Race Theory Counterstory: Stock Story versus Counterstory Dialogues Concerning Alejandra's 'Fit' in the Academy." *Composition Studies*, vol. 42, no. 2, 2014, pp. 33–55.

Martinez, Aja Y. *Counterstory: The Rhetoric and Writing of Critical Race Theory*. NCTE, 2020.

Melaku, Tsedale M., and Angie Beeman. "Black Women in White Academe: A Qualitative Analysis of Heightened Inclusion Tax." *Ethnic and Racial Studies*, vol. 46, no. 6, 2023, pp. 1158–81.

Ming Dariot, Wei, and Grace J. Yoo. "Care Work: The Invisible Labor of Asian American Women in Academia." *Fight the Tower: Asian American Women Scholars' Resistance and Renewal in the Academy*. Rutgers UP, 2022, pp. 300–24.

Museus, Samuel D., and Peter N. Kiang. "Deconstructing the Model Minority Myth and How It Contributes to the Invisible Minority Reality in Higher Education Research." *New Directions for Institutional Research*, no. 142, 2009, pp. 5–15, https://doi.org/10.1002/ir.292.

Newcomb, Michelle. "The Emotional Labour of Academia in the Time of a Pandemic: A Feminist Reflection." *Qualitative Social Work*, vol. 20, no. 1–2, 2021, pp. 639–44.

Ore, Ersula, et al. "Symposium: Diversity Is Not Enough: Mentorship and Community-Building as Antiracist Praxis." *Rhetoric Review*, vol. 40, no. 3, 2021, pp. 207–56, https://doi.org/10.1080/07350198.2021.1935157.

Padilla, Amado M. "Ethnic Minority Scholars, Research, and Mentoring: Current and Future Issues." *Educational Researcher*, vol. 23, no. 4, 1994, pp. 24–27, https://doi.org/10.2307/1176259.

Poon, Oiyan A., et al. "Asian Americans, Affirmative Action, and the Political Economy of Racism: A Multidimensional Model of Raceclass Frames." *Harvard Educational Review*, vol. 89, no. 2, 2019, pp. 201–26, https://doi.org/10.17763/1943-5045-89.2.201.

Tunguz, Sharmin. "In the Eye of the Beholder: Emotional Labor in Academia Varies with Tenure and Gender." *Studies in Higher Education* (Dorchester-on-Thames), vol. 41, no. 1, 2016, pp. 3–20.

Valverde, Kieu Linh Caroline, et al. *Fight the Tower: Asian American Women Scholars' Resistance and Renewal in the Academy*. Edited by Kieu-Linh Caroline Valverde and Wei Ming Dariotis, Rutgers UP, 2020, https://doi.org/10.36019/9781978806405.

Williams, Wendi. "Lightening the Burden." *Inside Higher Ed*, 17 June 2021, www.insidehighered.com/advice/2021/06/18/advice-how-colleges-can-lift-some-emotional-burden-bipoc-faculty-opinion. Accessed 21 Jan. 2024.

Section 3 Response

A Call for Progressive Leadership

Resisting Neoliberalism and Pluralistic Views of Tenure and Promotion

Staci Perryman-Clark

The chapters featured in section 3 of this collection are indeed timely in relation to current issues in higher education that require institutions of higher education to consider both the impacts of the COVID-19 pandemic on tenure and promotion requirements (Davis et al.; Krukowski et al.; Oleschuk), as well as the affordances and assaults to academic freedom (Caldwell; Kezar and Culver). These contributions are also timely in terms of my own self-reflection and experiences in academia and higher education leadership. As I sit to write my response to section 3, I am reminded of the parallels (some quite triggering) between the experiences discussed by Ana Ribero, Brad Jacobson and Tom Hong Do, and the just-released manuscript proofs of *The Black Feminist Coup: Black Women's Lived Experiences in White Supremacist Feminist Academic Spaces*, a book I collaboratively wrote with Western Michigan University colleagues Jennifer L. Richardson, Mariam Konate, and Richardson's former graduate students Olivia Marie McLaughlin and Keiondra Grace. In this book, we share through collaborative memory and feminist methodologies our stories of exiting a white supremacist gender and women's studies department, as well as experiences of misogynoir as scholars and leaders on campus.

The book, like the contributions in this section, urges us to consider intersectionality and equity in relation to the COVID-19 pandemic, the systemic challenges as connected to tenure and promotion expectations and standards, and the affordances and limits of academic freedom. Like the challenges and traumas endured while trying to fulfill institution's neoliberalist agendas to produce, or as Jacobson suggests, "cinch down and get it done," we, too, felt the pressure to continue producing both scholarship and credit hours. Meanwhile, our colleagues in gender and women's studies, were more concerned with who would run the department (hoping it would be one of them for purposes of economic benefit and power) and neoliberalist business as usual, while also co-opting the feminist struggle and #BlackLivesMatter movement for "their own personal gain" (Richardson et al. 30). In terms of the systemic challenges related to tenure and promotion, despite neoliberalist philosophies to add COVID-19 statements as part of tenure and promotion portfolios, these statements do nothing to address the culturally biased standards prescribed to tenure and promotion requirements, as both Ribero and Jacobson also acknowledge.

Similarly, in chapters 5 and 6 of *The Black Feminist Coup*, we share experiences of one of our colleagues (Jennifer) having to appeal an adverse tenure decision, despite having included her own COVID-19 impact statement and statement for stopping her tenure clock before the pandemic (70). And finally, as these contributions also affirm, academic freedom is now and always at stake. For us, the notion of sharing our stories in *The Black Feminist Coup* does not go without risks to academic freedom. While our institution's academic collective bargaining agreement affirms academic freedom for both faculty and others affiliated with the institution, noting that "both the protection of academic freedom and the requirements of academic responsibility apply to all persons associated with the University who exercise teaching and/or other professional responsibilities" it still poses risk to at least one of our coauthors who has included this book as part of her tenure cases, as well as me who, though tenured, is currently employed as an at-will administrator ("2021–2026 WMU/WMU-AAUP Agreement").

The notion of Black women's academic freedom being at risk also evokes a very timely discussion. At the moment of this writing, former Harvard University President, Claudine Gay resigned after only six months of her tenure as Harvard's first Black woman president in response to her testimony to Congress concerning antisemitism on Harvard's campus, as well as accusations of plagiarism that were deemed as not a violation of academic misconduct on Gay's part. Implications of academic freedom are at stake here as well. A petition of Harvard faculty supporters urged Harvard University officials to "resist political pressures that are at odds with Harvard's commitment to academic freedom." It added: "The critical work of defending a culture of free inquiry in our diverse community cannot proceed if we let its shape be dictated by outside forces" (qtd. in Blinder) in response to Gay's congressional testimony that encouraged academic inquiry and freedom of expression. While purposefully yet carefully referencing Gay's tenure and implications for academic freedom, I do not aim to relitigate Gay's testimony. Rather, my aim is to draw attention to the fact that Black women in particular are held to different ethos and standards of institutional leadership, including those where academic freedom is at stake. In *The Black Feminist Coup*, we also write about the implications of consequences for Black women who lead under public scrutiny (see chapter 5).

Indeed, the contributions in this section have led me to think and reflect through the lens of what it means to be a Black woman in academia and what liberation from neoliberal and overly capitalist institutions can look like for the next generation of scholars on the tenure track. As I reflect, three themes emerge from these contributions: (1) gender equity implications of parenting and mothering; (2) the urgency to revise tenure and promotion standards by any means necessary; and (3) the necessity to lead with a true commitment to equity and academic freedom. Through these themes, I will reference both my own personal experiences as well as examples from the contributing chapters in this section.

Gender Equity Implications for Parenting and Mothering

Clearly, caregiving and mothering are some of the many sacrifices women make when working in any profession, including academia. While reflecting on Ribero's discussions of parenting during the pandemic, I cannot help but reflect on my own experiences as a pregnant dissertator navigating the job market, albeit not during a pandemic. Like Ribero, I too hid my pregnancy while on the job market, even borrowing my mother's clothes to disguise my seven-month pregnant belly while on a campus visit for my tenure-track position as an assistant professor and WPA. The notion of sacrifice and mothering happens much earlier than the birth of a baby, like Ribero, one of the happiest times of my life had to be captured in silence. I couldn't celebrate publicly the pending arrival of my daughter, Jamison (Jami), until the third trimester of my pregnancy, after securing a tenure-track position. Sacrificing celebration and joy for career prospects is not simply something mothers and parents do after the birth of a child; rather, sacrificing often begins at the confirmation of a pregnancy.

Sacrificing continues, though, especially on the tenure-track. In "A WPA's Guide to Producing the First Book for Tenure," I shared my "success story" of traveling on weekends to secure childcare in order to write my first book needed for tenure with minimal interruption (74). But the part of the story not shared–and perhaps the part where I feel the most guilt–is by not taking any leave (I simply could not afford to) to bond or spend time with her and had pretty much outsourced (at least in my mind) the majority of the parenting duties to my husband who was a stay at home dad for the first two years of Jami's life. As I recall memories of my first year on the tenure track, I can only recall a few instances when I changed Jami's diaper. I'm sure I changed her more than I can remember, but I mostly remember nursing her as my primary form of caregiving. Still to this day, I feel like I sacrificed parenting her and even sacrificed not having more children for a career.

From a feminist perspective, Ribero's discussion affirms the need for counternarratives surrounding gender equity, especially as related to mothering. For one, mothering and caregiving are in fact labor. Ribero's discussion of "motherwork" further challenges us to resist traditional feminist dichotomies that create a false binary between private and public work. The COVID-19 pandemic clearly taught all of us that these lines are blurred and have never neatly fit into these binaries. As feminist scholars and educators who have often worked more than a typical forty-hour work week, we have always understood that our work has never simply fit within an office space, and even before a pandemic we have always taken on parenting and caretaking responsibilities. For me, the shift in parental responsibilities came during the pandemic. Because my husband was an essential worker, he was required to report to work daily and didn't have the luxury of staying home and protected. This meant, the parenting responsibilities including helping with school projects and interrupting work to help Jami complete her science project, which often required us to apply earth science and nature principles to outside activities, activities that also parallel Jacobson's own discussion of navigating parenting during a pandemic in chapter 9. Jacobson's chapter also effectively situates his own subject position as a cis, hetero white male within the context of caregiving and parenting, while also being candid about the implications on all caregivers who are expected to still meet institutional expectations for tenure and promotion.

As something that benefits all caregivers, including nonbinary parents and caregivers, Ribero's recommendation that institutions prioritize (and commit to subsidizing) early care education through fundraising, grant, or strategic planning measures is worthy of consideration, especially for women of color who not only parented, but also disproportionately had to care for (and bury) loved ones affected by and infected with COVID-19. As a college dean at an institution whose budget model rewards revenue, I know that childcare centers are expensive and often do not generate enough revenue to support their operations without the support of external funding, which may not be available. That said, Ribero offers other possibilities for incentivizing early care and education by incentivizing care work, including academic service through the tenure and promotion process, by creating flexible work arrangements for those with care work responsibilities while on the tenure track, and by protecting paid care workers from exploitation, including Black women and Latinas who are disproportionately affected by care work exploitation. Absent funding possibilities, a review and revision of institutional structures and policies is certainly attainable.

The Urgency to Revise Tenure and Promotion Standards by Any Means Necessary

Each of the contributions in this section identify key recommendations for revising tenure and promotion standards. The overarching theme across the three contributions is not simply the fact that we need to revise tenure and promotion, but the fact that it is the standards for tenure and promotion that need to change, not the concept of tenure itself. As a scholar who has written extensively about the notion of standards and their application to student writing, literacy acquisition and linguistic diversity, I am wary of any standard that is designed, defined, and/or enforced by a white and male-centered enterprise, including and especially higher education. One cannot afford to divorce any standard or policy from an institution or enterprise that was clearly designed to reinforce inequity and prioritize dominant and traditional discourses over nondominant discourses, and higher education is no exception. The elimination of equity gaps that continue to exist with women and BIPOC scholars earning tenure and promotion in comparison to their counterparts requires urgent transformation of the processes that award counterparts tenure and promotion at higher rates than women and BIPOC faculty.

Ribero suggests that care work and academic service, areas that disproportionately impact women and those from historically oppressed communities, be incentivized in tenure and promotion decisions. Jacobson encourages us to consider counting what others do not count in tenure and promotion decisions. And Do recommends that we find ways to make visible the emotional labor that BIPOC faculty often take on. What each of these suggestions has in common is the need to grant credit to things that typically do not award credit in tenure and promotion decisions. In order to award credit, the criteria for what gets counted must change. When we consider new and different criteria to the criteria that have typically been designed to exclude women and those from historically oppressed communities, we indeed must revise the standards for the criteria put into policy in the first place.

For Jacobson, collaborative scholarship must be weighed more heavily in revising tenure and promotion standards. Such a notion is similar to feminist calls to honor collaboration as equally important as single-authored publications. Jacobson's discussion of a request for him to quantify the percentages of contribution on collaborative projects is consistent with the absurdity that scholars, especially humanists, can place a percentage on the contribution of ideas to a project. Even if the number of words by each author could be quantified, what an absurdity that we measure productivity by the number of words produced in print without considering the numbers of hours devoted to discussing, researching and meeting about the written product. This brings me to another problem with tenure and promotion standards written from a white hegemonic lens: knowledge is not easily quantifiable and what gets quantified and counted often reinforces cultural biases toward individualist research or the securing of grants and other quantifiable external funding.

When we interpret tenure and promotion expectations in terms of quality and not quantity, Jacobson contends that it also enables scholars to focus more on careful scholarship, a slow form of scholarship that engages feminist resistance of a neoliberalism academy. Jacobson characterizes the necessity of producing slower scholarship in the following way:

> I believe that slowness and a humanizing ethos are about both institutional and individual change. We, collectively, must work to change ourselves and the culture that surrounds academic life. As Berg and Seeber suggest, the language of slow can connect to a larger political and social movement. Junior faculty need to hear from others across professional positionalities about changes they have made as scholars and leaders. While the democratic governance of yore may never have really existed . . . we need to know that there are leaders out there interested in counting differently, relating differently, and aligning the work with the democratic and civic missions of many institutions.

As Jacobson suggests, slower scholarship is a humanistic method that also deeply embeds principles of the humanities into the care and quality of scholarship that we produce as both citizens and humans. Slower scholarship also positions us as transferable to leadership development, a point I will return to later in this section. Through the use of slower scholarship, tenure and promotion expectations become doable, valued, and balanced in a way that acknowledges that there are circumstances that impact scholarly productivity in terms of quantity that are beyond our control. As humanists, we must resist tenure and promotion standards that emphasize quantity over quality in terms of publications only, and that do not take into consideration a holistic understanding of the applicant's body of work and quality across a variety of different forms and genres not limited only to academic publications.

As coauthors of *The Black Feminist Coup*, we had to help two of our pre-tenured collaborators respond to standards requiring authors to quantify their collaboration. One condition initially imposed upon Jennifer was to submit a book-length project where she was the sole or primary author (even though our stories were collaboratively written, even the chapters that focus mostly on one of our perspectives: collective memory was at work and our collaborative storytelling was purposefully crafted from a Black feminist methodological perspective). For Olivia, her review committee did not want to count/quantify this book as a monograph, but instead argued it was an edited collection. In other words, we were coeditors of a collection that consisted of our own contributions. We coedited our own authored chapters. We helped Olivia respond by stating that while each chapter may focus on a perspective or two at a time, each chapter was collaboratively written by each of us: we each went through every chapter and added layers of the story as we remembered when being told to us. Moreover, the publication itself lists coauthorship and not coeditorship.

In addition to collaboration, both Jacobson and Do advocate for community engagement being weighed more heavily in tenure and promotion decisions, for community engaged scholarship often impacts the work of public intellectuals from historically oppressed communities and benefits the public, the institutional community, and the academic community. For Jacobson, community engagement is a joyful practice, and one of pleasure. Community engagement as labor is often invisible, and department chairs as leaders and decision makers can be more intentional about outlining contributions for this labor in tenure and promotion decisions projects and scholarship then become helpful when not only tenure applicants provide rationales for counting these scholarly activities, but also and more importantly, when decision makers are also willing and able to reference these statements as valuable in the tenure and promotion decisions for which they provide recommendation.

For Do, community engagement occurs through what he calls "disruptive, strategic dialoguing," a practice where, "white allies are aware of mico- and macroaggressive behaviors in meetings and intentionally disrupt such behaviors... [and] strategically dialoguing with BIPOC faculty to speak in an otherwise hostile environment." Disruptive and strategic dialoguing doesn't suggest that white allies speak for BIPOC faculty. It is instead a practice cognizant of current power structures in our institution that acknowledges that sometimes BIPOC faculty need allies to speak with as we all collectively imagine shifts in our institutional and departmental politics.

Do's chapter reminds us that community engagement may take on public scholarship work and dissemination within the institution, work that often gets inappropriately classified simply as service only. While working on *The Black Feminist Coup*, one of our coauthors sought to count campus lectures and external to department expertise (e.g., dissertation and thesis committee; task force representations; campus workshops) as public scholarship and professional recognition because she was *the only* faculty member on campus with expertise in Black feminism and new media. Instead of counting these activities as professional recognition and scholarship, her dean's level review chided her for this work and recommended that she limit these service activities therefore, not counting them. These activities often get classified, especially for BIPOC women, as being part of the "service tax" (Arnold et al.; Baker-Bell; Griffin et al.), where such faculty are pressured and overextended to participate in these DEI-based activities because there is no one else on campus with the needed expertise, experiences we reference in *The Black Feminist Coup* (145). But without counting these activities as scholarship, they inequitably take time away from one's ability to produce traditional forms of scholarship and research, though they are often implicitly and explicitly expected.

The Black Feminist Coup also questions the notion of tenure standards, but also any decision-making concerning professional recognition of one's career. A need to revise standards is critical not only because the standards themselves are biased, but also, because even when the standards created by institutions are met, Black women often recount examples of imposing new or different standards upon the original ones, in a move that shifts the goal post (101). Even one of Jennifer's former graduate students and our coauthor, Keiondra, shares that she was not surprised about the outcome for her department not to award her funding even though she met all of the criteria, a decision that parallels how the goal post was moved even when "Pulitzer-Prize-winning journalist Nikole Hannah-Jones" met the requirements for tenure but was denied tenure anyway (101).

When revising tenure and promotion standards and expectations, we articulate the necessity this way: for us, "true healing not only requires a change in systems, but also a change in outcomes.... What good are these policies if the demographics for academic rank remain the same?" (145). When transforming tenure and promotion policies, we must keep in mind the purpose: to close equity gaps in those who achieve tenure and promotion. The recommendations outlined in section 3 of this book provide opportunities to include activities that disproportionately impact people of historically oppressed communities, but the goal should always be to advance equity.

The Necessity to Lead with a True Commitment to Equity and Academic Freedom

It is important to note that the previous discussion on equitable tenure and promotion practices is necessary because of the relationship between tenure and academic freedom. Each contribution of this section demonstrates how critical it is for community-engaged scholars, and scholars from historically oppressed groups to obtain tenure for economic security. For Do, it is important to reconceptualize the variety of work that BIPOC faculty take on so that their labor is rewarded, and not *only* viewed as a "cultural obligation," or as ways in which they show "good citizenship towards the institution." For Ribero, "despite the growing attempts to close the gender gap in promotion and tenure, academia continues to assume that workers are 'unencumbered' by dependents." For Jacobson, market-based principles that consider the economic impact of institutions through neoliberal structures, award competition in ways that often reinforce inequity:

> The modern university neoliberalizes academic life through discourses of "excellence" and competition, as well as the corporatization of governing structures that have centralized power in administration and created an employee/employer power imbalance at the expense of shared governance.... The notion that faculty are responsible for deriving supplementary income from external grants and contracts, also known as "academic capitalism," is another trend that further entrenches competition and distances next-gen faculty from civic, leadership, and equity efforts.

It is the affordance of tenure that leads to economic security, which neoliberal institutions reinforce through capitalistic and competitive practices that privilege certain activities over others. Academic freedom is critical because it is designed to enable scholars to use professional expertise to speak and write freely without employment consequence; tenure protects one from being fired because of one's academic right to speak and write in ways that align with one's professional expertise.

The act of tenure from a legislative perspective is at risk, as we see evidence of states seeking to end tenure protections (Bauer-Wolf), and I would suggest that it is not only the end of tenure that is at risk; rather, it is the end of tenure at risk in order to limit academic freedom. In terms of protecting the next generation against eliminations of tenure not only must we revise rules for affording tenure internally within our institutions, but we also must protect outside attacks from the elimination of tenure and assaults on academic freedom.

Each chapter in this section specifically directs responsibility at institutional leaders to protect tenure and academic freedom both from within as well as externally, and this protection has serious implications for closing equity gaps. In relation to childcare Ribero offers that

> childcare workers, particularly domestic care workers, can face financial hardship and are less able to meet basic needs, let alone build and pass down wealth. Building a system of care in academia must intentionally work towards anti-capitalist community care and away from the model of racialized exploitation that perpetuates inequality.... I realize this is not an easy ask. A possible start is to diversify childcare leadership and ensure that care providers at all levels have a voice in decision making that affects them. Considering the needs of care providers along with the needs of children, parents, and universities, can lead to more equitable solutions.

For Jacobson, it is crucial that untenured faculty "hear from others across professional positionalities about changes [those in leadership positions] have made as scholars and leaders." Moreover, scholars and scholar-activists must exert more pressure on leaders to uphold academic freedom in response to legislative and external attacks, for in many cases, especially within academic affairs, leaders themselves are often tenured and benefit from these protections.

As authors of *The Black Feminist Coup*, we also sought to provide a space for boldly using academic freedom to call out racism and white supremacy (10). While we also place pressure and responsibility on campus leaders to protect Black women from white supremacist assaults, we also believe that leadership more broadly be representative of those from the same historically oppressed groups we must commit ourselves as leaders to protect. We ask: "What good are policy changes if we do not increase the representation of Black women in faculty and leadership positions? What good are these policies if the demographics for academic rank remain the same?" (144). Finally, we must hold leaders accountable for the roles they play in advancing inequities and white supremacy, and we must protect leaders from historically oppressed groups from internal and external pressure, using the same forms of tenure and academic freedom that we afford to all members of a campus community.

Conclusion

The contributions in this section give us our marching orders to protect the next generation of scholars from internal inequities and external attacks facing tenure and promotion. As scholars and leaders who already benefit from academic freedom and tenure, we owe it to the next generation to protect the same freedoms we have had for decades. We also owe it to the next generation of scholars to close equity gaps in our tenure and promotion practices and decisions. We are humanists: we must leverage our knowledge against arbitrary numerical measures and criteria for tenure, criteria that privilege certain groups over others. And we must push back on the many forms that knowledge dissemination may take. As a senior scholar in the field, I am committed to the task and encourage other senior scholars to commit to the task when doing external reviews for junior scholars and also when making decisions on our own campuses. It is time and the time is now.

Works Cited

"2021–2026 WMU/WMU-AAUP Agreement—Western Michigan University." *Academic Labor Relations*, Western Michigan University, wmich.edu/sites/default/files/attachments/u510/2021/WMU_AAUP_Contract_2021-2026%20FINAL.pdf. Accessed 3 Jan. 2024.

Arnold, Noelle, Azadeh Osanloo, and Whitney Sherman Newcomb. "Paying Professional Taxes for Promotion and Tenure: The Costs of Justice Work for Black Faculty." *Journal of Research on Leadership Education*, vol. 16, no. 2, 2021, pp. 122–39.

Baker-Bell, April. *Linguistic Justice: Black Language, Literacy, Identity, and Pedagogy*. Routledge, 2020.

Bauer-Wolf, Jeremy. "5 State Plans to Restrict Faculty Tenure You'll Want to Watch." *Higher Ed Dive*, 13 Mar. 2023, www.highereddive.com/news/5-state-plans-to-restrict-faculty-tenure-youll-want-to-watch/643880/.

Blinder, Alan. "Why Defenders of Harvard's President Are Focused on Academic Freedom." *New York Times*, 11 Dec. 2023, www.nytimes.com/2023/12/11/us/academic-freedom-harvard-antisemitism.html.

Caldwell, Jimmy, Jr. "All Education Is Political: Critical Race Theory, White Power, and the Killing of Black Academic Freedom." *AAUP Journal of Academic Freedom*, vol. 14, 2023, pp. 1–9.

Davis, Jennifer C., Eric Ping Hung Li, Mary Steward Butterfield, Gino A. DiLabio, Nithi Santhagunam, and Barbara Marcolin. "Are We Failing Female and Racialized Academics? A Canadian National Survey Examining the Impacts of the COVID-19 Pandemic on Tenure and Tenure-Track Faculty." *Gender, Work, and Organization*, vol. 29, no. 4, pp. 703–22, https://doi.org/10.1111/gwao.12811.

Griffin, Kimberly A., Jessica Bennett, and Jessica Harris. "Marginalizing Merit? Gender Differences in Black Faculty D/discourses on Tenure, Advancement, and Professional Success." *The Review of Higher Education*, vol. 36, no. 4, 2013, pp. 489–512.

Kezar, Adrianna, and K. C. Culver. "Leadership Provocation: Silence Is Complicity." *Change: The Magazine of Higher Learning*, vol. 55, no. 3, 2023, pp. 2–3.

Krukowski, Rebecca A., Loneke T. Blackman Carr, and Danielle Arigo. "Pandemic-Related Tenure Timeline Extensions in Higher Education in the United States: Prevalence and Associated Characteristics." *Challenges*, vol. 13, no. 34, 2022, pp. 1–11, https://doi.org/10.3390/challe13020034.

Oleschuk, Merin. "Gender Equity Considerations for Tenure and Promotion during COVID-19." *Canadian Review of Sociology*, vol. 57, no. 3, 2020, pp. 502–14.

Perryman-Clark, Staci. "A WPA/First-time Mom's Guide to Producing the First Book for Tenure." *Explanation Points: Publishing in Rhetoric and Composition*. Edited by Danielle Nicole DeVoss and John Gallagher, Utah State UP, 2019, pp. 72–76.

Richardson, Jennifer, Mariam Konaté, Staci Perryman-Clark, Olivia McLaughlin, and Grace Keiondra. *The Black Feminist Coup: Black Women's Lived Experiences in White Supremacist Feminist Academic Spaces*. Peter Lang, 2024.

AFTERWORD

"Can't Be Stopped/Gonna Hit the Top"[1]

When Next-Gen Stands at the Threshold of Reinstated White Supremacist Departments and Institutions

CARMEN KYNARD

If you ain't real careful out here in these academic streets, the folx running your departments and institutions will get you so caught up that you mess around and forget that YOU are the ones resurrecting their politically compromised, discrimination-liable, culturally irrelevant, racially divided-into-zero, and centuries-outdated ideas, programs, and policies. Yup, that's one sentence. And I mean every word of it. Charles McMartin, Eric A. House, Sonia C. Arellano, and Thomas Miller have put together a stunning collection of next-gen perspectives that interrogate leading, living, breathing, and being in departments and institutions today.

The current regimes of white nationalist backlash against twenty-first-century Black Freedom Movements have given renewed life to what I call the resident-racists of departments and programs. For a moment all too brief, the resident-racists saw their oppressive shadows and burrowed back into the holes they came from. The current illusion of a dramatic season change has them thinking they can now come back out to play. They are going to have to learn all over again that we are still here and that we will still read their colonial paradigms for filth. I am so ecstatic that I get to witness the ways that next-gen will get them all-the-way together and join the magnificent responses

---

1. In 1979, Sha-Rock was the first woman to rap on a track released to the public on Funky Four Plus One More's "Rappin And Rocking The House." In the opening, she says "I'm Sha-Rock, and I can't be stopped. For all the fly guys, I'm gonna hit the top."

of Jennifer Sano-Franchini, Christina Cedillo, and Staci Perryman-Clark in supporting these scholars.

From the very first chapter by Sean Moxley-Kelly and Abigail Oakley, I was outraged and re-radicalized. They sparked a deep return to my memories of a freezing winter in Ohio where January–February temperatures remained –15° and below each day. Cold spells were not unusual for late winter, but that winter stands out because its chilling effect was extensive, and my mother's electricity bills were extremely high. When she couldn't pay in full, the electricity provider (there was/is only one in the city) turned off the electric supply to the heat, lights, hot water heater, and stove of our tiny one-bedroom apartment. My mother went to multiple social service agencies for help, including the utility company's offices, in an attempt to work out various payment plans despite the dangers of driving to these places in that weather in her dilapidated car, more affectionately known as our "hoopty." As just a little girl, the condescension and callousness of the white managers in each setting were very apparent to me. Not a single one of those people owned the actual company or saw even 1 percent of its profit-margins and yet they each sat there in offices as rundown as our "hoopty" acting like it was their sole job to protect and defend the brand from us. Those managers offered us no help and said truly dumb things like, "Yes, this is a serious issue," or, "You have to manage your money better," or, "We cannot afford to supply your electricity without full payment." They seemed rather nonchalant about letting my mother and me know—along with so many countless others in that city—that there was no aid for us during this risk of literally freezing to death. Their entire outlook and set of policies were designed to punish mothers, especially those bringing BIPOC children into the world, in exactly the ways that Ana Ribero points out in "Mothering in the Academy: Equity, Child Care, and the Tenure Clock."

Every institution during that freezing winter in Ohio performed the same white liberalist discourse of excuse-making, even though the company was amassing unprecedented profits given how much everyone was paying for heightened heating needs. When Moxley-Kelly and Oakley describe the process of getting salary increases for instructors in "Putting the Rhetorical Expertise of NTT Faculty to Work," I flash right back to these memories of winters with no electricity, not just because of salary suppression and lack of regard, but also based on the way administrators handled the material effects of the socioeconomic disparities that they were managing. Moxley-Kelly and Oakley explain that in 2014, more than seventy instructors taught five writing courses per semester (with twenty-five students per class) for $32,000 at their university.

They are a non-voting body represented by a small group–a trend far too many English departments support to protect the elitism of tenure (which is not always earned through research despite what so many claim). By 2022, there was an increase in the base salary for instructors from $49,000 to $60,000, but only after they pursued research studies and data to present to administrators to convince them that folx couldn't afford housing and other basic needs. To keep it on the cheap, the administration did not do an across-the-board $11,000 raise for all, so folx at the higher rank from years of service didn't see much increase. Meanwhile, if a household earns less than $4,395 per month in that state right now, they are considered low-income so the $60,000 can't raise a family either and the previous $32,000 was just $2,000 above poverty level. Like those Ohio managers who insisted they could not help us, while people literally froze to death, these university managers also acted like BooBoo the Fool in their utter surprise that their instructors were struggling materially and financially while doing most of the teaching labor in the department.

They remind me of what James Sledd would call "boss compositionists" who "maintain and defend the indefensible while tinkering with an iniquitous system just enough to obscure its iniquities but never enough to change it deeply" (147). And they play right in your face too with these excuses in this fake-nice White Mainstream English that we are then supposed to go back and teach in our classrooms as if it is not a vehicle of violence and silence (Baker-Bell). Whether it involves leaving poor communities in the dark and cold like I describe in my childhood in Ohio or super-exploiting writing instructors today, this is the logic of racial capitalism, and it undergirds all American institutions from the electric company to the university (Melamed). As Charisse S. Iglesias so brilliantly argues in "Navigating Industry Careers through Cultural Integration," colleges and universities are also industries and, as such, they are governed by these same logics of racial capitalism. As a socioeconomic and cultural logic rooted in plantation life and white setter occupation, racial capitalism does not care about the harm it causes or the value that it subtracts and extracts from our bodies and lives. And the white liberalist discourses in our departments seem to accommodate it.

While my narrative involves the power/electric industrial complex, it is never merely one institution causing harm but many working in tandem. Schooling is always deeply implicated. The teachers and administrators at my elementary school did not offer any more regard for my mother and me than the electric company who purposely left us in the dark and cold. Whenever my mother had to visit social aid offices, she did so before she went into work and before the school doors opened. This means I always went with her, usually an enjoyable experience since our time together was limited as she was a single mother always working and struggling to take care of us. During that blistering cold winter of visiting many social aid offices in the mornings, I would often arrive late to my second grade class. On such occasions, my white female teacher would reprimand me in front of the classroom, making comments about how my mother needed to do better. So, after spending the night in the cold, then getting ignored by social services, I went to school to get ridiculed by white teachers implementing a curriculum that didn't include me. I would get in even more trouble throughout the day, because I did what I always do when some silly fool tries to come for me (and there have been so, so, so many in every school): I refuse to respect anything they say or do. At that time in Ohio, schools were in the throes of racial-desegregation experiments, so all of the Black children were bussed in from the nearest housing projects and apartment developments. The absences of my friends that winter were obvious to me but didn't seem worth noting to the majority white adults running the school. I remember us always talking among ourselves about who was staying across town with aunties and uncles, who went back South to live with they granmomma and 'nem, and who moved to different cities and neighborhoods to get out of them heating bills. I was in second grade having these complex conversations about navigating poverty under white supremacy. The irony is that our teacher was a long-term substitute (who we called "sub-lady") in a position that could be terminated at any time, but that fact did not align her fate to ours in her teaching practices.

At the time of this writing, Brown and Black children are even more chronically absent in schools. David Kirkland traces these issues at *forwardED* in "Where Have Our Children Gone? Chronic Absenteeism and the Disappearance of Black, Latinx, and Economically Less Advantaged Students Post-COVID." Kirkland shares that in places like New York City, chronic absenteeism after COVID rose from 27 percent in 2019 to over 40 percent in 2022, especially impacting working class/working poor students of color. Meanwhile, in places like Los Angeles, absenteeism among Black students is at 57 percent while districts across the US report absenteeism spikes (Blume). As Kirkland argues, this absence of BIPOC students sits at the amalgamation of multiple forces: administrative failures; schools' disconnection from students' lives; refusals to meet the needs of the most vulnerable populations; social inequities related to housing, hunger, and trauma; lack of safety in schools; ongoing inability to offer a sense of belonging and identity affirmation for BIPOC, queer students, and disabled students; hostility and disregard from a still-too-white teaching force. In "Challenges and Opportunities for Teacher Leaders in K–12 Schools: Lessons Learned from Teachers of Color in K–12 Schools," Alice Hays, Shaylyn Marks, Alexandra Chapa-Kunz, and Amardeep (Rupsy) Bajwa beautifully take us inside the politics and practices of teachers of color who intervene in and disrupt white supremacy in these daily operations of classrooms and schools. Seeing these teachers educate and nurture Black and Brown children today is nothing short of inspiring, and they do so at detriment to themselves given the antagonisms they face.

The Boyer report of 2030 does not offer us a more promising glimpse of equity in higher education. Six-year completion rates for Black and Latinx students are significantly lower than they are for white students at R1 and R2 universities and across all four-year institutions. Meanwhile, the enrollment of Pell grant recipients, still the best marker of college students facing the most economic hardship, has decreased at R1 and R2 universities, and these students also have lower graduation rates. My focus on R1 and R2 universities is not an attempt to center these kinds of universities as the only or best kind. My point is to call attention to the fact that the very schools who produce the holders of PhDs have not figured out how to implement an education that honors folx who are of color and/or not wealthy and so cannot produce social change related to them. They are an inadequate role model and next-gen is not being quiet about it. It is why scholar-teacher-activists like Anicca Cox describe an untenable reality in "Crossing Over: Transitioning to Early-Career Leadership with Labor Equity in Mind." For Cox, it is like inventing a whole new world to create and maintain a writing program that directs and *actually evaluates* an evidence-based commitment to BIPOC success when it has never done so before, alongside a platform of labor justice and professional support for critical and creative anti-racist writing teachers. In many ways, it most certainly is a whole new world because R1/R2 schools can't prepare anyone for this when they struggle to achieve it themselves (if it is even a real goal and not apologized away by always referencing "stakeholders" and "parents" who supposedly only want the grammar and white formulaic styles that we can all now get from AI).

Robin Kelley, who I regard as the most brilliant historian of our time, reminds us of a critical point: "Certainly universities can and will become more diverse and marginally more welcoming for black students, but as institutions they will never be engines of social transformation."

In my time at multiple universities now, I have witnessed several first Black graduates with PhDs in rhet-comp get through programs and all are amazing teachers and scholars. The departments' racism in these cases, however, never once questions how and why it took so damn long. In one particular institution, I encountered the most racist and problematic white graduate students of my career with BIPOC students routinely reporting racist antagonisms to me when, already at pre-semester gatherings, they were confused for other BIPOC students standing nearby despite the fact that they were wearing name tags. BIPOC and/or queer students also describe how stunned they are by the racist graduate students who enroll in race-focused courses and must wonder if such students are "plants" from right-wing white supremacist groups. This is who R1s/R2s are sending out into college classrooms, and they look a lot like the hostile faculty who Tom Hong Do so chillingly describes in "Racialized Bodies Navigating White Institutional Spaces." This training of R1/R2 graduate students is also implicated in the experiences of Felicita Arzu-Carmichael and Mena Hannakachl who describe as many ethics-wayward faculty in the writing center and department in "Student-Faculty Coalition Building: Autoethnographic Perspectives on Leadership and Empowerment." Next-gen leaders remain the ones most committed to calling all this out! They do as Robin Kelley advocates: "become subversives in the academy, exposing and resisting its labor exploitation, its gentrifying practices, its endowments built on misery, its class privilege often camouflaged in multicultural garb, and its commitments to war and security."

Our post-COVID-19 schools represent more chronic absenteeism of BIPOC students, dismal progress at R1s/R2s, erasure of affirmative action and DEI offices, and targeted attacks on queer/ BIPOC/ immigrant/ undocumented students and teachers. White supremacy will always let you know that it hates you, especially when you are calling it out. Wilson Kwamogi Okello reminds us that in such contexts we must also seek out alternative models of joy, thriving, and imagining. Brad Jacobson's "(Trying to) Take it 'Slow': Navigating Productivity, Parenting, and Academic Life through COVID-19" is closely related in insisting that taking it slow is an important political act and this cannot be underestimated. Tricia Hersey, the Nap Bishop, has brilliantly mobilized her Nap Ministry to help us contest this kind of rundown of our bodies, time, and minds. Across social media, art installations, rest decks, and multiple books, Hersey keeps telling us to go "lay yo ass down" and "sit my ass down and daydream"; understand that rest is a divine human right for the sake of our bodies, souls, and the earth; refuse to donate our bodies to capitalism and white supremacy; and see rest as resistance and reparations for our ancestors whose stolen labor built nations. The right to rest and slowdown is revolutionary for folx whose labor has been super-exploited.

Today, corrupt companies cannot terminate heat and lights for non-payment in such harsh winters given these kinds of policies once resulted in so much loss of life. The only people who ever helped my mother and me back then were BIPOC folx in the community working towards mutual aid. The networks that gave my mother the money to pay up our bill were designed to offset the need for us to rely on predatory lenders, because, in the hood, poverty is still very lucrative for the people who don't look like us. My mom and I were considered "easy" cases because we lived in a dense apartment building with less expensive heating costs, unlike freestanding homes and rowhouses with freezing pipes and exorbitant plumbing repairs on top of bigger electric bills. I remember my mom being so scared when she heard more folx were even worse off than us. She took all the overtime she could get so that she could pay back into the fund very quickly. She was a keypunch operator at a downtown bank, a data entry type of job that no longer exists where my mother and multiple other BIPOC and/or immigrant women used a large keypunch machine to punch holes into paper cards to record the bank's data. I always went to her overtime shifts with her, because only the "keypunch girls," as they were called, were in the building at the time and never told when I accompanied her. They assigned me filing tasks, had me go get snacks for them, trained me to stack cards, and let me double-check and triple-check their punches. In exchange, I secured bubblegum treats for myself and was always told how smart and helpful I was. They even called me a "li'l keypunch girl," a term they re-inscribed as positive. This was a space where women shared information about community help (and other exciting things like soap operas) that I could eavesdrop on even when I didn't fully understand. It should come as no surprise that so many next-gen scholars like Adele Leon are centering such spaces in their work as the place where real mutuality can happen as she describes in "From Perfunctory to Practice: Creating an Administrative Identity as Early-Career Faculty through Community Partnership."

When I think back on my second-grade substitute teacher who ridiculed poor Black families for coming late to school during a winter where we were all just trying not to die, I remember that she did have one good thing: she had an interestingly pronounced last name. Her name and person are not worthy of repeating in print, so I will just say that it offered many wonderful rhyme schemes. "Rapper's Delight," one of our favorite songs at the time, ain't have nuthin on us second-graders with the way we tore up that "sub-lady's" whole character in our rhymes, a literacy event far more sophisticated than anything she ever provided. When the school finally found us a full-time teacher, the "sub-lady" announced her departure in class with big, ol' crocodile tears. Many of the white almost-middle-class kids, bless they little hearts, cried alongside her. Meanwhile, I excitedly raised my hand and asked how long 'til her last day, a memory that my childhood friends still tease me about. Whenever I see one of them at a local Walmart when I am in town, now some forty-plus years later, no matter if they are way down or across the aisle, they will reenact that second-grade scene by smiling, waving their hand in the air, and yelling out "Ooooo-when you leavin'?!" Them poor Walmart shoppers be so confused. That "sub-lady" is likely still alive, and I would ask her the same question today.

As a small child, I was never reprimanded or even side-eyed from any parent or community member when they learned about what I said to the "sub-lady" in her last days; all I saw was a weird smirk. As an adult, I now think they were holding back a laugh and agreed with my resistant stance. As small children, we were already developing a sharp critique against racist institutions that harmed us based on the everyday conversations in the homes where we congregated for heat, in the community organizations where we were welcomed and really educated, at our mother's extra jobs where we were seen as smart and helpful, and in the rhyming cyphers in the classroom and lunch room where we were highly creative-literate. For some of us, a critique of institutional racism/whiteness/anti-blackness and the people who defend it are an empowering inheritance we received long ago as a rite of passage into this cold world. Since I used to quote Sha-Rock as a little girl during the harsh winter I described here, I'll do so again with the fabulous next-gen cypher in this book in mind: "Can't Be Stopped/Gonna Hit the Top."

Works Cited

Blume, Howard. "As School Starts, LAUSD Faces Chronic Student Absenteeism." *Los Angeles Times*, 23 Aug. 2024. www.latimes.com/california/00000191-7cdb-d2c8-abfd-7dfb1b640000-123.

Boyer 2030 Commission. *The Equity/Excellence Imperative: A 2030 Blueprint for Undergraduate Education at U.S. Research Universities*. Association for Undergraduate Education at Research Universities (UERU), 2024.

Hersey, Tricia. *Rest Is Resistance: A Manifesto*. Little, Brown Spark, 2022.

Kelley, Robin D. G. "Black Study, Black Struggle." *Boston Review*, Mar. 2016. www.bostonreview.net/forum/robin-kelley-black-struggle-campus-protest/.

Kirkland, David. "Where Have Our Children Gone? Chronic Absenteeism and the Disappearance of Black, Latinx, and Economically Less Advantaged Students Post-COVID." *forwardED*, Sept. 2024. www.forward-ed.com/post/where-have-our-children-gone-chronic-absenteeism-and-the-disappearance-of-black-latinx-and-econom.

Melamed, Jodi. *Represent and Destroy: Rationalizing Violence in the New Racial Capitalism*. U of Minnesota P, 2011.

Okello, Wilson Kwamogi. "Unspeakable Joy: Anti-Black Constraint, Loopholes of Retreat, and the Practice of Black Joy." *Urban Education*, 2024, https://doi-org.ezproxy.tcu.edu/10.1177/00420859241227956.

Sledd, James. "On Buying in and Selling out: A Note for Bosses Old and New." *College Composition and Communication*, vol. 53, no. 1, 2001, pp. 146–49.

Acknowledgments

We would like to acknowledge the service of those who have stepped up to support our students, coworkers, and communities in the years since the great recession and global pandemic. Our dependence on such leaders has deepened as student support programs have been targeted, free speech rights have been rolled back, and immigrants and other marginalized groups have been attacked and criminalized. Many of the students, faculty, staff, and community organizers upon whom our future depends have gone unrecognized and unrewarded, and some have been jailed, fired, expelled, and deported.

These leaders have helped us to recognize and learn from our interdependencies and the mutual benefits of caring for ourselves and others. Some of these lessons have been hard-earned. We have lost students, coworkers, and friends who have stepped away, including colleagues who collaborated on this collection. Several agreed to contribute and then decided to withdraw from the collection and leave the academy. We wish to take note of their absence from these pages, our departments, and our communities. We also want to acknowledge both their rights to self-determination and our obligations to learn from their experiences.

Acknowledging these mutual interdependencies is a vital part of the sorts of coalitional leadership that this collection addresses. We have come to realize how vital these reciprocities are in our work, our jobs, and our lives in our own individual ways as we will briefly take note of here...

FROM CHARLIE: When we began this project in fall 2021, I was overwhelmed by the stories of next-gen leaders who were showing up for their students, their communities, and their families. They were working within and beyond the confines of their roles, navigating systems that often asked too much and gave too little. As I begin my career, their leadership sustains me in ways I could not have anticipated. Their resolve to resist institutional harm has sharpened my own focus on the work that matters most, and I am reminded that I must be as honest as I am hopeful about the path ahead for our profession. Our shared generational challenges make me more grateful than ever to the family and friends who have carried me through these uncertain times. To Michael and Cathy McMartin, Kellen and Bob Hix, Jack McMartin and Nikolass Colpaert, Bryan and Lauren McMartin, Will and Meghan McMartin, Geraldo and Erica Boldewijn, Jorge Pizano, and Yesenia Monroy—thank you for making home feel like just a phone call away. Your love and steadiness continue to be my tower of strength.

FROM ERIC: The last moments of the publishing process for this collection paralleled the schedule for my tenure process almost perfectly. It was interesting to theorize and build with the contributors of this collection in our unified calls for a different type of leadership discourse to inform our institutions while also thinking through the ways in which my own academic career was living out the arguments we were raising. Sometimes those moments were inspirational, sometimes they were anxiogenic; either way, they were important parts of the process for both realizing the collection and working through tenure, and I want to briefly shout out a few people who have held me up, worked with me, inspired me, and built with me along the way. Shout out to Tom and Charlie for the initial vision for the collection, and for trusting both my critiques and visions for leadership and administration enough to invite me to edit the collection. Shout out to Sonia, who's been my academic big sis since back in the days of Arizona's RCTE program. I've always learned so much from you and valued your friendship, and it has been an honor to work with you in this capacity. Shout out to the colleagues (both former and current) at my institution who have helped me think through this process, specifically Kellie Sharp-Hoskins, Kerry Banazek, Kathleen Weisse, and Suban Nur Cooley. And last but certainly not least, shout out to Ethi and Quinn, whose love and support sustains me and reminds me of the necessity of effective work/life balance.

FROM SONIA: One of many lessons I carry with me from exiting academia is to choose your community wisely because it will support and sustain you throughout the years. I am thankful for the community I built with colleagues in academia and meaningful friendships that continue beyond my time as a professor. I am in awe of how many former colleagues reach out, check in, and catch up regularly. I'd like to acknowledge these friendships that have played a key role in my life, my career, and my overall well-being as a human. I'd like to thank many of the contributors in this collection because our one-on-one conversations through the years have been incredibly impactful. I'd especially like to thank my coeditors for their patience, guidance, and support as I left this career and as we finished this collection. Charlie and Eric, your friendship throughout the years has meant more than you know, and I appreciate any time we get to hang out in person. Importantly, I'd like to thank Tom as the senior member of this editorial team, because he kept us moving along during these difficult times. Additionally, Tom has been an incredible mentor to me since day one of graduate school, and he continues to care for and advise me holistically. I hope everyone experiences even a sliver of the love and friendship that continues to fuel me. ¡Adelante!

FROM TOM: As I prepared to retire and step away from my job, my recognition of all the privileges I had enjoyed deepened. I have long realized that I was part of the last generation in which most faculty could have a hope of such benefits, and I felt remorse for not having done more to support my students and coworkers in more precarious positions. I would like to acknowledge that debt and renew my commitment to continuing to do what I can to support the first-gen and new-majority leaders whose vision and aspirations must be acknowledged to sustain the role of liberal education in a liberal democracy.

Index

A4BL Anti-racist Tenure Letter Working Group, The, 224, 237
academia, 29, 91, 214, 261; careers in, 52; careers outside, 85, 86; culture of, 203–4; industry and, 83, 84, 95, 96, 103; leaving, 79, 81–82, 99; mothering in, 209–13; parenthood and, 224; personal/professional split for, 202; productivity in, 211
Academia Insider, 83
academic freedom, 67, 253, 254; assaults on, 259, 260, 268; commitment to, 267–69; equity and, 261; racism/white supremacy and, 268; tenure and, 261, 267, 269
Academic Labor: Research and Artistry (Melançon, Mechenbier, and Wilson), 36, 41
academic life, 100, 103, 138, 211, 228
accountability, 69, 70, 85, 90, 91, 95, 96, 119, 166, 167, 169, 180, 181, 229, 230; community, 94; core values and, 84; reciprocity and, 178
accreditation, 5, 6, 71, 236
activism, 154; anti-racist, 167; labor, 13; student, 7
Adler, Laura, 127
administration, 57, 65, 82, 109, 110, 170; anti-racist, 165; challenges from, 150, 153–54; managing up/down and, 49; meetings with, 46; navigating, 74; NTT faculty and, 50, 51; traditional, 119; working with, 40–41, 48–50
advisory boards, 173, 176
affirmative action, 276
agency, 139; collective, 118; exercising, 115, 118; relationality and, 76
Ahmed, Sara, 76, 94, 121
alternative academic (alt ac), 81, 85, 96, 100
American Association of University Presses, 9
annual faculty review (AFR), 246
Antecol, Heather, 212
anti-blackness, 126, 278
anti-DEI mandates, 5–6, 135
anti-racism, 8, 10, 16, 70, 164, 165, 166, 167, 169, 178, 180
Anwer, Megha, 223
Arellano, Sonia C., 4, 6, 13, 14, 271; professionalization and, 17
Arizona State University (ASU), 34–35; NTT faculty strategies at, 33–34, 36, 37
Arzu-Carmichael, Felicita, 12, 116, 117, 138, 141, 186, 188, 189–90, 276; autoethnography of, 123, 142; coalition building and, 171; problems for, 187
Asian Americans, 241, 243; invisible labor by, 242; microaggressions and, 244, 254;

racialized bodies of, 242; stereotypes and, 244; workplace experience of, 244
assessment, 57, 165, 255
ASU. *See* Arizona State University
ASU Charter, 38, 51
Atlantic, The, 223
austerity, 71, 100, 109

Bajwa, Amardeep (Rupsy), 116, 117, 148, 149, 151, 167, 189, 191, 275; challenges for, 150, 160; curriculum/students of color and, 153; invisible labor and, 155; leadership and, 192; PLC group and, 152, 158; social climate and, 154; teacher-educator programs and, 12
Baker-Bell, April, 68
Basford, Tessa, 190n1
Berg, Maggie, 227, 230, 264; embodiment/affect and, 233; pedagogy of pleasure and, 233; slow food and, 226; slow professor and, 235
Beyond Academia (webinar), 82
Beyond Guilt Trips: Mindful Travel in an Unequal World (Taranath), 87
bias, 180, 211; cultural, 264; political/ideological/personal, 250, 251
biological clock, tenure clock and, 219
BIPOC faculty, 15, 76, 203, 204, 246, 251–53, 263; bodies of, 242; cultural taxation and, 245; dialoguing with, 266; discrimination and, 253–54; emotional labor of, 254–55, 264; goals/expectations and, 16; hidden tax on, 244; knowledge-making and, 250; labor of, 13, 243, 267; microaggressions and, 254, 255; policing and, 249–51; silencing, 245; success for, 275; well-being of, 253; white allies of, 255
BIPOC students, 263, 274–75; attack on, 276; identity information for, 274
BIPOC women, 213, 266, 277
Birdsong, Mia, 90
Bishop, Nap, 276
Bishop, Rudine Sims, 151
Black faculty, 126, 129, 130, 187; working conditions for, 241
Black Faculty Association (BFA), 130
Black feminism, 66n1, 121, 122, 140, 169, 266
Black Feminist Coup: Black Women's Lived Experiences in White Supremacist Feminist Academic Spaces (Perryman-Clark, Richardson, Konate, and McLaughlin), 259, 260, 261, 265, 266, 268
Black Freedom Movements, 271
Black Lives Matter, 4, 260
Black Marxism, 69

Black Power, 69
Black students, 5, 7, 149, 193; absenteeism among, 274; completion rates for, 275
Black women, 130, 168, 213; academic freedom of, 260; exploitation of, 263; standards for, 266; status of, 219; systems of power and, 66n1
Black Women's Liberatory Pedagogies (Spencer), 168, 180
Blue Lives Matter, 154
Boo Boo the Fool, 273
boundaries, 18; disrupting, 9; personal/professional, 204; setting, 205; violation of, 192
Boyer, Ernest, 235, 236, 275
Brannon, Lil, 210–11
Brown, Wendy, 202–3
Brydon-Miller, Mary, 40
burnout, 45, 73, 75

capitalism, 216, 276; academic, 10, 226; labor and, 215; racial, 273; white patriarchal, 204
care: collectivizing, 216; community, 110, 219, 268; crisis of, 14; domestic, 268; early, 218, 263; family-oriented, 222; home, 210; institutional, 212; mothering and, 209; rethinking, 213–15. *See also* childcare; daycare; early care and education
care work, 213, 261, 262; exploitation and, 263; incentivizing, 217, 263; models of, 16; protecting, 219
Carey, Tamika, 188
Carmichael, Arzu, 128
CCCC. *See* Conference on College Composition and Communication
"CCCC Position Statement of Professional Guidance for Mentoring Graduate Students," 72
CCSS. *See* Common Core State Standards
Cedillo, Christina, 272
Center for Excellence in Teaching and Leaning, 132
Center for Multicultural Initiatives (CMI), 140
Chadwick, Jocelyn, 10
change: advocating for, 122, 155, 195; behavioral, 208; cautions/contexts for, 58, 59–60; collective, 101, 107–9; cultural, 238; effective, 108–9; 4R's and, 140–42; ideological stances of, 71; institutional, 56, 75, 104, 207, 238; macroeconomic, 42; meaningful, 102, 109; political, 9; resistance to, 66; structural, 254
Chapa-Kunz, Alexandra, 116, 117, 148, 149, 151, 167, 188, 193, 275; challenges for, 150, 160; curriculum options and, 153, 157;

experiences of, 157; invisible labor and, 154–55, 191; PLC and, 158; teacher-educator program and, 12
childcare, 205, 207, 210, 211, 215, 218, 224, 263, 268; affordable, 209; compensation for, 219; full-time, 208; heteronormative, 208; losing, 209
childcare deserts, 218
Chronicle of Higher Education, The, 13
cinch down, 222, 223, 224, 260
citizenship, 244, 267
Ciurria, Mich, 134
civic missions, 238, 264, 267
civil rights movement, 99
classrooms, 58; hybrid/online, 174, 231; interaction in, 136; subjectivity of, 11; virtual, 230, 232. *See also* working conditions
Coalition for Community Writing, 15
coalitions, 67, 73, 126, 141, 186, 196; building, 10, 27, 30–31, 60, 105, 123, 127, 132, 137, 138, 139, 142, 187; microaffirmations and, 18; microaggressions and, 204
collaboration, 3–4, 5, 11, 12, 30, 40, 57, 58, 59, 70, 83, 92, 103, 118, 123, 125, 127, 141, 160, 165, 167, 171, 172–73, 174, 177; building, 53, 64, 76; communication and, 94; community, 232; envisioning, 18; face-to-face, 6; faculty, 139; focus on, 235; grassroots, 29; labor of, 230; leadership, 169; opportunities for, 232; prioritizing, 228–29; relying on, 71; slow and, 230
collective action, 8, 9–10, 18, 47, 100, 265; building, 234
College Composition and Communication, 16
College Made Whole (Gallagher), 8
College Uncovered (podcast), 8
colonialism, 81, 84, 116, 271
Colorado Department of Education Office of Language, Culture and Equity, 166
Combahee River Collective, 71
comics, 80
commitments, 17; actionable, 123; personal, 15; valuing, 216
Common Core State Standards (CCSS), 147, 157, 188
communication, 8, 44, 57, 88, 105, 133, 222, 234; collaboration and, 94; constructive, 95; data-driven, 46; strategies for, 85
communities, 31, 119, 137; campus, 132; changing, 196, 197; connecting with, 89; departmental, 75; extended, 211; in-class, 236; individualism and, 238; marginalized, 84; oppressed, 267; programmatic, 108

communities of color, 124, 189
community building, 117, 123, 204, 205, 216, 237, 255
Community-Campus Partnerships for Health (CCPH), 86
community writing programs, 165, 166, 168–69, 172; coordinating, 12–13; establishing, 167
composition, 86, 99, 175; courses, 251; critiquing, 68; multimodal, 231; program, 65; teaching, 163
Composition, Communication and Rhetoric division, 59
composition sequence, 246–47, 248
Conference on College Composition and Communication (CCCC), 125, 237, 249
consensus, navigating, 40–41, 45–47
Consortium of Doctoral Programs in Rhetoric and Composition, 72
contexts, 58, 59–60; importance of, 65–70; institutional, 105, 205; observing, 86–88; organizational, 93; spatiotemporal, 104, 105
Cooper, Brittney, 129
Cortez, José Manuel, 6, 14
Council of Writing Program Administration (CWPA), 247
counterstories, 13, 147, 242, 245
counterstrategies, 187, 195–97
Covarrubias, Rebecca, 16
COVID-19 pandemic, 3, 39, 49, 57, 91, 99, 108, 123–24, 133, 142, 154, 163, 177, 188; absenteeism during, 274; education during, 233; impact of, 14, 128, 132, 135–36, 137, 189, 208–9, 228, 260; leadership and, 122; life during, 38, 223–24; parenting and, 14; response to, 225; spread of, 232; women and, 210; working through, 222
Cox, Anicca, 10–11, 100, 102, 105, 201, 275; coalitional action and, 108; graduate students and, 28; institutional structures and, 82–83, 101; positionality and, 104; possibility and, 107; precarity and, 16
critical race theory (CRT), 27, 242, 243
critical thinking, 169, 173, 178
Crow, Michael, 35, 50–51
CRT. *See* critical race theory
cultural integration, 80, 81, 83–84, 87, 93, 95, 96, 103, 105, 148, 158; as lens, 85; strategies for, 85; study of, 84
cultural norms, 89, 107, 116, 117
cultural taxation, 241–42, 249, 254; microaggressions and, 243–45

culture, 66, 83, 85, 89, 117, 131, 132, 137, 202, 203–4, 238, 250; academic, 224; care, 215; company, 94; dominant, 188; institutional, 11, 59, 64, 65, 76, 136; organizational, 105; patriarchal, 118; white supremacy, 224; workplace, 88, 94, 95
curriculum, 29, 56, 57, 69, 75, 125, 148, 151, 197, 247; approval of, 153; challenges of, 153–54, 157–58; changes for, 11, 149, 153, 155, 158; culturally-affirming, 191, 193; developing, 153, 155, 158, 159; diversification of, 117; humanizing, 147; implementing, 274; pedagogy and, 147; planning, 152; requirements of, 151; students of color and, 153

data, 5, 92, 229; gathering, 34, 40, 41, 42, 43, 50–51, 53; qualitative/quantitative, 42, 43
Davila, Bethany, 13
Davison, April, 130
daycare, 205, 207, 213, 224, 234
decision-making, 36, 110, 153, 159, 176, 219, 223, 229; collaborative, 31; NTT faculty and, 49–50; political/social aspects of, 44
Dedoose (software), 40
Defining, Locating, and Addressing Bullying in the WPA Workplace (Elder and Davila), 13
DEI. *See* diversity, equity, and inclusion
Delgado, Richard, 243
demographics, 7, 9, 203, 269; shift in, 156
Department of English (ASU), 35, 39, 48; NTT faculty at, 34, 36, 44, 45–46
Dewi Oka, Cynthia, 210, 216, 219
Diab, Rasha, 122
DiAngelo, Robin, 249
digital testimonios, 231, 232
Dirty Dozen, 68, 69
discrimination, 193, 211, 271; combatting, 255; racial, 244, 253–54; wage, 209
dissertations, 91, 92, 93, 229, 266
diversity, 4, 13, 146, 147, 160; cultural, 130, 140; ethnic, 130; linguistic, 130, 140, 263; racial, 130
diversity and equity programs, 3, 5–6, 30
diversity, equity, and inclusion (DEI), 41, 164, 171, 178, 192, 195, 212, 266; attack on, 186, 276; committees, 217; goals, 168, 187, 220; initiatives, 3, 5–6, 30, 116, 119, 142; opposition to, 121; work, 94, 169, 179–80, 253
Do, Tom Hong, 14, 16–17, 203, 259, 276; BIPOC faculty and, 267; collaboration and, 265; community engagement and, 265; emotional labor and, 263–64; microaggressions and, 13; mismatches and, 16

Docka-Filipek, Danielle, 212–13, 217
Doleža, Joshua, 13
Dugan, Jamila, 180

early care and education (ECE), 218, 219, 262
Echelbarger, Margaret, 83–84
education: communally engaged, 5; experiential, 180; people of color and, 147; pre-service, 147, 158; prioritizing, 218; public, 3, 5; special, 156; tools, 173; whitestreaming, 250. *See also* early care and education; graduate education; higher education
ELD. *See* English Language Development
Elder, Cristyn, 13
elitism, 169, 273
embedded writing specialist (EWS), 133, 134, 136, 139, 140, 141
emotional labor, 43–44, 156, 175, 252, 254–55, 263–64; assessment protocols for, 255
empowerment, 122, 139; Black feminist, 142; collective, 27; leadership and, 129–32; personal, 129; perspectives on, 123; student, 138
engagement, 11, 106, 124, 141, 236; community, 15, 83, 84–85, 87, 91, 95, 96, 118, 119, 167, 231–33, 235, 266; institutional, 28; labor, 265; looking for, 17; stakeholder, 173; student, 151
English as a second language (ESL), 132
English education, 231, 232, 247
English Language Development (ELD), 156, 192
entrepreneurship, 202, 225–26
environment, 81, 126, 138, 154–55, 255; educational, 13; political, 13; school, 157; transforming, 94. *See also* working conditions
equity, 4, 28, 60, 73, 109, 117, 118, 187, 211, 219; academic freedom and, 261; advancing, 180, 267; approaches to, 57, 70; commitment to, 267–69; gender, 209, 261–63; racial, 87, 124, 140; work, 147. *See also* labor equity
"Equity, Justice, and Anti-Racist Teaching" (NCTE conference), 127
Equity Toolkit for Administrators, 166
ethnicity, 4, 236, 244
EWS. *See* embedded writing specialist

faculty: diversity of, 121; early-career, 12, 13, 16, 19, 28, 59, 181; life of, 204, 235; morale of, 51; underrepresented, 187. *See also* next-gen faculty; non-tenure-track (NTT) faculty; tenure-track (TT) faculty
faculty of color, 14, 109, 126, 149, 187
family medical leave act (FMLA), 201
"Fast Food Nation" (Berg and Seeber), 226

feedback, 73, 139, 160, 166, 169, 179, 232
Feigenbaum, Paul, 179
feminists of color, 213
feminist theory, 11, 58, 81, 164
First-Generation Faculty of Color: Reflections on Research, Teaching, and Service (Lachica Buenavista, Jain, and Ledesma), 14
first-year composition (FYC), 249, 251
First-Year Writing Program (FYW), 57, 64, 70, 75, 108, 124, 141, 248
flexibility, 174–75, 218, 223
Flores, Lisa A., 123
Floyd, George, 124, 186, 188–89
forwardED (Kirkland), 274
Foucault, Michel, 226
four R's (recognize, reveal, reject, and replace), 123, 142
Freire, Paulo, 129
Fujiwara, Lynn, 244, 245
funding, 30–31, 110, 193; federal, 110; grant, 222, 228; internal/external, 173, 263, 264
Funk Four Plus One More, 271n1
FYW. *See* First-Year Writing Program

GADs. *See* graduate assistant directors
Gallagher, Chris, 8, 58, 71, 107
García, Romeo, 6, 14
gatekeeping, 87, 88, 134, 189
Gather, Read, Analyze, and Make (GRAM) model, 28, 34, 40, 41, 50
Gay, Claudine, 260, 261
Gay Straight Alliance, 149
gender, 58, 236; disparities, 212–13; hierarchies, 5; race and, 217; studies, 260; subjectivity of, 11
gender affirming care, 216
gender gap, 209, 210, 212, 217
GI Bill (1944), 99
Gildersleeve, Ryan Evely, 225–26
Gonzales, Leslie D., 237
González, Juan Carlos, 116, 117
governance: flows of, 101; shared, 52, 53, 64, 70; structure, 100, 225, 226
graduate assistant directors (GADs), 175–77
graduate education, 38, 57, 59, 67, 76, 82; considering, 71–73; defunding of, 5; market demands and, 11
GRAM model. *See* Gather, Read, Analyze, and Make model
grant proposals, 79, 82, 110, 173, 235
Great Resegregation, 4
Great Resignation, 99
Grutter v. Bollinger (2003), 99

Haddix, Marcelle, 147
Hannah-Jones, Nikole, 128, 266
Hannakachl, Mena, 12, 116, 117, 121, 122, 132, 140, 186, 189, 191, 276; coalition building and, 171; problems for, 187; writing instruction by, 190
Harding, Sandra, 58, 104
Harper, Jordan, 18
Harris, Jessica, 5
Hart-Davidson, Bill, 101
Harvard University, antisemitism at, 260
Hays, Alice, 12, 116, 117, 148, 167, 187, 191, 196, 275; next-gen teachers and, 188
Hernández-Johnson, Monica, 214
Hersey, Tricia, 276
Hesford, Wendy, 203
Hicklin Fryar, 13
higher education, 164, 216, 222, 223, 227, 263; access to, 99; activism and, 7; attacks on, 100; austerity measures and, 100, 109; changes in, 99, 170; community engaged, 236; exclusionary practices of, 164; interventions in, 5; issues in, 259–60; neoliberal logics of, 237; service aspects of, 165
Hill Collins, Patricia, 66n1, 214; motherwork and, 213; "outsider within" framework and, 66; social justice and, 142
Holcombe, Elizabeth, 18, 19
Hong, Eunice, 245
hooks, bell, 59, 164, 207; scholarship of, 117–18; sense of place and, 135; service and, 170
House, Eric A., 4, 7, 18, 271
How We Show Up: Reclaiming Family, Friendship, and Community (Birdsong), 90
Hurston, Zora Neale, 119
hustle, avoiding, 6–7, 14–16, 16–18, 205

identity, 103, 128, 185, 190, 191, 203, 204; academic, 205; administrative, 165, 167, 177–79; as asset, 131, 132; building, 161, 177–79; cultural, 116; intersectional, 89, 96, 137–38; linguistic, 147; marginalized, 170; mother, 214; pedagogy and, 125; personal, 79, 180; professional, 38; programmatic, 167, 178; racial, 147; student, 151, 214; teacher, 70; values and, 91
ideology, 132, 133; liberal, 245; patriarchal, 203; political, 193; racialized, 125, 250; teaching, 148
Iglesias, Charisse S., 11, 80, 100, 108; informal leadership and, 101; institutional structures and, 103; leadership competency and, 106; positionality and, 104; strategies by, 28; transformation and, 105

immigrants, 125, 140, 186, 277
individualism, 35, 47, 72, 89, 186, 204; community and, 238; normalization of, 225; valuing, 224
indoctrination, 246, 247, 248, 251, 254
industry: academia and, 81, 83, 84, 95, 96, 103; adapting for, 90, 91
inequalities, 211, 227; exacerbating, 210; gendered, 47, 212–13; perpetuating, 268; racial, 242; researching, 47; social, 116, 242; systemic, 138
inequities, 11, 205, 273; advancing, 269; health, 124; internal, 269; passivity and, 168; reinforcing, 267; root cause of, 186; social, 274
injustice, 186; racial, 167, 189; recognizing/rejecting/replacing/revealing, 141
Inside Higher Ed, 35
institutional memory, invoking, 193–94
institutional structures, 38, 58, 86, 105, 107, 108, 263; feeling for, 101, 102, 103; redressing, 29; revision of, 71
institutions: capitalist, 261; care-full, 235, 236; racist, 278; resistance to, 214
instruction, 102; designing, 82, 152, 158; skills-based, 151; supplemental, 57
instructor representatives, 41, 47, 49, 50; leadership from, 51–52; role of, 45, 46, 48
internships, 11, 127, 251
interventions, 10, 71, 205, 209; institutional, 15; one-off, 94; grassroots, 110; possible, 215–19; state, 15
interviews, 27, 166; process for, 39, 45, 150, 158
invisible labor, 149, 154–56, 191–92; Asian Americans and, 242, 245
Irving, Maxwell, 80
isolation, 156, 193, 204, 215
Issues in Writing and Rhetoric (course), 125, 127, 189–90

Jacobson, Brad, 14, 259, 267, 276; cinch down and, 222, 223, 224, 260; collaboration and, 264, 265; community engagement and, 265; corporate models and, 15; on untenured faculty, 268
Jain, Dimpal, 14
Jimenez, Miguel F., 252
jobs, 19, 29, 72, 82, 208, 261; centering on, 17, 31; nonprofit, 87; searching for, 27; security, 13; summer, 127; work and, 31, 205
Johnston, Emily Ronay, 181
Jones, Natasha N., 9, 106, 180
justice: linguistic, 68, 134; racial, 4, 124, 129, 246. *See also* social justice

Kahn, Seth, 13, 37
Kelley, Robin, 275, 276
Kendi, Ibram X., 167, 168
Keon, Thomas, 241
Kezar, Adrianna, 16–17, 18, 19
Kim, Jennifer Y., 244
King, Martin Luther, Jr., 140
Kirkland, David, 273
Kirsch, Gesa E., 40n1
Knoblauch, Abby, 126
knowledge, 28, 37, 141; administrative, 172; cultural, 147; dissemination of, 269; distinctive kinds of, 58–59; funds for, 30–31; producing, 81, 250
Kohli, Rita, 12, 146, 147, 159
Konate, Mariam, 259
Kynard, Carmen, 4, 14, 69, 119, 205; Black student protests and, 7; Black thought/Black life and, 29; labor conditions and, 202–3; racial violence and, 126–27; student activism and, 7; on work/jobs, 7, 16, 31, 194

labor: advocacy, 102–3; capitalism and, 215; care-full, 228; community-engaged, 195; conditions, 74, 202–3; gendered division of, 211; household, 211; organization, 11, 67; issues, 58, 104, 205; sphere of, 214; teaching, 70; time/care and, 205. *See also* emotional labor; invisible labor
labor equity, 64, 68, 71, 72, 73, 76, 108, 217; work of, 69
Lachia Buenavista, Tracy, 14
language, 132, 139; differences, 93; role of, 90
Latinas: exploitation of, 263; status of, 219
Latinx faculty, working conditions for, 241
Latinx students, 5, 125, 193; completion rates for, 275
leadership: academic, 202, 205, 209, 235; actionable, 179–81; adaptive, 28–29, 39; advocating, 219–20; anti-racist, 165, 166, 169; Black feminist, 142; building, 6–7, 177; challenges for, 4, 16–17, 149, 150, 153; coalitional, 15, 16, 116, 139; collective, 9, 10, 18–19, 110; community, 15, 178; core, 103, 104, 105, 106, 107, 108; distributive forms of, 100, 110; effective, 105, 107–8; empowerment and, 129–32, 158; envisioning, 17, 27, 30; institutional, 122, 235, 261; next-gen, 166, 167, 170–71, 172, 178, 179, 180, 181; opportunities for, 38–39, 171; perspectives on, 123, 194; racist obstacles to, 12; time/care and, 204–5; understanding, 109, 110–11, 142; values and,

17; work of, 12–14
leadership development, 16, 18–19, 167, 265; plans, 6, 7, 18, 169; service/resistance and, 170–71
leadership roles, 18, 38, 100, 104, 108, 139, 155, 175; risking, 102
leadership strategies, 3, 7; work/job/hustle and, 16–18
leadership studies, 7; integrating, 8; writing studies and, 8
learning, 81, 122, 141, 173; affective dimensions of, 233; coalitional, 9, 106; collaborative, 8, 18; community-engaged, 233, 235; conditions for, 59, 74, 76; distance, 174; emotions and, 233; management systems, 99; public, 16, 236; service, 170, 180
LeBlanc, Symonds, 214
Ledesma, Maria C., 14
Leon, Adele, 118, 119, 186, 194, 195, 277; community and, 12–13, 196; leadership qualities and, 117; social justice and, 188
LGBTQ+ community, 154, 193
LGBTQ+ students, 3, 149, 186, 193, 218
liberation, 69, 167–68, 177, 178
Licona, Adela C., 203
"Lightening the Burden" (Williams), 254
listening, 9; research and, 40–43
literacy, 4, 152, 263, 278; data, 108; institutional, 59, 71, 107; learning, 7; race-radical, 7
Living a Feminist Life (Ahmed), 79
Lochler, Holley, 253
Lussier, Mark, 35
Lynch-Biniek, Amy, 13

Macguire, Patricia, 40
macroaggressions, 266
Mapping Police Violence, 189
marginalization, 4, 9, 125, 129, 150, 164, 168, 170, 181, 185, 187, 242, 245; racial, 250; theory of, 47
Marks, Shaylyn, 12, 116, 117, 148, 167, 275
Martell, Luke, 238
Martinez, Aja Y., 127, 243
materialist feminism, 58, 69
maternity leave, 207, 209
Mathieu, Paula, 168–69, 179
McAlister, Joan Faber, 219
McLaughlin, Olivia Marie, 260, 265
McMartin, Charles, 3–4, 17, 100, 115, 271
Mechenbier, Mahli, 36
Meikle, Paulette A., 186
Melonçon, Lisa, 34, 36, 40, 41
mentoring, 9, 17, 93, 141, 159, 160, 213, 218;

programs, 192; recognizing, 6
mentors, 14, 31, 91, 93, 181, 194, 215; coalitional, 195; identifying, 204; partnership, 172, 174–75; white, 156
mentorship, 156, 185, 236, 237; collaborative, 164; community building and, 255; importance of, 167; informal, 137
methodology: ethnographic, 11; PAR, 39, 40; research, 69, 86; theoretical, 39
Micciche, Laura, 71
microaffirmations, 119, 122, 130–32; coalitional actions and, 18; helpfulness of, 136–40; racial, 142
microaggressions, 13, 189, 251, 253, 266; coalitional actions and, 204; creating, 135; cultural taxation and, 243–45, 254; departmental, 242; experiencing, 12, 137, 160, 190; interpersonal, 242; naming/defining, 204; navigating, 255; non-verbal, 133; persistence of, 133–34; racial, 121, 122, 123, 125–29, 133, 137, 139, 140, 142, 147, 244; writing instruction and, 125–29
microinsults, 244, 254
microinvalidations, 190n1, 254
microprotections, 138
microrecognitions, 130
microtransformations, 138
Miller, Thomas, 3–4, 100, 115, 271
Minter, Debbie, 60, 76
Modern Language Association, 82
Moeller, Marie, 126
Moomau, Glen, 46
Morris, Lekeitha R., 186
Morrison, Toni, 169
motherhood, 14, 214; penalty, 209
mothering, 218; academic, 215, 219–20; care and, 209; gender equity and, 261–63; political/activist goals around, 216; private/public dichotomy and, 213, 214; rethinking, 213–15; sacrifice and, 261
Mother-Scholars, 214, 216
motherwork, 14, 213, 214, 262
Mountz, Alison, 227, 230, 237
Moxley-Kelly, Sean, 10, 38, 39, 45, 46, 49, 50, 51, 88, 100, 102, 104, 106, 272; coalitional action and, 108; collective strategies/rhetorical expertise and, 101; "homegrown" status of, 52; inequalities and, 47; labor organizing and, 28–29
Muhammad, Gholdy, 148
Muhlhauser, Paul, 30

Nadasen, Premilla, 215, 217

Nakano Glenn, Evelyn, 214, 215
Nap Ministry, 276
National Center for Educational Statistics, 146
National Council of Teachers of English (NCTE), 127, 162
National Writing Project (NWP), 166, 172, 178, 181, 194
Native American women, political conquest of, 213
NCTE. *See* National Council of Teachers of English
neoliberal imperative, slow scholarship and, 225–27
neoliberalism, 29, 30, 108, 109, 129, 202, 216, 223, 225–26, 227, 260; slow scholarship and, 264
neoliberal logics, 225, 230, 235, 237
neoliberal regimes, 15; service work and, 16
networks: action-oriented, 12, 122; building, 6, 12–14, 117, 118, 119; collaborative, 9; intersectional, 8; leadership-oriented, 122; professional, 204
New American University, 35
New Work of Writing Across the Curriculum: Diversity and Inclusion, Collaborative Partnerships, and Faculty Development, The (Perryman-Clark), 8
next-gen faculty, 16, 29, 83, 116, 118, 119, 164, 186, 188, 197, 275; community partnerships and, 13; expectations for, 15; precarities of, 15
non-tenure-track (NTT) faculty, 10, 40, 57–58, 60, 64, 73, 102, 201; administration and, 50, 51; advocating for, 44, 45, 46; career faculty and, 36, 38; collaborating with, 51, 53; data on, 42–43; decision-making and, 49–50, 67; dismissal of, 52; evaluation of, 193; institutional literacy and, 71; labor market for, 65; leadership and, 37; observing, 67; precarity for, 16, 46; priorities for, 28, 51; representation for, 100–101; resources for, 74; roles for, 34–35; strategies for, 33–34; working conditions for, 41, 42, 48, 49, 68
NTT faculty. *See* non-tenure-track (NTT) faculty
Nuñez, Anne-Marie, 237
NWP. *See* National Writing Project

Oakley, Abigail, 10, 28, 38, 39, 45, 46, 49, 50, 51, 88, 100, 102, 104, 106, 272; coalitional action and, 108; collective strategies/rhetorical expertise and, 101; labor organizing and, 29
Of Mice and Men (Steinbeck), 152

Okello, Wilson Kwamogi, 276
Olivas, Bernice, 75
O'Meara, Kerry Ann, 235, 236
onboarding, 88, 94, 95
Ore, Ersula, 189, 204, 250, 255
outcomes, 61, 86, 100, 106, 108, 160, 167; career, 52; changes in, 266–67; improving, 102; learning, 57, 142, 172, 175, 231; post-graduation, 104
outreach, 9, 13, 253; community-involved, 163

Padilla, Amado, 242, 243
parental leave, 218
parenting: academia and, 224; employment and, 212; gender equity and, 261–63; pandemic and, 14
Parks, Stephen, 179
participation, 34, 39, 52–53, 92; grassroots, 110; institutional, 73
participatory action research (PAR) methodology, 39, 40
partnerships, 176, 231, 232–33; community, 9, 11, 13, 14, 15, 18, 93, 164, 177, 178, 180, 181; community-academic, 11, 85, 86, 92, 94; mentoring, 172, 173, 174–75
patriarchy, 14, 129, 168, 170, 180, 202, 203, 204, 205, 214
Peace Corps, 80, 84, 88, 91, 93
pedagogy, 85, 148, 157–58, 175, 233, 249; Black feminist, 125, 128, 190; critical, 164, 167–68; curriculum and, 147; embodiment/affect and, 233; humanizing, 147; identity and, 125; liberatory, 167, 168; multimodal, 231; slow, 236; sustaining, 148, 151; undermining, 251; writing, 68, 174
people of color, 186, 190; cultural norms of, 122; education and, 147; experiences of, 187–88; invisible labor and, 191; skills for, 196
Perlow, Olivia N., 168
Perryman-Clark, Staci, 8–9, 272
persistence, 61, 64, 66, 68, 225
Phelan, Sean, 225
PLC. *See* professional learning community
political life, 121–22, 192
politics, 5, 230; evolving, 205; feminist, 227; institutional, 28; racialized, 125; university, 126
positionality, 37, 90, 96, 101, 141, 168, 201; minoritized, 250; racialized, 250; re-sensing, 108; reflecting on, 103; sensing, 103–5, 108
possibility: of conduct, 225; discerning, 101, 105–7, 108; location of, 127; understanding,

207
Powell, Katrina, 92
power: dynamics, 84, 86; imbalance in, 267; liminal space of, 37; relations, 227; structures of, 52, 227. *See also* empowerment
precarity, 4, 28; financial, 46; long-term, 12, 16
Principles of Partnership, 86
private/public binary, 213, 214
problem-solving, 158, 159, 160, 173, 191; collaborative, 5; pedagogical, 195
Probst, Barbara, 39
productivity, 95, 205, 211, 223; explosive, 225; labor, 203; scholarly, 265; valuing, 224
Profession (MLA), 82
professional development, 36, 38, 68, 82, 149, 156, 161, 166, 173, 176; guidance for, 75; opportunities for, 174; workshops for, 124
professionalization, 14, 17, 41, 72, 116, 164, 188
professional learning community (PLC), 151–52, 157, 158
promotion, 17, 30, 230, 234; achieving, 267; challenges of, 260; changes to, 216–18; gender gap for, 209, 210, 217; institutional reward system and, 243; process, 263, 264, 265; reviewers, 237; tenure and, 269
promotion standards, 261, 263–67
publications, 28, 29, 79, 115, 134, 235
public health, 84, 86, 87, 103
Pullias Center for Higher Education, 10, 17, 18, 19

queer students, 274–75, 276
quiet quitting, 100
quit lit, 99

race, 58, 123, 137, 187–88, 189, 191, 236, 242; addressing, 161, 248, 249, 250; anxiety and, 250; conversations about, 124; discussing, 196, 247, 248; gender and, 217; intentional talk about, 160–61; issues of, 141, 249, 250; relevance of, 126; silencing discussions about, 245–54; studying, 128–29; subjectivity of, 11
Race, Social Justice, and Professional Writing (course), 128, 129
racial battle fatigue, 253–54
racial matters, 123, 154, 166, 249, 250
racism, 4, 29, 68, 122, 126, 154, 169, 179, 187–88, 191, 196, 243, 276; anti-Asian, 241, 244–45, 254; calling out, 268; challenging, 242; colorblind, 246; discussing, 247, 248, 249; enacting, 190; experiencing, 147; exposure to, 253; gendered, 181; institutional, 9, 136,

166, 180, 278; legacies of, 70; researching about, 246; resident, 271; structural, 96, 179, 189; systemic, 70, 180, 186, 245, 246; teaching about, 249; topic of, 154
"Rapper's Delight," 277–78
"Rappin And Rocking The House" (Funky Four Plus One More), 271n1
RCWS. *See* rhetoric, composition, and writing studies
Read, Brock, 4–5
Real World Writing, 252
reciprocity, 92, 119, 139, 177; accountability and, 178
Red for Ed movement, 177
reflection, 47, 51–52, 169; critical, 180; questions, 88
reforms: equitable, 17; institutional, 75, 100; market-based, 225; social, 100
relationships, 28, 71, 93; building, 31, 76, 85, 89, 92, 137; collaborative, 148; collegial, 66, 109; personal, 93; social, 69
repurposing, 91, 92, 93, 95
Repurposing Composition: Feminist Interventions for a Neoliberal Age (Stenberg), 10
research, 9, 109, 115, 137, 170, 193; community-engaged, 81, 87, 89, 92; connections from, 92; disciplinary specific, 86; ethnographic, 69; experience in, 169; industry goals and, 82, 83–85, 93; instrumentalizing, 226; listening and, 40–43; public health, 87; RCWS and, 165; repurposing, 91, 92; skills sets and, 92; supermarket model of, 226
research hierarchies, 5, 13; challenging, 117; traditional, 12
resistance, 66, 168, 177, 179, 180; communities of, 118, 158–60, 195; enthusiasm and, 67; leadership development and, 170–71; networks of, 116, 118, 119; sense of, 139; transformation and, 119
responsibilities, 100, 104; academic, 260; administrative, 109; care work, 236, 263; collective, 215; individual, 35, 214; job, 30; parental, 262; social, 215
retention, 61, 66, 68, 73, 75, 94, 121, 192, 220, 255
retention, tenure, promotion (RTP), 253, 254
rhetoric, 41, 65, 87, 99, 133; collaborative, 18; power of, 30; race, 190; teaching, 247; writing and, 125
rhetoric, composition, and writing studies (RCWS), 165, 167, 180
rhetoric studies, 27, 83, 111, 125, 246, 249
Rhetoric(s) of Race and Ethnicity (course),

123, 124, 127–28, 188
Rhoades, Gary, 9
Ribero, Ana, 201, 205, 259, 260, 261, 271; care work/academic service and, 263; on childcare/domestic care, 268; early care education and, 262; institutional interventions and, 15; motherwork and, 14, 262; patriarchal ideologies and, 203
Richardson, Jennifer L., 259, 260, 266
Ridolfo, Jim, 99
Robbins, Stephanie Troutman, 84, 164
Rolón-Dow, Rosalie, 130
Ropers-Huilman, Rebecca, 253
Royster, Jacqueline Jones, 40n1
RTP. *See* retention, tenure, promotion

salary issues, 42, 51
Sano-Franchini, Jennifer, 16, 272
scholarship, 67, 202, 212, 233; anti-racist, 167; care-full, 227, 230, 234, 264; collaborative, 230; public, 266. *See also* slow scholarship
Scholarship Reconsidered (Boyer), 235
Schreiber, Joanna, 34, 40, 41
Seeber, Barbara K., 227, 264; collaboration and, 230; embodiment/affect and, 233; slow food and, 226; slow professor and, 235
self-evaluation, 89–90, 91, 93, 254, 259
service work, 164, 165, 169, 177, 180, 181, 193, 212, 217, 263; commitment to, 172; devaluation of, 12, 16, 170; early-career faculty and, 13; importance of, 100; leadership and, 170–71, 226; recognizing, 6; teaching and, 212; undervaluing of, 163; women's, 213
Serwer, Andrew, 4
Sha-Rock, 271n1, 278
Shah, Rachel, 167
Sheffield, Jenna, 30
Shelton, Christina D., 125
skills, 85, 92, 156, 161; administrative, 195; collaborative, 148, 150, 167; conflict resolution, 196; cultural integration, 87; leadership, 150; listening, 197; management, 179–80; negotiating, 162, 196; organizational, 179–80; practical, 28, 172; problem-solving, 158, 159; professional, 165; repurposing, 28, 91, 92, 93, 95; transferable, 73, 173–76, 178
Sledd, James, 273
slow professor, 227, 235
slow scholarship, 264, 265; neoliberal imperative and, 225–27
slow(er) academy, 234–38
slowness, 227, 228, 238, 264, 277
Smith, Barbara, 140

Smith, Dorothy, 69
social change, 9, 87, 128
socialization, academic, 116, 117, 118
social justice, 4, 8, 10, 70, 94, 109, 128–29, 137, 142, 149, 164, 172, 189, 190, 193, 245, 246; goals of, 16; principles of, 186; rhetoric of, 188; teaching, 153. *See also* justice
social location, 10, 11, 104
social norms, 88, 89, 91
social reproduction, 215, 217, 218
solidarity, 44, 75, 76, 104, 118, 255; building, 60, 61, 105
Solórzano, Daniel G., 122, 139
Souza, Tasha, 135
space: classroom, 136; educational, 158; problem-solving, 159; traditional, 89; virtual learning, 131, 132; white, 188–189
Spencer, Zoe, 180
stakeholders, 41, 48, 71, 90, 167, 197, 205, 275; community, 166, 193; participation of, 39; partnership, 174; privileged, 192–93; redefining, 196
Stapleton, Andrew, 83
Stenberg, Shari, 10, 60, 76
stereotypes, 122, 147; Asian American, 244; minority, 243; positive, 244; racist, 241
Stone, Lindsey, 212–13, 217
strategies, 99, 121, 195; practical, 172–77, 227; rhetorical, 136
strengths, weaknesses, opportunities, and threats (SWOT), 174
stress, 4, 44, 47, 95, 170, 189, 227; racial, 249–50
student leaders, learning with, 6, 7–9
students of color, 14, 151, 187; achievement gaps and, 146; curriculum and, 153; environment for, 154–55; experiences of, 156, 157, 161
Sutherland, Jean-Anne, 211
systemic challenges, 76, 93–94, 137, 267

Takayoshi, Pamela, 92
Taranath, Anu, 87
TAs. *See* teaching assistants
teacher education programs, 12, 158, 161; anti-racist, 167–68; recommendations for, 159; teachers of color and, 157; whiteness of, 147
teacher residency programs, 147, 149, 155
teachers of color, 158, 159, 187; challenges for, 148, 150, 156–57, 160, 161; experiences of, 147, 156, 161; politics/practices of, 275; representation of, 156; resistance by, 252; success for, 146, 192
Teachers of Color: Resisting Racism and

Reclaiming Education (Kohli), 146
teaching, 170, 193, 226, 236; anti-oppressive, 70; anti-racist, 141; burnout from, 45; community-engaged, 235; conditions for, 59, 74, 76; independent, 149; online, 231; re-professionalization of, 41; service and, 212
teaching assistants (TAs), 9, 27
technology, 9, 37, 174, 177
tenure, 29, 30, 50, 60, 219, 234, 265; academic freedom and, 261, 267, 269; academic service and, 263; challenges of, 260; changes to, 216–18; elimination of, 212, 268; gender gap in, 209, 210, 212; institutional reward system and, 243; promotion and, 269; protections from, 268; requirements for, 266–67; reviewers, 212, 237; sacrifices for, 261–62; safety of, 3; securing, 229, 262, 267
tenure clock, 208, 260; biological clock and, 219; female-only, 212; gender-neutral, 212; stopping, 217
tenure process, 59, 263, 264, 265; guidelines for, 217
tenure reviewers, 212, 237
tenure standards, revising, 261, 263–67
tenure-track (TT) faculty, 3, 28, 36, 56, 57, 58, 64, 70, 73, 82, 109, 115, 125; challenges for, 263; evaluation of, 193; journey for, 81; lecturers and, 67; NTT faculty and, 52; service load for, 217; stories of slowness and, 228; work-life balance for, 224
Teston, Christa, 203
traditional students, euphemism of, 248, 249
training, 94, 95; leadership, 161; mentor, 174; opportunities, 161
transformation, 5, 60, 94, 105, 118, 188, 195; institutional, 79, 186; perpetual, 102; resistance and, 119; social, 275
transparency, 88, 178, 180, 181
Trump, Donald, 3, 5, 13, 76, 146, 222
TT faculty. *See* tenure-track (TT) faculty

Ueda, Natsumi, 18, 19
undocumented students, attack on, 276
University of California, Berkeley, 81, 82, 166
University of Southern California, 10, 17
US Department of Education, 5, 222
US Department of Government Efficiency, 5

values, 35, 37, 80, 84, 224; abstract, 171; community, 90, 164; critical, 164; economic, 210; feminist, 164; identity and, 91; job searches and, 81; leadership and, 17; maintaining,

89, 96; negotiating, 88–91; skill sets and, 85; social, 210; working toward, 30–31; workplace environment and, 95
Vigil, Darsella, 18, 19, 30
violence, 273; community, 124; epistemological, 29, 185; racial, 126–27

Walton, Rebecca, 123, 140, 141, 142
Wells, Jaclyn, 167
Wenner Moyer, Melinda, 223
Wergin, Jon, 28–29, 37, 39
Whalen, Tracy, 37
white comfort, 250
white equilibrium, 249
white fragility, 249, 250
white innocence, 189–91
White Mainstream English (WME), 68, 132, 133, 273; acceptance of, 189; argument against, 135; enacting/enforcing, 134; writing in, 139
white nationalism, 271
whiteness, 130, 156, 189, 192, 242, 278
whitestream status, 196
white supremacy, 118, 122, 141, 170, 180, 189, 196, 224, 276; countering, 168, 268
white time, maintaining, 188–89
Wildcat Writers, 163–64, 171, 172, 175, 176, 188, 195
Williams, Wendi, 254
Wilson, Laura, 36, 44
WME. *See* White Mainstream English
women of color, 109, 262–63; feminist, 81; immigrant, 138; motherwork and, 214
women's studies, 4, 260
Wootton, Lacey, 46
work: adaptive, 36–39; affective, 43–45; care-full, 237; community-based, 28, 188, 193–94, 193n2, 197; empowering, 27; flexible arrangements for, 218–19; institutional, 74; interdisciplinary, 87; jobs and, 31, 205; sustaining, 31
work ethic, 93, 135
working conditions, 41, 42, 48, 53, 58, 76, 89, 95, 238, 241, 258; arguing for, 51; battle for, 44–45; degradation of, 13; equitable, 6, 9–11; focusing on, 36; improving, 37, 49
work-life balance, 91, 100, 202, 205, 216, 224, 225
workshops, 17, 224, 266
WPAs. *See* writing program administrators
writing, 27, 41, 137, 190; collaborative, 117; cultures of, 57; genres, 119; professional, 251;

rhetoric and, 125; technical, 41
writing instruction, 68; racial microaggression and, 125–29; traditional models of, 60
writing program administrators (WPAs), 10–11, 27, 28, 50, 60, 64, 69, 73, 74, 261; middle management and, 37; work of, 39, 59
writing programs, 8, 35, 39, 67; staffing, 71–72

Writing Spaces, 229
writing studies, 3, 28, 83, 246, 249; development of, 4; leadership studies and, 8; purposes/ paths of, 111

xenophobia, 68, 190

Young, Vershawn Ashanti, 135
Yu, Min, 214

About the Authors

Sonia C. Arellano is an independent scholar, technical writer, and director of the Migrant Quilt Project. Her scholarship engages tactile methods, tactile rhetorics, and mentoring of BIPOC students and faculty and has been recognized with the 2021 Biennial Kathleen Ethel Welch Outstanding Article Award, the 2022 CCCC Richard Braddock Award, and the 2022 Theresa J. Enos Anniversary Award. She resides in Tampa, FL with her menagerie and her partner.

Felicita Arzu-Carmichael (she/her/ella) is associate professor of writing and rhetoric and associate director of the First-Year Writing Program at Oakland University in Rochester, Michigan. She is also an associate editor of *College English*, the flagship journal of the College Section of NCTE. Felicita's teaching and research center race and inclusion, Black feminist thought, and online literacies. Her work can be found in journals and edited collections in technical and professional communication, rhetoric and composition, and cultural rhetorics.

Amardeep (Rupsy) Bajwa teaches high school English at the Kern High School District in Bakersfield, California, and graduated from California State University Bakersfield's Kern Teacher Residency program.

Christina V. Cedillo is an associate professor of writing and rhetoric at the University of Houston-Clear Lake. Christina's research draws from cultural rhetorics, critical race theory, disability studies, and decolonial theory to focus on embodied rhetorics and rhetorics of embodiment at the intersections of race, gender, and disability.

Alexandra Chapa-Kunz teaches high school English at the Kern High School District in Bakersfield, California, and graduated from California State University Bakersfield's Kern Teacher Residency program.

Anicca Cox is an assistant professor in a small English Department at a two-year college. Her research and publications include works on pedagogy, academic labor and WPA concerns, food justice, and feminist ethnographic methodologies. She has published in *College Composition and Communication*, *Peitho*, *College English*, *Across the Disciplines* and in several edited collections in writing studies. She lives in New Mexico, her home place.

Tom Hong Do is an assistant professor of rhetoric and writing at California State University, Long Beach. His research examines the relationship between language and race. He is the recipient of the Richard Ohmann Award. His works have been published in *College English*.

Mena Hannakachl (she/her/hers) is an alumna of Oakland University with a degree in Writing and Rhetoric. As an undergraduate, she focused on DEI-related topics in writing studies, particularly her passion for linguistic justice and diversity. Mena is also a published author, having written a memoir essay on her cultural identity and immigrant experiences. She is currently an incoming law student for Fall 2025, aspiring to become a civil and human rights attorney.

Alice Hays is an associate professor and department chair of the Teacher Education Department at California State University, Bakersfield. After nineteen years of teaching high school English, she recognizes the amazing power of secondary students to be agents of change. Her research interests focus on young adult literature and its impact on adolescent pro-social behavior in addition to teacher preparation and residency programs.

Eric A. House is an associate professor of critical composition and writing studies at New Mexico State University. His current research examines how Black rhetoric remixes perceptions of writing and intervenes in the politics of representation. His work places Black rhetoric and writing in conversation with scholarship in writing studies, rhetoric, literacy studies, linguistics, and cultural studies. He is invested in both teaching and research practices that address systemic inequities by centering on and theorizing through experiences often marginalized in academic spaces, and both his teaching and research are informed by conversations in black feminism and critical race theory.

Charisse S. Iglesias (she/her) is a training and resource director at Community-Campus Partnerships for Health (CCPH), has a PhD in rhetoric and composition with an emphasis on facilitating equitable community–academic partnerships. Her passion and expertise in community–academic partnerships stemmed from her experience as a Peace Corps volunteer co-creating educational programs and directing a college-pathway writing program that partnered economically marginalized public high schools with a research university. At CCPH, Charisse leads teams to create, facilitate, and evaluate technical training workshops and resources for international and US-based community partners, researchers, and academics.

Brad Jacobson is an assistant professor of English at The University of Texas at El Paso, where he teaches writing studies and English education courses. Brad's work on academic writing development, teacher development, and school-based writing opportunities has been featured in *Written Communication* and the *Journal of Literacy Research*, and in other journals and edited collections.

Carmen Kynard is the Lillian Radford Chair in Rhetoric and Composition and professor of English at Texas Christian University. Before TCU, she worked in English and gender studies at John Jay College of Criminal Justice as well as English, urban education, and critical psychology at the Graduate Center of the City University of New York. She interrogates race, Black feminisms, AfroDigital/Black languages and cultures, and the politics of schooling with an emphasis on composition, rhetoric, and literacies studies. Carmen has taught high school with the New York City public schools/Coalition of Essential Schools, served as a writing program administrator, and worked as a teacher educator. She has led numerous professional development projects on language, literacy, and learning and has published in *Harvard Educational Review*, *Changing English*, *College Composition and Communication*, *College English*, *Computers and Composition*, *Reading Research Quarterly*, *Literacy in Composition Studies*, and more. Her award-winning book, *Vernacular Insurrections: Race, Black Protest, and the New Century in Composition-Literacies Studies*, makes Black Freedom a twenty-first-century literacy movement.

Adele Leon (she/her) is an assistant professor of Writing and Communication at Nova Southeastern University and is the founding director of the SoFlo Writing Project. Her research engages structural and organizational issues related to diversity, equity, and inclusion in higher education, reciprocity in community-university partnerships, and feminist, liberatory, and anti-racist pedagogies.

Dr. Shaylyn Marks is an assistant professor in the Teacher Education Department at California State University, Bakersfield. With culturally responsive and sustaining pedagogies at the core of her work, her research interests include evolving educator preparation practices, using literature as a means to support and enact social justice, and advocating for equitable systems of practice and structures within educational spaces.

Charles McMartin is an assistant professor of English at Florida State University. He earned his PhD in rhetoric, composition, and the teaching of English from the University of Arizona. His research on culturally sustaining pedagogies, community writing, student activism, and next-gen faculty leadership has been published in *Peitho Journal, College English, Composition Studies*, and other journals and edited collections.

Thomas Miller is professor emeritus at the University of Arizona, where he served as WPA, graduate director, and vice provost for faculty affairs. He received awards for his diversity leadership, teaching, mentoring, advocacy for shared governance, and research. He is a recipient of the Mina Shaughnessy Award for his book *The Formation of College English* (1997).

Sean Moxley-Kelly is an instructor in the Department of English at Arizona State University. His interests include technical communication, narrative studies, gender and identity. As teacher and researcher, he examines the ways people rhetorically position themselves as valuable contributors to teams and organizations.

Abigail Oakley is an instructor in the Department of English at Arizona State University. She specializes in teaching writing in various forms, but primarily academic styles of writing. She earned her PhD in writings, rhetorics, and literacies from Arizona State University in 2019. Her research specializations focused on digital pedagogy, institutional ethnography, online identity, and gender studies.

Staci Perryman-Clark is a professor of English and African American studies at Western Michigan University and serves as the director of the Institute for Intercultural and Anthropological Studies at Western Michigan University. Her work focuses on Afrocentric pedagogies in relation to language rights afforded to writing students. Her work has appeared in numerous journals including *College English* and *College Composition and Communication*, and she has published several books including *Afrocentric Teacher-Research, Black Perspectives in Writing Program Administration*, and *Writing Across the Curriculum and Faculty Development*.

Ana Milena Ribero is an associate professor of rhetoric and writing at Oregon State University. Her research and teaching focuses on rhetorics of im/migration, rhetorics of race, critical literacies, women of color feminisms, and critical race and feminist pedagogies. Her latest book is *Dreamer Nation: Immigration, Activism, and Neoliberalism* and her scholarship can be found in *Rhetoric Review, Peitho: Journal of the Coalition of Feminist Scholars* in the *History of Rhetoric and Composition, Performance Research, Present Tense: A Journal of Rhetoric in Society,* and in edited collections.

Jennifer Sano-Franchini (she/her) is the Gaziano Family Legacy Professor of Rhetoric and Writing Studies and an associate professor of English at West Virginia University. Her research and teaching interests are in the relationships between culture, meaning-making, power, and technology. She has published widely in journals and collections across rhetoric and composition and technical communication. She serves as chair of the Conference on College Composition and Communication.

www.ingramcontent.com/pod-product-compliance
Lightning Source LLC
Chambersburg PA
CBHW060551080526
44585CB00013B/525